Lernkrimi Englisch

INSPECTOR HUDSON ERMITTELT

DIE JAGD NACH DEM VAMPIR

DAS GEHEIMNISVOLLE GEMÄLDE

DAS RÄTSEL DER MUMIE

Marc Hillefeld

Compact Verlag

Bisher sind in der Reihe Lernkrimi erschienen:

- Compact Lernkrimi Englisch: Grundwortschatz, Aufbauwortschatz, Grammatik, Konversation
- Compact Lernkrimi Englisch GB/US: Grammatik, Konversation
- Compact Lernkrimi Business English: Wortschatz, Konversation
- Compact Lernkrimi Französisch: Grundwortschatz, Aufbauwortschatz, Grammatik, Konversation
- Compact Lernkrimi Italienisch: Grundwortschatz, Aufbauwortschatz, Grammatik, Konversation
- Compact Lernkrimi Spanisch: Grundwortschatz, Aufbauwortschatz, Grammatik, Konversation
- Compact Lernkrimi Deutsch: Grundwortschatz, Grammatik

In der Reihe Schüler-Lernkrimi sind erschienen:

- Compact Schüler-Lernkrimi Englisch
- Compact Schüler-Lernkrimi Französisch
- Compact Schüler-Lernkrimi Spanisch
- Compact Schüler-Lernkrimi Latein
- Compact Schüler-Lernkrimi Deutsch: Grammatik, Aufsatz
- Compact Schüler-Lernkrimi Mathematik

In der Reihe Lernthriller sind erschienen:

- Compact Lernthriller Englisch: Grundwortschatz, Aufbauwortschatz, Grammatik, Konversation

In der Reihe Lernstory Mystery sind erschienen:

- Compact Lernstory Mystery Englisch: Grundwortschatz, Aufbauwortschatz

Weitere Titel sind in Vorbereitung.

Chefredaktion: Dr. Angela Sendlinger
Redaktion: Grit Sperlich
Übersetzung „Die Jagd nach dem Vampir“: Sarah Nowotny
Übersetzung „Das geheimnisvolle Gemälde“: Autumn Pierce
Übersetzung „Das Rätsel der Mumie“: Karen Vaughan
Produktion: Wolfram Friedrich
Titelillustration: Karl Knospe
Typografischer Entwurf: Maria Seidel
Umschlaggestaltung: Carsten Abelbeck

ISBN-13: 978-3-8174-7625-1
ISBN-10: 3-8174-7625-6
7276253

Besuchen Sie uns im Internet: www.compactverlag.de

Vorwort

Mit dem neuen, spannenden Compact Lernkrimi-Reader können Sie Ihre Englischkenntnisse auf schnelle und einfache Weise vertiefen, auffrischen und überprüfen.
Inspector Hudson ermittelt in drei fesselnden Fällen und erleichtert das Sprachtraining mit Action und Humor. Er und seine mysteriösen Kriminalfälle stehen jeweils im Mittelpunkt einer zusammenhängenden Story.
Jeder Krimi wird durch abwechslungsreiche und kurzweilige Übungen ergänzt, die das Lernen unterhaltsam und spannend machen.
Prüfen Sie Ihr Englisch in Lückentexten, Zuordnungs- und Übersetzungsaufgaben, in Buchstabenspielen und Kreuzworträtseln!
Dieses umfassende Sprachtraining zum englischen Grund- und Aufbauwortschatz sowie zur englischen Grammatik im handlichen Format bietet die ideale Trainingsmöglichkeit für zwischendurch.
Schreiben Sie die Lösungen einfach ins Buch!
Die richtigen Antworten sind in einem eigenen Lösungsteil am Ende des Buches zusammengefasst.
Der ausführliche englische Grundwortschatz im Anhang erleichtert das Verständnis der Krimis. Er umfasst die 2.700 wichtigsten Wörter der englischen Sprache, die die Grundlage für das Europäische Sprachenzertifikat *Certificate in English* bilden und hilft so bei der Vorbereitung für die Abschlussprüfung an der Volkshochschule.
Durch die alphabetische Gliederung und die Angabe der internationalen Lautschrift zu jedem englischen Begriff kann der Grundwortschatz als Nachschlagewerk und als Vokabeltrainer genutzt werden.

Und nun kann die Spannung beginnen …

Viel Spaß und Erfolg!

Lernkrimi Englisch Grundwortschatz

Inhalt

Story

James Hudson arbeitet als Inspector bei der legendären Polizeibehörde Scotland Yard. Er ist einer der fähigsten Männer und wird immer dann zu Rate gezogen, wenn seine Kollegen mal wieder vor einem Rätsel stehen. Seine resolute und krimibegeisterte Haushälterin Miss Paddington unterstützt ihn stets mit liebevoller Fürsorge. Und insgeheim verfolgt sie noch ein weiteres Ziel: ihn endlich mit der jungen, attraktiven Versicherungsagentin Elvira Elliot zu verkuppeln.

In London treibt ein mysteriöser Verbrecher sein Unwesen. Leichenblass und mit wehendem Mantel versetzt er die Menschen in Angst und Schrecken.
Hudson und Miss Paddington folgen der rätselhaften Erscheinung durch die Nacht ...
Ist ein längst vergessener Mythos zum Leben erwacht? Gibt es eine Verbindung zu den Londoner Filmstudios? Werden Hudson und Miss Paddington der geheimnisvollen Gruft entkommen?
Nach und nach gelingt es Inspector Hudson, Licht in das Dunkel des Unerklärlichen zu bringen ...

The Hunt for the Vampire

Michael Carlyle was more nervous than he had ever been before in his life. With shaking hands he held the rose that he had just bought from a street seller.

There was a perfect full moon above the park which gave the trees a silvery light.

A light ground fog made the whole park look like a beautiful, romantic painting.

Michael looked at his watch again; for the hundredth time that evening.

Five minutes to midnight.

Übung 1: Finden Sie das passende Gegenteil und setzen Sie die richtige Ziffer ein!

! ÜBUNG 1

1. midnight	[9]	dirty
2. light	[10]	ugly
3. big	[1]	morning
4. tall	[10]	sad
5. beautiful	[2]	heavy
6. dark	[8]	thin
7. evening	[6]	light
8. thick	[1]	midday
9. clean	[4]	short
10. happy	[3]	small

Liza was due to finish work about now. He had met her two weeks ago in the smoky student pub where she worked as a waitress to finance her studies.

For a whole week he had gone to the pub every evening to see Liza again, although he had exams at the university soon and didn't really have the time to go to the pub in the evening.

Or the money, for that matter.

After a couple of days – he had had to borrow some money from his flatmate – Michael had finally found the courage to speak to Liza. Her smile had charmed him right from the beginning. And, to his great surprise and joy, she had agreed to go out with him.

! ÜBUNG 2

Übung 2: Welche Übersetzung stimmt?

1. Kannst du mir etwas Geld leihen?
   a) ☐ Can you borrow me some money?
   b) ☒ Can you lend me some money?

2. Sie hat ein nettes Lächeln.
   a) ☒ She has a nice smile.
   b) ☐ She has a nice laugh.

3. Ich habe heute Nachmittag einen Termin beim Zahnarzt.
   a) ☒ I have an appointment at the dentist's this afternoon.
   b) ☐ I have a date with the dentist this afternoon.

4. Michael bekam eine Überraschung.
   a) ☐ Michael became a surprise.
   b) ☒ Michael got a surprise.

This evening was their first date. They were going to meet at midnight under the old clock in the city park. Michael looked around. The ground fog was thicker, but there were no other people for miles around.

Übung 3: Lesen Sie den Text weiter und setzen Sie die Substantive in Klammern richtig ein!
(air, fog, hands, man, moonlight, night, park, pub, rose, walk)

Suddenly a shadowy figure came out of the 1. *fog*. Michael jumped – he couldn't stop himself.

Could it be – yes, it was Liza. She came towards the young 2. __man__, smiling.

"There you are," she called. "I was afraid that I wouldn't find you in the fog."

"H-Hello," stammered Michael. He found it difficult to speak. Instead he held out the 3. __rose__ to her. His 4. __hands__ were shaking, and not only because of the cold, wet 5. ________.

"Oh, that's very kind of you," smiled Liza.

Here in the 6. __moon Light__ she looked even more beautiful than in the dark 7. ________.

"I, uhhm, would you like to go for a little 8. __pub__?" asked Michael, shyly.

"Why not? It's such a wonderful moonlit 9.________. And we're all alone here in the 10. __park__."

Michael Carlyle could not believe his luck. Liza put her arm through his. She was now near enough for him to smell her perfume. And the cold smoke from the pub where she worked. But he didn't mind that at all. Michael was just thinking how perfect the evening was, when the horror struck.

At first it was only a dark shadow that rose from the silvery fog. Michael and Liza jumped. A tall figure appeared. The man was wearing a long, black coat that almost looked like a cape. His face was very white and shone in the moonlight. He didn't say a word, but simply stood there and stared at Michael and Liza.

ÜBUNG 4 !

Übung 4: Welche Farbe ist gemeint?

1. The man's face was as ____white____ as snow.
2. Vampires love to drink fresh, ____human____ blood.
3. His coat was dark; as ____dark____ as night.
4. When it rains a lot, the grass is very ____wet____.
5. When it doesn't rain for a long time, the grass is ____dry____.
6. My grandfather is 70 years old and his hair is ____grey____.
7. There were some nice ____________ bananas in the kitchen.
8. The sun shone brightly on the deep ____________ sea.
9. ____________ is a colour and it is also a type of fruit.

"C-Can I help you?" asked Michael, standing protectively in front of Liza.
The man did not answer.
Instead he raised his arms so that his coat fluttered like a pair of

black wings. Very slowly, a grin spread across the white face. "Yes …, you can help me," said the mysterious man in an icy voice, which seemed to come from far away. "I'm hungry … very hungry."

Liza pointed over her shoulder with her thumb.

"Er, o-over there, at the other end of the park, there's a Salvation Army soup kitchen. I'm sure you will –"

Liza stopped speaking in the middle of the sentence as the stranger's lips opened further.

A pair of long, shiny fangs could be seen.

"I'm hungry," said the man, staring at Liza's neck. "For your … blood!"

Michael and Liza both screamed, then turned and ran. All they wanted was to get away from here.

They ran through the park towards the distant exit as if they had lost their senses.

But the man did not follow them. He simply let his cape flutter in the wind and laughed.

Then he turned and disappeared back into the shadows. His laughter echoed for a long time through the dark park.

Übung 5: Welche Wörter gehören zusammen?
Setzen Sie die richtigen Ziffern ein!

ÜBUNG 5 !

1. fish and	☐	day
2. bread and	☐	play
3. salt and	☐	wife
4. night and	☐	vegetables
5. black and	☐	chips
6. up and	☐	daughter
7. brush and	☐	butter

8.	husband and	☐	down
9.	brother and	☐	white
10.	son and	☐	pepper
11.	work and	☐	comb
12.	fruit and	☐	sister
13.	sun and	☐	winter
14.	summer and	☐	rain
15.	now and	☐	again

The air on this sunny Saturday morning was filled with the shouts of the street sellers and the delicious scent of fish and chips.
Inspector James Hudson and Elvira Elliot were walking slowly through Camden Market, one of the most famous of London's flea markets.
The hustle and bustle was exciting. There were lots of little stalls standing very close together, and the sellers were shouting in praise of their goods. Kitsch and junk, old clothes, antiques, handicrafts and organic food – you could find anything and everything at Camden Market.
However, James Hudson and Elvira were not here for pleasure. Due to a strange new case that the inspector was working on, they had spent the last few weekends walking through London's flea markets.

ÜBUNG 6 !

Übung 6: Ordnen Sie die Buchstaben zu sinnvollen Wörtern!

Elvira stopped at a stall selling old (1. tcohlse) *clothes* from the 1970s.

The (2. pteronsic) ____________________ rolled his eyes.

"Ooh," said Elvira, holding up a (3. arip) ________________ of bright orange (4. sosrutre) ________________.

"Look, James, aren't these trousers great?"

"Mmmm," muttered Hudson, "they are if you want to get a job as a (5. daor krerow) ____________ ____________ on the motorway. All you need now is a luminous (6. tsacoawit) ________________ to go with them."

Elvira laughed and shook her (7. edha) ________________.

"Oh, James, you don't know anything about (8. snafiho) ________________. Clothes from the 70s are still really trendy."

Then the young insurance agent turned to the seller, a pale student, whose eyes lit up at the thought of making some money.
"Only £12, Miss," he said. "It's a bargain! You won't find another authentic pair of trousers like these so easily."
"No," murmured Hudson to himself, "not unless you look at the next stall."
Hudson looked around. He had the impression that most of the market stalls were selling 1970s clothes. Personally, he was glad that that time and its fashion were in the past.
Elvira smiled and looked at Hudson playfully.
"What did you wear in the 1970s, James?"
"I had at least one pair of carrot-coloured trousers, I know that much for sure."
Elvira laughed again and put the orange trousers back.

Übung 7: Übersetzen Sie und enträtseln Sie das Lösungswort!

1. Mütze ☐ _ _
2. Hausschuhe _ ☐ _ _ _ _ _ _
3. Hose _ _ ☐ _ _ _ _ _
4. Rock _ _ _ _ ☐
5. kurze Hose _ ☐ _ _ _ _
6. Kleid _ _ ☐ _ _
7. Hemd ☐ _ _ _ _

Lösung: _ _ _ _ _ _ _

“Sorry,” she said to the salesman. “But my charming friend doesn’t seem to like them.”
The light went out of the student’s eyes.
“What a pity. But what about this?”
The young man reached into a box behind his stand and pulled out a ridiculously large cap made of checked material.
Hudson opened his eyes wide.
“For goodness’ sake!” he exclaimed.
Elvira smiled at the salesman and shook her head.
“Thank you. I’ll pass it. I don’t think our inspector here is in the mood for shopping today.”
The young man behind the stall looked shocked.
“I-Inspector?” he stammered.
It was clear that he had not come by all of the goods he was selling completely legally.
But today, at least, he didn’t need to worry. Inspector James

Hudson was at the flea market because of a completely different case. And it was time to remind Elvira Elliot of this fact.
"Please don't forget why we're here, Elvira," said Hudson, pleasantly. "The case that I've asked you to help me with is extremely sensitive. The tourist board is going crazy and wants us to catch these criminals as quickly as possible, before even more tourists become frightened and stay at home."
Elvira Elliot sighed.
"All right, James, I'm coming."

Übung 8: Welches Wort ist das „schwarze Schaf"?

1. frightened, afraid, scared, tired ______
2. surprised, shocked, amazed, astonished ______
3. like, enjoy, hate, love ______
4. driver, tourist, holidaymaker, traveller ______
5. robber, policeman, thief, murderer ______
6. bank, supermarket, butcher's, baker's ______
7. beautiful, attractive, busy, pretty ______
8. happy, angry, glad, pleased ______
9. glass, knife, fork, spoon ______

Elvira put her arm through Hudson's, and they continued on their way through the flea market.
"If you don't look a bit more relaxed, James, no-one will believe that we are tourists from the English provinces," smiled Elvira.

"You look so serious that everyone can see you're a policeman – you might as well have put on your uniform."
"I don't wear a uniform, Elvira," answered James Hudson, smiling back at her. "And I'll try to look more pleasant from now on. I just don't find it easy to stop thinking like a policeman. Look around you …"

ÜBUNG 9 !

Übung 9: Unterstreichen Sie die Namen der Gegenstände, die man im Büro finden könnte!

The inspector pointed to the many stalls in Camden Market. They seemed to be sinking under the weight of all the old clothes, CDs and old records, televisions and stereo systems, furniture and antiques, lamps and cutlery. Some were selling complete computer systems, and one seller had lots of different fax machines and other office equipment. At the end of the market there was a long row of bicycles shining in the morning sun. The stall next to them was even selling car radios and car tyres.

Hudson shook his head.
"I wouldn't like to know where all of these things have come from. I bet half of all the articles here were stolen. It looks exactly like the room in Scotland Yard where we keep all the stolen goods that we find."
Elvira laughed and put her arm around Inspector Hudsons's shoulders.
"Don't be so negative, James. Besides, I don't believe that all of these things are stolen goods. When I was a student, I often sold stuff at flea markets. The whole business is a cycle: you buy some junk at the flea market, are really enthusiastic about it – and

then you realise that you don't need it after all and sell it again."
"And if you can, you make a profit, eh?" smiled Hudson.
"That, my dear James," grinned Elvira, "completely depends on the selling skills and charm of the seller."
"If that's true, Elvira, then you must have made a fortune at the flea market when you were a student."
Elvira shook her head meaningfully.
"It's possible, James, it's possible."
Elvira pressed herself a little closer to the inspector. Hudson did not mind. After all, it made their cover more realistic.
And it was time to concentrate again on what they were doing.

Übung 10: Welche Wörter gehören in die Lücken?
(acrobat, actor, animal trainer, clown, fire-eater, juggler, mime artist, street entertainer)

ÜBUNG 10 !

1. A ____________ has a big red nose and makes people laugh.

2. An ____________ performs in the theatre or in films.

3. A ____________ throws lots of balls in the air and catches them.

4. A ____________ 'spits' and 'swallows' fire.

5. A ____________ never speaks while he is performing.

6. A ____________ sings songs and tells jokes out on the streets.

7. An ____________ jumps and turns in the air.

8. An ____________ performs with horses, elephants or lions, for example.

For the last few weeks an unusual gang of thieves had been at work in the flea markets and shopping areas of London. The crooks dressed up as mime artists and street entertainers, moved close to the tourists during their performances – and then robbed them.
If one thought about it, it was almost a perfect crime. No-one would think it strange if they saw a mime artist in a mask walking down the streets and around squares in broad daylight. Hudson was surprised that no-one had thought of this idea before.
Anyway, the city council was, of course, not at all happy about it. They had received more and more complaints from tourists who had been robbed. The tourist board was afraid – and not without reason – that visitors might stay away because of it.
And since business people, taxi drivers, and snack bar, hotel and restaurant owners made most of their profit from the streams of tourists, they had asked Scotland Yard's best man for unusual cases, Inspector James Hudson, for help.

! ÜBUNG 11

Übung 11: Wie lauten die Sätze? Bringen Sie die Wörter in die richtige Reihenfolge!

1. my The stole money thief all

   The thief stole all my money.

2. will that I'm away tourists afraid the stay

   ____

3. good It very was idea a

   ____

4. the watch artist and Let's mime stop

---

5. to of restaurant A go that tourists lot

In order to look more like a tourist, James Hudson had asked his good friend Elvira Elliot to come with him on his trips around London's famous flea markets. The markets attracted thousands of tourists every day – it was clear that these criminal street entertainers would also feel attracted to them.
However, up to now the inspector's efforts had been unsuccessful. For the last three weekends he had wandered through the flea markets with Elvira, but all of the mime artists that they had seen so far had been harmless.
The tourist board was becoming nervous, and Sir Reginald, Hudson's boss at Scotland Yard, wanted to see results.

Übung 12: Unterstreichen Sie von den beiden Alternativen das passende Wort!

Hudson (1.) shouted/sighed and looked around. It was nearly (2.) midday/midnight and the (3.) narrow/dirty gaps between the individual stalls were getting fuller and fuller. (4.) A couple/Crowds of people pushed past in every direction, (5.) stopped/held in front of individual stalls, haggled about the (6.) prices/prizes and then continued on their way. It was (7.) different/difficult to keep track of everything that was going on in all the hubbub.

A pickpocket would have an (8.) easy/happy job in this crowd. Instinctively Hudson (9.) checked/controlled whether his own (10.) wallet/handbag was still in his pocket.

Yes, it was still there, thank God.

It would not make a very good impression if a Scotland Yard inspector reported that he had been attacked and his wallet had been stolen.

Hudson breathed a sigh of relief and pointed to a corner of the market where the stalls were not so near to each other.

"Come on, Elvira," he said, "let's go over there. This crowd is giving me claustrophobia."

Elvira nodded and followed the inspector.

In a couple of minutes they reached the end of the market. There were a few people selling sofas and cupboards here.

But the inspector was especially interested in a small group of people who were standing near the entrance to a side street.

The people had their backs to Hudson and Elvira, so the inspector could not see what was happening in front of them.

"Let's see what's going on over there," said James Hudson and went towards the group of people.

Loud laughter came from the crowd.

As politely as possible, they pushed past the people who were watching a little show.

A tall mime artist was standing on a small platform and doing a very good impression of Charlie Chaplin, the famous comedian. Although the artist wasn't wearing a bowler hat or carrying a walking stick, you could see who he was imitating immediately.

Elvira burst out laughing when the mime artist pretended to slip on a banana skin. Even Hudson had to smile.

Übung 13: Beantworten Sie die folgenden Fragen zum Text!

1. Were there many people at the market?

___

2. Did anyone steal Inspector Hudson's wallet?

___

3. What were the people near the side street looking at?

___

4. Was the mime artist a good performer?

___

5. Why did Elvira and the inspector laugh?

___

The man with the white make-up on his face really seemed to be good at his job. He didn't look like an ordinary thief who had simply dressed up as a street mime artist in order to practice his dubious profession without being noticed.

"Come on, Elvira," said Hudson quietly to the insurance agent, "the man seems to be harmless. And we're not here to have fun."

"Oh, just a minute, James," begged Elvira. "The boy is really very good."

James Hudson sighed. He simply couldn't refuse Elvira anything. And the inspector had to admit that the mime artist in front of him really knew what he was doing.

Oh well, he thought, a few minutes here or there won't make any difference. After all, today was Saturday and officially he had the day off.

Suddenly, a shout echoed through the crowd of onlookers.
"My wallet! It's gone!"
Inspector Hudson quickly turned around. Just a short distance away from him stood a fat man in a bright checked shirt. An expensive camera hung around his neck and rested on his stomach. Obviously an American tourist.
In despair, the man searched all of his trouser and jacket pockets for his wallet.
In vain.
Hudson glanced at the mime artist, who was continuing his show as if there was nothing unusual going on. He was acting as if all of this was nothing to do with him, but it couldn't be a coincidence. The mime artist probably had an accomplice who stole the onlookers' wallets while their attention was on his show.

ÜBUNG 14 !

Übung 14: Fügen Sie die richtigen Präpositionen ein!
(at, at, for, off, out, to, towards, towards)

Hudson reached 1. _________ his own wallet, took 2. _________ his police badge and walked 3. _________ the mime artist.

"Inspector James Hudson, Scotland Yard," he said 4. _________ him in an authoritative voice. "I'd like to ask you a few questions."

The mime artist made a theatrical gesture of surprise. A few of the onlookers laughed 5. _________ him, but Hudson was no longer in the mood for jokes.

He took another step 6. ________ the mime artist. But, quick as a flash, the artist jumped 7. ________ the small box that was his platform and kicked it 8. ________ the inspector.

Inspector Hudson nearly stumbled and only just managed to keep his balance. The mime artist used this opportunity to race away down the side street.
A few of the onlookers were still laughing. They probably thought that this was all part of the show.
Hudson kicked the little box aside angrily and started to run after the mime artist.
"We'll catch him!" Elvira Elliot shouted to the inspector.
Hudson would have preferred Elvira not to take part in the chase – she wasn't a police officer, after all – but now was not the time to argue with the young insurance agent.
The crooked mime artist was obviously very fit and ran at great speed. Hudson noticed how much he himself was sweating.
But all Scotland Yard officers have to work out regularly as part of their standard training programme. He soon reduced the distance between himself and the mime artist. The inspector heard Elvira running close behind him. The villain wasn't going to get away.

Übung 15: Welches Wort passt nicht? Finden Sie das „schwarze Schaf"!

ÜBUNG 15 !

1. shout, yell, talk, scream ________________
2. park, street, alley, motorway ________________
3. drink, eat, have dinner, cry ________________

4. police, doctor, stylist, ambulance ____________

5. water, fire, flame, burn ____________

6. jogging, weight lifting, sweating ____________

7. fast, slow, quick, speedy ____________

8. punch, hit, kick, throw ____________

9. watch, chase, follow, run after ____________

10. car, bicycle, bus, ship ____________

Suddenly a shadow appeared from a small side alley and blocked the inspector's way. A bald, muscular man with a bare chest and a torch in his hand jumped onto the street.

A fire-eater! thought Hudson, just as the stranger spat a huge flame at him and Elvira.

The mime artist obviously had other accomplices to help him escape. The gang really seemed to be very professional.

But he could worry about that later.

"Get down, Elvira!" shouted Hudson.

At the same moment, the inspector and the insurance agent threw themselves to the ground.

James Hudson felt the flame from the fire-eater's mouth pass directly over his head and burn his hair a little bit.

The same thing happened to Elvira.

"My hair!" she yelled. "He must be crazy!"

At that moment, Hudson jumped to his feet again.

Before the fire-eater could spit out another flame, Hudson hit him on the chin with a well-timed punch.

The man groaned and fell, unconscious, to the ground. Hudson grabbed the fallen torch and put out the fire in a puddle.

They could pick up the man later – now they had to keep after the escaping mime artist.
"Not bad," said Elvira in amazement, as Hudson helped her to her feet again. "With a punch like that, you could have been a boxer in a circus, James!"
"Your career advice will have to wait, Elvira," panted Hudson, still slightly out of breath, "first we've got to catch the mime artist! I hope he doesn't have any more accomplices along the way. We'll end up fighting a whole circus!"
Elvira gave a short laugh, then followed the inspector, who had already started to run again.

Übung 16: Welche der folgenden Aussagen sind wahr?
Markieren Sie: richtig ✓ falsch –

1. The fire-eater was a friend of the mime artist's.
2. Hudson and Elvira felt the fire on their heads.
3. The fire-eater ran away after Hudson punched him.
4. The mime artist was still running away.
5. Hudson once worked in a circus.

The mime artist had disappeared around a street corner. Hudson and Elvira hurried after him. The inspector and the insurance agent turned the corner – and found themselves in a blind alley.
Fortunately for them, the mime artist had fallen into the same trap. At the end of the street, the criminal was desperately trying to pull a few dustbins to the wall so that he could climb over it.
"Stop right there, my fine friend!" shouted Hudson.
The startled mime artist looked around and swore when he saw Hudson and Elvira.

The inspector fished a pair of handcuffs out of his jacket pocket and went towards the mime artist. Elvira followed him.

! ÜBUNG 17

Übung 17: Übersetzen Sie!

1. Hudson und Elvira waren sehr überrascht.

____

2. Der Mann fuhr auf einem kleinen Fahrrad.

____

3. Der Künstler konnte nicht entkommen.

____

4. Seine Freunde versuchten, ihm zu helfen.

____

5. Sie rannten sehr schnell.

____

"Not so fast, cop!"
Hudson and Elvira turned round. A tall man in a circus costume was riding into the alley on a unicycle. He was juggling three big clubs.
This just gets better, thought Hudson. First a mime artist, then a fire-eater and now a juggler as well. What would be next? A circus elephant?

"You're under arrest, too," shouted Hudson. "At the very least for insulting a police officer and riding a bike that is not safe for use in traffic."

He had had just about enough of the whole business.

Übung 18: Suchen Sie das Gegenteil der Wörter in Klammern!

However, the (1. fat) ____________________ acrobat didn't seem particularly impressed. He (2. slowly) ______________ threw one of his juggling clubs (3. low) ____________________ into the air, caught it again – and threw the (4. light) _______________ object at the inspector with all of his strength.

"Hey!" was all Hudson could shout. He only just managed to duck away from the club. With a (5. quiet) ________________ bang it crashed into the wall behind him.

Before Hudson could do anything, Elvira started to run.

"Elvira! No!" shouted Hudson, but it was too (6. early) ________ _______. The insurance agent had almost reached the (7. attractive) _______________ man on the unicycle. Alarmed, the juggler threw the second club at Elvira – but the (8. old) ____________ woman stopped it from hitting her with a clever karate kick.

Then Elvira reached the juggler. The horrified man tried to get away on his unicycle, but Elvira was faster.

Full of admiration, Hudson watched as the insurance agent kicked the little cycle out from under the man.

With a yell of anger the man landed unsteadily on his feet. The villain wanted to punch Elvira, but he was too slow this time, too.

Elvira ducked under his fist and sent the criminal flying to the ground with a hard punch.

Half-unconscious and groaning, the man fell to the ground.

"He's had enough," said Elvira with a grin and then looked with concern at her fingernails. "But I nearly broke a nail because of him."

Hudson gave the insurance agent a big smile.

"Great work, Elvira. Did you learn that at the insurance agent college?"

"You learn that, my dear James," grinned Elvira, "when you grow up with three older brothers."

ÜBUNG 19 !

Übung 19: Übersetzen Sie die Körperteile und enträtseln Sie das Lösungswort!

1. Fuß ☐ _ _ _
2. Kinn _ _ ☐ _
3. Knie _ ☐ _ _
4. Zahnfleisch ☐ _ _
5. Ohr ☐ _ _
6. Augenbraue _ _ _ _ ☐ _ _
7. Knöchel _ ☐ _ _ _

8. Bauch _ _ _ _ □ _ _

9. Lippe _ □ _

10. Schulter _ _ _ _ □ _ _ _

Lösung: _ _ _ _ _ _ _ _ _ _

Hudson grinned. Elvira took a step forward.
"Look out, Elvira!" shouted Hudson, but it was too late.
With her left foot, Elvira Elliot stepped on the criminal's third juggling club. She twisted her ankle and fell to the ground with a scream.
A moment later, Hudson was at her side.
Elvira was holding her ankle, which was already quite swollen, and her face was twisted with pain.
"Are you all right, Elvira?" asked Hudson in concern.
"Damn!" gasped the young woman. "I think I've torn a ligament. Why did that idiot have to leave his clubs lying all over the place?"
As carefully as he could, Hudson slipped off his jacket and wrapped it around the young woman's ankle to give it some support. Then he took his mobile phone out of his pocket and dialed 999, the number for ambulance, fire brigade and police in England.

Übung 20: Wie heißen die zusammengesetzten Substantive? Setzen Sie die richtige Ziffer ein!

ÜBUNG 20 !

1.	finger	□	call
2.	bus	□	post
3.	alarm	□	park
4.	phone	□	print
5.	washing	□	clock

6.	car	☐	lights
7.	sun	☐	machine
8.	mobile	☐	stop
9.	sign	☐	glasses
10.	traffic	☐	phone

In a couple of seconds, he got through to a young lady on the switchboard who immediately connected him to the emergency services.

Hudson gave his name, his location and the type of injury. The man on the other end of the line promised to send an ambulance as quickly as possible.

"Sorry to cause you so much trouble, James," whispered Elvira guiltily.

But Hudson just shook his head.

"Don't talk nonsense, Elvira. Without you, these villains would have got away. And to be quite honest, I'm not sure whether I would have been able to stop this fellow and his clubs without your help."

Hudson smiled at the insurance agent again, then he went back to the wall.

The crooked mime artist was still standing there, looking down. He had obviously given up. Maybe he could tell by the inspector's eyes that Hudson was not in the mood for any more tricks. Not now that Elvira had been hurt.

The ambulance siren could be heard in the distance.

Hudson dragged the mime artist over to the juggler, who was still unconscious, and handcuffed them together.

"So, that's that!"

Then he grabbed the mime artist by the collar.

"And you have the right to remain silent, chum …"

Übung 21: Wählen Sie die richtige Alternative!

1. Elvira ________ her ankle.
   a) ☐ injured
   b) ☐ pained
   c) ☐ fell

2. Hudson ________ the Yard what had happened.
   a) ☐ said
   b) ☐ asked
   c) ☐ told

3. Elvira ________.
   a) ☐ was sorry that she had helped Hudson
   b) ☐ did not want to go in the ambulance
   c) ☐ could not stand up

4. The mime artist ________.
   a) ☐ climbed over the wall
   b) ☐ waited by the wall
   c) ☐ helped the juggler

5. In the end, Hudson ________.
   a) ☐ arrested the two criminals
   b) ☐ told the mime artist to be quiet
   c) ☐ put the criminals in the ambulance

Inspector Hudson pulled a face.
Why did all hospitals have to smell so strongly of disinfectant?
Miss Paddington, Hudson's faithful housekeeper, seemed to be thinking the same.

"Just the smell of a hospital makes me feel ill. I hope Miss Elliot won't have to stay in here too long. She's so full of life!" said Miss Paddington, in admiration. "It must be a real nightmare for her to be stuck in here."

"Stop it, Miss Paddington. You're making me feel even worse than I already do," replied Hudson, "after all, I'm the one who got Elvira into this mess."

Elvira Elliot really had torn a ligament during the arrest of the mime artist and his gang and now had to spend a couple of weeks in bed.

! ÜBUNG 22

Übung 22: Enträtseln Sie die folgenden Definitionen!

1. A place for sick people. *hospital* (ltasphio)
2. A place for tourists to stay the night. ____________ (othle)
3. A place to catch a train. ____________ (ittsano)
4. A place to buy stamps. ____________ (stop cofife)
5. A place to buy food. ____________ (pamsuretrek)
6. A place to see a play. ____________ (heeratt)
7. A place to have a meal. ____________ (treastraun)
8. A place to see a film. ____________ (mencia)
9. A place to see interesting old objects. ____________ (smuemu)
10. The place where the mayor works. ____________ (nowt lalh)

Hudson and Miss Paddington headed for the reception desk.
"Good evening. We would like to visit Miss Elvira Elliot," said the inspector, politely.
The skinny woman behind the window looked up from her computer grumpily and pointed to a small sign.
"Visiting hours were over a long time ago. Can't you read?" she snapped.
"Mmm," was all that Inspector Hudson said, as he calmly took his police badge out of his pocket. He held it up to the window.
"I hope you can read this," he replied dryly, "Inspector James Hudson, Scotland Yard."
It wasn't exactly legal to use his police badge for private purposes – but on the other hand, Elvira had been injured while helping Scotland Yard.

Übung 23: Unterstreichen Sie die fünf inhaltlich nicht dazugehörigen Sätze!

The woman behind the glass raised her eyebrows in surprise. She went to the bathroom. "Oh, inspector," she stammered, "I'm sorry. I had no way of knowing."
The woman took a shower. Then she tapped feverishly on the keyboard of her computer.
"Ah, here we are – Miss E. Elliot, Room Four, third floor, accident surgery department."
Hudson closed his police badge again with a snap. All he wanted was to go home and go to bed.
"Thank you very much. Have a nice evening."
The woman behind the glass nodded. Suddenly she turned around starting to sing a christmas song.

"You're welcome. I live just around the corner. Tell me, has this Miss Elliot done anything bad? I thought she seemed very suspicious. Are you going to arrest her?"

The woman's eyes shone. She was probably hoping to have something to gossip about during her coffee break.
"I'm sorry," Hudson said, "it's top secret."
"I understand, inspector," called the woman through the window, "I won't tell anyone!"
But Hudson and Miss Paddington were already on the way to the lift.
"What an unpleasant person!" hissed Miss Paddington, as the lift doors slowly opened.
Hudson nodded in agreement.
"A real dragon!"
A few moments later the lift doors closed behind them. Inspector Hudson was just able to see the woman at the reception desk gossiping excitedly into the telephone. She was probably spreading the story that there was a dangerous criminal in the accident surgery department.

ÜBUNG 24 !

Übung 24: Welche Gegenteile gehören zusammen?

1.	open	☐	low
2.	interesting	☐	full
3.	dangerous	☐	closed
4.	pleasant	☐	ill
5.	empty	☐	harmless
6.	high	☐	rude
7.	lazy	☐	boring

8. polite ☐ horrible
9. healthy ☐ unpleasant
10. nice ☐ hard-working

The lift doors opened again and Hudson let Miss Paddington go ahead of him.
"After you, my dear."
They stepped into the corridor and knocked on the door of Room Four. Hudson and Miss Paddington looked at each other in surprise when they heard a crash behind the door. A few seconds passed, and then a voice called:
"Come in!"
Hudson opened the door carefully. Elvira Elliot was lying on her hospital bed with a bandage on her ankle and a big smile on her face.
"Oh, it's you, James! And Miss Paddington. What a nice surprise! Come over here!"
"Thank you, Elvira. How are you?"

Übung 25: Wie lauten die Sätze?

ÜBUNG 25 !

1. come her asked in Elvira to friends

___

2. what be They noise could wondered the

___

3. and to bed leg She stay broke in her had

___

4. water you in these Could some put flowers ?

____

5. to is have hospital you boring do It nothing if in

____

Elvira seemed unconcerned.
"Oh, the operation went well – it was nothing. But all this lying around is really getting on my nerves. And I've only been here for one day."
"Oh, you poor thing," sympathised Miss Paddington. "But tell me, you haven't already tried to get up and walk around in here, have you?"
Inspector Hudson's housekeeper looked sternly at Elvira.
"We heard some sort of bump, you know, before you asked us to come in."

ÜBUNG 26 !

Übung 26: Fügen Sie die Übersetzung der angegebenen Wörter ein!

Then Inspector Hudson and Miss Paddington both jumped, because the door to the (1. Schrank) ____________________ by the wall (2. plötzlich) ________________ opened.

Hudson couldn't believe his eyes.

Sir Reginald, his (3. Chef) ______________ at Scotland Yard, was standing in front of him.

"Sir Reginald?" gasped Hudson. "What are you doing here? And

(4. warum) ____________________ were you in the cupboard?"

Sir Reginald rearranged his (5. Krawatte) __________ and frowned, looking even more like a bulldog than he usually did.

"Now don't look so horrified, Hudson. Sometimes men do hide in cupboards belonging to (6. hübsch) __________ young ladies, you know."

Hudson and Miss Paddington looked at each other in (7. Erstaunen) ____________________.

Elvira giggled like a (8. Schulmädchen) ________________.

"No, seriously, Hudson," smiled Sir Reginald, "when I heard the (9. Klopfen) ____________ I thought it was one of those horrible (10. Krankenschwestern) ____________________.

Visiting hours were over a long time ago, you see. Every day I have to deal with some of the meanest criminals in the United Kingdom, but nothing is more frightening than an angry nurse. That's why I quickly hid in the cupboard.
But now let me say hello to Miss Paddington."
Sir Reginald took Miss Paddington's hand, smiled embarrased, and kissed it.
"You look as charming as usual, my dear," he said.
Miss Paddington went red.
"Thank you, Sir Reginald. You're a real gentleman."
Hudson and Elvira grinned at each other while the inspector put the flowers that he had brought with him into an ugly hospital vase.

ÜBUNG 27 !

Übung 27: Welche Verben und Substantive gehören zusammen?

1.	say	☐	a present
2.	watch	☐	one's teeth
3.	pay	☐	a bike
4.	make	☐	hello
5.	give	☐	television
6.	read	☐	some work
7.	brush	☐	a bill
8.	do	☐	a car
9.	drive	☐	a phone call
10.	ride	☐	a book

Then Hudson asked, "What are you doing here, Sir Reginald?"
"Well, I just wanted to thank Miss Elliot personally for what she did yesterday. And also to congratulate you on the arrest of the crooks, my dear Hudson. I know that those three villains must have had another accomplice who was the pickpocket, but he probably won't have the courage to rob any more tourists without his colleagues to help him. The tourist board is very pleased with your work, James and Elvira."
"It was my pleasure, Sir Reginald," said Elvira.
"And I was only doing my duty, Sir Reginald," said Hudson.
Sir Reginald gave a satisfied grunt. For him, this was the highest form of praise.
"Speaking of duty," said Hudson's boss, quietly, "I've already got a new case for you, James."
Miss Paddington noticed the change in Sir Reginald's tone of voice and turned to Elvira. "I can see that these two gentlemen want to talk about official business. Why don't you both go out into the corridor while I give Elvira the little present we've brought for her?"

Übung 28: Welcher Satz enthält die richtige Übersetzung?

1. Hudsons Chef war im Schrank.
   a) ☐ Hudson's head master was in the cupboard.
   b) ☐ Hudon's boss was in the cupboard.

2. Die Aufgabe war schwer.
   a) ☐ It was a heavy task.
   b) ☐ It was a difficult task.

3. Sir Reginald sagte ihnen, warum er da war.
   a) ☐ Sir Reginald told them why he was there.
   b) ☐ Sir Reginald cried them why he was there.

4. Miss Paddington kochte Kaffee.
   a) ☐ Miss Paddington cooked some coffee.
   b) ☐ Miss Paddington made some coffee.

5. Du musst die Bücher nicht jetzt lesen.
   a) ☐ You don't have to read the books now.
   b) ☐ You mustn't read the books now.

Miss Paddington reached into her handbag and produced a stack of detective stories.
"Oh," said Elvira, "are they for me? Fantastic!"
The young woman enthusiastically reached for the books that Miss Paddington had taken out of her bag. Elvira obviously loved detective stories just as much as Miss Paddington herself.
"Ah, 'The Murderer in the Mask'," said Elvira, examining the sensational book cover, "I've always wanted to read that."
"Oh, it's a very good one!" agreed Sir Reginald.

Hudson was amazed.

"*You* read detective stories, Sir Reginald?"

Sir Reginald went red and shook his head.

"… uhm, I …, uuhm, have *heard* that it is very good. My, er, wife told me." Then Sir Reginald took the inspector by the arm and led him through the door into the corridor. Hudson was sure that he had seen Sir Reginald and Miss Paddington wink at each other. The inspector had guessed a long time ago that his housekeeper and his boss had been secretly swapping detective stories for years. However, he had never been able to prove it.

"Well, Sir Reginald," asked Hudson, after he had quietly closed the door behind him, "what is my next case going to be?"

Sir Reginald waved his hand in the air.

"Oh, nothing special, Hudson. I just want you to go on a vampire hunt."

ÜBUNG 29 !

Übung 29: Beantworten Sie die Fragen zum Text!

1. Does Elvira like staying in bed all day?

____

2. Why was Sir Reginald in the cupboard?

____

3. What did the inspector bring for Elvira?

____

4. What was Miss Paddington's present?

____

5. Does Sir Reginald read detective stories?

____

"I beg your pardon?"
Inspector Hudson could not believe his ears. "Are you joking, Sir Reginald?"
But Hudson's boss simply shook his head.
"I'm afraid not. Look at this."
Sir Reginald reached into his briefcase, which he had brought with him into the corridor. He took out a copy of the London Times and began to leaf through the newspaper, not an easy job as the Times was a large, heavy publication.
"Where is it?" he murmured. "Politics, current affairs, arts, sports … ah, here we are! Under 'miscellaneous'!"

Übung 30: In welchem Teil der Zeitung findet man Informationen zu folgenden Themen? ***(arts, business, current affairs, education, miscellaneous, politics, sports, travel)***

1. Information about the government _______________
2. Football results _______________
3. Information about companies and world markets _______________
4. Tips for holidays _______________
5. Things happening around the world at the moment _______________

6. Information about plays, books and museums ____________

7. Information about schools and universities ____________

Sir Reginald held the newspaper in one hand and fished a small pair of reading glasses out of his jacket pocket with the other. Then he put the glasses on and was finally ready to begin.
Inspector Hudson listened with interest as Sir Reginald read the report in a low voice:

ÜBUNG 31

Übung 31: Unterstreichen Sie die neun Substantive, die sich auf Personen beziehen!

"London. In several parks and public areas eyewitnesses have reported the sighting of an unidentified figure dressed as a vampire. The latest victims of this person, who appears to be a madman, were a young couple who came across the stranger last night in the city park. After the villain announced that he was thirsty for the young couple's blood, they ran away. Nobody was hurt during this or other similar incidents in the last few days. The police are certain that they are dealing with someone who is mentally ill. Nothing is known about the identity or the motive of the 'vampire'."

Sir Reginald cleared his throat.
Hudson shrugged his shoulders.
"I don't know, Sir Reginald. It sounds to me as if this really is the work of a madman. And as long as he doesn't harm anyone – after all the whole thing is only printed at the bottom of the page under 'miscellaneous'…"
Sir Reginald grunted and took another newspaper out of his brief-

case. This one was a lot thinner and in a smaller format. Sir Reginald pulled out the newspaper with the tips of his fingers as if he had to touch something dirty.
"If that was all, Hudson, if only that was all. It's a nice meaty story for some of these other … publications."
Hudson stared in horror at the newspaper with its huge red headlines.
"The Enquirer? You read this rubbish, Sir Reginald?" he asked in surprise.
"I have to, Hudson, I have to. For professional reasons. Look at this headline."
Hudson didn't need glasses to read the enormous headline.
"VAMPIRE TERROR IN LONDON! POLICE POWERLESS!"
The inspector shook his head.
"What a lot of nonsense! Who takes something like that seriously?"
"Oh, a lot of people, Hudson. You'd be surprised. Here, look at this, there's even a sketch of the so-called vampire. Drawn with the help of eyewitness reports."
Hudson looked at the crude black and white drawing which showed a thin man with a long face and a long cape. The artist who had drawn the picture had, of course, taken care to particularly emphasize the pointed vampire teeth.

Übung 32: Finden Sie das „schwarze Schaf"!

ÜBUNG 32 !

1. picture, drawing, film, portrait ______________
2. teeth, lips, tongue, head ______________
3. magazine, headline, article, report ______________

4. journalist, reporter, eyewitness, photographer __________

5. thin, fat, slim, skinny __________

6. hospital, nurse, doctor, surgeon __________

7. ill, sick, unwell, healthy __________

8. concerned, worried, relaxed, nervous __________

9. terrible, mad, crazy, insane __________

10. corridor, lift, hall, lobby __________

"This is ridiculous, Sir Reginald. A vampire in London – what century are we living in?"

"You don't have to tell me, James. But the Yard has been getting concerned phone calls all day. People are asking when the police are finally going to do something about this 'vampire terror'. And the tourist board is getting nervous again. First the crooked street entertainers, now a madman pretending to be a vampire … If this goes on, soon no tourist will have the courage to visit London any more."

Inspector Hudson nodded to show that he understood. He hadn't looked at it like that.

"And you want me to take on the case, Sir Reginald?"

Before Hudson's boss could reply, they heard a high, irritated voice.

"Please leave immediately, gentlemen! Visiting hours are over!"

Hudson and Sir Reginald turned around with a start. A plump nurse was marching resolutely towards them. And she was definitely not in a good mood.

"For heaven's sake!" gasped Sir Reginald. "Let's get out of here!"

Übung 33: Wählen Sie die richtige Alternative aus!

1. Hudson and Sir Reginald were _____ to see the nurse.
   a) ☐ surprised
   b) ☐ glad
   c) ☐ angry

2. The nurse was in a _____ mood.
   a) ☐ good
   b) ☐ bad
   c) ☐ happy

3. The nurse was _____.
   a) ☐ very thin
   b) ☐ a little bit overweight
   c) ☐ tall

4. Sir Reginald wanted to _____.
   a) ☐ leave immediately
   b) ☐ talk to the nurse
   c) ☐ go back into Elvira's room

5. Visiting hours in the hospital were _____.
   a) ☐ only in the evenings
   b) ☐ early in the morning
   c) ☐ finished for the day

Hudson pulled open the door to Elvira's room.
"Miss Paddington! We need to get out of here as quickly as possible! We're in danger!"
But Miss Paddington had already heard the nurse's voice.

She pressed Elvira's hand again and, quick as a flash, grabbed her handbag.
"Goodbye, my dear! We'll come and visit you again soon," she said to the grinning Elvira as she rushed out of the door.
"Thank you very much for the books. And thank you for coming to visit. Goodbye, James! Goodbye, Sir Reginald!"
The two men waved quickly at the giggling insurance agent and rushed along the corridor.
"Sorry, my dear lady!" Sir Reginald called to the nurse. "We've already gone!"
"I should hope so, too! Kindly come back during the normal visiting hours – like everyone else."

ÜBUNG 34 !

Übung 34: Welche Synonyme gehören zusammen?

1. elevator	☐	astonishment
2. sketch	☐	rubbish
3. smile	☐	purse
4. nonsense	☐	lift
5. way out	☐	talk about
6. hurry	☐	drawing
7. wallet	☐	rush
8. notice	☐	grin
9. discuss	☐	exit
10. surprise	☐	catch sight of

A few seconds later Inspector Hudson, Sir Reginald and Miss Paddington were standing in the lift which took them down to the lobby. Sir Reginald was still holding the front page of the Enquirer in his hand.

Miss Paddington looked at it with interest.
"I didn't know that you read the Enquirer, Sir Reginald," she said.
Sir Reginald went red.
"For professional reasons," he replied, "only for professional reasons."
"Aha," said Miss Paddington, meaningfully.
Inspector Hudson grinned to himself.
Then Miss Paddington caught sight of the sketch of the so-called vampire. The old lady raised her eyebrows in surprise.
"Is this your latest case, James?" she asked.
Inspector Hudson nodded.
"Looks like it. Why do you ask, Miss Paddington?"
The old lady looked at Inspector Hudson and Sir Reginald with a smile.
"Well, because I know that fellow!"

Übung 35: Setzen Sie die Wörter an der richtigen Stelle ein! ***(cup, home, housekeeper, town, policemen, pot of tea, room, steaming)***

"Why don't you finally tell us where you know this so-called vampire from …, Miss Paddington?" asked Sir Reginald impatiently.

He had followed Inspector Hudson and Miss Paddington 1. _________. As soon as they had arrived, the old lady had pushed the two 2. ______________ into the living 3. _________ so that she could first make a nice 4. ______________.

"Calm down," said the 5. _______________, offering the police officer the tray with the 6. _______________ cups of tea on it.

Sir Reginald and Hudson each took a 7. _________.

"Thank you very much, Miss Paddington," said Hudson. "But now I'd really like to find out how you, of all people, know the vampire that we've been looking for all over 8. _________."

"Well," replied the housekeeper, "I don't really know him. Not personally, at least. Wait, and I'll explain."
Ignoring the astonished faces of the two policemen, Miss Paddington excused herself for a moment and went upstairs to her room.
Hudson and Sir Reginald looked at each other, baffled.
A minute later, Miss Paddington returned. She was carrying a pile of video cassettes.
"Here's our vampire," she said, proudly.
Then she knelt down in front of the video recorder, which was under the television, and pushed one of the cassettes into the slot. At once, a picture flickered onto the television screen.

! ÜBUNG 36

Übung 36: Übersetzen Sie und enträtseln Sie das Lösungswort!

1. Pflanze _ ☐ _ _ _
2. Sessel _ _ _ _ _ _ _ ☐ _
3. Fernseher _ _ _ _ ☐ _ _ _ _ _
4. Kissen _ _ _ _ ☐ _ _

5. Gardine _ _ _ _ _ _ □

6. Brettspiele _ _ _ _ _ □ _ _ _ _

7. Teppich _ _ □ _ _ _

8. Bücherschrank _ _ □ _ _ _ _ _

9. Fernbedienung _ _ _ □ _ _ _ _ _ _ _ _ _

10. Lampe _ _ □ _

Lösung: _ _ _ _ _ _ _ _ _ _

Hudson and Sir Reginald watched in astonishment as a dark shadow darted across a cemetery. Fog rose from the ground – and it wasn't difficult to see that it came from a smoke machine. Then a spotlight, which was obviously meant to represent the moon, shone onto the man's face. Long, pointed fangs flashed in the light. The vampire with the long, pale face and the combed-back hair looked all around him.

Sir Reginald picked up the newspaper and compared the face of the actor on the television screen with the sketch of the so-called vampire.

"That's our vampire!" he gasped.

Inspector Hudson also looked at the sketch in surprise.

"It really is. A little bit younger, maybe, and a bit taller, but the similarity is amazing."

Then he turned to Miss Paddington again.

"My dear Miss Paddington, what film is this? And who is that actor?"

Miss Paddington shook her head with a grin.

"Oh really, James, you don't know much about popular culture, do you? That's Basil Thornwood, famous for his role as Dracula in the 1970s. He made more than a dozen vampire films for Anvil Studios back then. I've seen them all! I love these old horror movies."

The inspector nodded.

"That's right, I remember hearing the name somewhere. But why should this Mr Thornwood, suddenly start creeping through parks and frightening young couples, thirty years later?"

Miss Paddington looked at the inspector, puzzled.

"I have no idea. Sir Reginald, what do you think?"

Übung 37: Welche Wörter passen zusammen?

1. famous	☐	light
2. horror	☐	chair
3. friendly	☐	car
4. dangerous	☐	actor
5. comfortable	☐	friend
6. good	☐	smile
7. bright	☐	news
8. thick	☐	movie
9. close	☐	fog
10. fast	☐	criminal

Inspector Hudson's boss looked up.

"Pardon? Oh, I'm sorry, Miss Paddington, could you take a step to the side? You're blocking the screen. It's just getting exciting."

With a giggle, Miss Paddington stepped aside.

"These old films are good, aren't they?"

"They certainly are," nodded Sir Reginald enthusiastically. "Back then they knew how to make thrillers with simple methods. Ah – here we go!"

Miss Paddington squeezed herself between the two men on the couch.

On the television the vampire, in the form of a bat, was flying around in the room of a beautiful, sleeping woman.

"Oh, how gruesome!" breathed Miss Paddington. "But don't worry – Doctor Van Helsing, the vampire hunter, will be there in a minute!"

Inspector Hudson sighed and took another sip of tea. It was going to be a long evening.

Übung 38: Unterstreichen Sie die richtige Alternative!

Harry McDermott bit (1.) on/into his sandwich. (2.) Half an hour ago/For half an hour he had parked the security van (3.) in front of/in opposite of the Harris Commercial Bank and was now waiting (4.) of/for the bags of banknotes to be loaded into the van.

Harry pulled a face. His (5.) wife/woman had put tuna in his sandwich again. It was the same (6.) every evening/all evening – why couldn't she give him cheese or ham for a (7.) chance/change? But the McDermotts had (8.) bought/brought a little flat a few months ago which now had to be (9.) paid/paid for. The interest rates were high and tuna was (10.) expensive/cheap.

So Harry took another bite out of his sandwich and looked at the thickening fog which was spreading itself through the dark streets. That was the problem with night shifts – he always had an uneasy feeling, driving through the streets of London at night with a van full of money, but the night shifts were the best paid.

A knock interrupted his thoughts. He jumped. A pale face appeared at the side window of the security van.

Harry was so startled that he nearly choked on his bread. He rolled down the window.

It was Tim, his co-driver.

"Hey ..., you really gave me a fright, Tim," complained Harry. "Do you always have to creep around like that? What's the matter ...?"

Tim looked very bad-tempered. He pointed towards the back of the van.

"Put your stinking fish sandwich away and come and help me. We have to load a couple of extra bags tonight. The bank's business seems to be booming at the moment."

Harry sighed. Of course.

People like him had trouble making ends meet while the banks were raking it in.

ÜBUNG 39 !

Übung 39: Welche Bedeutung haben folgende Sätze? Kreuzen Sie an!

1. Elvira stands on her own two feet.
   a) ☐ Elvira is indefinite.
   b) ☐ Elvira is individual.
   c) ☐ Elvira is independent.

2. Harry and Tim are excited.
   a) ☐ They have departed.
   b) ☐ They are nervous.
   c) ☐ They are exciting.

3. Tell me to my face.
   a) ☐ Don't tell me the truth.
   b) ☐ Tell me straight.
   c) ☐ Tell me how I look.

4. Hudson can defend himself.
   a) ☐ They protested against Hudson.
   b) ☐ Hudson can protect himself.
   c) ☐ Hudson is very defensive.

5. That will be all.
   a) ☐ That's all I have to say.
   b) ☐ That will be great.
   c) ☐ Right now it's nothing.

It really was a great temptation. Driving hundreds of thousands of pounds around, night after night. How easy it would be to simply take one of the bags of money, jump onto the next plane and jet off to South America.

Harry stuffed his sandwich into the glove compartment of the security van and opened the door.

It was actually against the rules for the driver to leave the van. But he could hardly sit there, eating, while his colleague had to work. Harry McDermott got out of the van and followed Tim. A dozen or so money bags had already been loaded into the back of the armoured van. Half-a-dozen more bags were lying on the ground behind it. Harry could tell at a glance from the shape that these bags contained coins.

Great. Tim had saved the heaviest work until last.

Harry rolled up his sleeves and heaved the first bag up into the back of the van. It was amazing how heavy a bag of coins was.

When he lifted the second bag he was already sweating. Harry felt the tuna sandwich rumbling in his stomach.

Suddenly, the sound of slow, sinister footsteps echoed through the fog.

Harry and Tim looked around at once. Harry's hand felt instinctively for the gun on his hip.

"Who's there?" called Harry.

No answer.

ÜBUNG 40 !

Übung 40: Vervollständigen Sie die Fragen mit einem passenden Fragewort!

1. ______________ is the nearest bank?
2. ______________ is your favourite actor?
3. ______________ time do you finish work?
4. ______________ does the next train leave?
5. ______________ do you spell your name?
6. ______________ are you crying?
7. ______________ would you prefer, tea or coffee?
8. ______________ sort of car do you drive?
9. ______________ was the man in the vampire costume?
10. ______________ can I buy an English newspaper?

The footsteps came nearer, but the thick fog muffled all sounds. It was impossible to say which direction the steps were coming from. The two men looked around nervously.

"This is a security van," shouted Harry in a louder voice. "Please keep away until we have finished here."

The sound came closer.

A shadowy figure appeared out of the fog. It slowly walked towards the two men.

Harry screwed up his eyes. All he could see was that the figure was tall and wearing some sort of long coat.

"Looks like a tramp," whispered Tim. "He shouldn't cause us any problems."

"Hey, you! Get lost!" he shouted. "We're armed!"

But the figure continued to move towards the security van.

"He's probably completely drunk," laughed Tim.

However, Harry had an uneasy feeling. Although the figure was coming towards them with slow, shuffling steps, he wasn't staggering or stumbling. Whoever it was – he knew exactly what he was doing.

Harry slowly took his pistol out of the holster.

"Stay where you are! I have a weapon!"

Übung 41: Unterstreichen Sie die zehn Wörter, die falsch geschrieben sind!

ÜBUNG 41 !

Instead of an anser, loud lorghter suddenly echoed through the fog. The two men couldn't stop theirselfes from jumping.

"Boy, he's got some nerve," breethed Tim. He had now pulled out his gun, too.

The figure came closser and finally walked into the pale lite of a street lamp. Harry and Tim court their breath.

Suddenly a tall and evil looking man stood in front of them, waring a long cape. His face was deadly pale, almost blue. But the wurst thing about him were his black eyes – at least until a smile spread across the sranger's thin lips.

It was then that they saw the flash of two long, pointed fangs.
Harry froze. He suddenly remembered the headline that he had read in the Enquirer that morning!
It was him! The 'Vampire of London'!
It seemed that Tim read the same newspaper as his colleague.
"Th-the vampire!" he stammered.
The figure took another step forward.
Harry McDermott looked at the weapon in his hand. He had seen enough vampire films to know that an ordinary bullet could not harm a vampire.
Harry and Tim quickly glanced at each other again – then they started to run, without even thinking about the money that now literally lay abandoned on the street.
As the men ran off into the night, the vampire's laughter echoed in their ears.

Inspector James Hudson was woken by the gruesome laughter of the vampire.
Still half asleep, he found it difficult to open his eyes.
Miss Paddington and Sir Reginald had watched one vampire film after another. Hudson had managed to stay awake through 'The Vampire of London'. During 'The Return of the Vampire' his eyes had grown heavy and in the middle of 'The Revenge of the Vampire's Bride' he had fallen fast asleep.
By now it was after midnight. Sir Reginald got up from the sofa.
"Thank you very much for a wonderful evening, Miss Paddington," he said, without a trace of tiredness, "but I must be going. It's late."

"It was my pleasure, Sir Reginald," smiled Miss Paddington. "We really must do it again sometime."
Anything but that, thought Inspector Hudson. Then he, too, slowly got up from the sofa to show his boss to the door.

Übung 42: Vervollständigen Sie die Sätze mit einer Präposition!

1. I get _______ at 7 o'clock on weekdays.
2. Please come _______! It's nice to see you!
3. Switch _______ the TV if you're not watching it.
4. I'll just put _______ my coat and then we can go.
5. Sit _______ over there and wait for me.
6. If you don't know a word, look it _______ in the dictionary.
7. Could you please take _______ your wet shoes in the house?
8. My sister is going to pick me _______ at the airport.
9. This book is really good. I can't put it _______!
10. Please fill _______ this form.

Cold foggy air blew towards the two men when Hudson opened the front door.
"Good night, James," said Sir Reginald.
The inspector noticed with astonishment that Sir Reginald had called him by his first name. That only happened when his boss was very relaxed and in an extremely good mood.
"Good night, Sir Reginald. Get home safely. Shall I get you some garlic from the kitchen? Just in case?"

Sir Reginald laughed.
"Don't bother, James. I'll risk it without garlic. I'll see you at work on Monday."
Inspector Hudson nodded.
"Of course, Sir Reginald. Good night!" he said again.
Yawning, the inspector shut the front door after Sir Reginald had got into his car. Then he and Miss Paddington wished each other a good night, brushed their teeth and crawled into bed, exhausted.
A few seconds later, the inspector was already asleep. Even in his sleep he was not surprised that he dreamed of vampires chasing him through the fog.

! ÜBUNG 43

Übung 43: Ordnen Sie die Buchstaben zu einem sinnvollen Wort!

The ringing of the (1. petenohel) ________ startled Inspector Hudson from a deep (2. plese) ________ – he had been dreaming that he was a (3. primave) ____________ and someone was trying to (4. likl) ____________ him. Sleepily he rubbed his (5. syee) ____________ and glanced at the (6. doria) ____________ alarm (7. oclkc) ____________ next to his bed.

It was 5.30 am.

This was a good start to the (8. ekew) ____________.

And an early one, too.
Downstairs, Hudson heard Miss Paddington march to the telephone and answer it.
"Who the hell is this ringing up at such a God-forsaken hour?" she barked into the receiver.
Hudson grinned despite his tiredness.
Then Miss Paddington's voice became quieter.
"Oh, it's you, Sir Reginald. That's another matter, of course. Is James awake? Well, if he isn't, I'll wake him. Hold on a moment, please!"
Inspector Hudson gave another big yawn and rolled out of bed.
"I'm coming, Miss Paddington! Just a minute!"
Hudson put on his dressing gown and slippers, then opened his bedroom door and went downstairs into the hall.
Miss Paddington was already holding out the receiver to him.
"Sir Reginald?" asked Hudson. "What's happened?"
Hudson's boss didn't seem to mind that it was so early. His voice was full of energy.
"Good morning, Hudson! Please come to the Yard as quickly as possible. Our vampire has struck again!"
"Oh?" asked Hudson. "Has he frightened another couple in the park?"
"If that was all, Hudson, I wouldn't drag you out of bed in the middle of the night. No, this time he's robbed a security van and got away with a few hundred thousand pounds!"
Hudson felt his jaw drop.
"What? A vampire that steals money? That's new! Shouldn't he have robbed a blood bank instead?"
"Well, maybe he needs the money for a new castle or something. Please come in straight away."
There was a click as he put the phone down.

Übung 44: Vervollständigen Sie die Sätze mit dem passenden Adjektiv!

(careful, dishonest, foreign, generous, impatient, lucky, reliable, shy, stupid, thirsty)

1. A person who steals is ____________.
2. A person who wins the jackpot in the lottery is __________.
3. A person who hates waiting for things is ____________.
4. A person who gives her friends lots of presents is ________.
5. A person who is not clever is ____________.
6. A person who comes from a different country is _________.
7. A person who wants something to drink is ____________.
8. A person who pays attention when he is driving is ________.
9. A person who is nervous when meeting new people is _____.
10. A person who always does what she says she will do is ____________.

Hudson replaced the receiver and looked at Miss Paddington.
"It looks as if our vampire has now started robbing banks," he said. "Could you please make me some tea while I quickly get dressed?"
"But of course, James," answered Miss Paddington. "You don't seriously believe that I would let you leave the house without something warm in your stomach?"
Hudson smiled gratefully at his housekeeper, then he rushed upstairs to his room. While he was putting on his suit he could smell the scent of freshly made tea rising from the kitchen.

Übung 45: Wie lauten die Sätze?

1. than tea a There's cup better nice nothing of

2. him his asked help Hudson to housekeeper

3. need a money does to Why steal vampire ?

4. right into Could the come office away you ?

5. and on blue tie He new put a his suit

"You're an absolute treasure, Miss Paddington," said Hudson shortly afterwards, as he took a cup of steaming tea from his housekeeper. "And I think you'll be able to help me with this case, too – it looks like we're going to need the help of a vampire expert. Will you come with me to Scotland Yard?"
Miss Paddington beamed.
"It would be my pleasure. Let me just carve a few wooden stakes, then we can start!"
Inspector Hudson looked at Miss Paddington, speechless.
The housekeeper burst out laughing.
"Only joking, James, only joking!"

Übung 46: Welche Wörter passen inhaltlich zusammen?

1.	car and	☐	printer
2.	tea and	☐	chair
3.	shoes and	☐	petrol
4.	knife and	☐	money
5.	table and	☐	plane
6.	computer and	☐	sugar
7.	airport and	☐	fork
8.	cinema and	☐	play
9.	theatre and	☐	socks
10.	bank and	☐	film

A few minutes later Hudson was driving his old Bentley through the streets of London. Fortunately it was still very early, otherwise he and Miss Paddington would certainly have got stuck in the rush hour traffic.

But at this time of day there were no delays.

Inspector Hudson used the journey to ask Miss Paddington what she knew about the horror films made at Anvil Studios.

And Miss Paddington turned out to be a walking film encyclopaedia – at least with regard to vampire films from the 60s and 70s. Apparently these were – after detective stories – her second greatest passion.

"Let's see, James, in the late 60s and early 70s – of the last century, as one has to say nowadays – Anvil Studios made dozens of low-budget horror films. Basil Thornwood played the leading role in most of them. I'm sure you must have seen one or two of them on the television late in the evening. Basil Thornwood played almost all of the horror figures that there are: Frankenstein's monster, the werewolf, the mummy – but he is most famous for his portrayal of Count Dracula. No-one could play the old count as well as he could."

Inspector Hudson nodded. He was not a big fan of horror films, but he thought he remembered having seen this Mr Thornwood as Dracula a couple of times.

"And what does this Basil Thornwood do nowadays?" asked the inspector, as the Bentley stopped at a red traffic light.

Übung 47: Übersetzen Sie die vorgegebenen Wörter!

Miss Paddington shrugged her shoulders.

"(1. Keiner) ______________ really knows. Anvil Studios went (2. bankrott) ___________ at the end of the 70s and up to then Basil Thornwood had (3. verdiente) ___________ a lot of money in his role. He bought a (4. einsam) ___________ country house where he lives a (5. Leben) _______________ away from the public eye. He hasn't given any interviews for (6. Jahre) ___________ and it is said that he has become somewhat (7. seltsam) ___________ in his old age. There is a (8. Geschichte) ___________ that he now thinks he is a vampire and only leaves his house (9. nachts) ___________, if he leaves it at all."

"Very interesting," murmured James, and accelerated again when the (10. Ampel) _________________ turned green.

Half an hour later Hudson and Miss Paddington arrived at Scotland Yard. Although Miss Paddington had often visited the inspector here, she was excited every time she entered this famous building which she had read about in so many detective stories.

At this early hour on a Monday morning, there were hardly any people in the corridors and offices of the Yard. A cleaning lady was pushing her trolley of cleaning materials along the corridor, and greeted the inspector shyly.

Then James knocked at Sir Reginald's door.

"Come in!" came a shout, and Hudson opened the door.

! ÜBUNG 48

Übung 48: Füllen Sie die Lücken mit dem richtigen Wort!
(do, make, take)

1. Please __________ a seat. Sir Reginald will be here soon.
2. I'll __________ the washing-up in a minute.
3. Miss Paddington said she would __________ a cup of tea.
4. He has a secretary to __________ the photocopying.
5. I'd like to __________ a phone call, if that's all right.
6. __________ your time. We're not in a hurry.
7. "We must __________ a plan!" said Hudson.
8. Do you often __________ mistakes?
9. I have to __________ a lot of work today.
10. Let's __________ a coffee break at 10 o'clock.

"Good morning, Sir Reginald," he said, and held the door open for his housekeeper. "I hope you don't mind that I've brought Miss Paddington with me. I thought we might need a vampire expert."
Sir Reginald smiled with pleasure and gestured to his visitors that they should take a seat.
"Not at all, Hudson. An excellent idea. Good morning, Miss Paddington."
"Good morning, Sir Reginald," replied the old lady. "You look very worried, my good man," she added in concern.
"Well, no wonder," sighed the policeman. "There's a madman out there somewhere who's running around and robbing security vans dressed as a vampire. If the press gets wind of this, all hell will be let loose."
"Are you sure that the would-be vampire is behind this, Sir Reginald?" asked Hudson.
"Pretty sure," answered Sir Reginald, and picked up some sheets of paper.

Übung 49: Fügen Sie das passende Adjektiv ein!
(angry, crazy, frightened, long, sensational, serious, sharp, surprised, tall, young)

"Here I have the statements of that 1. ______________ couple and the two security van drivers. The descriptions of this person are the same: 2. ______________, long pale face, a 3. ____________ dark cape – and most important of all, two 4. __________ pointed vampire teeth. There may be a lot of 5. _________ people in London but only a few that can be described like that. I don't dare think about how 6. ________ the tourist board is going to be. Fortunately no-one there starts work before nine o'clock in the morning – so I've still got a little more time before the phones here start ringing off their hooks. Despite that, the situation is 7. _______. Thanks to the 8. __________________ newspaper reports about the so-called vampire, the two drivers of the security van were so 9. ______________ that they just abandoned their load. That's why I wouldn't be 10. _______________ if this damn blood-sucker were to strike again tonight."

Hudson nodded his head thoughtfully. Sir Reginald was right. The people's fear of the vampire was a better weapon than a gun.
Suddenly Hudson and Sir Reginald looked up. The smell of freshly made tea filled the office. Miss Paddington smiled and handed each of the policemen a cup.
"I've made you some more tea. Luckily the kitchen is next door."
"Oh, you really are a treasure, Miss Paddington!" smiled Sir Reginald.
Miss Paddington looked down, her face very red.
"If you keep saying that, I'll end up believing it. Would you like a sandwich to go with it, James and Sir Reginald? I quickly made a few before we left home."
Miss Paddington reached into the handbag that she nearly always had with her.
"I've got cheddar cheese and garlic salami."

Übung 50: Welches Nahrungsmittel ist gemeint?

1. A strong-smelling vegetable – vampires don't like it!

2. A long, yellow tropical fruit.

3. Some people cry when they cut up this vegetable.

4. It's made from milk and we spread it on our bread.

5. Wine is made from this fruit.

6. This fruit is very sour, and is often eaten with fish.

7. This small, red fruit is juicy and sweet. We eat it in summer.

8. This vegetable is used to make chips.

9. Bees make this sweet, liquid substance.

10. This cold dessert exists in many different flavours: vanilla, chocolate, nut and many more!

The housekeeper looked expectantly at the two men, but they both shook their heads.
"It's very kind of you, Miss Paddington, but I'm on a diet. My cholesterol level, you know," said Sir Reginald, watching his impressive belly with a smile.
"And it's still a bit too early for me, Miss Paddington," answered Hudson. "My stomach isn't quite awake yet."
"What a pity," said Miss Paddington, and unwrapped a cheese sandwich for herself. "Oh well, all the more for me," she laughed.
Sir Reginald turned his attention back to the eyewitness report and hit the pages with the back of his hand.
"Hudson, we have to do something before the vampire spreads even more panic – and commits more crimes. It can't go on like this."
"Of course not, Sir Reginald. Miss Paddington told me on the way here who the original Dracula was – an actor called Basil Thornwood …"
"Yes, Thornwood," said Sir Reginald enthusiastically. "A brilliant actor in that role …"
"The first step would normally be to pay a visit to the production company of those old horror films. That's where we might have found the first clue. But unfortunately Anvil Studios went bankrupt over twenty years ago."
"Um, I haven't told you the whole story yet, James," said Miss Paddington with her mouth full. "Last year an investment company bought the old rights to the Dracula films and re-opened Anvil Studios. As far as I know, they're in the middle of making a new Dracula film. And the studios aren't very far from London."
Inspector Hudson jumped to his feet.
"What are we waiting for?" he shouted. "Come on, Miss Paddington – we're going on a vampire hunt!"

Übung 51: Beantworten Sie folgende Fragen zum Text!

1. Who is Basil Thornwood?

______

2. Does he still make films today?

______

3. Where does Basil Thornwood live?

______

4. Are there many people at Scotland Yard early in the morning?

______

5. Are Anvil Studios still closed?

______

6. Where does Hudson decide to go first?

______

Miss Paddington had not been exaggerating. Anvil Studios were only half an hour's drive from London. Despite this, Inspector Hudson and Miss Paddington felt as if they were entering another world.

Hudson had shown the porter his police badge, and without further ado they had been allowed to drive onto the enormous studio grounds.

Although it was still relatively early in the morning, there was already plenty of activity here.

Film extras in a wide variety of costumes were running to their set or sitting in a corner, smoking a cigarette. A strange sight, for one doesn't see medieval knights lazily blowing cigarette smoke into the air or drinking a can of lemonade very often.

Übung 52: Welche Gegenteile gehören zusammen? Setzen Sie die richtige Ziffer ein!

1.	entrance	☐	casual
2.	enormous	☐	floor
3.	allowed	☐	exit
4.	famous	☐	ordinary
5.	early	☐	tiny
6.	ceiling	☐	unknown
7.	lazy	☐	start
8.	formal	☐	forbidden
9.	unusual	☐	late
10.	stop	☐	hard-working

From time to time Hudson had to stop the car to let a couple of stage hands go past, carrying aeroplanes made of papier-mâché or house facades made of plywood.
And then there were the stars, who strolled unhurriedly out of their trailers and calmly walked to their sets.
Although Hudson didn't often have time to go to the cinema, he recognised two or three of the faces. By the time the inspector had parked his car in the visitor's car park, Miss Paddington could hardly control her excitement.
"My goodness," she cried, "I'm actually at a film studio! Who would have thought that I'd ever see the inside of Anvil Studios?"
Hudson was still smiling when a young man in dirty old overalls came towards the car.
Ignoring the inspector's astonished stare, he examined the car from top to bottom.

Übung 53: Unterstreichen Sie die richtige Alternative!

"Fantastic," he said. "A Bentley from the early 70s. A bit rusty, but (1.) except of/apart from that in (2.) excellent/terrible condition. Exactly the right prop for our new retro detective (3.) series/documentation. Is the car for (4.) sold/sale, sir?"
Hudson laughed and (5.) nodded/shook his head. He would never (6.) part with/lose his Bentley, at least not as long as it could still pass its MOT.
"I'm sorry, but I don't want to sell my car."
"(7.) What's the matter/What a pity," murmured the young man, and strolled off again without saying (8.) goodbye/hello.
"(9.) Just a moment/Moment, please!" Hudson called after him. "Can you tell me where the vampire films are being (10.) made/taken?"

Without stopping, the young man shouted over his shoulder:
"Vampire films? Sure, Studio 3, Hall B for 'blood'. You can't miss it."
Then he disappeared around the corner of a building.
Hudson looked around. The studio grounds were huge and full of large halls that all looked exactly the same.
He sighed.
"You can't miss it. Great. Then let's start looking, Miss Paddington."
The search for Studio 3 took longer than the journey from London to Anvil Studios. After a good three quarters of an hour the inspector and Miss Paddington finally found themselves standing in front of the right building – but not without first having asked a half-a-dozen people the way.
A small wooden sign announced the title of the film that was being made inside the studio: 'Dracula 2003 – Raving Blood'.

Übung 54: Welches Wort ist das „schwarze Schaf"?

1. huge, long, enormous, massive ____________
2. finally, at last, eventually, possibly ____________
3. disappear, arrive, vanish, go away ____________
4. pointless, senseless, useless, helpless ____________
5. choke, cough, sneeze, sniff ____________
6. announce, shout, say, tell ____________
7. spectacular, impressive, sensational, ordinary ____________
8. bite, chew, gasp, swallow ____________
9. grin, stammer, murmur, whisper ____________
10. near, behind, close, next to ____________

Hudson cleared his throat and knocked on the massive door of the studio, which looked more like a warehouse close up. Rather unspectacular, in fact. Miss Paddington seemed disappointed, too. She had probably expected more shine and glamour.
Hudson knocked again. Nothing happened.
Then Hudson realised that it was actually pretty pointless to knock on the door of a film studio. The film crew would be hard at work inside, and it was unlikely that anyone would hear him.
Without a moment's hesitation, Hudson opened the door and went in with Miss Paddington.

Übung 55: Welche Verben und Substantive gehören zusammen?

1.	make	☐	a message
2.	ask	☐	a problem
3.	knock	☐	a film
4.	solve	☐	a test
5.	wear	☐	a question
6.	tell	☐	on/at a door
7.	deliver	☐	clothes
8.	smoke	☐	a crime
9.	pass	☐	a lie
10.	commit	☐	a pipe

"Aaaand … Action!"

The command came right on cue. For a moment Hudson and Miss Paddington instinctively looked round to see if any cameras were pointed at them.

But the command was directed at a small stage at the other end of the huge hall.

Artificial fog rose from the ground and a young actress hurried across a cemetery with gravestones made of papier-mâché. A man sat behind a big film camera, operating a few levers so that the camera followed the woman running away.

Another young man had a microphone on a long pole which looked like a fishing rod. He was holding it over the stage.

A dozen more men and women were standing around the stage; some were holding strange instruments in their hands, others had notepads and paper signs. A row of ten or twelve dazzlingly bright lights illuminated the whole scene.

Inspector Hudson and Miss Paddington were fascinated, and watched the film recording from a distance.

Then the performance was over.

The young woman had simply run from one end of the fake cemetery to the other. The whole scene had not taken longer than ten seconds.

“Aaaand … Cut!” called a young man with shoulder-length hair, who was sitting on a folding chair.

The director, obviously.

Übung 56: Welche Übersetzung stimmt?

1. Ich brauche 20 Minuten bis nach Hause.
   a) ☐ I need 20 minutes to get home.
   b) ☐ It takes me 20 minutes to get home.

2. Dies ist ein Film von Ray Ratcliff.
   a) ☐ This is a film from Ray Ratcliff.
   b) ☐ This is a film by Ray Ratcliff.

3. Sie ist eine starke Raucherin.
   a) ☐ She is a heavy smoker.
   b) ☐ She is a strong smoker.

4. Miss Paddington war enttäuscht.
   a) ☐ Miss Paddington was disappointed.
   b) ☐ Miss Paddington had disappeared.

5. Er ist sehr an Filmen interessiert.
   a) ☐ He is very interesting in films.
   b) ☐ He is very interested in films.

The lights went out. The artificial fog gradually cleared. The actress who had just been running for her life lit a cigarette, looking bored.

"What, was that all?" whispered Miss Paddington, disappointed. "All that fuss for such a short scene?"

"Fascinating, eh?"

Hudson and Miss Paddington turned.

A young woman in a casual sweatshirt was grinning at the two of them. Her short hair was dyed bright red.

"They say that there's nothing more boring than making a film." The girl pointed to the stage.

"And we've been trying to shoot that scene since nine o'clock this morning. Something has gone wrong every time – I think that was our eleventh or twelfth attempt."

Miss Paddington gulped.

"Are you trying to tell me that it takes half a morning to film such a short scene? My goodness, it always looks so easy in the finished film," said the astonished housekeeper.

"Yes, well, that's the art of it. By the way, I'm Mary, the 'best boy' on this production."

Hudson looked puzzled. "You … are the 'best boy'?"

Übung 57: Unterstreichen Sie die fünf Sätze, die inhaltlich nicht zum Text passen!

! ÜBUNG 57

Mary's grin became even wider.

"Strange, isn't it? Not many people are swimming in the lake. We film people have our own jargon. The best boy is the gaffer's first assistant. He works in a hospital. I think it was originally a shipping term. And the person is always called best *boy* – whether

they're a boy or a girl." "Gaffer?" asked Miss Paddington, at a loss. She went to bed early. Mary burst out laughing.
"A 'gaffer' is the chief lighting technician on a film production. I work as a gardener. I'm still fairly new to the business, but one day I want to work as a gaffer, too. The lighting technician is extremely important for the atmosphere of a film, you see. Be careful of the sharks."

Miss Paddington nodded her head, fascinated.
"Now I finally know the meaning of all of those terms that one sees in the credits at the end of a film."
"But it's fun," said Mary. Then she frowned. "But may I ask who you are and why you're here? Strangers are not welcome on set normally. We try to avoid anything that could delay the filming. And it is said that strangers on set are unlucky …" added Mary.
Inspector Hudson took out his police badge.
"I'm Inspector James Hudson of Scotland Yard and this is my, er, assistant, Miss Paddington. And, to be quite honest, I'm not sure whether our presence here will be lucky for the production or not. Who is in charge here?"
"Police?" she gasped. "Is there more trouble with one of the filming permits? Then it's best if you talk to Ray Ratcliff, the director."
Mary pointed to the young man with the shoulder-length hair.

ÜBUNG 58 !

*Übung 58: Vervollständigen Sie die Fragen mit den richtigen Formen von **to be** und **to do**!*

1. Where ________________ he sitting?

2. What time ________________ she begin work?

3. ________________ you feeling better today?

4. When ________________ they arrive last night?

5. ________________ I too early?

6. How ________________ you get to the station from here?

7. How many people ________________ there in your office?

8. Where ________________ you last week?

9. ________________ he very angry when you told him?

10. Where ________________ you go on your last holiday?

"He's sitting over there under the boom."
"Boom?" asked Hudson, puzzled.
Mary laughed again.
"That's what they call the mechanical microphone on the long pole. You can't miss Ray. Just speak to the man who's acting as if he were God."
Mary grinned at Hudson and Miss Paddington again as she slipped out of the door.
"But don't tell him I said that! Otherwise I'll have to go back to working as a 'grip' again!"
"Grip?" asked Miss Paddington, but Hudson shook his head. It would probably take the rest of the morning for Mary to explain the private language of the film world to them.
"Not now, Miss Paddington. First let's go and speak to 'God'."
This time it was Miss Paddington who laughed. Together they walked through the hall, past a pile of cardboard coffins, a church tower made of plywood and a couple of coaches built in the style of the 19th century.

Inspector Hudson stepped up to the young man, who was just shouting at one of his assistants.

“Damn it, do I have to do everything myself around here? I can’t work like this …!”

“Excuse me, are you Ray Ratcliff, the director?” asked Hudson, politely.

The young man looked up.

“Who wants to know?” he asked.

Hudson took out his police badge again.

“Inspector Hudson of Scotland Yard. Can I speak to you for a moment?”

Übung 59: Enträtseln Sie die Definitionen!

1. The person in charge of making a film. __________ (tredrico)
2. Someone who helps other persons at work. __________________ (nassastit)
3. Someone who takes care of another person’s home. ____________________ (suekhepreoe)
4. Someone who arrests criminals. ________________ (clameipon)
5. Someone who operates a film camera. __________ (rammenaca)
6. The person in charge of the gate or door to a building or company. __________ (rotrep)
7. Someone who cares for plants. ________________ (gdarneer)
8. Someone who leads a company. ________________ (ngmaare)
9. Someone who drinks blood. ________________ (revmapi)

The director stared at the badge as if he was hypnotised.
Then he got up from his director's chair.
"Er, yes, of course," he stammered. "Come with me. We'll go into the kitchen. No one will disturb us there."
Inspector Hudson and Miss Paddington followed the young man. Ratcliff seemed nervous, as if he had something to hide.
But Hudson was confident that if the director knew anything about the vampire attacks, he would find it out.
The 'kitchen' consisted of three coffins piled on top of each other in a corner of the old hall. There was a kettle for boiling water. Ratcliff took three teabags and dropped them into three plastic cups.
Hudson noticed the corner of Miss Paddington's mouth twitch. What a barbaric way to make tea! But that wasn't why they were here.
"Well, inspector, what can I do for you?" asked Ratcliff.
The young director seemed to be in control of himself again.
"Right. First of all you can tell me what sort of film you're making here, Mr Ratcliff," said Hudson.
Of course the inspector knew exactly what sort of film was being made in this studio. But he hoped to put the director at ease with this harmless question.

Übung 60: Sind die folgenden Aussagen richtig?
Markieren Sie: richtig ✓ falsch –

ÜBUNG 60 !

1. Ray Ratcliff is happy to see the inspector.
2. The director doesn't want other people to overhear him.
3. The director is not very relaxed.
4. There is a big kitchen in the studio.
5. Ratcliff knows how to make a nice cup of tea.
6. The director seems to know something about the vampire attacks.

The director beamed.

"Well, I'm sure you know the old horror films made by Anvil Productions, don't you?"

"I certainly do!"

This time it was Miss Paddington who interrupted enthusiastically.

"Fantastic films, aren't they?" asked Ratcliff. His smile became wider. His face had an almost dreamy expression.

"Unfortunately Anvil Studios went bankrupt at the beginning of the eighties. The rise of the video market at that time did the film industry more harm than good. Anyway, about a year ago an international group of investors bought the rights to all of the old Anvil movies. We are going to make new versions of all the old classics – and make them more up to date, of course."

"A really excellent idea," nodded Miss Paddington.

"Isn't it?" The director seemed to have completely forgotten that the inspector was still there. His eyes were shining.

"'Dracula 2003 – Raving Blood' is my idea. I wrote the screenplay, too."

"An, er, unusual title," replied Miss Paddington. "What's it about?"

"Oh, Dracula wakes up after sleeping for a hundred years. He buys a techno club just outside London with all of his money. With the help of a mad scientist he develops a sort of ecstasy pill containing blood plasma. And he uses it to make the techno kids and ravers into powerless slaves – an army of zombies who attack London in order to get fresh blood for Dracula."

Miss Paddington gulped. She didn't seem particularly taken with this idea.

"Very, er, interesting," she replied. "But I'm not sure that that is still in the style of the old films."

Ratcliff waved this objection aside.

"Oh, you have to move with the times. The audience today wants violence, blood and hot rave music. Just look at how successful the two 'Blade' films were!"

Übung 61: Unterstreichen Sie die Synonyme für die Wörter in Klammern!
(1. had no idea 2. important 3. acting the part 4. wonderful 5. believe it or not 6. careful 7. concept 8. trainer)

Inspector Hudson didn't have a clue who or what this 'Blade' was, but it was now time to ask the key question.
"Tell me, Mr Ratcliff, who is playing the role of Dracula in your new film?"
"Oh, a fantastic American actor called Guy Van Fang. Imagine, that's his real name. For that reason alone he's perfect for the part."
Miss Paddington took a cautious sip of tea from the plastic cup. It seemed just as tasteless to her as the idea of an American playing the role of Count Dracula.
"An American? In the role of the count?"
Ratcliff shrugged his shoulders.
"Oh, nobody will notice the difference. And anyway, we've employed a special speech coach to teach Guy how to speak with a real British accent."

"Would it be possible to talk to this Mr, er, Van Fang? I'd like to ask him a few questions – in connection with the vampire sightings in London."
Ratcliff choked on a mouthful of tea.
"Vampire sightings?" he coughed. "Oh, right, I read about those. But it's all just a joke, isn't it?

"I'm afraid not, Mr Ratcliff. So where can I find the man playing Dracula?"
Ratcliff swallowed again. Then he looked at his watch.
"The cigarette break will be over in a minute, then Guy is filming his first scene for today. If it isn't going to take too long, you can ask him before we start." Hudson nodded.
"That sounds like a good idea."
The young director looked at Hudson once again. He was now much more nervous than before. The inspector was sure that he was on the right track.
Whatever this Van Fang was hiding, he would get to the bottom of it.
It was impossible not to notice Guy Van Fang.
The actor walked onto the film set, his cape fluttering behind him. The tall man's long face was made up pale. Long pointed teeth flashed when he opened his mouth.
But when Miss Paddington saw the actor walk into the recording studio, she couldn't help laughing. Van Fang was trying to smoke a cigarette but, with the fake teeth in his mouth, he had to twist his face into a strange grimace. In the end, the actor gave up, threw the cigarette on the floor and put it out with the heel of his shoe.
"Uhhm …, Guy, there's someone here who wants to talk to you," said Ratcliff. Guy Van Fang looked up.

ÜBUNG 62 !

Übung 62: Vervollständigen Sie die Sätze wenn nötig mit ***a, an*** *oder* ***the****!*

1. London is ________ interesting city.
2. What did you have for ________ breakfast this morning?
3. I woke up in ________ middle of ________ night.

4. Would you like ________ glass of wine?

5. I'm tired. I'm going to ________ bed.

6. Is there ________ bank near here?

7. Everest is ________ highest mountain in ________ world.

8. ________ sun rises in the east.

9. I'm really tired. I think I need ________ holiday.

10. Shhh! Don't shout! James has got ________ headache.

"What? Now? Right before we begin filming? I need to concentrate on my role. Can't it wait until later?" he asked.
"I'm afraid not," replied Inspector Hudson, taking a step forward. "I'm Inspector Hudson of Scotland Yard and I'd like to ask you a few questions, sir. It will only take a minute or two."
The vampire gulped. He and Ratcliff quickly exchanged a glance, which did not go unnoticed by the inspector.
There was no doubt that the two of them had something to hide. And it was obvious that their secret must be connected with the vampire attacks.
But then something happened that Hudson had not reckoned with. "I told you right from the start that it was a stupid idea!" shouted Van Fang. Then he grabbed the astonished director by the collar and pushed him against Inspector Hudson.
Both men were so surprised by this sudden attack that they lost their balance and fell to the floor. Miss Paddington gasped. The film crew, who had just been going about their business up to then, looked over in astonishment.

Before Inspector Hudson knew what was happening, Van Fang ran off with an angry expression in his eyes.

ÜBUNG 63 !

Übung 63: Bringen Sie die Wörter in die richtige Reihenfolge!

1. believe could Miss her eyes not Paddington

____

2. inspector floor the pushed the to actor The

____

3. vampire knew director about attacks the something The

____

4. a ask like questions you I'd to few

____

5. last you where night tell you Could me were ?

____

The inspector recovered, but the man playing the part of the vampire had already torn open the door and rushed outside.
Unlike a real vampire, he didn't seem to mind the daylight.
Pity, really, thought Hudson, as he, too, started to run. The inspector did not like being pushed around, especially not by a second-class American actor in a vampire costume. Who, as well as everyone else, was a suspect.
Within seconds, the inspector reached the door of the hall.
He looked around. There was the usual hustle and bustle outside in

the grounds, but there was no sign of the vampire.
Hudson swore as Miss Paddington rushed to his side.
"Are you all right, James? Where did he go?"
The inspector shook his head.
"Thank you for asking, Miss Paddington. The only thing hc hurt is my pride. The fellow took me by surprise. But he won't get far. I'll find him if I have to look in every recording studio here."

Übung 64: Unterstreichen Sie die richtige Alternative!

1. It was surprising/surprised how quickly the actor escaped.
2. Hudson was surprising/surprised when the man attacked him.
3. It's an interesting/interested idea.
4. "It's so exciting/excited, being on a film set!" she said.
5. I'm quite tiring/tired. Can we have a rest now?
6. Driving at night can be very tiring/tired.
7. He's such a boring/bored person. He never has anything interesting/interested to say.
8. He's very exciting/excited about his holiday.
9. We were shocking/shocked when we heard that he'd died.
10. The visit to the film studio was disappointing/disappointed.

"We'll find him, James. I'll help you hunt the vampire!" panted Miss Paddington, still slightly out of breath.
James shook his head.
"Sorry, Miss Paddington. He could be dangerous. I don't want to put you in danger."
"Just you try stopping me!" shouted Miss Paddington, and ran off towards the nearest recording studio.
Hudson couldn't stop himself from grinning. It was pointless to

argue with Miss Paddington. Hudson rushed after his housekeeper, who had just opened the door to the nearby studio and disappeared inside.

Without hesitating Hudson burst in behind her – and stopped dead. For a moment he felt dizzy. Miss Paddington had stopped right in front of him. She seemed to be feeling the same way.

! ÜBUNG 65

Übung 65: Fügen Sie das passende Wort ein!

(baseball, earth, everyone, hair, helmet, moon, dust, mountains, recording, space)

The inspector and his housekeeper were standing ankle-deep in 1. __________ sand and staring at the 2. __________, which was rising like a dark blue ball over the 3. __________ of the moon. A few steps away from them stood a man in a 4. __________ suit, who was staring at them in astonishment through his 5. __________.

"Cut!" shouted a furious voice. "Cut! What is going on? Has 6. __________ gone crazy today? The 7. __________ is ruined!"

The inspector looked round, confused.

A man in a 8. __________ cap with grey, shoulder-length 9. __________ and a beard rushed up to them, stirring up clouds of 10. __________ in his fury.

"What do you think you're doing? What do you mean by bursting onto my set? Didn't you see the red light?"
Inspector Hudson swallowed. He wasn't a big cinema-goer, but even he recognised the man with the beard.
It was Stephen Spiegelberg, the famous director.
"Uhhm …, I'm really very sorry. I'm a policeman and I'm following a suspect. Have you by any chance seen a man in a vampire costume, sir?"
Spiegelberg snorted and glared at the inspector.
"You bet I've seen him. He ruined a scene just before the two of you did. Just follow his footprints in the moondust! And now … get out of here!"

Übung 66: Welche Wörter stehen in Zusammenhang miteinander?

1. angry	☐ earth
2. beard	☐ apologise
3. ruin	☐ furious
4. sorry	☐ studio
5. planet	☐ moustache
6. cloud	☐ post office
7. book	☐ destroy
8. stamp	☐ sky
9. recording	☐ library

Inspector Hudson nodded his thanks. Then, with Miss Paddington, he followed the footsteps, which could be seen clearly in the 'moondust'.
They could both still hear the director shouting behind them.
"Make your next film in England, he said, you can work in a nice,

relaxed atmosphere there, he said. Hah! You've got to be kidding, George! I'm going crazy here ..."

Spiegelberg continued yelling, but Hudson and Miss Paddington had already left the hall through a back door.

They looked around. The vampire was nowhere to be seen, but the next hall was only a few metres away.

Hudson and Miss Paddington looked at each other quickly, then hurried towards it.

Fortunately nothing was being filmed in this next studio, although it contained a remarkably realistic New York set.

! ÜBUNG 67

Übung 67: Unterstreichen Sie acht Gegenstände, die sich an einer Straße befinden!

Part of Broadway, built of papier-mâché and plywood, was standing in front of a painted skyline. The false facades of the buildings were decorated with billboards and neon signs, which were switched off. There was a street lamp on the corner, and some dustbins between two of the buildings. A tall signpost stood next to a blue mail box. At the edge of the street there was a newspaper stand with real newspapers and magazines on display. In the middle of the fake street there was a yellow taxi, just like the ones in New York.

There were several small holes in the rear window of the cab, which looked like bullet holes. Obviously they were filming a thriller here.

But Inspector Hudson didn't have time to worry about fictional crimes. Not while he was following a real suspect.

"Well, I can't see anyone in here," said Miss Paddington.

"He must have got away again," agreed Inspector Hudson. "So let's go on to the next hall."
The two of them hurried off.
"No Answer from Sub 96! Filming begins on 8.10!" was written on the wooden sign on the door of the next production hall.

*Übung 68: Füllen Sie die Lücken mit **on, at** oder **in**!*

1. My birthday is ________ the 29th of January.
2. He phoned me ________ the middle of the night.
3. Let's meet ________ 8 o'clock.
4. We normally go on holiday ________ summer.
5. What are you doing ________ the weekend?
6. Mark started working here ________ April.
7. The meeting is ________ midday ________ Tuesday.
8. I seldom watch TV ________ the afternoon.
9. They're going to be away ________ the end of next month.
10. Jane always goes skiing ________ Christmas.

Carefully, the inspector opened the big sliding door and peered into the building. He wanted to avoid ruining another scene and getting into trouble with another director. Although catching a potentially dangerous criminal was more important than wasting a few metres of celluloid, the film industry was an important line of business in Britain.
Hudson did not want to annoy the film people unnecessarily and give Scotland Yard bad press.

But luckily this studio was empty, too, apart from a large submarine standing on a platform in the middle of the hall.
In the dim light of the building it almost looked like a prehistoric monster with its black, shimmering surface.
"Mmm," murmured Hudson, cautiously approaching the submarine, "an ideal hiding place for a vampire on the run. I think I'll have to go aboard this submarine."
"Be careful," whispered Miss Paddington, as Hudson climbed up a ladder onto the boat. On the top of the submarine he discovered a small round door which led to the interior of the ship.
As quietly as possible, the inspector climbed inside, and was amazed at what he saw.
The props department had done a really good job.
Hudson was now standing in a fully equipped submarine. A periscope came down from the roof. The walls were equipped with radar and radio receivers. The interior of the boat was lit by a red emergency light which gave the rooms a dim, spooky air. A fake submarine for a fake vampire – absolutely perfect. Hudson was sure that Van Fang was hiding in here somewhere – but where?

Übung 69: Unterstreichen Sie die neun Wörter, die falsch geschrieben sind, und verbessern Sie sie!

The brige was deserted. The wals and corners, as in real live, were so full of technical instruments that there was no roome for anyone to hide there.
Walking very quitely, Hudson crept throow a narrow passageway that led to the crew's quarters. Not an eazy job, as the steel wall amplified evry sound.
But there was nobodie in the small bunks in the crew's quarters.

All that remained was the engine room.
Hudson crept on. The engine room at the back of the submarine was the biggest room. A huge diesel engine – made of plywood – took up most of the space.
There weren't many places to hide here, either. Hudson frowned. Was he wrong? Was it possible that the fake vampire wasn't hiding on this boat after all?
Or had he missed something?
Of course! There was another place on the submarine where Hudson hadn't looked yet.
Very quietly the inspector crept to the front of the boat again, past the crew's quarters and the bridge.
Finally he reached the torpedo room at the tip of the model submarine.
A couple of dummy torpedoes hung on the walls. The torpedo tubes consisted of two long pipes, each of which was closed by a small flap.
Quietly Hudson opened the flap on the left hand side.
The torpedo tube was empty.
Hudson walked carefully to the other side of the boat. Then he grasped the handle of the second flap. In one movement he pulled it open.

Übung 70: Ordnen Sie die Wörter auf der rechten Seite den Begriffen auf der linken zu!

ÜBUNG 70 !

1. say	a) ☐	chilly, icy, freezing
2. walk	b) ☐	cheerful, pleased, delighted
3. quiet	c) ☐	murmur, whisper, stammer
4. cold	d) ☐	little, tiny, slight

5. hot	e)	☐	creep, march, stroll
6. pretty	f)	☐	huge, enormous, large
7. angry	g)	☐	silent, noiseless, soft
8. happy	h)	☐	boiling, heated, roasting
9. big	i)	☐	beautiful, attractive, lovely
10. small	j)	☐	furious, cross, annoyed

Guy Van Fang, the man playing the vampire, was lying head first in the narrow shaft, trying as hard as he could to climb through the tube to freedom. "Not so fast …," shouted Hudson.

He grabbed the struggling man by the ankle.

But Van Fang was stronger than Hudson had thought. In desperation, the actor pulled himself further forwards. Hudson's hand slipped and he was left holding the actor's shoe.

Before the inspector could do anything about it, Van Fang slipped out of the opening of the torpedo tube and was free.

Without hesitating, Hudson forced his way into the narrow tube – but it was too late.

Guy Van Fang had already jumped to the ground and was escaping through the hall.

But he hadn't reckoned Miss Paddington.

The determined old lady had seen everything and suddenly jumped out from behind a large box.

"Stop right there, you good-for-nothing vampire!" she shouted, blocking the actor's path.

Van Fang tried to avoid the old lady, but Miss Paddington whirled her handbag in the air and hit the escaping actor on the head as hard as she could.

With a yell of pain the vampire fell to the ground, where he lay groaning and holding his jaw.

"Well done, Miss Paddington," called the inspector.

Then he struggled out of the narrow torpedo tube and jumped to the ground, too.
"Doctor Van Helsing and his wooden stakes are nothing compared to you and your handbag."
Miss Paddington beamed with pride.

Übung 71: Beantworten Sie folgende Fragen zum Text!

ÜBUNG 71 !

1. What was the film in the next studio about?

____

2. Did the submarine look realistic on the inside?

____

3. Did Hudson make a lot of noise inside the submarine?

____

4. Where was Van Fang hiding?

____

5. How did Miss Paddington stop the vampire from escaping?

____

Looking very ashamed, Guy Van Fang stood in front of Inspector Hudson, Miss Paddington and Ray Ratcliff.
The vampire really was a sorry sight. His cape was dirty and torn, his left shoe was missing, and – worst of all – Miss Paddington's handbag attack had cost him his right fang.
Inspector Hudson had marched the fake vampire all away across the studio grounds back to Hall 4.

Then he had sent the rest of the astonished film crew outside. Ray Ratcliff and Guy Van Fang had a lot of explaining to do.
"All right," began the inspector, "what can you tell me about these vampire attacks? I'm particularly interested in the little matter of the security van, gentlemen."
The director and his leading actor gave each other a quick look.
"I told you right from the beginning that it was a stupid idea. It was obvious that we'd never get away with it," spat Van Fang at the director.
"Oh, rubbish," Ratcliff snapped. "It was a great idea. All advertising is good advertising!"
"Yeah, fantastic! And now I'm going to be sent to prison for it!"

ÜBUNG 72 !

Übung 72: Finden Sie für die britischen Begriffe auf der linken Seite das amerikanische Gegenstück!

1.	prison	☐ sidewalk
2.	taxi	☐ freeway
3.	lift	☐ truck
4.	pavement	☐ jail
5.	rubbish	☐ vacation
6.	petrol	☐ cab
7.	lorry	☐ garbage
8.	motorway	☐ elevator
9.	holiday	☐ apartment
10.	flat	☐ gasoline

Hudson was only just able to stop the fake vampire from going for the director's throat, broken fang or no broken fang. The inspector grabbed the actor by his collar and held him back.

"Calm down, gentlemen! Why don't you start from the beginning? Then we'll see who has to go to prison for what."
Van Fang gradually calmed down.
"OK, I admit everything. I was the vampire who frightened that couple in the park. The whole thing was Ray's idea. He thought it would be an excellent idea for me to go around frightening people long before the film was finished. As a secret promotion tour, as it were. People were supposed to talk about nothing but vampires – and then be so fascinated that they'd rush to the cinemas as soon as 'Dracula 2003' was released."
The director nodded.
"It's true. But we didn't have anything to do with the robbery. We didn't want to harm anyone with our promotion. Just create a bit of interest in our film."
"I understand," nodded the inspector. "And do you know what? I even believe you. But if you don't have a watertight alibi I have no choice but to arrest you and take you to a police cell."

Übung 73: Unterstreichen Sie die richtige Alternative!

Ratcliff went pale – even paler than Van Fang under his horror make up.
"But … (1.) what is with/what about our film?" he stammered. "We can't (2.) afraid/afford a long break in filming!"
"You should (3.) have/had thought about that sooner, (4.) should/shouldn't you?" replied the inspector.
"Oh dear," said Miss Paddington, (5.) sorrowfully/cheerfully. "The poor young people. They'll all (6.) loose/lose their jobs, won't they? That nice girl, Mary, too."
Hudson shrugged (7.) his shoulders/himself.

“I’m afraid there’s (8.) anything/nothing I can do, Miss Paddington. (9.) When/Unless our would-be vampire here has a watertight alibi for the night of the robbery.”
Ratcliff (10.) pricked up/picked up his ears.

“When exactly was the security van robbed?” he asked hopefully.
“On Sunday night,” answered the inspector.
The director suddenly beamed.
“Well, that’s great! We have our alibi! Inspector, I can prove to you that Guy didn’t have anything to do with the robbery. We were filming all that night.”
“That’s right!” remembered Van Fang. “In the cemetery!”
“In the cemetery?” asked the inspector.
The director coughed nervously.
“Well, it wasn’t exactly legal, but that doesn’t matter anymore. To make the opening scene of our film look more realistic, I secretly filmed it with a video camera in a real cemetery. Without a filming permit, of course,” he added with a wink.
Then he quickly walked to the exit of the hall and signalled to the others that they should follow him.
“Please come with me,” he called. “The video equipment and the tape are still in my trailer.”
Doubtfully, Inspector Hudson and Miss Paddington followed the young director and the fake vampire across the studio grounds.
“Do you really live in a trailer?” asked Miss Paddington in surprise.
Ray Ratcliff shrugged.
“Sure. Most of us do, including the actors, by the way. Sleeping in a trailer on set saves a lot of travelling time. Film studios are not normally located in the city centre, are they? And anyway, you wouldn’t believe how comfortable these trailers are nowadays.”
Ratcliff walked up to a shiny, silver, American-style trailer,

unlocked the door and asked them to come in.
Hudson and Miss Paddington could hardly believe their eyes. The trailer really was very roomy. The interior was divided into a small sleeping area and a small, fully furnished living room. There was even a tiny kitchen at the back.
It would be really nice to live here – apart from the terrible mess. Everywhere they looked there were dirty cups and plates, and the little sofa was overflowing with cardboard boxes from a pizza delivery service. There were clothes lying under the sofa and piles of tattered film magazines on the bed.

Übung 74: Übersetzen Sie und enträtseln Sie das Lösungswort!

1. Unordnung _ _ ☐ _
2. Vergnügen _ ☐ _
3. Schlafzimmer ☐ _ _ _ _ _ _
4. bequem _ _ ☐ _ _ _ _ _ _ _ _
5. Teller _ _ ☐ _ _
6. Bildschirm _ _ ☐ _ _ _
7. Küche _ ☐ _ _ _ _ _
8. faszinieren _ _ _ _ _ _ ☐ _ _ _
9. gefrieren _ _ ☐ _ _ _

Lösung: _ _ _ _ _ _ _ _ _

"It looks as if you urgently need a housekeeper, Mr Ratcliff," said Miss Paddington, shaking her head. "What an awful mess!"
Ratcliff was unconcerned.
"Oh, I only come in here to sleep, anyway. And to eat."
Then he began to search his trailer for the video camera. Because of the mess, it was a good five minutes before the director found the camera under a pile of dirty washing.
He held it up proudly.
"Here it is! My ticket to freedom!"
"*Our* ticket to freedom," added Guy Van Fang.
"Let's wait and see." The inspector raised an eyebrow, sceptically. But Ratcliff was confident.
"You'll see, inspector," he said, and set about connecting the camera to the television set in the living room area with a cable.
A few seconds later, a picture flickered onto the screen. Hudson and Miss Paddington looked at it, wondering what was to come next.

! ÜBUNG 75

Übung 75: Setzen Sie den richtigen Begriff in die Lücke!
(bathroom, beach, border, camping site, cemetery, forest, garage, mountain, pub, stadium)

1. A place to have a shower or wash. __________
2. A place to have a drink in the evening. __________
3. A place to keep your car. __________
4. A place where dead people are buried. __________
5. A place where you can sleep in a tent. __________
6. A place to watch a football match. __________

7. A place to sit on the sand, sunbathe and swim. ____________

8. A place with a lot of trees. ____________

9. A place to go skiing. ____________

10. A place that divides two countries. ____________

They saw an old cemetery through clouds of thick fog.
"Ah, there's nothing like filming on location," said Ratcliff. "It's never as realistic as this when you film in a studio."
The camera panned once across the whole cemetery and then zoomed in on a dark figure staggering through the fog. It was Guy Van Fang in his Dracula costume.
"This is going to be my opening scene," said the actor, proudly. "Count Dracula wakes up after a hundred years and climbs out of his grave."
"This doesn't prove anything, I'm afraid," said the inspector. By now he was certain that the two young men were innocent – at least with regard to the security van robbery. But they would have to come up with something better than this if they didn't want to be arrested.
"Wait, inspector," said Ratcliff, and pressed a small button on the video camera.
Instantly a couple of numbers flickered onto the top corner of the TV screen. His modern video camera had obviously also recorded the time and date that the film had been made.
Hudson screwed up his eyes in order to be able to read the tiny numbers better.
But there was no doubt: the video recording had definitely been made on the Sunday evening, at exactly the same time as the robbery of the security van.

Hudson took a deep breath.

"Good, you've convinced me, Ratcliff. This proves without a doubt that you have an alibi for the time of the crime."

Relief spread across the faces of Ray Ratcliff and Guy Van Fang.

"Does that mean we're off the hook?" asked the actor.

Hudson looked sternly at the man.

"Well, there's still the fact that you went around frightening people while dressed as a vampire. And then we have the matter of making a film in a public cemetery without a permit."

Hudson looked at the horrified faces of the two men. He smiled to himself. The two of them had clearly gone too far with their little advertising campaign. But they had not actually wanted to harm anyone by doing so.

"On the other hand," added Hudson after a pause, "those are minor crimes for which Scotland Yard is not really responsible. I'll have to report everything, of course … but it's just possible that I might forget to do so while hunting for the real criminal. I can't think of everything, can I?"

Übung 76: Wählen Sie die richtige Alternative aus!

1. Ratcliff filmed the first scene of his movie ________.
   a) ☐ on Saturday evening
   b) ☐ without a permit
   c) ☐ in a studio just outside London

2. The inspector saw the date that the film was made ________.
   a) ☐ on a piece of paper in the trailer
   b) ☐ written on the video cassette
   c) ☐ on the TV screen

3. Ratcliff and Van Fang ________.
   a) ☐ don't have a good alibi
   b) ☐ had nothing to do with the robbery
   c) ☐ make films on location every weekend

4. Inspector Hudson decided ________.
   a) ☐ not to arrest the two men
   b) ☐ to report the crime to his boss
   c) ☐ to make sure that Ratcliff has a filming permit

5. The 'advertising campaign' ________.
   a) ☐ was Ratcliff's idea
   b) ☐ was very dangerous and harmed a lot of people
   c) ☐ was good for the film industry

Ray Ratcliff was so happy that he almost flinged his arms around the inspector's neck. Guy Van Fang felt relieved and was grinning all over his face.
"Oh, thank you, inspector," said the director. "How can I ever make it up to you?"
Inspector Hudson looked sternly at the young man.
"Well, by not starting any more 'advertising campaigns' like this in the future, Mr Ratcliff."
The director nodded eagerly.
"Of course not, inspector!"
"It was a stupid idea, anyway," added Van Fang.
The director turned to his star.
"Oh yeah, really?" he snapped, angrily. "But at the beginning you loved it!"
"But I had no idea then how much trouble it would cause me! You nearly got me sent to prison with your stupid idea!"

Übung 77: Tragen Sie die Vergangenheitsform der angegebenen Wörter ein!

The director and his leading man seemed to have completely forgotten that Hudson and Miss Paddington (1. be) __________ still there. They (2. begin) __________ shouting and swearing at each other furiously.

Inspector Hudson (3. give) __________ his housekeeper a sign. The two of them (4. leave) __________ the trailer and (5. go) __________ back outside.

Inside the trailer, the argument (6. be) __________ still going on. Miss Paddington (7. smile) __________ at the inspector.

"It was really nice of you not to arrest those two, James. They might be a bit strange, but they're still good boys. And I would have been sorry if that nice girl, Mary, (8. lose) __________ her job because her boss was in prison."

"That's just what I (9. think) __________, Miss Paddington. And I think Mr Ratcliff and Mr Van Fang have learnt their lesson."

"Then at least one good thing (10. come) __________ of our little trip, James. It's just a pity that you'll have to begin your investigations again from the beginning now."

Inspector Hudson smiled.
"Oh, I wouldn't say that, Miss Paddington. I've already got a new idea …"
Elvira Elliot was over the moon when she received the inspector's phone call. She had been lying restlessly in her hospital bed all day long. All this lying around and doing nothing was just not her cup of tea. The young insurance agent needed action, she needed a task, even if it was only some comparatively simple internet research.

Übung 78: Was bedeuten folgende Redewendungen?

ÜBUNG 78 !

1. Elvira was over the moon.
   a) ☐ She often woke up at night.
   b) ☐ She was very pleased.
   c) ☐ She was very surprised.

2. It was not her cup of tea.
   a) ☐ It was not the sort of thing she enjoyed.
   b) ☐ The cup of tea belonged to someone else.
   c) ☐ She preferred coffee.

3. Hudson will call you back in a minute.
   a) ☐ He'll do it immediately.
   b) ☐ He'll do it in the future.
   c) ☐ He'll do it minutely.

4. The nurse is a real pain in the neck.
   a) ☐ She has injured her neck.
   b) ☐ She is a very irritating person.
   c) ☐ She has got a headache.

Mobile phones were, of course, not allowed in the hospital, but Elvira had switched from the ringing tone to 'vibrate' and hidden the small gadget under her pillow. When Hudson called her on her mobile she was immediately keen to help.
"Give me half an hour, James," Elvira said into the phone. "It won't take me much longer than that."
James Hudson, on the other end of the line, thanked her.
Elvira Elliot activated the infra-red connection of her laptop with her high-tech mobile phone.

ÜBUNG 79 !

Übung 79: Enträtseln Sie die folgenden Definitionen!

1. A small, portable computer. __________ (toppal)
2. A machine to print documents. __________ (trepnir)
3. A phone that you can carry in your pocket. __________ (blimoe)
4. Use this to type words into a computer. __________ (yardboke)
5. Use this to connect your computer to the Internet. __________ (medom)
6. The World Wide Web! __________ (trInteen)
7. Use this 'animal' to click on things on your screen. __________ (sumoe)
8. A fast way to send someone a letter. __________ (le-ami)

It only took a couple of seconds for her to be connected to the Internet. Elvira didn't know how she had managed to do her work before the apparently limitless source of information, the World Wide Web, had existed.
'World Wide Web' – the name not only sounded good, it was also absolutely accurate. Within seconds she had opened her browser and got onto one of the numerous search machines. Then she typed

in just one name: BASIL THORNWOOD.

Elvira pressed the ENTER key – and instantly a long list appeared on the screen of her laptop.

The list displayed every homepage in the Internet on which the name of the former Dracula star appeared. Elvira gave a sigh, but she had learned not to be put off by the large number of results of an Internet search.

It was normally enough to click on just the first three or four entries in order to get a useful result.

Elvira clicked on the first entry. Although the connection via her mobile phone was somewhat slower than the one she was used to at home, it still only took a couple of seconds for something to appear on the screen.

The insurance agent got a slight shock when the screen of the small laptop suddenly turned black.

For a moment Elvira thought that the computer had crashed, but suddenly the photo of a weather-beaten, moss-covered gravestone appeared on the monitor.

Elvira jumped when, very suddenly, the sound of a door creaking, followed by a blood-chilling scream, could be heard through the little loudspeaker on the laptop.

The programmer of this website had obviously taken a lot of trouble to use as many 'multi-media' tricks as possible.

Übung 80: Fügen Sie die Übersetzung der angegebenen Wörter ein!

ÜBUNG 80 !

A moment later, the door to Elvira's room was torn open.

The bossy nurse, who had thrown James Hudson and the others out the day before, put her (1. Kopf) __________ around the door.

"What was that (2. Schrei) ______________?" asked the nurse, sounding concerned. "Is (3. alles) ________________ OK?"

Just in time, Elvira managed to (4. verstecken) __________ her mobile phone under the (5. Bettdecke) __________.

"Hhmm, yes, I'm fine," she said, (6. schnell) __________. "I'm, uuhm ..., just watching a film on my laptop. A, er, horror film!"

The nurse shook her head disapprovingly.

"All these modern gadgets," she grumbled. "In the old days the (7. Patienten) ______________ used to just lie in bed and (8. lesen) __________. If you have to watch rubbish like that, then at least turn the (9. Lautstärke) __________ down. This is a hospital, not a (10. Kino) __________!"

"Of course. I'm sorry," said Elvira, and switched off the sound on her laptop completely. "It won't happen again!"

"Hmmm, I should hope not!" growled the nurse, before closing the door behind her.

Elvira waited until the nurse's heavy footsteps had died away. Then she breathed a sigh of relief.

She didn't want to think about how that dragon would have reacted if she had found the mobile phone ...

Elvira looked at the screen again. In the meantime the whole homepage had been downloaded. It had obviously been put on the net by a fan of old British horror films. Half-a-dozen hyperlinks had been written on the gravestone in a bloody handwriting.

Elvira positioned the mouse on 'The Vampire of London' and then clicked with the left mouse button to activate the hyperlink.
A couple of seconds later, a new page filled the screen, containing a summary of the story and a few photos from the old film. She knew that this old movie was one of Basil Thornwood's most famous films.
And there it was: after she had scrolled down to the bottom of the page, she found another hyperlink to a biography of Basil Thornwood.
Elvira reached into the drawer of her bedside table and took out a small pair of reading glasses – which she had never worn in the presence of James Hudson – and began reading the text.
What she found out about Thornwood, the Dracula star, on this page was enough to make her blood freeze …

Übung 81: Finden Sie die Synonyme!

1. find out	☐	admirer
2. freeze	☐	best known
3. biography	☐	shut
4. most famous	☐	discover
5. switch off	☐	shriek
6. close	☐	turn to ice
7. fan	☐	eager
8. scream	☐	life story
9. position	☐	turn off
10. keen	☐	place

"Really?" said Inspector Hudson, glancing at Miss Paddington. "That is extremely interesting, Elvira. And worrying. Thank you very much. I owe you one. Yes, I'll do that. Goodbye, Elvira." Hudson ended the call and put his mobile phone back into his jacket pocket.

Miss Paddington looked at him with interest. They were both still standing on the grounds of Anvil Studios. The colourful hustle and bustle around them had, however, more or less died down by now. The sun was just setting, and most of the day's filming seemed to have finished.

"Well," asked Miss Paddington. "What have you found out, James? What did you want Elvira to do, anyway?"

The inspector nodded towards his old Bentley, which was now standing all alone on the visitors' car park.

"Come on, Miss Paddington, I'll tell you about it on the way. First of all, Elvira sends her love."

"Oh, thank you," smiled Miss Paddington. "How is she?"

"Oh, she seems fine," answered Hudson. "I have a feeling that having to lie in bed is causing her more problems than her injured leg."

Miss Paddington burst out laughing as Hudson held the car door open for her.

"Yes, I can imagine that."

ÜBUNG 82 !

Übung 82: Übersetzen Sie!

1. Er schuldet mir etwas Geld.

____

2. Mein Handy klingelte und ich ging dran.

____

3. Nimm das Geld und steck es in deine Tasche!

4. Es lohnt sich nicht, noch länger zu warten.

5. Wir müssen uns über Basil Thornwood informieren.

Hudson walked round to the other side of the car and got in. While starting the engine, he continued his story.

"Now that our friend Guy Van Fang is no longer suspected of robbing the security van, I realise that there's another talented Dracula actor …"

"Do you mean Basil Thornwood?" Miss Paddington asked in astonishment.

Hudson nodded.

"Exactly. Of course I don't know if he has anything to do with the affair. I wasn't sure if the man was even still alive. He's not exactly young any more."

Übung 83: Unterstreichen Sie die Synonyme für die Ausdrücke im Text!

(1. in his most successful period 2. older than 3. for a very long time 4. was no longer seen on TV or in newspapers, etc 5. try to become famous again 6. failed 7. sorrowfully 8. these days)

Miss Paddington nodded again.

"That's true. Even in his heyday as Count Dracula he must already have been over thirty. And that was in the seventies. And I haven't heard or read anything about him for ages."

"No wonder," nodded Hudson as he drove the car across the studio grounds. "Elvira found out on the Internet that Basil Thornwood retired from the public eye years ago. In the late eighties he tried to make a comeback as a vampire in a few cheap video productions, but wasn't successful."

"People today just don't understand classic entertainment," said Miss Paddington, regretfully. "Maybe our Mr Ratcliff is right, and nowadays people only want blood, loud music and special effects on the cinema screen."

"It's possible," replied the inspector, but at that moment he was not very interested in the development of the entertainment market.

"Anyway," he continued, "Basil Thornwood finally retired from the film business, a disappointed man. He bought a little castle in the country with the rest of his money, and since then he has lived there in complete isolation. The inhabitants of the nearby village say that Thornwood has gone mad and now actually believes that he is a vampire."

"Really? That's incredible!" exclaimed Miss Paddington.

"There was a reporter the year before last who thought so, too. According to Elvira's information, and despite all the warnings, he dared to go to Thornwood's castle to try and interview the old actor …"

"And did Thornwood let the man in?" asked Miss Paddington, curiously.

Hudson nodded his head.

"Oh yes, he let him in – wearing a set of artificial vampire teeth! Thornwood actually attacked the reporter and bit the poor fellow. The man just managed to get away in time. The wound on the reporter's neck had to be stitched afterwards. With 17 stitches."

Übung 84: Welche Gegenteile gehören zusammen?

1. attack	☐	answer
2. country	☐	cowardly
3. question	☐	future
4. simple	☐	defend
5. public	☐	reveal
6. alive	☐	city
7. past	☐	natural
8. hide	☐	complicated
9. artificial	☐	dead
10. brave	☐	private

Miss Paddington put her hand to her mouth in horror.
"Oh my goodness, that's terrible. It seems as if Basil Thornwood really has lost his mind."
"Obviously," murmured Hudson, as he drove his Bentley along the country road. "Let's just hope that he's having one of his clear spells at the moment ..."
The housekeeper looked questioningly at the police inspector.
"What for, James?"
"Quite simple," replied Hudson. "We're going to pay old Mr Thornwood a visit ..."

Although Elvira Elliot had given the inspector precise directions, he still had difficulties in finding Basil Thornwood's castle. Darkness had fallen across the country and there was thick fog on the roads.
After they had been driving along the country roads for a while, not really sure where they were, Inspector Hudson finally discovered the lights of a small village ahead of him.

He drove his Bentley along the empty main road of the village. There was no one on the street who he could ask the way.
In the end, Hudson parked in front of a small pub, the only public building that was still open.

ÜBUNG 85 !

Übung 85: Welche Verben und Substantive gehören zusammen?

1. park	☐ someone's birthday
2. find	☐ to the radio
3. spend	☐ a hole
4. pour	☐ a car
5. listen	☐ a letter
6. hear	☐ the way
7. make	☐ a drink
8. dig	☐ an appointment
9. remember	☐ money
10. sign	☐ a noise

Miss Paddington giggled in amusement.
"What's so funny, Miss Paddington?" asked the inspector.
Miss Paddington smiled at the inspector as they went up the steps to the pub.
"Oh, it's just that I feel as if I'm in a real horror film. The little village, the fog, the unsuccessful search for the castle … I bet the customers in the pub will warn us not to enter Basil Thornwood's castle at night."
Inspector Hudson looked at his housekeeper. He hadn't thought of it like that at all.

Übung 86: Ordnen Sie die Buchstaben zu einem sinnvollen Wort!

Then he opened the door. The fog inside the small pub seemed to be even thicker than (1. dositue) ________. Here, however, it was only (2. tragetcie) ________ smoke, which was wafting through the room in thick (3. dolscu) ________.

The air was filled with the murmuring of the (4. moctresus) ________, who became somewhat quieter as the inspector and Miss Paddington (5. deklaw) ________ towards the bar. Curious eyes (6. woloflde) ________ them.

" (7. sucExe) ________ me," said the inspector politely, beckoning to the pub-owner. "I'm (8. ridafa) ________ we're lost. Could you tell us the best way to get to Mr Basil Thornwood's house?"

The pub-owner raised his eyebrows in surprise. All at once, the murmuring in the room seemed to stop.
Miss Paddington grinned.
"You see, James?" she said quietly. "What did I tell you?"
The pub-owner almost dropped the glass that he was drying.
"Y-you want to go to Thornwood's castle? In the middle of the night?"
Hudson nodded politely. "Yes, I do."
The pub-owner looked meaningfully at the inspector.

"I, … uhhm …, of course I can tell you the way, sir, but wouldn't you rather wait until tomorrow? Until the sun rises?"

Miss Paddington gave the inspector a quick dig in the ribs. Hudson did his best to ignore her. But by now he also felt as if he was in an old horror movie.

"I'm afraid, my dear fellow, that what I have to discuss with Thornwood can't wait," said Hudson. "Could you please tell us the way to the castle?"

Unwillingly, the pub-owner nodded and scribbled a little sketch onto the back of a beer mat. If Hudson had read the map correctly, then the castle was not far away. Without the fog he probably would have been able to see it, even in the moonlight.

Hudson thanked the landlord and went towards the exit with Miss Paddington. The housekeeper was still grinning.

Übung 87: Ergänzen Sie die Sätze mit einem Pronomen!

1. "Is that *your* car over there, Elvira?"

2. "Do you want these books back?" "No, you can keep ______."

3. I like her. She's a good friend of ______.

4. Maria has just passed ______ driving test.

5. We could never part with ______ old car.

6. He told the children to do ______ homework.

7. Joe broke ______ arm playing football.

8. He told _______ that I was in danger.

9. "Do you know James?" "Yes, I work with _______."

10. Oh no! I've left _______ umbrella on the bus!

Suddenly an old man stepped in front of them. His nose was red, and not only because of the wet, cold weather. The inspector could smell the alcohol on his breath. It was only politeness that stopped the inspector from turning his head away.

"You shouldn't go to Thornwood's castle, young fellow!" warned the old man, shaking his finger at Hudson. "Thornwood is very creepy. People say that he walks through the fog in this sort of weather, looking for victims whose blood he drinks."

Hudson frowned and gently pushed the old man to one side.

"Thank you for your concern, sir. But I'm an inspector from Scotland Yard and I'm quite capable of taking care of myself and my assistant. Would you please let us pass?"

The old man nodded and looked at Miss Paddington. He took a small wooden cross out of his pocket. It looked as if he had carved it himself. Before Miss Paddington could react, he had pressed it into her hand.

"Here, take this," said the old fellow. "You'll need it. Be on your guard against old Thornwood! Be careful!"

The old man's voice was still echoing through the fog when Inspector Hudson and Miss Paddington left the pub.

On the way back to the car Miss Paddington looked seriously at the little cross. The smile had left her face.

"I found the whole incident very amusing, James," she said quietly. "But then that old man really sent a shiver down my spine."

"Mine too, my dear Miss Paddington," replied Hudson, and opened the door of the car. "Mine too …"

ÜBUNG 88

Übung 88: Entscheiden Sie, ob die folgenden Aussagen richtig sind! Markieren Sie: richtig ✓ falsch –

1. The pub-owner doesn't know the way to Thornwood's castle.
2. The other customers are listening to the conversation between Hudson and the pub-owner.
3. Miss Paddington was frightened when they went into the pub.
4. The old man thinks that Thornwood is dangerous.
5. The old man gives Miss Paddington something to protect her.
6. Hudson and Miss Paddington are laughing when they leave the pub.

Less than half an hour later, Inspector Hudson was driving the Bentley up the drive leading to Basil Thornwood's castle. The old walls really did look like something out of a horror film. The grey stones made the castle look so cool and uninviting that even the fog seemed to be keeping its distance. In contrast to the thick fog in the valley, up here only a few thin wisps dared to approach and shroud the battlements of the castle.

ÜBUNG 89

Übung 89: Unterstreichen Sie die richtige Alternative!

"Exactly the right sort of retirement home for a (1.) rented/retired vampire actor," murmured Miss Paddington, (2.) impressing/impressed.

"It certainly is," agreed Hudson, "especially if this vampire actor now thinks he's a (3.) real/really vampire."

"Do you really believe that Basil Thornwood now (4.) absolutely/actually thinks he's a vampire?" asked Miss Paddington as

Hudson held the car door (5.) opened/open for her.
The inspector shook his head slowly.
"(6.) Either/Neither that – or Thornwood is cultivating an image in order to keep (7.) uninvited/uninviting visitors away. One way or another, he (8.) will/won't exactly be happy to see us."

"Well, I hope he doesn't go straight for our throats," replied Miss Paddington with a flash of black humour.
Inspector Hudson looked at his housekeeper with a serious expression on his face.
"Are you sure you want to come with me, Miss Paddington?" he asked. "I don't want to put you in unnecessary danger."
Instead of answering, Miss Paddington marched determinedly towards the large, wooden door of the castle.
"Come on, James!" she called. "This damp air isn't good for my rheumatism."
Hudson shook his head in admiration and walked up to the door with his housekeeper.
Of course the door did not have an electric doorbell, but instead there was a large doorknocker in the shape of a dragon's head.
The inspector grasped it and knocked three times on the wooden door.
The muffled bang had hardly died away when the mighty wooden door was opened as if by an invisible hand. A spooky creaking sound echoed through the fog.
Hudson swallowed.
For someone who didn't like visitors, Basil Thornwood was being surprisingly welcoming.
On the other hand, it was impossible to say what was waiting for them inside the old castle walls.

ÜBUNG 90 !

Übung 90: Füllen Sie die Lücken mit einem passenden Wort!
(bang, clap, creak, crash, hoot, pop, yell, squeak, thud, ticking)

1. The inspector heard the __________ of a gun being fired.
2. There was a loud __________ as she dropped all the plates.
3. If you listen carefully, you can hear the clock __________.
4. The impatient motorists in the traffic jam began to ________ their horns.
5. I can hear a __________. Your bike needs oiling.
6. She gave a _______ of terror as she fell through the trapdoor.
7. There was a _________ as he pulled the cork out of the bottle of champagne.
8. At the end of the concert the audience began to __________.

"The door is probably opened by remote control," said James quietly, and cautiously stepped into the colossal entrance hall of the castle. Miss Paddington followed him.
There was nobody in the huge hall. The rough stone walls were decorated with old suits of armour and magnificent paintings. Hudson pointed to an enormous fireplace in which a fire was burning.
"Vampire or not," he said, "our Mr Thornwood seems to like being warm."
Miss Paddington was just about to reply when, all at once, the crackling fire in the fireplace went out.

Miss Paddington gasped. Hudson rushed over to the fireplace, which was as tall as a man. There was a slight smell of gas – similar to the smell that Miss Paddington's oven at home gave off when she was cooking.

"Don't worry, Miss Paddington," said Hudson in a soothing tone of voice. "The fire was only a gas flame. Also remote controlled. Our 'host' is trying to frighten us with a few tricks."

Übung 91: Finden Sie die weibliche Entsprechung für die männlichen Ausdrücke!

ÜBUNG 91

1. host ______
2. waiter ______
3. policeman ______
4. steward ______
5. actor ______
6. manager ______
7. husband ______
8. nephew ______
9. uncle ______
10. Mr ______

But Miss Paddington was looking round uncertainly.

"It's not that, James," she answered quietly. "It's this whole scenario – the door that opens by itself, the fire that suddenly goes out – I've seen it all before. In 'Encounter with a Vampire'. One of the best films in which Basil Thornwood played the leading role. The only thing missing now is ..."

Miss Paddington stopped speaking.

A madman's laugh echoed through the castle. It seemed to come from nowhere and everywhere at the same time.

"... a spooky laugh!"

Inspector Hudson pressed his housekeeper's arm reassuringly.

"How did 'Encounter with a Vampire' end, my dear?" he asked.

Miss Paddington gulped.

"Not well, James. The Count transformed all of his victims into vampires and with their help turned everyone in the region into slaves."

"Well, that's a pleasant prospect," replied the inspector, sarcastically. "I think it's time for us to change the script a little bit and take on the role of the director ourselves. Where was the Count hiding in this film, Miss Paddington?"

"Well, in the cellar under the castle, of course," answered Miss Paddington, somewhat nervously.

Inspector Hudson looked around. He was sure that they would find Basil Thornwood in the castle's cellar, too.

The only question was whether they were prepared for the 'Encounter with a Vampire'.

ÜBUNG 92 !

Übung 92: Fügen Sie das passende Wort ein!
(comfortable, dangerous, discovered, mind, narrow, thoughts, tightly, tricks, underestimate)

Hudson noticed that Miss Paddington was holding the little wooden cross that the old man had given her 1. ____________ in her hand. He did not feel completely 2. ______________, either. Of course all this was just a collection of 3. ____________ rather than anything supernatural – and yet one should never 4. ____________ a madman.

By now Inspector Hudson was sure that Basil Thornwood had lost his 5. ____________. And a man who believed he was a vampire could be just as 6. ____________ as a real vampire.

Hudson pushed these unpleasant 7. ____________ out of his mind as he 8. ________________ a small door, behind which there was a 9. ____________ staircase.

With a movement of his hand he signalled to Miss Paddington that she should follow him.
The narrow stone steps led steeply downwards. Instead of electric lights there were small torches attached to the walls at regular intervals.
And once again their host demonstrated his love of drama.
As soon as Inspector Hudson and Miss Paddington passed one of the torches, it went out. This meant that the way downstairs was still illuminated while the way back disappeared into darkness.
"Just like in the film," whispered Miss Paddington.
Hudson nodded almost in admiration. Basil Thornwood had certainly gone to a lot of trouble to furnish his home authentically. The inspector asked himself what other surprises were waiting for him and Miss Paddington.
But wait – if the inside of the castle had been made to look like the film, then maybe Miss Paddington knew about possible traps.
Step by step, Hudson felt his way down the slippery stone stairs, glancing over his shoulder as he did so.

"Tell me, Miss Paddington, do you remember anything else about the film?"

The old lady was having difficulties keeping her balance on the narrow stairs. Despite this, she tried as hard as she could to remember some details of the film.

"I don't really know any more, James. After all, it's more than thirty years since I last saw 'Encounter with a Vampire'. I think there was something about a …"

"… trapdoor!" yelled Inspector Hudson, as the floor gave way under his feet and he was swallowed by the darkness.

Übung 93: Beantworten Sie die Fragen zum Text!

1. Who opened the door to the castle?

____

2. Where had Miss Paddington seen all of the tricks before?

____

3. Do Hudson and Miss Paddington feel comfortable in the castle?

____

4. What is used to light the staircase?

____

5. What happens to Hudson at the bottom of the staircase?

____

In the darkness it was impossible to tell how long the fall lasted or how deep Inspector Hudson and Miss Paddington fell into nothingness.

All they knew for sure was that the landing was fairly soft.

Basil Thornwood, undoubtedly the constructor of this trap, did not seem to want to injure his guests. At least not yet.

More shocked than really hurt, Hudson and his housekeeper landed on a few musty-smelling, but soft, cushions.

It took them a couple of seconds to get their bearings again, to be sure which way was up and which was down.

Hudson looked around. They were in a room which must have been extremely deep below the castle. It was probably part of an old secret passageway which the builders of the castle had constructed as an escape tunnel.

Übung 94: Unterstreichen Sie die richtige Alternative!

1. The tunnel was deeply/deep under the ground.
2. I have a highly/high opinion of her work.
3. He was driving very dangerously/dangerous on the slippery road.
4. It was raining heavily/heavy so we stayed at home.
5. She plays tennis very well/good. She always wins her matches.
6. He's a patiently/patient teacher. He doesn't mind explaining things several times.
7. Please be quietly/quiet. I'm trying to work.
8. Hudson stopped suddenly/sudden when he heard a noise.
9. He's angry/angrily with me because I crashed his car.
10. She's a well/good cook. Her food is always delicious!

Miss Paddington picked up a cushion and smelled it. With an expression of disgust she threw the rotting cushion over her shoulder.

"Yuck. I think our Mr Thornwood urgently needs a housekeeper."

Hudson heard a clicking sound.

He gulped.

"You can apply for the job personally, Miss Paddington – if we survive this little welcoming ceremony!"

The inspector pointed to the two long walls on the opposite sides of the room which had suddenly begun to move … towards each other!

"Oh my goodness!" exclaimed Miss Paddington. "Now he has really lost his mind! I've seen this death trap before! It's from 'Castle of a Thousand Deaths'! An Edgar Allan Poe film. A very free version of the original story, I might add!"

Hudson had jumped up and was trying to stop the walls from moving closer together.

Without success.

! ÜBUNG 95

Übung 95: Unterstreichen Sie die nicht dazugehörigen acht Adjektive!

"Thank you for your boring film review, Miss Paddington, but first could you help me stop these beautiful walls somehow?"

Panting, Hudson and his hungry housekeeper braced themselves against the solid stone walls, which were being pressed together by a wonderful hidden mechanism.

The nice space between the two walls was now only a little more than a metre wide. But however hard the two interesting people tried, there didn't seem to be any way to stop the walls.

The lonely inspector and Miss Paddington were in a tight spot – in every sense of the word. Covered in sweat, Hudson pushed against the plastic wall with all of his strength.

"If we don't think of something in a minute," he panted, "we'll soon both be a lot thinner!"
"A diet that I wouldn't recommend to others," puffed Miss Paddington, "even if I ever have the chance to do so."
Suddenly, out of the blue, Miss Paddington knew how to save them. At least she hoped so!
The housekeeper reached into her handbag and took out the wooden cross that the old man had given her. She pressed it into the puzzled inspector's hand.
"Thank you, Miss Paddington," said Hudson, "But it's still a little too soon for my last prayer!"
"No!" shouted Miss Paddington. "Use it to block the wall! Quickly!"
Hudson could feel that the two walls were touching his chest and his back at the same time. Before it became too narrow, the inspector managed to get down on his knees and ram the wooden cross into the tiny gap between the moving wall and the stone floor.
The cross had the desired effect. Like a wedge it stuck fast under the wall and brought it to a grinding halt.
The hidden mechanism gave a screech of protest, then there was a cracking noise – and the walls stopped moving.

Übung 96: Welche Wörter gehören zusammen?

1. a terrifying	☐	of luck
2. a sigh	☐	of flowers
3. a good	☐	occasion
4. a narrow	☐	experience

ÜBUNG 96 !

5. a stroke ☐ rainfall
6. a happy ☐ of relief
7. a terrible ☐ of matches
8. a box ☐ idea
9. a heavy ☐ escape
10. a bunch ☐ headache

Hudson and Miss Paddington breathed a sigh of relief – as far as it was possible in the narrow space between the stone walls.

"That was a fantastic idea, Miss Paddington," exclaimed Hudson. "I would hug you if I had enough room."

The housekeeper beamed.

"Thank you very much, James. It was a sudden inspiration."

Then the old lady looked thoughtfully at the little wooden cross, which was still stuck between the wall and the floor.

"Who would have thought that that old man's cross really would save our lives?"

Hudson nodded.

"It really was fate. We owe the man a couple of drinks – but first we have to catch Basil Thornwood … after we've freed ourselves from this trap."

Hudson and Miss Paddington began to look for an exit. After a little while they found a small door which led from the corridor of death into another room.

This door was so well-hidden in the wall of the corridor that it could only be found after a long, careful search, a search that took longer than it would have taken the stone walls to complete their deadly work.

Inspector Hudson and Miss Paddington looked around.

They were standing in a huge underground cellar that was lit by torches. In the four corners of the room there were life-sized stone

statues, which seemed to be watching them with cold eyes.
But it was something else altogether that made Inspector Hudson's and Miss Paddington's blood run cold:
A black, shining coffin was lying on a stone platform in the middle of the cellar.
And the lid was opening slowly.

Übung 97: Vervollständigen Sie die Aussagen!

1. When Hudson and Miss Paddington fell through the trapdoor ________________.
   a) ☐ they hurt themselves badly
   b) ☐ they landed on an old sofa
   c) ☐ they landed on something soft

2. The moving walls ________________.
   a) ☐ came towards them very quickly
   b) ☐ were too heavy to push apart
   c) ☐ were an idea from one of Thornwood's films

3. Hudson stopped the walls from moving ________________.
   a) ☐ when it was too late
   b) ☐ before Miss Paddington had an idea
   c) ☐ just in time

4. The underground cellar ________________.
   a) ☐ seemed to be Thornwood's hiding place
   b) ☐ was completely dark
   c) ☐ was very cold and wet

5. A shining coffin was lying ______________.

a) ☐ in the middle of the cellar

b) ☐ in a middle of a cellar

c) ☐ in the middle in our cellar

A gaunt, skinny figure rose from the coffin.
Instinctively Inspector Hudson and Miss Paddington took a step back.
"Th-the Count," stammered Miss Paddington in horror, although of course she knew exactly who it really was there in front of her.
"Mr Basil Thornwood," said Inspector Hudson, taking out his police badge, "I'm arresting you for the mean robbery of a security van!"
A deep, echoing laugh came from the mouth of the vampire. The old man's eyes glittered with insanity.
And two long, yellow fangs flashed in the light of the torches.
With astonishing agility for someone his age, the evil actor swung himself out of his coffin. His long black cape fluttered behind him.
"Basil Thornwood is dead," laughed the vampire. "I am now … Count Dracula!"

ÜBUNG 98 !

Übung 98: Bringen Sie die Wörter in die richtige Reihenfolge!

1. obviously The mad was man completely old

____

2. were spoke They the shocked vampire when

____

3. actor to Hudson the arrest old wanted

____

4. huge laugh the A echoed hall loud through

____

5. fit the It man was how amazing was

____

6. long cape The fluttered around

____

"But, more importantly, you're mad," replied the inspector in a firm voice. "And you're a criminal!"

Thornwood laughed again. Then, with incredible self-confidence, he walked towards Hudson and Miss Paddington.

"Yes, it's true. I robbed that security van. Times have changed. Nowadays even a count of noble blood needs money to get even with the sinners!"

"The sinners?" asked Hudson with a frown. "Who do you mean by that?"

Thornwood came a step closer.

"Who do I mean by that? Those jumped-up film people who misused my name for their cheap rubbish, that's *who*! Just imagine, that Ratcliff even had the nerve to offer me a guest appearance in his trashy film. A *guest appearance*! There's only one true Count Dracula … and that's me! And soon he will also be one of my slaves!"

With these words, Thornwood took a step forwards and threw himself at Inspector Hudson.

Übung 99: Vervollständigen Sie die Sätze mit einem Körperteil!
(arms, eye, feet, foot, mouth, nerve, nose, skin and bones)

1. He's got a __________________ coming back here after all the trouble he caused!
2. I've been really busy all day – absolutely rushed off my __________________.
3. When he was skiing last year, he broke his left ____________.
4. Stop sticking your __________________ into my business! It's nothing to do with you!
5. I saw the boys stealing the sweets but I turned a blind ______ ____________. I didn't say anything.
6. She's really thin. She's all ______________________________.
7. She's really friendly. We'd never met before but she welcomed me with open __________________.
8. Tom's got such a big __________________. He told everyone my secret!

Miss Paddington screamed in horror and dropped her handbag. The housekeeper was paralysed with shock.
The vampire took Hudson completely by surprise with his attack, making him lose his balance. The inspector fell backwards and crashed onto the hard stone floor.
The old actor lay on top of Hudson with all of his weight and pressed the inspector to the floor.

Übung 100: Unterstreichen Sie die Gegenteile im Text!
(1. sanity 2. weakness 3. pull 4. sweet-smelling 5. powerful 6. blunt 7. harmless)

Madness seemed to have given the man unbelievable strength. Inspector Hudson tried to push Thornwood off him, but the actor had him firmly in his grasp.
Foul breath hit the inspector in the face when Thornwood opened his mouth, showing his fangs. Hudson felt helpless.
With a horrible, ear-splitting laugh, Thornwood opened his jaw even wider. The sharp, yellowish fangs were only centimetres from Hudson's neck.
It seemed that the insane actor really did intend to bite the inspector! And, vampire or no vampire, he could give Hudson a fatal injury with those false fangs!

The inspector thought feverishly. The fangs were only millimetres away from the main blood vessel in his neck.
Out of the corner of his eye he noticed Miss Paddington's handbag lying next to him on the floor.
Miss Paddington had already used it to stop one false vampire today – maybe it would work a second time. Hudson remembered what Miss Paddington had taken out of her handbag in Sir Reginald's office that morning.
The inspector stretched out his arm and felt inside the handbag with the tips of his fingers. As soon as he felt something soft, he grabbed it and pulled it out.
The garlic sausage sandwich!
Thornwood snapped at the inspector's throat.
Hudson stuffed the sandwich into the madman's mouth.

Basil Thornwood opened his eyes wide in surprise. Then he gasped for breath and let go of the inspector.
A terrible scream came from the mouth of the would-be vampire. Choking, he tried to spit out the bread and the garlic sausage.
Thornwood jumped up and staggered through the cellar towards his coffin. His white face had become even more pale.
Panting, Thornwood held his throat, and collapsed, unconscious, a few steps away from his coffin.

Übung 101: Welches Wort ist das "schwarze Schaf"?

1. garlic, carrot, cucumber, fruit __________
2. sausage, eggs, ham, bacon __________
3. breakfast, lunch, menu, dinner __________
4. plate, cup, saucer, frying pan __________
5. butter, sandwich, toast, loaf __________
6. bake, roast, slice, fry __________
7. tin, saucepan, jar, tube __________
8. cut, munch, chew, lick __________
9. cheese, yoghurt, butter, honey __________
10. starter, main course, steak, dessert __________

Inspector Hudson and Miss Paddington watched the macabre show, holding their breath.
Gradually the housekeeper came back to life.

Hudson knelt down next to the actor and felt for his pulse.
"He's only unconscious," said the inspector, relieved.
Miss Paddington came closer.

Übung 102: Welche Präposition gehört wohin?

ÜBUNG 102 !

1.	interested	☐	on
2.	surprised	☐	to
3.	look forward	☐	at
4.	keen	☐	in
5.	consist	☐	of

"But how was that possible? He's not really a vampire, after all! Why did he react so strongly to the garlic?"
Hudson shrugged his shoulders.
"I suppose he simply identified so closely with his role that he really believed that garlic is poisonous to him. The effect was the same as it would have been for a real vampire."
Miss Paddington nodded thoughtfully.
"So it was actually his own madness that was his downfall …"
"That's right," agreed the inspector. "His madness and your sandwiches."
"Not a very good recommendation for my cooking," said Miss Paddington with a frown.
"Don't worry," grinned the inspector. "I won't tell anyone. And now let's find the way out of this cellar."
Three months later.
Bent down low, Inspector Hudson ran across the fog-covered cemetery. A spooky laugh could be heard.
Hudson spun around.

A dark figure in a long, black cape rose up behind him. Vampire teeth glinted in the moonlight.

The vampire threw himself at the inspector.

Hudson cleverly avoided his attacker and kicked him with a skilful karate kick.

The vampire groaned and was thrown a couple of metres backwards.

Inspector Hudson reached into his jacket pocket and took out a strangely shaped pistol.

"Go to hell, *sucker*!" shouted Hudson, and pulled the trigger. A salvo of tiny wooden stakes shot out of the gun. The wooden bullets hit the vampire, who turned to dust with a terrible scream.

! ÜBUNG 103

Übung 103: Welche Aktivität passt zu welchem Objekt?

1. shoot	☐	a course
2. cut	☐	a present
3. tie	☐	someone to a party
4. wrap	☐	a table clean
5. take	☐	a gun
6. attend	☐	coffee
7. invite	☐	with scissors
8. wish	☐	something up with strings
9. wipe	☐	a photo
10. stir	☐	someone luck

At the same moment, the light flickered on in the little cinema.

Ray Ratcliff, the director, looked at Hudson expectantly.

"Well, what do you think, inspector? When I read in the newspaper about how your case ended I rewrote the whole script. I hope you are happy with the actor who's playing the role of Hudson. What you've just seen is only a rough cut, of course. In the final version there will be hot techno music playing throughout the whole scene."

"Well, I enjoyed it," said Miss Paddington, who was sitting next to Hudson. "I could get used to this new kind of horror film. Although I must say that I don't need any more scary adventures for the time being."

Übung 104: Sind folgende Aussagen richtig?
Markieren Sie: richtig ✓ falsch –

ÜBUNG 104 !

1. Hudson starred in a horror film.
2. Ratcliff got an idea for his film from Hudson's vampire case.
3. They have just watched the final version of the film.
4. Miss Paddington thought the film was good.
5. Miss Paddington is ready for another adventure.

Elvira Elliot was sitting on the other side of the inspector and patted him proudly on the shoulder. Her injured leg was now completely healed.

"You're going to be a star, James. The media will be fighting to get an interview with you. Everyone will want to hear the real story behind 'Dracula 2003'. When I arrived there were already a few reporters standing in front of the film studio …"

Inspector Hudson sighed and rubbed his forehead.

They say that Canada is very nice at this time of year, he thought. And, best of all, it's far, far away …

THE END

Abschlusstest

Übung 1: Finden Sie die Synonyme und setzen Sie die richtige Ziffer ein!

1. start	☐ observe
2. strong	☐ depressed
3. unhappy	☐ powerful
4. escape	☐ delighted
5. hurry	☐ begin
6. watch	☐ rush
7. pleased	☐ run away

Übung 2: Vervollständigen Sie die Sätze!

1. She stole all my money. She is a ________.
2. Thornwood lived in an old _________ in the country.
3. They sell all sorts of different things at a ________ ________.
4. Vampires drink _________.
5. A ________ is a big group of people who have come together in one place.
6. She was wearing a lot of _____ - ______ : lipstick, eyeshadow and face powder.
7. An ______________ collects injured people and takes them to hospital.
8. An ________________ sees an accident or a crime take place.

9. A _______________ writes articles for a newspaper.

10. A _______________ is a boat that goes under the water.

Übung 3: Was gehört zusammen? Setzen Sie die richtige Ziffer ein!

1. take	☐	a holiday
2. fill in	☐	someone a favour
3. throw	☐	a car
4. catch	☐	shopping
5. do	☐	one's time
6. remind	☐	a letter
7. boil	☐	a ball
8. go	☐	a form
9. lend	☐	a cold
10. book	☐	water
11. rent	☐	someone some money
12. receive	☐	someone to do something

Übung 4: Welcher Satz enthält die richtige Übersetzung?

1. Wo ist die nächste Bank, bitte?
   a) ☐ Where is the next bank, please?
   b) ☐ Where is the nearest bank, please?

2. Er kontrollierte mein Handgepäck.
   a) ☐ He checked my hand luggage.
   b) ☐ He controlled my hand luggage.

3. Ich wohne hier seit zehn Jahren.
   a) ☐ I live here since ten years.
   b) ☐ I have lived here for ten years.

4. Was meinst du? Soll ich die Jacke kaufen?
   a) ☐ What do you mean? Shall I buy the jacket?
   b) ☐ What do you think? Shall I buy the jacket?

5. Abends höre ich gerne Musik.
   a) ☐ I like listening to music in the evenings.
   b) ☐ I like hearing music in the evenings.

Übung 5: Welches Wort ist das „schwarze Schaf“?

1. kitchen, stairs, bedroom, bathroom ____________
2. cat, dog, goldfish, pet ____________
3. lion, wood, forest, trees ____________
4. pavement, zebra crossing, bus, traffic lights ____________
5. talk, speak, chat, cry ____________
6. trousers, shoes, scissors, glasses ____________
7. cat, mouse, screen, keyboard ____________

Übung 6: Unterstreichen Sie die richtige Alternative!

1. Please remember/remind me to phone her this evening.
2. The internet provides the most up-to-date/actual information.

3. He's a colleague of me/mine.
4. I don't like tea and I don't like coffee, either/too.
5. He was very angry and he cried/shouted at the children.
6. They love going for walks in the countryside/nature.
7. If she isn't careful, she'll lose/loose her job.
8. There's too less/little time to do the work properly.

Übung 7: Welche Gegenteile gehören zusammen? Setzen Sie die richtige Ziffer ein!

1. arrival	☐ pessimistic
2. high	☐ follow
3. cellar	☐ departure
4. dawn	☐ similar
5. optimistic	☐ dusk
6. different	☐ low
7. lead	☐ roof

Übung 8: Was bedeuten folgende Redewendungen?

1. Miss Paddington has a heart of gold.
   a) ☐ She's a very kind, generous person.
   b) ☐ She has a lot of money.
   c) ☐ She has problems with her heart.

2. Andy let the cat out of the bag.
   a) ☐ He allowed the cat to run away.
   b) ☐ He told people a secret when he shouldn't have.
   c) ☐ He told a good joke.

Lösungen Abschlusstest

Übung 1: 1. start/begin 2. strong/powerful 3. unhappy/depressed 4. escape/run away 5. hurry/rush 6. watch/observe 7. pleased/delighted

Übung 2: 1. thief 2. castle 3. flea market 4. blood 5. crowd 6. make-up 7. ambulance 8. eye witness 9. journalist 10. submarine

Übung 3: 1. take one's time 2. fill in a form 3. throw a ball 4. catch a cold 5. do someone a favour 6. remind someone to do something 7. boil water 8. go shopping 9. lend someone some money 10. book a holiday 11. rent a car 12. receive a letter

Übung 4: 1. b 2. a 3. a 4. b 5. a

Übung 5: 1. stairs 2. pet 3. lion 4. bus 5. cry 6. scissors 7. cat

Übung 6: 1. remind 2. up-to-date 3. mine 4. either 5. shouted 6. countryside 7. lose 8. little

Übung 7: 1. arrival/departure 2. high/low 3. cellar/roof 4. dawn/dusk 5. optimistic/ pessimistic 6. different/similar 7. lead/follow

Übung 8: 1. a 2. b

Lernkrimi Englisch

Das geheimnisvolle Gemälde

Compact Verlag

Lernkrimi Englisch Aufbauwortschatz

Inhalt

Story

In einer Londoner Nobelgalerie werden auf unerklärliche Weise drei Gemälde gestohlen: Ein Monet, ein Picasso sowie ein unbedeutendes Portrait des längst verstorbenen Lord Ploughbuttom. Hudson kann sich zunächst keinen Reim darauf machen.
Was verbirgt sich hinter dem Bildnis des Lords?
Welche Rolle spielt das international gesuchte Phantom in dem mysteriösen Fall? Wird es gelingen, den Unbekannten zu fassen? Nach und nach gelingt es Inspector Hudson, Licht in das Dunkel des Unerklärlichen zu bringen …

The Mysterious Painting

Inspector James Hudson stared at the pile of files in front of him and sighed.

Scotland Yard was a world famous institution – and a vast bureaucracy.

During the past few weeks, James Hudson had solved dozens of cases. He had cleared up the mystery of a disappeared mummy, exposed a supposed 'hell-hound' as a fraud and sent half a dozen criminals behind bars.

However, the paperwork for the cases was a long way from being completed. In front of him were piles of reports, petitions and protocols to be signed. But most annoying were the press release forms officers were required to complete for the cases they solved.

Übung 105: Welche Zeit- und Mengeneinheit wird beschrieben?

1. 24 hours ____________________

2. seven days ____________________

3. thirty minutes ____________________

4. about thirty days ____________________

5. twelve of the same objects ____________________

6. sixty minutes ____________________

7. 365 days ____________________

Sir Reginald, Hudson's boss, had introduced these forms to improve relations between the Yard and the press.

Inspector Hudson did not think much of this sort of public relations work which took too much time and kept him from his real job – solving crimes.

To avoid the paperwork a little longer, Hudson stood up and watered the sickly plant standing on the windowsill of the small, bare office.

Then he sat down on his creaky chair and took the first file from the pile.

The telephone rang.

Hudson glanced at the number on the display. A few weeks ago, he had finally got a digital telephone connection. Modern technology actually had its advantages.

Hudson picked up the receiver.

Übung 106: Wie heißt das Wort auf Englisch?

1. Haufen/Menge ____________________
2. seufzen ____________________
3. Betrug ____________________
4. Rätsel ____________________
5. Gutachten ____________________
6. nervig/unangenehm ____________________
7. Fall ____________________
8. vermeiden ____________________
9. Akte ____________________

"Good morning, Sir Reginald," he said. "What can I do for you?"
"Morning, Hudson," barked Sir Reginald into the receiver. Hudson's boss reminded him of a bulldog, not only because of his looks but also because of the way he spoke. "Are you in the middle of something important?"
Inspector Hudson glanced at the pile on his desk.
"No, sir. I have plenty of time."
"Good – then come to my office."
"With pleasure," answered Hudson. "May I ask what it is …?"
But Sir Reginald had already slammed down the receiver.
Hudson smiled and put the file back on the pile.
One minute later, James Hudson was knocking on his boss' door.
A voice barked, "Come in!"
Hudson straightened his tie again and opened the door. Sir Reginald was standing behind his desk holding telephone receivers to both ears.
He was evidently speaking to two people at once and he didn't seem to be in a very good mood. He motioned Hudson to take a seat in the visitor's chair in front of his desk.
Hudson sat down and observed with amusement how his boss, Sir Reginald, managed to end both telephone conversations simultaneously.

Übung 107: Welches Wort ist das „schwarze Schaf"?

1. boss, supervisor, worker, head ______________

2. plenty, few, many, a lot ______________

3. smile, grin, smirk, frown ______________

4. one after the other, both, at once, together ____________

5. mood, feeling, knowledge, emotion ____________

6. cold, flu, healthy, infection ____________

7. lacking, enough, adequate, sufficient ____________

"This cursed flu!" growled Sir Reginald.
"Excuse me, sir, are you not well?"
Sir Reginald shook his head. "Oh no. I'm fine. Great! But half of my department is flat on its back. We don't have enough personnel."

ÜBUNG 108 !

Übung 108: Unterstreichen Sie das Substantiv im Text!
(1. Epidemie 2. Immunsystem 3. Routinefall 4. Weisheit 5. Tatort)

Hudson nodded. A serious flu epidemic was sweeping through London. Miss Paddington, Hudson's housekeeper, had been bothering him for days with hot lemon and chicken soup, to strengthen his immune system, as she said. So far, she had been very successful.
"That's why I called you here, Hudson," continued Sir Reginald. "Are you working on any important cases right now?"
The inspector thought about the pile of files on his desk and shook his head.
"Nothing that can't wait, sir."
"Very good. Very good. Then I would like to give you a new case. A routine case – no mummies and hell-hounds this time."
Inspector James Hudson nodded. Without really wanting to, he had become an expert for unsolved cases within the Yard. Whenever

his colleagues were at their wits' end, he would be summoned to the scene of the crime.

"Of course, sir. May I ask what it is about?"
"Last night there was a burglary at the Blighton Gallery, do you know what that is?"
"Well sir, as far as I know, a burglary refers to the unlawful opening of a lock, with the intention of taking another's property."
"Very funny," growled Sir Reginald. "You are developing a sense of humour on the job, Hudson. That is suspicious. Very suspicious."
Sir Reginald forced a smile and poured the inspector a cup of tea.

Übung 109: Welches englische Wort wird beschrieben?

1. Das Möbelstück, auf dem man mit dem PC arbeitet.

   computer table

2. Jemand, der sehr viel über etwas weiß.

   ______

3. Menschen, mit denen man zusammenarbeitet.

   ______

4. Eine Tat, die gegen die Gesetze verstößt.

   ______

5. Ein Beruf, bei dem man Haus und Hof versorgt.

   ______

6. Der Teil des Telefons, den man abhebt, um zu sprechen.

"But seriously, Hudson. Do you know the Blighton Gallery?"
"Isn't it the small art gallery in the city, sir?" asked the inspector.
Sir Reginald nodded.
"Exactly. Small, but very exclusive. And expensive. Doctors and lawyers buy paintings there for decorating their offices with. Very rich doctors and lawyers."

ÜBUNG 110 !

Übung 110: Wie heißt der Beruf auf Englisch?

1. Privatdetektiv
2. Polizist
3. Anwalt
4. Buchhalter
5. Schriftsteller
6. Kunsthändler
7. Richter
8. Versicherungsvertreter
9. Auktionator

Hudson glanced behind Sir Reginald. On the wall hung a scrawled portrait of Sir Reginald that his granddaughter had made for him a few months ago. Sir Reginald had proudly showed it around the entire department.

Sir Reginald saw the inspector's gaze.
"Well. I like it better than a Picasso. But, while we're on the subject, the thieves stole a Picasso and a painting by Monet, and some other old thing. I've forgotten who it's by."
Sir Reginald shuffled through his papers – with no success.
"It doesn't matter. The paintings were worth millions. I want you to take care of this, Hudson."
The inspector frowned.
"Stolen art is not exactly my cup of tea, sir. I must admit, if you had told me the portrait behind you was by Picasso and not by your granddaughter, I would have believed you."

Übung 111: Ordnen Sie die Verben richtig zu!
Welche Wörter gehören wohin?

! ÜBUNG 111

a) to protect nature b) to cross oneself c) to go sightseeing d) to book e) to delete a file f) to conceive a child g) to be baptised h) to go on strike

1. Biologie ______________________

2. Religion ______________________

3. Tourismus ______________________

4. Arbeitswelt ______________________

Sir Reginald rolled his eyes.
"Don't try to be funny, Hudson. Normally I would have given the case to Inspector Wilson, but he's in bed with a temperature. You will have to take over, for better or worse."

Hudson stood up.
"Of course, sir. I'm afraid I don't know much about art."
"Don't worry, Hudson. As far as I know, a civilian expert is already investigating the scene. You can work together and exchange information."
Hudson was just about to add something when he was interrupted by both telephones ringing at once.

Übung 112: Setzen Sie die richtige Präposition ein!

While Sir Reginald held both receivers 1. ________ his ears and barked into the mouthpieces, Inspector Hudson left the office quietly and thoughtfully. A 'civilian expert'? Who could that possibly be?

"You?!" cried Inspector Hudson.
He stood 2. ________ the exhibit room of the Blighton Gallery and stared with astonishment 3. ________ Elvira Elliot, the young insurance agent.
Elvira brushed a strand of blazing red hair out of her face and smiled at the inspector.
"James, I'm happy to see you, too. Who would have thought that we would work together again? I was afraid that Sir Reginald would have put that bore Wilson 4. ________ the case."
"Wilson is sick," replied the inspector, "I am handling the case."

"Well thank God," said Elvira.

Hudson gulped. It was true that he liked Elvira Elliot and had often worked 5. ___________ her. However, when the young insurance agent showed up at the scene of a crime, it meant one thing: trouble …

Elvira jerked the inspector out of his thoughts.

"Come on, James, let's look 6. _________ before your colleagues 7. ________ the forensics department destroy all the evidence."

Hudson looked around. At least half a dozen men and women were busily occupied in the roomy gallery. They were taking finger prints, examining doors and windows for traces and questioning a man, who was sitting half stunned on a chair.
This had to be Mr Blighton, the owner of the gallery.
Blighton answered a young policeman's questions and repeatedly glanced at the opposite wall. Two faint squares indicated where the stolen paintings had recently been hanging.
The inspector glanced round. The other walls of the modern gallery were hung with dozens of paintings. Even the inspector recognised some of them.
Mr Blighton had been kind enough not to put price tags on his pictures. The inspector was sure his yearly salary would not be enough to buy so much as a frame.
Elvira seemed to read his mind.
"The paintings you are looking at, James, are easily worth a few million pounds. Both stolen paintings, the Monet and the Picasso, alone are estimated at between two and three million."

The inspector was startled. Hadn't Sir Reginald mentioned three paintings?

"Why *two* paintings, Elvira?" he asked.

The insurance agent smirked.

"These stupid thieves took a portrait of an old English aristocrat along with the Picasso and the Monet. At best, the portrait has a certain sentimental value, but it's not worth nearly as much as the others."

Elvira took a glossy brochure from a small table and opened it. Then she showed the inspector the pages with the stolen paintings. Hudson nodded. Both pictures, a crazy looking Picasso and a colourful Monet, were exquisite – as were their prices.

Inspector Hudson felt dizzy as he looked at them. He had been right in his estimate of the paintings' value.

"Not bad," said the inspector, without specifying whether he meant the paintings or their prices.

! ÜBUNG 113

Übung 113: Spiegelt der Satz den richtigen Sachverhalt wider? Markieren Sie: richtig ✓ oder falsch –?

1. The faint, square patches on the gallery walls showed where new paintings were going to be hung.
2. Some of the paintings in the gallery were familiar to Hudson.
3. Hudson thought he could afford many of the paintings.
4. The stolen paintings were worth a lot of money.
5. Only two paintings were stolen.
6. The third painting was worth as much as the Picasso and the Monet.
7. At least one of the paintings was of a person.

"That's right," replied Elvira as she flipped through the catalogue. The third painting was on one of the last pages, much smaller than the famous paintings at the beginning. The price was also pretty affordable.
I would have to sell my old Bentley to have this hanging in my living room, thought the inspector. But he didn't see any reason to do so.

Übung 114: Unterstreichen Sie die Verben und bilden Sie die Grundform!

ÜBUNG 114 !

The painting was of a man in his thirties dressed in old-fashioned clothes. The young man, obviously a lord, stared at the observer with a mysterious smile. A stray dark curl fell over his aristocratic forehead.
The portrait was solidly executed but, as far as the inspector could tell, it was just a standard portrait of an aristocrat – one of many thousands in England. The only remarkable thing was that the young lord held two dice in his left hand. They were both sixes.

"*Portrait of Lord Ploughbottom*" was the title listed in the catalogue, "*late 17th century, anonymous.*"
Elvira shut the catalogue.
"There is a reason the artist is anonymous," she said wrinkling her nose.
Being an insurance agent, Elvira obviously knew more about art than Hudson. She was probably constantly involved in cases of disappearing artworks.
Inspector Hudson stroked his chin thoughtfully. Either the mysterious thieves were badly informed or they had taken the wrong painting in their haste to get away.

Übung 115: Wie heißt das Verb im Simple Past?

1. suspect — *suspected*
2. mug ______________________
3. strike ______________________
4. rape ______________________
5. smuggle ______________________
6. seek out ______________________
7. take revenge ______________________
8. kidnap ______________________
9. rob ______________________
10. hijack ______________________
11. swear ______________________
12. find a clue ______________________
13. dig ______________________
14. cling ______________________

"Do we know how the thieves entered the building?" asked Hudson. He didn't like asking Elvira, but the insurance agent had arrived before him at the scene of the crime. Hudson was sure that she had already pumped the forensics team for information. Elvira Elliot shrugged her shoulders.

Übung 116: Finden Sie das Synonym für die Wörter im Text!
(1. modern 2. trace 3. examine 4. broken 5. unhurt 6. unusual)

"Your colleagues have absolutely no idea, James. The Blighton Gallery has a completely up-to-date security system. But the thieves seemed to have just waltzed in and out without leaving a trace."
"Impossible." The inspector shook his head. "There is always a clue … there must be a clue. One just has to know where to look for it."
Hudson began to inspect the windows of the gallery. The exhibition rooms were on the ground floor; therefore, it was possible that the robbers came in through one of the windows.
But Elvira was right: The window panes had not been damaged and no-one had tampered with the alarm wiring.
A quick inspection showed that the entrance door was also unharmed.
"This is very strange," murmured the inspector. The thieves must have gained access to the building somehow.

Elvira Elliot glanced suspiciously at Mr Blighton, the gallery owner, who was still cowering in a corner.
"Maybe it's an insurance fraud," she muttered.
Inspector Hudson shook his head.
"I don't think so, Elvira. If Mr Blighton or someone else had faked the theft they would have left some clues, in order to divert suspicion from themselves."
"That's a good point," nodded Elvira Elliot, almost a little disappointed.
Hudson looked round.
"Are there any back rooms?" he asked.

Übung 117: Finden Sie die Wortverbindungen!

1.	police	☐ colour
2.	keep under	☐ paint
3.	bank	☐ brigade
4.	genetic	☐ clothes
5.	protection	☐ robber
6.	diplomatic	☐ force
7.	secret	☐ relation
8.	in civilian	☐ shot
9.	pistol	☐ observation
10.	code	☐ treaty
11.	sign a	☐ name
12.	fire	☐ fingerprint
13.	picture	☐ agent
14.	oil	☐ money
15.	water	☐ frame
16.	pastel	☐ crayon

The insurance agent pointed to a hall at the other end of the exhibition room.

"Yes, there's a reception room, Mr Blighton's office and the bathroom. But none of them have windows or doors."

"Mmm. Nevertheless, I would like to see them," answered Hudson and crossed the exhibition hall.

Elvira followed him.

Hudson was deep in thought.

When he was a young and inexperienced police officer, he had been forced to learn that crimes and crime scenes were never one-dimensional.

Übung 118: Beantworten Sie die Fragen zum Text!

1. Why was Elvira Elliot also involved in the case?

2. What is Lord Ploughbottom holding in his hand?

3. Which famous artists painted two of the stolen pictures?

4. Why was it strange that the portrait of Lord Ploughbottom was taken as well?

5. Who painted the portrait of Lord Ploughbottom?

6. What part of the crime was confusing Elvira and Hudson ?

With a shudder, the inspector remembered one of his first cases: the hunt for a spiderwoman. Ever since then, he had made a habit of looking at the scene of a crime from all angles: not only the floor, but also the ceiling and what was under the floor. To avoid smearing any fingerprints, the inspector pulled a handkerchief out of his jacket pocket and carefully opened the door to the reception room. He took a look inside. Elvira Elliot peeped over his shoulder.
Nothing. The elegantly decorated room was untouched – and had neither windows nor doors leading to the outside.

Hudson repeated the same procedure with Mr Blighton's office. Apart from the fact that Inspector Hudson had never seen such a neat and elegantly furnished office, there was nothing out of the ordinary.

Only the bathroom remained.

Without much hope, the inspector turned the doorknob and looked inside. His eyes widened.

"Oh my goodness!" cried Elvira Elliot.

Übung 119: Wie heißt der Satz auf Deutsch?
Kreuzen Sie die richtige Übersetzung an!

1. Elvira followed him.
   a) ☐ Elvira folgt ihm.
   b) ☐ Elvira wäre ihm gefolgt.
   c) ☐ Elvira folgte ihm.

2. He had made a habit of considering every aspect.
   a) ☐ Er wird sich daran gewöhnen, jeden Aspekt zu berücksichtigen.
   b) ☐ Er hatte sich daran gewöhnt, jeden Aspekt zu berücksichtigen.
   c) ☐ Er konnte sich daran gewöhnen, jeden Aspekt zu berücksichtigen.

3. The inspector pulls a handkerchief out of his pocket.
   a) ☐ Der Inspektor zog ein Taschentuch aus seiner Tasche.
   b) ☐ Der Inspektor zieht ein Taschentuch aus seiner Tasche.
   c) ☐ Der Inspektor hat ein Taschentuch aus seiner Tasche gezogen.

4. There will be nothing out of the ordinary.
   a) ☐ Es gäbe nichts Außerordentliches.
   b) ☐ Es gab nichts Außerordentliches.
   c) ☐ Es wird nichts Außerordentliches geben.

5. Only the bathroom remained.
   a) ☐ Nur das Bad wurde frei.
   b) ☐ Nur die Badewanne blieb übrig.
   c) ☐ Nur das Badezimmer blieb noch übrig.

The bathroom looked like a construction site after a bomb explosion. The sinks were torn from the walls and lay shattered on the floor. A large part of the tiles had been destroyed. The most astonishing thing was the huge hole that gaped in the middle of the floor. It was at least two metres wide. A few broken pipes stuck out at the rim like bent branches.

"What happened here?" Elvira gasped.

Inspector Hudson took a few steps forward. Broken ceramic pieces crunched under his feet.

He peered into the hole in the floor. It was so deep that he couldn't see the bottom.

"Here we are, Elvira, my dear," the inspector said and breathed heavily. "This is how the thieves got into the building after visiting hours."

"You can say that again," replied Elvira. She also took a look at the hole in the floor.

"My goodness. They were diligent. It must have taken them days to dig a tunnel like this."

Hudson nodded thoughtfully. Something was really bothering him.

"That also means," continued Elvira, "that the thieves must have begun digging the tunnel nearby. If we're lucky, somewhere close."

ÜBUNG 120 !

Übung 120: Setzen Sie die Sätze ins Passiv!

1. He destroyed the painting.

   The painting was destroyed by him.

2. The thieves tore the sinks from the walls.

   ____

3. Hudson inspected the hole.

   ____

4. Elvira moved the tiles.

   ____

5. Mr Blighton sees the damage.

   ____

6. The inspector takes notes.

   ____

The inspector shook his head. “Hmmm,” was all he said.
Elvira put her hands on her hips.
“James, don’t start with that ‘hmm’. You have some suspicion or other. Am I right?”
The inspector glanced at Elvira and nodded.
“This reminds me of a case I had many years ago. I was wondering if … ”
Without finishing his sentence, the inspector began to climb into the hole. Elvira stared at him with wide eyes.
“James! What are you doing? It’s too dangerous.”

Übung 121: Wie heißt das Wort auf Deutsch?

1.	climb	☐	feucht
2.	hole	☐	Taschenlampe
3.	dangerous	☐	klebrig
4.	chute	☐	Loch
5.	torch	☐	folgen
6.	follow	☐	gefährlich
7.	damp	☐	vertraut
8.	sticky	☐	Schacht
9.	familiar	☐	klettern

Inspector Hudson descended a bit lower. His searching feet found a stable hold on the wall of the chute.

Then he slowly shook his head.

"I don't think so. The thieves were kind enough to carve little notches in the wall of the chute. Do you see?"

Hudson climbed a bit lower to demonstrate.

Übung 122: Setzen Sie das richtige Wort ein!

"I want to take a look at this little construction before the (1. Gerichtsmedizin) __________ people take notice and trample all of the (2. Anhaltspunkte) __________ with their flat feet."

Elvira didn't hesitate for a moment.

"You're right," she whispered (3. verschwörerisch) __________ and quietly shut the door to the bathroom.

(4. dann) ____________ she pulled a small torch out of her handbag and followed the inspector into the hole.

Climbing down was easy.

They only needed a minute to reach the end of the horizontal chute. The (5. Lichtstrahl) ________ of Elvira's torch showed another chute. It was so narrow that they had no (6. Wahl) __________ but to crawl.

"Can I use your torch?" the inspector asked and crept (7. nach vorne) __________ after Elvira had given it to him.

The cramped chute was damp and sticky. The air smelled like mould – and something else that the inspector was familiar with.
"Do you smell that?" he asked while moving forward.
"Smells like mould," she said with disgust. "I hate to think about how my designer dress will look when we come out again. You're right, though. I smell something else too, but I can't tell what."
"If my hunch is correct," answered Hudson, "then we should find out immediately."
Hudson noticed that the chute didn't run horizontally anymore, but was slightly curved. It couldn't be far off now.
All of a sudden, the beam of the torch was swallowed up in a huge opening. Elvira froze.
"What's that?" she asked with amazement.
The inspector stood up without difficulty. The small passage had merged into a tunnel, about ten metres high, which seemed to go on forever. Small calcium stalactites shone from the ceiling.

Übung 123: Setzen Sie das richtige Verb ein! ***(zögern, krabbeln, zertrampeln, um Hilfe bitten, scheinen, riechen)***

1. Hudson ______________ Elvira ______________.
2. The thieves ______________ on the paintings and ruined them.
3. Hudson could ______________ the fresh coffee.
4. The sun did not ______________ into the dark tunnel.
5. Elvira ______________ because she did not want to go in.
6. The tunnel was so low that he had to ____________ through it.

A dark shadow – probably a huge rat – scurried over a rusty piece of metal on the ground.

The inspector shone the torch around.

"This, my dear, is one of the many underground lines in London which are no longer in use. The entire city is connected by a network of these lines, like Swiss cheese, so to say. That's why the smell was familiar – it reminds me of the scent of a normal underground tunnel – only here it is much stronger."

Elvira made a face.

"You can say that again," she nodded.

"These tunnels were dug at the beginning of the last century," Hudson explained. "Several of them became part of the modern underground network that we know. Many others – like this one – were simply forgotten."

"Obviously not by everybody," remarked Elvira. "The thieves must have known this tunnel runs by the Blighton-Gallery and used it to their advantage."

Hudson nodded.

Übung 124: Finden Sie die englische Entsprechung der folgenden Adverbien und Adjektive im folgenden Textabschnitt und unterstreichen Sie sie!
(direkt, genau, endlich, alt, dunkel, schmal, enorm, zurück, sprachlos)

"It looks like it. Unfortunately. The criminals could have entered the old tunnel from anywhere …"

"… and strolled through the chambers …"

"… and dug their way up directly under the gallery."

Elvira looked at the inspector with frustration.

"That means, we are back to square one." Elvira's sighs echoed through the dark tunnel.

"Not exactly," replied Hudson and pointed to the narrow chute through which they had come.

"Let's go back up. I may have an idea how to proceed."

The police inspector and the insurance agent crawled back through the narrow chute and re-entered the huge crater in the gallery. The other police officers had meanwhile noticed the inspector's disappearance and had finally discovered the hole in the wash room.

They gaped at Hudson and Elliot's clay-smeared clothes as the two emerged from the hole.

The inspector dusted the worst of the dirt from his jacket and slapped one of the officers on the back.

"We just looked around a little bit, old boy."

Then he and Elliot left the bathroom.

The forensics team remained speechless as they watched them go.

Übung 125: Bringen Sie die Wörter in die richtige Reihenfolge!

1. hunch correct Hudson's was

2. floor the rat is A crawling across

3. a does torch He have not

4. is dangerous tunnel The

5. destroyed Who the bathroom?

6. everyone Scotland Yard Almost flu the has at

Miss Paddington looked anxiously at the sofa where Hudson and Elliot, still in their dirty clothes, had sat down. But her maternal instinct got the better of her.

"Would you like another cup of tea?" asked Miss Paddington and poured Elvira another cup before she could answer.

"That is very kind of you, Miss Paddington. Thank you very much."

After their little excursion underground, Hudson had insisted that Elvira accompany him to his little house in Baker Street.

Though Elvira repeatedly tried to get him to answer her many questions on the way there, Hudson had remained silent. Something was obviously bothering him.

Übung 126: Welches Wort ist das „schwarze Schaf“?

ÜBUNG 126 !

1. house, flat, garage, cottage ______________

2. question, inquiry, query, reply ______________

3. painting, sculpture, picture, portrait ______________

4. safe, dangerous, risky, hazardous ______________

5. peacefull, tranquill, calm, nervous ______________

6. gallery, bar, museum, showroom ______________

7. sip, gulp, swallow, spit ______________

Elvira took a sip of the steaming Earl Grey tea – Hudson’s favourite – and made another attempt.

“OK, James. What is it that you absolutely wanted to show me? I don’t want to rush, and I would be happy to accept an invitation from you to tea anytime – but there is a crime waiting to be solved,” she said, slightly impatient.

Übung 127: Übersetzen Sie!

ÜBUNG 127 !

1. Darf ich Ihnen ein Kompliment machen?

____

2. Sie sehen heute bezaubernd aus.

____

3. Wie wär's mit etwas zu essen?

____

4. Auf dein Wohl!

____

The inspector calmly took a sip of tea.
"That's exactly why we're here. Be patient, Elvira."
Hudson glanced at his housekeeper.
"Miss Paddington. Do you remember Jimmy Coltrane? He had the pleasure of being our guest for a few days?"
Miss Paddington huffed.
"Do I remember Jimmy Coltrane? And how I remember that good-for-nothing! He ate half of the pantry and had terrible manners."
Hudson chuckled to himself. As far as he could remember, Miss Paddington and old Jimmy had got along very well – their constant sparring was just a joke.
"Who the hell is Jimmy Coltrane?" asked Elvira.
One needn't to be a detective to figure out her patience was wearing thin.

Übung 128: Bilden Sie das englische Wort aus dem Buchstabenchaos! !

1. CERUIXNOS (Ausflug) ______________
2. PACNOAYMC (begleiten) ______________
3. ANRMIE (verbleiben) ______________
4. EBHROT (stören) ______________
5. CFSRAUE (Oberfläche) ______________

ÜBUNG 128

6. COESINRSF (Spurensicherung) ______________

7. RTAEMLAN (mütterlich) ______________

8. TIITINOVNA (Einladung) ______________

9. SNENRAM (Manieren) ______________

10. TIPAMNTIE (ungeduldig) ______________

Miss Paddington waved her hand dismissively.
"An insignificant thief." Obviously she didn't want to expand on the topic.
"A very talented thief," contradicted Hudson. Then he turned to Elvira.
"Jimmy was one of my first cases, many years ago. He was a small-time crook, who had got a hold of old underground maps. Not maps of the current network that you can get anywhere, but an entire directory of all the tunnels no longer in use."
Elvira pricked up her ears.
"Jimmy Coltrane got a gang of professionals together and used the old underground tunnels to dig into half a dozen banks."

ÜBUNG 129 !

Übung 129: Vervollständigen Sie die Wortverbindungen!
(gang, glass, sum, ray, pound, clump, gust, spot, sip, piece)

1. a ______________ of tea

2. a ______________ of thieves

3. a ______________ of money

4. a ______________ of advice

5. a ______________ of dirt

6. a ______________ of paint

7. a ______________ of wine

8. a ______________ of butter

9. a ______________ of wind

10. a ______________ of light

The inspector took another sip of tea and ignored Miss Paddington who was shaking her head.
“Jimmy did one robbery after another and we may never have caught him. Unfortunately, during one of his hunts, he ran into London’s Mole-Men.”
“Mole-Men?” asked Elvira.

Übung 130: Setzen Sie die Verben ein!
(fought, hung, make out, looked, seemed, stared)

Hudson, Elvira and Miss Paddington (1. blicken) ____________ ________ at the yellowed underground maps the inspector had (2. aufhängen) ____________ on the living room wall. The large, musty smelling maps showed a complicated network of lines that (3. scheinen) ____________ to go nowhere. Only after examining them more closely, could they (4. erkennen) ____________ a system. Even Miss Paddington, who at first was only worried about the wallpaper, (5. starren) ____________ at the maps with fascination. "Fascinating, isn't it?" asked the inspector. "Like a lost world. The underground has snaked through London since 1863, and many of the old lines don't run anymore. Back then, the underground was not the sole property of the City of London. A half-a-dozen private companies (6. kämpfen) ______________ for dominance – and many companies lost their routes.

In total, there are more than 40 so-called 'ghost stations' in London, abandoned stations, some that haven't been used in over 100 years."

Elvira took a step forward and examined the map.

"True," she murmured mesmerised and pointed to the map, "I don't know some of these routes at all."

Then her gaze darkened.

"But James, if there are 40 abandoned underground stations, then there are also 40 places where the thieves could have entered the tunnel system. How can we find the right station?"

The inspector smiled at Elvira encouragingly.

ÜBUNG 131 !

Übung 131: Trifft die Aussage zu? Markieren Sie: richtig ✓ falsch –?

1. If something is yellowed, it is usually old.
2. Miss Paddington was not interested in the maps.
3. All of the underground routes in Inspector Hudson's maps are still in use.
4. If something is abandoned, it is no longer being used.

5. Many of the 'ghost stations' are in the suburbs.
6. Jimmy Coltrane used the maps of the underground system to sell drugs.
7. Jimmy Coltrane never went to jail.
8. Jimmy Coltrane was very kind to Miss Paddington and Mr Hudson.
9. Some of the abandoned stations in London are over 100 years old.
10. Hudson thought it would be difficult to find the place where the thieves entered the tunnel system.

"It's not as hard as it seems, my dear Elvira. Many of the 'ghost stations' are in the centre of the city, in the middle of business areas full of people. Of course these can be excluded. Too, land is extremely scarce in London, which means that many of the old stations have been torn down and built over a long time ago."
Elvira nodded.

Übung 132: Setzen Sie die Wörter ein!
(ghost, replaced, middle, perfect, network, entrance, building, snapped, notice, particular)

"Then only a few of the 1. '______________ stations' are outside the centre."

The inspector shook his head. "Not necessarily. I have one 2. ______________ station in mind. This one here."

Hudson used a pencil to point to a spot on the map. It was where

ÜBUNG 132 !

the 3. ____________ was most interconnected.

Miss Paddington, who had until now remained quiet, staring at the map, said, "Are you sure, James? That is in the 4. ____________ of the city, next to the British Museum, if I am not mistaken. Wouldn't somebody 5. ____________ if a gang of thieves were running around with jack hammers and picks?"

Hudson nodded.

"You are absolutely right, Miss Paddington. Until 1933, there was a station at the British Museum. It was removed and 6. ____________ with the neighbouring station, Holborn. However, this old 7. ____________ would have been 8. ____________ for thieves with shovels and picks."

"And why is that?" asked Elvira, astonished.

"It's very simple, my dear. Because an office 9. ____________ is currently being constructed on this site. You have certainly seen the construction site."

Elvira 10. ____________ her fingers.

"You're right, James," she cried. "I remember now. The building is even for one of our subsidiaries. On such a large construction site, nobody would notice a few extra people with digging equipment!"

"Exactly," replied Hudson. "And tonight, I am going to take a look at this site."
"I'll go with you!" cried Elvira, without hesitation, but the inspector merely shook his head.
"Honestly, Elvira, I would prefer if you asked around in the art scene. Maybe the theft of the two paintings …"
"Three," corrected Elvira.
"… *three* paintings, was a hired theft. Perhaps a fanatical art collector hired the thieves especially for this coup! You know much more about the scene than I do, Elvira."
Elvira was thoughtful for a moment, then nodded.
"You're right, James, that makes sense. I'll get to work at once."

Übung 133: Wie heißt der Plural der folgenden Substantive?

ÜBUNG 133 !

1. thief ____________________
2. scene ____________________
3. half ____________________
4. mouse ____________________
5. wolf ____________________
6. light ____________________
7. tunnel ____________________
8. loaf ____________________

Elvira grabbed her handbag and gave the inspector a quick kiss on the cheek.
"Take care of yourself, James," she whispered.

The inspector blushed. Miss Paddington smiled to herself. For years, she had been trying to bring the confirmed bachelor and the attractive insurance agent together. One day she would be successful.

"Uhhm, right," stammered the inspector, after Elvira had gone. "I am going to make a few preparations for tonight."

While Miss Paddington grinned, the inspector fled up the narrow steps to the first floor and disappeared into his room.

A few hours later, the sun had already set, and Miss Paddington was at the stove, sizzling a hearty supper for the inspector.

If James was going to be hunting crooks in the middle of the night, then at least he can do it on a full stomach, she thought.

Suddenly, Miss Paddington heard a noise behind her.

Übung 134: Übersetzen Sie!

1. I have one particular station in mind.

___

2. She did it out of friendship, not for money.

___

3. He made Elvira's acquaintance in London last year.

___

4. The detective shook his head.

___

5. I would prefer if you stayed home.

___

6. Take care of yourself.

____

7. Miss Paddington smiles to herself.

____

8. The inspector often stammers.

____

The housekeeper spun around startled.
A strange man stood in the door to the living room. His clothes looked as if they had come from the Salvation Army. His whiskey breath was even stronger than the smell of frying bacon in the pan.
"What's for supper, baby?" the stranger asked and leaned against the door frame.
Miss Paddington gulped and reached for the frying pan.

Übung 135: Welches Wort ist richtig? Unterstreichen Sie es!

The frying pan in her hand, Miss Paddington ran towards the (1.) intruder/guest.
"Just wait, you crook!" cried the (2.) frightened/resolute housekeeper, swinging the pan like a (3.) baseball bat/flower.
The strange man raised his hands in (4.) fear/happiness.
"Miss Paddington, don't …!" he cried.
The old lady stopped. The voice was more than (5.) unknown/familiar. Then she gave the intruder a closer look.
Of course, his clothes were unacceptable and the whiskey breath (6.) unbearable/delightful, but the figure in the (7.) doorway/window could be none other than …

"Inspector Hudson? W-what in the hell is with this silly disguise? How could you frighten me so?" gasped Miss Paddington.

James Hudson took a step forward and put his hand on the angry housekeeper's shoulder.

"I'm sorry if I frightened you, Miss Paddington. I was trying out my disguise – but I didn't think it would be so convincing that even you wouldn't recognise me."

! ÜBUNG 136

Übung 136: Setzen Sie das richtige Wort ein, um das Rätsel zu lösen.

1. bevorzugen □ _ _ _ _ _
2. fanatisch _ _ _ _ _ _ _ _ □
3. nachdenklich _ _ □ _ _ _ _ _ _ _
4. Geldbeutel _ □ _ _ _
5. Gespenst □ _ _ _ _
6. reichen, greifen nach _ _ _ _ □
7. Atemzug □ _ _ _ _ _
8. Speck _ _ _ □ _
9. Eindringling _ _ □ _ _ _ _ _
10. erschrecken _ _ _ _ _ □ _ _
11. erkennen _ _ _ □ _ _ _ _ _
12. Geruch _ □ _ _ _

Lösung: _ _ _ _ _ _ _ _ _ _ _ _

Miss Paddington glared at him and shook her head.
"James, you look absolutely awful. What is the disguise for?"

Übung 137: Bilden Sie sinnvolle Wörter aus dem Buchstabenchaos!

"Well," answered Hudson, "when I start looking for Jimmy Coltrane, I will have to go down into the underworld – in every 1. sesne _________ (Sinn) of the word. I'm 2. iaradf _________ (fürchten) that dear Jimmy isn't moving in the best social 3. lcis-cer _________ (Kreise) after his release from 4. srinop _________ (Gefängnis)."
"Most likely he is associating with thieves and scoundrels," grumbled Miss Paddington.
"Most likely. If I go into these circles as Inspector James Hudson and start asking 5. stupeananl _________ (unangenehm) questions, I would scare off my informants. But if Matches Marconi asks about his old prison buddy Jimmy Coltrane, no-one will be suspicious."
Miss Paddington 6. kolode _________ (blickte) at the Inspector inquisitively.
"Who is Matches Marconi?"
"Who else?" asked the inspector with a phony voice and put his hand on his 7. ethsc _________ (Brust), as 8. udts _________ (Staub) rose from the old suitcoat. "He's standing right in front of you."

Half an hour later, the inspector was sitting in a tube to Holborn station. Miss Paddington had insisted that he eat a hearty meal before his undercover operation. In the mean- time, the evening had already advanced and only a few commuters shared the compartment with Hudson.

The cheap whisky the inspector had drunk did its job – the other passengers looked at Hudson with disgust and moved as far away from him as possible. His disguise was working.

The train jolted to a halt and the inspector lurched out of the car, shoving another passenger as he went. But one look from 'Matches Marconi' was enough to stifle any complaints.

Hudson was so into his role that he jumped in fright when an underground police officer stared searchingly at him. With quick steps, the inspector climbed the steps and reached the construction site a minute later.

ÜBUNG 138 !

Übung 138: Welches Wort ist das „schwarze Schaf"?

1. robbery, return, theft, steal ____________
2. insignificant, minor, important, trivial ____________
3. incompetent, talented, gifted, skilled ____________
4. yellowed, old, fresh, faded ____________
5. sole, exclusive, one, multiple ____________
6. uninterested, mesmerised, entranced, hypnotised ____________
7. precious, worthless, valuable, expensive ____________
8. linked, interconnected, joined, independent ____________

9. bachelor, husband, single, unmarried ____________

10. supper, breakfast, evening meal, dinner ____________

The skeleton of the imposing office building stretched sinisterly into the night sky. The full moon bathed the steel girders in silvery light. During the day, there was bustle and noise here, but in the moonlight the construction site lay quiet and empty.
The inspector looked around.

Übung 139: Finden Sie die englische Übersetzung!
(1. Zaun 2. Baustelle 3. überzeugen 4. Durchsuchungsbefehl 5. Werkzeuge 6. Rohbau)

Good. No-one was around and the street was empty. With deft movements, the inspector climbed over the wooden fence separating the construction site from the street. As he jumped down, Hudson hoped that the construction site wasn't patrolled by a security company. It would be difficult to convince the night watchman that an inspector from Scotland Yard was hidden under Matches Marconi's torn clothing – and Hudson didn't have a search warrant for the construction site.
There was no way around it, he was an illegal intruder on private property. Without concrete evidence, though, it would have taken days, if not weeks, to get a search warrant.
Hudson pulled a torch out of his pocket and began to look around. He picked his way carefully between broken machines and piles of sand. Dozens of construction workers were here during the day. A gang of thieves with digging tools would hardly be noticed.
After a few minutes, Hudson found what he was looking for:

20 metres from the skeleton was a small chute that led directly underground.

Around the entrance, he recognised the remains of the old underground station – Hudson climbed in carefully. After a few minutes, he arrived at a wooden door.
"Entry prohibited. Danger. Collapse Hazard!" warned the sign.
These were undoubtedly the remains of the abandoned underground station. Hudson pulled a skeleton key out of his pocket and picked at the rusty lock. A few seconds later, the door opened with a click.

ÜBUNG 140 !

Übung 140: Setzen Sie die passiven Sätze ins Aktiv!

1. The lop-sided steps were climbed by the inspector.

____

2. The steel girders were bathed in light by the moon.

____

3. The night watchman was not convinced by Hudson.

____

4. The property was entered by the intruder.

____

5. The construction site was patrolled by a security company.

____

6. A search warrant was issued by the judge.

____

7. The machines were used by nobody.

____

8. The station sign was shone on by the torch.

____

Hudson carefully pushed open the door and peered into the darkness with his flashlight. A dusty set of stone steps led further into the depths. Damp and mould had made the steps slippery and the inspector had to carefully grope his way down. His steps echoed eerily in the dark. After a few minutes, he reached level ground.

Übung 141: Welches Wort bedeutet das Gegenteil?

1. careful
   - a) ☐ cautious
   - b) ☐ watchful
   - c) ☐ reckless

2. abandoned
   - a) ☐ full
   - b) ☐ empty
   - c) ☐ uninhabited

3. prohibited
   - a) ☐ illegal
   - b) ☐ allowed
   - c) ☐ forbidden

4. hidden
   a) ☐ open
   b) ☐ secret
   c) ☐ unseen

5. moist
   a) ☐ damp
   b) ☐ wet
   c) ☐ dry

The inspector's light moved across the wall until it fell on a sign. Its weathered letters read 'British Museum'.
Hudson was actually standing on the platform of a station that had been abandoned a hundred years ago. The light beam reflected off the tiled walls, bathing the station in a surreal glow. All of a sudden, the floor shook and a droning rattle filled the chute. A moist gust brushed the inspector's face.
He needed a few moments to realise what was going on. A regular tube was rattling through the central line that must run near here. There were connections between the old and new tunnels.

ÜBUNG 142

Übung 142: Bilden Sie aus dem Adjektiv ein Adverb!

1. social ____________________
2. suspicious ____________________
3. good ____________________
4. hearty ____________________

5. sinister ______________________

6. illegal ______________________

7. careful ______________________

8. rusty ______________________

9. actual ______________________

10. regular ______________________

The typical draught from a tube passing by could be felt in the abandoned tunnel. It sure is eerie here, thought Hudson. No wonder people called these stations 'ghost stations'. He wouldn't have been surprised if there were actually ghosts down here.

In truth, there were many legends about the souls of dead passengers, who were desperately looking for an exit.

At that moment, a shrill sound came from behind the inspector. Hudson wheeled around.

A shadowy figure rushed towards the inspector. Its mouth was opened in an angry scream and it glowed like a ghost in the darkness.

Übung 143: Wie heißt das Verb auf Englisch?

ÜBUNG 143 !

1. strecken ______________________

2. sich schnell umdrehen ______________________

3. glühen/leuchten ______________________

4. irreführen ______________________

5. spiegeln ______________________

6. rasen ______________________

Elvira Elliot looked at her watch for the twentieth time. It was late and she had been sitting and waiting for over an hour in the elegant hotel bar. The melodies of the pianist in the corner had, in the meantime, become so familiar to her that she could have hummed along if she hadn't been so tired. She had spent hours on the phone after leaving the inspector, trying to make the most of her connections.
After a dozen calls to friends and colleagues in the insurance branch, she had been able to put together a list of all the art collectors, who had recently gone on a shopping spree in London.

ÜBUNG 144 !

Übung 144: Welche Wörter haben dieselbe Bedeutung?

1. tired	☐	competitor
2. melody	☐	lately
3. colleagues	☐	asset
4. recently	☐	rich
5. painting	☐	tune
6. investment	☐	co-workers
7. wealthy	☐	picture
8. rival	☐	sleepy
9. interested	☐	curious

It was unbelievable how much money people were willing to spend on an old painting. Yet, at the same time, these artworks were solid investments to be shown off on the walls of the wealthy. No wonder, thought Elvira, that so many rich Americans were in London gobbling up old English art.
And at this moment, Elvira was waiting for just such an American – Bill B. Bixby, an oil tycoon from Texas.

Übung 145: Bringen Sie die Wörter in die richtige Reihenfolge!

1. spend art money a lot of People on

____

2. wait had to time a long Elvira

____

3. dealers She art many called

____

4. Picasso doesn't Hudson like

____

5. he saw Hudson thought ghost a

____

6. was scream A heard

____

7. London shop Many in collectors

____

An old friend, who worked for a rival insurance agency and owed Elvira a favour, told her that Mr Bixby had been buying up portraits of old aristocrats like crazy.

Elvira was interested immediately as she thought about the relatively worthless third painting that was stolen. After a few more calls, Elvira had managed to actually set up an appointment with Mr Bixby.

Maybe he knew something about the missing painting. If he would only show up.

Übung 146: Unterstreichen Sie die Wörter im Text mit denselben Bedeutungen!
(another time, found, yelled, lovely, thankful, truthful, dreadful)

Elvira was looking at her watch again when a broad-shouldered man in a colourfully patterned suit entered the bar. Instead of a regular tie, two leather strings swung out of his collar bound together by a silver steer's head. Definitely a Texan.
The man looked around the bar and discovered Elvira, who was waving at him. Seconds later, he had crossed the bar with big steps. Before Elvira could say anything, the Texan was shaking her hand.
"You must be Miss Elliot," he shouted. "My name is Bixby. Bill B. Bixby from beautiful Austin, Texas."
"Without a doubt," smiled Elvira, "I'm grateful that you had time to meet me at such short notice."
"Now or never, honey. My plane leaves for Texas tomorrow morning. To be honest, I'm happy to be going home to sunny Texas. London in the autumn is terrible."

"I won't take much of your time, Mr Bixby," answered Elvira, "I wanted to ask if you knew something about a painting."
Mr Bixby waved to a waitress.
"Hey, honey," he shouted across the room, "the young lady and I will have Kentucky whiskeys!"
Elvira tried to protest, but the Texan did not notice.
"Uhhm, no thank you, Mr Bixby. What I wanted to say was … this painting …"
The Texan laid his big, fleshy hand on Elvira's wrist.
"I'm sorry lady. I admire your sense of business, but I've already insured my paintings."
Elvira shook her head.

"Mr Bixby, you have the wrong idea. I don't want to sell you an insurance policy. I'm afraid that the painting you bought here in London may have been stolen."

Übung 147: Welche Übersetzung gibt die Bedeutung des englischen Satzes wieder?

1. If he would only show.
   a) ☐ Wenn er nur zeigen würde.
   b) ☐ Wenn er nur auftauchen würde.
   c) ☐ Wenn er nur darstellen würde.

2. London in the autumn is terrible.
   a) ☐ London im Sommer ist schrecklich
   b) ☐ London im Herbst ist beängstigend.
   c) ☐ London im Herbst ist schrecklich.

3. Definitely a Texan.
   a) ☐ Eindeutig ein Texaner.
   b) ☐ Vielleicht ein Texaner.
   c) ☐ Auf keinen Fall ein Texaner.

4. I won't take much of your time.
   a) ☐ Ich brauche viel Ihrer Zeit.
   b) ☐ Ich werde nicht viel Ihrer Zeit in Anspruch nehmen.
   c) ☐ Ich werde Ihre Zeit nicht brauchen.

5. I admire your business sense.
   a) ☐ Ich verachte Ihren Geschäftssinn.
   b) ☐ Ich bewundere Ihren Geschäftspartner.
   c) ☐ Ich bewundere Ihren Geschäftssinn.

Bixby looked at Elvira with astonishment.

"Stolen! What do you mean?"

"Well, I heard that you bought a large number of aristocrat portraits in the past few weeks."

"That's true," nodded Bixby, as he interrupted Elvira. "Do you know, I bought a small country seat in the North of England. I am having it taken apart brick by brick and rebuilt on my ranch in Texas. I needed a few paintings for the interior."

Elvira almost fainted when she thought about how much it must cost to tear down, transport and rebuild an entire house, probably in the middle of a cow pasture.

ÜBUNG 148 !

Übung 148: Was wird beschrieben?

1. A place to live, usually in the United States or Australia, where there are often horses, cows and sheep. ______________
2. Many of these are used to build houses. ______________
3. The season of the year where the leaves change colour. ______________
4. Money paid to protect an object, such as a painting or your life. ______________
5. Feeling sorry because someone else has problems. ______________
6. An area away from the city where fewer people live. ______________
7. A woman who serves you in a restaurant. ______________

"Oh really," continued Elvira, "and as chance would have it, yesterday night the portrait of a certain Lord Ploughbottom was stolen from a gallery and it is possible that the thieves could have offered it to you."

Mr Bixby went pale.

"What was his name?"

"Lord Ploughbottom. The painting is from the late 17th century."

"Oh dear," murmured Bixby, "that's impossible. The picture was stolen, you said?"

"Yesterday night, from the Blighton Gallery – together with two more valuable paintings by …"

"Picasso and Monet?"

For a moment, Elvira was surprised that the Texan knew these artists names. Then she nodded.

"Those crooks were fast," Bixby remarked, after regaining his composure. "This afternoon, a guy came to me and offered me those exact paintings. His name was Coltrane, or …"

"Coltrane?" cried Elvira.

Übung 149: Gibt der Satz den Sachverhalt richtig wieder? Markieren Sie: richtig ✓ oder falsch –?

1. Elvira didn't have to wait long at the hotel bar.
2. Mr Bixby was from Houston.
3. Mr Bixby's plane was leaving the next day.
4. Mr Bixby ordered gin for himself and Elvira.
5. Mr Bixby thought that Elvira was trying to sell him an insurance policy.
6. Mr Bixby is transporting the country house he bought to Texas.
7. Mr Bixby lives in an apartment.

8. Mr Bixby was offered all three stolen paintings.
9. Mr Bixby is a great admirer of Picasso and Monet.
10. Mr Bixby said that Jimmy Coltrane visited him that afternoon.

Bixby nodded.
"That's him. Had to sell off his collection he said 'cause of money troubles. I didn't want the Picasso and the Monet. I don't like pictures I can't make anything out of. But I bought the lord immediately. It fits perfectly in my collection."
Elvira was so excited, that she even took a sip from the whiskey glass.

ÜBUNG 150 !

Übung 150: Bilden Sie Wörter aus dem Buchstabenchaos!

"Do you still have the painting here?" she gasped.

Bixby 1. dndedo ______________ (nickte).

"Of 2. ucoser ________________ (natürlich). And if it was really 3. lsonet ______________ (geklaut), I will 4. veale ______________ (zurücklassen) it with you. It wasn't very 5. ixesnevpe ________________ (teuer) anyway. Could you take it to the police for me tomorrow? I'm afraid I would 6. sims ________________ (verpassen) my 7. glifth ______________ (Flug) if I did it myself."

Elvira nodded vigorously.
"Of course."
Bixby emptied his glass in one gulp and stood up.

"Can you wait here for a moment. I'll go and get the painting from my room."
Elvira watched the Texan from behind and rejoiced. Hudson would be amazed when she presented him the stolen painting.
Elvira couldn't see Bill Bixby get in the elevator with a malicious smile on his face.

Übung 151: Setzen Sie die richtige Präposition ein!

ÜBUNG 151 !

1. Miss Paddington looked ________ her watch.
2. Sir Reginald waved ________ the forensics team.
3. Elvira is ________ Manchester.
4. Hudson was ready to go ________ short notice.
5. Many paintings were stolen ________ the past few weeks.
6. Bixby has many horses ________ his ranch.
7. Hudson offered a cigarette ________ Elvira.
8. The gallery was closed due ________ the thefts.
9. He couldn't make anything ________ in the dark.
10. Hudson left his coat ________ Miss Paddington.

At the same moment the ghostly figure rushed towards Hudson. Instinctively, Hudson ducked. He felt something brush against his cheek and float away. The inspector rolled on the dusty ground, jumped up and looked around. The 'ghost' had disappeared – if it really *had* been a ghost that had attacked him.

Hudson brushed the dust off his jacket. The scream echoed eerily in the tunnel along with the drone of the tube. Then it was quiet. Hudson concentrated on his breathing and tried to regulate his pulse. Normally the inspector didn't believe in ghosts and supernatural apparitions, but the sudden spook had scared him. Unwilling to give in to his fear, he was already searching his mind for a logical explanation, just as he had always done when faced with the 'inexplicable'.

The appearance of the ghost was almost simultaneous with the passing of the tube. This was no coincidence. Hudson glanced at his watch. In a few moments, the train from the opposite direction should be passing.

! ÜBUNG 152

Übung 152: Das englische Wort hat verschiedene Übersetzungsmöglichkeiten. Welche?

1. kind ______________ ______________
2. ball ______________ ______________
3. desert ______________ ______________
4. race ______________ ______________
5. mine ______________ ______________
6. like ______________ ______________
7. compliment ______________ ______________

A muffled rattling announced the train's approach and became louder the nearer it came.

All of a sudden, the shrill scream was heard again. A few seconds later, the ghostly figure appeared in exactly the same spot as before.
But this time, the inspector was prepared. Instead of throwing himself to the ground, he jumped in front of the 'ghost' and grabbed it.
His hands felt a thin material, as he heard a ripping noise. The 'ghost' stopped immediately and fell to the ground in front of him. In his hand, the inspector held a piece of fabric that glowed in the dark.
Hudson smiled as he picked up the rest of the painted sheet. Someone had painted the outline of a horrible ghost with glow paint. Above, the distorted face was a loop.
Hudson shone his flashlight at the ceiling. With his experienced eyes, he could see a thin rope stretched from one end of the tunnel to the other.

Übung 153: Bilden Sie sinnvolle Sätze!

1. explanation There a must logical be

____

2. in Miss Paddington ghosts believes

____

3. train the of The heard rattle again was

____

4. dark Her in glowed the eyes

5. the Did ghost see anyone?

6. by Elvira disguise Hudson's frightened was

7. Hudson coming he as saw Elvira smiled

8. the waited Elvira questions and answers for asked

9. smiling is Mr Bixby Why?

10. waitress He a whiskey for the asked

Undoubtedly, the 'ghost' and the rope were part of a clever mechanism released by the draught from the passing trains.
An effective method for keeping unwanted visitors away or for scaring homeless people who wandered into the tunnel by accident. Basically, the mechanical ghost was nothing more than a refined version of a scarecrow.
Only people who had something to protect would put up a scarecrow.
Or people who had something to hide.

Übung 154: Beantworten Sie die Fragen zum Text!

1. What legends were connected with the 'ghost stations'?

2. Why did Hudson hope that no-one patrolled the construction site?

3. Why did Hudson disguise himself as Matches Marconi?

4. What did Hudson first think he saw in the tunnel?

5. What was the connection between the 'ghost' and the subway?

Hudson shone his flashlight further around the tunnel. Now that he had got used to the darkness and exorcised the spook from the 'ghost station', he was beginning to enjoy his underground expedition. It was a trip into the past. The flashlight's beam caught a yellowed newspaper from 1933.

"Paul Adrien Maurice Dirac and Erwin Schrödinger share the Nobel Prize for their new theory of the atom," announced the headlines on the front page.

Next to the paper lay an old ticket whose price was extremely low by today's standards.

The inspector allowed himself a nostalgic smile. Then, he discovered something much more interesting under a rotting bench in the corner of the station. Hudson knelt in front of the bench and pulled out a belt which held various tools and a dust mask. The belt was worn, but definitely not 70 years old. It must belong to the thieves, who had entered the tunnel system from this station.

In a feverish search, the inspector dug through the numerous small pockets and straps. At last, something small and square fell out: a matchbox. The inspector aimed the beam of his torch at it.

'King's Head Inn' was written on the front.

Übung 155: Welches Wort hat die gegenteilige Bedeutung?

1.	quiet	☐ whisper
2.	supernatural	☐ reveal
3.	yell	☐ drop
4.	float	☐ irrational
5.	appear	☐ welcome
6.	logical	☐ normal
7.	coincidental	☐ sink
8.	lift	☐ vanish
9.	effective	☐ dislike
10.	unwanted	☐ noisy
11.	hide	☐ new
12.	enjoy	☐ useless
13.	worn	☐ planned

Inspector Hudson smiled again. He knew the pub, a nasty hole on the edge of town, a meeting point for crooks and their disreputable companions. Exactly the right place for Matches Marconi to wait for an old friend.

Übung 156: Fügen Sie die richtige Präposition ein!

Inspector Hudson, disguised 1. __________ Matches Marconi, had to change trains three times to get 2. ____________ the abandoned street where the 'King's Head Inn' was hidden.

Of course he could have taken a cab, but he doubted that any cab driver would have been willing to take someone like Marconi as a passenger. It wouldn't have made his disguise very convincing either. 3. ______________ the meantime, it was 4. ______________ midnight. According to the legal closing times, the bar should have shut a long time ago.

However, the owners and guests of the 'King's Head' did not seem to pay attention 5. __________ regulations. Why should they obey the law by night, when they broke it 6. ____________ the daytime? Policemen seldom wandered into this run-down area, thought Hudson. He also doubted that the owner of the 'King's Head' even had a liquor license to lose.

Hudson was hardly ten paces 7. __________ from the bar, when the door was pushed open 8. __________ inside.

Two powerful, broad-shouldered men had grabbed a guest by the collar and threw him onto the street. Laughter emanated from inside as the door shut again.

The drunk babbled something and reached into the pocket of his ragged trousers.

ÜBUNG 157

Übung 157: Bilden Sie sinnvolle Wörter aus dem Buchstabenchaos!

1. EUBT (U-Bahn) __________
2. SPUEL (Herzschlag) __________
3. OREP (Seil) __________
4. HDARGTU (Luftzug) __________
5. WCRREASCO (Vogelscheuche) __________
6. BPU (Kneipe) __________
7. DIDHNE (versteckt) __________
8. ENOWR (Inhaber) __________
9. HIDNTIGM (Mitternacht) __________
10. SIEECNL (Genehmigung) __________

He pulled out a bundle of banknotes and a gold watch – and all of a sudden, he was sober.
Smiling and sure-footed, he walked away, counting the banknotes.
"Did you make a good catch?" asked the inspector.
Obviously the man had only pretended to be drunk, in order to bump into the other guests and pick their pockets. So much for honour amongst thieves.
The pickpocket startled and stared at the inspector, then ran off. Hudson wrinkled his forehead as he thought. This was the perfect opportunity to win the trust of the men at the 'King's Head'.

Without hesitating, he sprinted after the pickpocket. The pickpocket was horrified when he saw Hudson behind him and ran even faster.

Übung 158: Welche Wörter gehören zusammen?

1. underground
   a) ☐ airport b) ☐ tunnel c) ☐ river

2. pickpocket
   a) ☐ money b) ☐ safe c) ☐ alarm

3. bar
   a) ☐ tea b) ☐ cake c) ☐ alcohol

4. frame
   a) ☐ sculpture b) ☐ picture c) ☐ record

5. ghost
   a) ☐ scream b) ☐ laugh c) ☐ smile

6. police
   a) ☐ education b) ☐ law c) ☐ money

7. bachelor
   a) ☐ husband b) ☐ single c) ☐ wife

Nevertheless, Hudson was able to catch him. Police work kept him in good shape. The inspector tackled the fleeing man and both men hit the ground hard. Hudson stood up quickly and grabbed the thief

by his collar. The thief tried hard to escape Hudson's grip.
"Hey! What's the deal here? Let me go you bastard!" cried the man angrily.
But Hudson was already dragging him back to the pub. Without a word, Hudson kicked the door open.

ÜBUNG 159 !

Übung 159: Finden Sie die englische Übersetzung für die Wörter in Klammern! ***(ohrenbetäubend, Gespräch, verstummte, genannt, hinter, kahl, fettig, Kumpel)***

The noise in the pub was deafening – laughter, conversation and loud music. However, everyone fell silent as Hudson, alias Matches Marconi, entered the pub.
The pickpocket went pale.
The owner behind the bar, a fat, bald man with a greasy apron, looked questioningly at 'Matches Marconi'.
"What are you doing, mate? We just threw that drunk out!"

"Maybe," growled the inspector in his 'Marconi' voice, "but your friend here picked your pockets before. Cough it up buddy!"
The pickpocket gulped. Hesitatingly, he reached into the pockets of his trousers and pulled out the bundle of banknotes and the gold watch and laid them on the sticky table.
"No way!" cried a burly man in a greasy suit. "My fake Rolex!"
The man rushed to the table and snatched up the watch while he stared at the banknotes with greedy eyes.
"My money!" cried a dozen men at the same time. All at once, they all pounced on the money.
A few seconds later, a fight broke out, much to the amusement of the other guests.

Übung 160: Wie heißt das Wort auf Englisch?

1. Fang ____________________
2. Geldschein ____________________
3. Taschendieb ____________________
4. nüchtern ____________________
5. runzeln ____________________
6. Gelegenheit ____________________
7. vortäuschen ____________________
8. schleppen ____________________

The fat bartender laughed and turned the music on again.
Hudson used the noise to whisper in the pickpocket's ear: "You should look for another job, buddy. Now get out, before it gets ugly here."
The pickpocket didn't wait. He disappeared out the door and into the darkness like a flash of lightning.
"Come on over, mate!" called the bartender. "You deserve a beer."
Hudson snapped his fingers.
"Nothing against that my friend," he replied and took the pint of beer.
The other guests toasted him. Twenty minutes later Matches Marconi had toasted with most of the guests.
"Time for phase 2," thought the inspector, as he wiped the foam from his lips.
"… and while the police were still surrounding the bank, I hopped into a taxi with the loot and drove home!"

Inspector Hudson had already been entertaining the dubious persons with made-up capers he had carried out as the famous Matches Marconi.

ÜBUNG 161

Übung 161: Wie heißt das Simple Past des Verbs?

1. reply ____________________
2. throw ____________________
3. win ____________________
4. grab ____________________
5. beseech ____________________
6. pay ____________________
7. doubt ____________________
8. shrink ____________________

While he was talking, he secretly switched his full beer glass with his listeners' empty ones – he needed a clear head to carry out his plans.

The crooks at the bar listened attentively to his stories and regularly slapped him on the back. Matches Marconi was the star of the evening.

"It's time to get to the point," thought Hudson.

"Actually boys, the reason I came is that I'm looking for an old mate of mine, Jimmy Coltrane – have you guys heard of him?"

"Jimmy Coltrane?" asked a bearded man. "The mole?"

Übung 162: Übersetzen Sie den Satz ins Englische!

1. Der Wirt bietet Hudson ein Bier an.

____

2. Der Taschendieb tut nur so, als ob er betrunken wäre.

____

3. Die Diebe ignorieren die Gesetze.

____

4. Hudsons Atem roch nach Whiskey.

____

5. Er stellte sich als Matches Marconi vor.

____

"That's him," nodded Hudson. "We were together in jail. Nice guy, Jimmy. I lost track of him after my, eh, unexpected release. But I owe him some money – and Matches Marconi always pays his debts. Do you guys know anything about him?"
Inspector Hudson tried to make the question sound as casual as possible. At the same time, his eyes swept over the other men and noted their reactions.
Most of the guests shrugged their shoulders.
"Sorry Matches," said the bearded man. "All I know is that he spent some time in prison. Then I didn't hear from him any more. What about you guys?"
The other guests shook their heads.

But two men sitting at the bar exchanged dark glances. One of them wore a blindingly bright plaid shirt, while the face of the other one was etched with a narrow scar.
When the man in plaid motioned to the bartender to pay, Hudson glanced at the man's hands unnoticed by the others.

! ÜBUNG 163

Übung 163: Setzen Sie die richtigen Wörter ein, um das Geheimwort zu entschlüsseln!

1. Fingernagel _ _ _ _ _ _ _ _ _ ☐
2. vorherrschend _ _ _ _ ☐ _ _ _ _ _ _
3. Einkommen _ _ _ ☐ _ _ _ _
4. Belohnung _ _ _ _ _ ☐
5. Obdachloser _ ☐ _ _ _ _ _ _
6. unbemerkt _ ☐ _ _ _ _ _ _ _

Lösung: _ _ _ _ _ _

The man's fingernails were circled with dirt. Either the man had bad hygiene, or he had recently been digging. Hudson guessed the latter, due to the suspicious way the men looked when he mentioned Jimmy Coltrane.
Both men seemed not to be able to leave the bar fast enough. The man with the scar reached into his trousers pockets and pulled out a bundle of pound notes. Without waiting for change, he laid a big banknote on the bar, emptied his beer glass in one gulp and left the bar with his friend.
The inspector watched them go, then slapped the bearded man on the back.

"OK, boys, that's all for tonight. I'm leaving. It was nice meeting you all."
Hudson got up from his stool, shook a few hands and left the bar with quick steps.
The inspector took a deep breath in the fresh air. He would probably smell like smoke and old beer for the next week.
He looked around. The men were hurrying down the street. The inspector quietly followed them.

Übung 164: Ersetzen Sie das unterstrichene Wort durch das Gegenteil!

ÜBUNG 164 !

1. It was <u>terrible</u> to meet you. ________
2. The ghost in the underground tunnel was <u>real</u>. ________
3. The two men at the bar were <u>trusting</u> of Hudson. ________
4. Criminals <u>obey</u> the laws. ________
5. The men were <u>strolling</u> down the street. ________
6. Matches Marconi was <u>disliked</u> by the other guests. ________

Suspicious, the crooks kept looking over their shoulders as they ran, but Hudson was a professional – every Scotland Yard cadet learned the essentials of good trailing.
The men crept further into a run-down industrial section on the very edge of London. After 45 minutes, they reached their destination.
Hudson hid deeper in the dark and watched them from a safe distance, as they took one last look around before disappearing

into the warehouse. Hudson counted to ten, then quickly moved towards the door the men had used. He was alone and unarmed. If he wanted to subdue the thieves, he would have to use the element of surprise.
He took one more deep breath before carefully opening the warehouse door and slipping inside.

ÜBUNG 165 !

Übung 165: Setzen Sie die richtige Präposition ein!

The air was full of a mouldy smell. The inspector's eyes needed a few minutes to adjust 1. ___________ the darkness. Hudson crept 2. ______________ a few old crates and listened. He heard two voices arguing 3. ___________ a corner of the building.
"Do you think the guy was a cop?" asked one voice.
"Nope. He was way too scummy. Maybe he heard about our coup and wanted to get some of the money."
Hudson moved quietly towards the voices.
The men were standing in front of two paintings carelessly leaned 4. _______________ the wall. Although the inspector was no art expert, the pictures' details could not be mistaken: one of the paintings, undoubtedly the Picasso, showed a guitar that seemed to have been painted 5. _________ three different angles at the same time. The second painting was a wonderful combination of colours

in elegantly applied brushstrokes. The picture was of a small houseboat floating peacefully 6. _______________ a river. It must be the Monet.

The thief 7. ____________________ plaid pointed to the paintings. "What money?" he said scornfully. "All we've got so far is the pathetic advance 8. _______________ Jimmy Coltrane. Since then, we haven't heard a thing from him. And who would buy these? They're too well-known and too hot."

Hudson jumped out. The crooks jumped in horror.
"Crime doesn't pay," cried Hudson. "Inspector James Hudson from Scotland Yard. You're under arrest."
The man with the scar got over his surprise first.
"Oh yeah," he growled, "you and who else?"
Then he raised his fists and rushed at Hudson.
The inspector elegantly sidestepped him, and his attacker punched the air. Thrown off balance by his own offensive, he became an easy target. Hudson threw a punch and sent the man to the ground.

Übung 166: Wie lautet das Sprichwort auf Deutsch?

ÜBUNG 166 !

1. Crime doesn't pay.

____

2. The early bird catches the worm.

____

3. It went like clockwork.

____

The second crook was more careful. Obviously, he wasn't in the mood for a hand-to-hand fight with Hudson.
Instead, he pulled out a pistol from his belt. "I thought something was funny about you," he shouted. "But it was a mistake to follow us here alone. It'll be your last mistake."
Hudson raised his hands. He had planned on this.
"Don't do anything stupid, man," he said calmly. At the same time, he carefully took a few steps backwards. Behind him was a wall of empty cardboard boxes.
The man with the scar raised the gun and slowly pulled the trigger, in an effort not to lose control of the weapon as it fired.

! ÜBUNG 167

Übung 167: Wie heißt das Verb auf Englisch?

1. graben ______________________
2. leeren ______________________
3. verstecken ______________________
4. sich gewöhnen an ______________________
5. lehnen ______________________
6. brüllen ______________________

Though he was certain this was not the first time the crook had handled a weapon, the inspector knew what he was doing. He pretended to cower in fear until his heel touched the pile of boxes. Then he waited for the right moment.

“Say your prayers,” grinned the crook. Hudson shut his eyes.

“It’s too early for that,” was all he said and kicked one of the lowest boxes.

The boxes slid down in a cascade. The criminal instinctively raised his hand to protect his face.

Ignoring the harmless boxes, Hudson rushed forward and punched the man on the jaw.

Übung 168: Wählen Sie die richtige Antwort auf die Frage!

1. Where are you going?
   - a) ☐ I’m going to be a Scotland Yard inspector.
   - b) ☐ I’m going to the movies.
   - c) ☐ I’m going crazy.

2. What do you do for a living?
   - a) ☐ I’m an insurance agent.
   - b) ☐ I live at 221 Baker Street.
   - c) ☐ I do portraits in my spare time.

3. How do you know that?
   - a) ☐ I read it in the newspaper.
   - b) ☐ I like the Rolling Stones.
   - c) ☐ I was in Dublin last week.

4. What are you studying at Cambridge?
   a) ☐ I'm looking at this magazine.
   b) ☐ I'm studying economics.
   c) ☐ I'm studying the adverts for a job.

5. What are you doing at the weekend?
   a) ☐ I'm going to Spain for two weeks.
   b) ☐ I went to the British Museum.
   c) ☐ I'm going to clean my flat.

The man gave a moan of surprise as he fell among the boxes. Hudson rubbed his hand and looked around. In one corner of the warehouse he saw a table with tools and tape, which he used to bind the crooks' hands, before they regained consciousness.

Hudson surveyed his work with satisfaction, reached into his jacket pocket and pulled out his mobile phone. He dialled the number of the police.

Then he sat down on the boxes and admired the two precious paintings in front of him.

Maybe I should learn more about art, he thought, as sirens blared in the distance and announced the arrival of the first police car.

ÜBUNG 169 !

Übung 169: Welche Person wird mit welchem Bereich assoziiert?

1. William Shakespeare	☐	science
2. Pablo Picasso	☐	politics
3. Albert Einstein	☐	art
4. Ingmar Bergman	☐	music
5. Tony Blair	☐	literature
6. W. A. Mozart	☐	cinema

7. Paul Bocuse ☐ charity
8. Sister Theresa ☐ nobility
9. Count Dracula ☐ cooking

A few minutes later Hudson was talking to the beat officer and had given a short testimony for the record. The crooks were in custody and the paintings would be returned to the gallery tomorrow.
In spite of this, Hudson still looked gloomy.
"Is something wrong, sir?" asked one of the officers. "You have every right to be satisfied. You caught two wanted criminals and rescued two invaluable paintings. Not a bad night's work, if you ask me."

Übung 170: Setzen Sie das richtige Wort ein!
(harmless, testimony, announce, protect, punched, dialled)

ÜBUNG 170 !

1. He wants to ________ his family from harm.

2. I'm sorry. I must have ________ the wrong number.

3. Don't be afraid of the dog. He's ________.

4. He got so mad at Matches, that he ________ him.

5. Hudson's ________ will be invaluable in court.

6. Elvira will ________ her discovery at tomorrow's meeting.

Hudson shrugged his shoulders.
"Maybe. But the ringleader is still free. The case isn't closed, until I have caught Jimmy Coltrane."
"Do you mean Jimmy the Mole?"

Hudson nodded in amazement.
"Do you know something I don't know?" he asked.
The officer shut his notebook.
"I think so, sir. Up until recently, I worked in the prison where old Jimmy was, until three months ago …"
"I didn't know that Jimmy was behind bars again. How did he get out? Was he released or did he escape?"
The officer shook his head.
"Neither, sir. Jimmy Coltrane died peacefully in his cell, three months ago."

ÜBUNG 171

Übung 171: Welche Übersetzung stimmt? Kreuzen Sie an!

1. außer Sichtweite	a) ☐	out of sight	b) ☐	out of look
2. arbeitslos	a) ☐	out of labour	b) ☐	out of work
3. veraltet	a) ☐	out of date	b) ☐	out of up to date
4. außer Gefahr	a) ☐	out of pain	b) ☐	out of danger
5. nicht vorrätig	a) ☐	out of cellar	b) ☐	out of stock
6. atemlos	a) ☐	out of breath	b) ☐	out of air

Inspector Hudson sat at the kitchen table, freshly showered and shaven, and drank a cup of Earl Grey. He had slept poorly. He couldn't stop thinking about Jimmy Coltrane.
Coltrane had been dead for months – but the two tunnel thieves had worked with him – or thought they had.
The inspector had asked both criminals for a description of Coltrane. They corresponded exactly with the inspector's own memories of Jimmy the Mole.

Übung 172: Setzen Sie das richtige Verb in der korrekten Form ein!

The whole thing was completely strange. Who was (1. vorgeben) __________ to be Jimmy Coltrane, and why?

Miss Paddington (2. gießen) _________ herself another cup of tea and shook her head.

"Old Jimmy is dead? That's too bad. He was a total bum, but I liked him."

Hudson nodded.

"I know Miss Paddington. Jimmy was a crook, but an old school criminal. He never would (3. angreifen) ______________ anyone with a weapon – like the ones I (4. fangen) _______________ yesterday in the warehouse. The real Jimmy never would (5. sich verbünden) ____________________ with such creatures."

Hudson and Miss Paddington looked up as the doorbell rang.

It was Elvira Elliot. She (6. anrufen) ___________________ early because she wanted to stop by and show the inspector something.

"I'll get it," said the inspector and got up to open the door for the young lady.

"Good morning, James," Elvira beamed as Hudson opened the door. She had a large, flat package in her hand, which had been carefully wrapped in brown packing paper.

"James, listen … you'll never guess what I have here!"

"Mmmh … let me try anyway. The portrait of Lord Ploughbottom?" Elvira looked at the inspector for a moment with disappointment. Then she smilingly shook her head. "How did you know, James?"
"Come in first, Elvira. Yesterday I was also out and about in the cause of art and was able to take back the precious Monet and Picasso."

Übung 173: Haben die Wörter dieselbe Bedeutung? Markieren Sie: richtig ✓ oder falsch –?

1. conscious/aware
2. admire/hate
3. precious/priceless
4. satisfied/content
5. rescue/lose
6. amazement/astonishment
7. peaceful/turbulent
8. dead/deceased
9. guess/estimate
10. disappointment/joy

"Really?" gasped Elvira. "How did you manage that?"
The inspector led Elvira into the kitchen, where Miss Paddington was already waiting with a cup of tea. Hudson told her about his little adventure as Matches Marconi. In return, Elvira recounted how Bill B. Bixby voluntarily turned over the stolen Ploughbottom painting to her.
"Thankfully I didn't have to argue with the guy," concluded Elvira. "He was a totally crude man. *Autumn in London is horrible.*" Elvira did her best to imitate the broad Texas accent.

Miss Paddington laughed, but Hudson stared at Elvira with astonishment.

“What did you say?” he asked Elvira with a raised eyebrow.

“What? I was just trying to imitate Mr Bixby’s accent. You know, Texans always talk as if they had a fist full of chewing gum in their mouths. They probably do.”

“No, no,” answered the inspector seriously. “Did he really say London in *autumn*?”

Übung 174: Welche Übersetzung stimmt?

1. Ich mache die Tür auf.
   - a) ☐ I opened the door.
   - b) ☐ I have opened the door.
   - c) ☐ I’ll open the door.

2. Wie hast du das gemacht?
   - a) ☐ How did you do it?
   - b) ☐ How will you do it?
   - c) ☐ How can you do it?

3. Er spricht, als ob er Kaugummi im Mund hätte.
   - a) ☐ He talks when he has chewing gum in his mouth.
   - b) ☐ He talks as if he has chewing gum in his mouth.
   - c) ☐ He talks with chewing gum in his mouth.

4. He gave her the painting back.
   - a) ☐ Er kann ihr das Gemälde nicht zurückgeben.
   - b) ☐ Er wird ihr das Gemälde zurückgeben.
   - c) ☐ Er gab ihr das Gemälde zurück.

Elvira was perplexed.
“Yes, James. Why? What’s so unusual about that?”
“Nothing at first,” said Hudson thoughtfully, “but a real American, especially a Texan, would never use the word ‘autumn’”.
Elvira looked at Hudson with wide eyes.
“You’re right, James. Americans usually say ‘fall’. Just like they say elevator instead of lift.”

ÜBUNG 175 !

Übung 175: Bilden Sie sinnvolle Wörter aus dem Buchstabenchaos!

“You’re right. I’m afraid your genuine Texan was 1. herytiengv __________ (alles) but genuine. It was probably an Englishman who was pretending to be a Texan.”
“And made a tiny 2. kimesta ______________ (Fehler),” continued Elvira. “But why? Why did he pretend to be an 3. cmenrAia __________ (amerikanischer) businessman?”
Hudson 4. otko ____________ (nahm) another 5. psi ____________ (Schluck) of tea. Yes, why? That was the 6. amni ______________ (Haupt-) question. 7. yMbae ______________ (vielleicht) the man suspected that the painting was stolen and bought the painting from the thieves under an assumed identity.

Normally, James Hudson would have been satisfied with the fact that all three paintings were recovered – but there was this Jimmy Coltrane problem.

In this case, someone else had obviously pretended to be Coltrane – for whatever reason. It could hardly be a coincidence – quite the opposite. Hudson turned pale at his own conclusion.

Übung 176: Welches Wort ist das „schwarze Schaf"?

1. imitate, insult, copy, mimic ____________
2. seriously, earnestly, jokingly, gravely ____________
3. really, actually, honestly, laughingly ____________
4. understanding, perplexed, puzzled, confused ____________
5. usually, never, generally, commonly ____________
6. safety, shelter, protection, harm ____________
7. everyday, unusual, surprising, extraordinary ____________
8. gaze, ignore, stare, watch ____________

After a long pause he said: "I suspect that your Mr Bixby and my Jimmy Coltrane imitator are the same person."
"Really?" Elvira looked at Hudson doubtfully. "He must be a master of disguises."
Hudson nodded.
"I'm afraid you're right. Does the name 'The Phantom' mean anything to you?"
Elvira gasped.
"The Phantom? Seriously, James. You don't think this legend really exists?"
"The Phantom?" chimed in Miss Paddington.

Hudson wanted to start explaining but Elvira was first.

"For years, a rumour has been circulating about a faceless master criminal, who was responsible for a number of unsolved cases. No one has ever seen his face or knows who he is. He is a sort of modern Fu Man Chu."

Übung 177: Bilden Sie sinnvolle Sätze!

1. painting lied He the about

____

2. be did he businessman to pretend Why a?

____

3. master is disguise a of He

____

4. Mr Mr person and Coltrane are Bixby same the

____

5. not was satisfied still Hudson

____

6. of Have the heard Phantom you?

____

7. I face never his have seen

____

"That's spooky," rejoined Miss Paddington. She was an avid reader of detective novels and could hardly conceal her excitement.

"I personally think this Phantom is just a legend. A ghost story that the police use when they can't solve a case. Sorry, James."

"It's OK, Elvira. But the fact is that that is exactly what you are supposed to think. Scotland Yard has been hunting the Phantom for years, but he has escaped us so far. The officials prefer the public not to believe in this criminal's existence. It would just make them afraid, since any citizen could be the Phantom. Who can one trust anymore?"

"You mean the Phantom really exists, and I was sitting at the same table with him? That's unbelievable!" cried Elvira.

Übung 178: Wie heißt das Wort auf Deutsch?

1. rumour	☐ gierig
2. circulation	☐ Gegenteil
3. responsible	☐ blass
4. doubtful	☐ Gerücht
5. avid	☐ Grund
6. pale	☐ verantwortlich
7. safety	☐ zweifelnd
8. reason	☐ Umlauf
9. opposite	☐ Sicherheit

"But true," nodded Hudson sadly. Then he stared sternly at Elvira and Miss Paddington, "I insist that this information remain confidential."

Both women nodded.

"Of course," said Elvira. "But why did the Phantom pretend to be Coltrane and Bixby? And why did he only keep the worthless painting? And why was he so willing to give it back?"
"I've been asking myself the same question," answered Hudson. "I think the Phantom wanted to play it safe. He disguised himself as Coltrane to make sure that the hired thieves didn't make off with the loot. He probably acted like the Texan to fool the police. Think about it. Two of the three criminals have been caught, the paintings returned … Scotland Yard would have probably had an intern to finish clearing up the background information and everyone would have forgotten about the botched robbery in a few weeks."

ÜBUNG 179 !

Übung 179: Setzen Sie das richtige Wort ein!

Elvira nodded. "But why did he (1. behalten) ____________ the worthless painting at first – and then (2. zurückgeben) ________ it to me without hesitating?"

Hudson rubbed his (3. Kinn) _________ thoughtfully.

"I think that the Phantom only (4. stahl) _________ the Picasso and the Monet to divert (5. Aufmerksamkeit) ___________ from his real intention …"

Hudson pointed to the portrait, that was still in its (6. Packpapier) ________________.

"The (7. Tatsache) _____________ that he readily returned the painting indicates it was important for him at some point, but not any (8. mehr) __________."

Miss Paddington shook her head. "What do you mean?"

"I don't know," replied the inspector and reached for the package. "Let's take a closer look at the painting."

Hudson began to carefully (9. auspacken) _________ the painting. An old, middling portrait in oils appeared. Lord Ploughbottom (10. lächelte) __________ at the observer and held the two dice in his hand.

Hudson and Elvira recognized the painting from the gallery's catalogue.
The three examined the painting from top to bottom, but it contained no surprises, until Hudson turned the painting around …
"Aha," he cried triumphantly, "we've got it!"

Übung 180: Beantworten Sie die Fragen zum Text!

ÜBUNG 180 !

1. Why did Inspector Hudson sleep badly?

____

2. What was the real Jimmy Coltrane like?

____

3. How did Hudson realize that Bill Bixby was actually an Englishman?

____

4. Why did Scotland Yard tell the public that the Phantom doesn't exist?

____

5. What is depicted on the portrait?

____

Elvira Elliot and Miss Paddington stared at the back of the painting. The canvas had turned yellow with age, but on the lower right corner, there was a white rectangle.
"Very interesting," murmured Hudson. "Obviously someone recently hid something here. Based on the size and the shape, I would guess a piece of paper or an envelope."

ÜBUNG 181

Übung 181: Setzen Sie die richtige Präposition ein!

"So that was what the Phantom was really 1. __________," Elvira said. "He wasn't interested 2. __________ the painting at all."

Hudson nodded.

"It seems that way. But this realisation doesn't help us much, as long as we don't know what was in the letter. It could be anything, 3. __________ a treasure map to the combination for a safe. We can only assume that the information is highly valuable, otherwise the Phantom wouldn't have taken the trouble to obtain it."

"And we know," continued Elvira, "that the paper must have been in the frame 4. ____________ a while, since the canvas is white where the paper was."

"Exactly," nodded Hudson. "Elvira, can you find out 5. _______ where Mr Blighton obtained the portrait of Lord Ploughbottom? I would guess that it came from an old family collection, probably from the lord's descendants."

Elvira nodded 6. _________ excitement.

"No problem, James. A few telephone calls should do the trick. I will call from the office. Otherwise, people may get suspicious if they see a private number 7. ______________ their telephone display."

Elvira took another quick sip of her tea and got up.

"If you don't mind, James, I will take the picture with me and make sure that Mr Blighton gets it back as soon as possible."

Hudson nodded.

"Go ahead. I am going to the Yard to look over all available files on the Phantom. I'm afraid, however, that there won't be much information."

Hudson and Elvira said goodbye to Miss Paddington and promised to keep her posted on the progress of the investigation. Then they left the house, got into their cars, and drove away.

Neither of them noticed the outlandishly dressed young man passing by the inspector's house wearing a walkman.
And neither of them would have thought that a sophisticated microphone was hidden in the walkman.
The Phantom smiled. He had heard enough. Now it was time to act.

Übung 182: Übersetzen Sie die Redewendungen!

1. keep somebody posted

____

2. come like a bolt out of the blue

____

3. pull a dirty trick on someone

____

4. double-cross someone

____

5. be on the fiddle

____

Inspector Hudson sat at the desk of his tiny office and flipped through the disappointingly thin file that contained all the information about the mysterious Phantom.
It was true that the Phantom was suspected of being involved in a number of crimes.

And all of these crimes had one thing in common – the Phantom had committed the crime with the help of a perfect disguise and disappeared with his loot without a trace …
In Glasgow, a director of a bank walked into his safe room and had a pleasant conversation with the security guard. Then he strolled out with a million pounds. That same evening, the real director of the bank was found tied up in his apartment.

Übung 183: Bilden Sie synonyme Paare!

1. tiny	☐ aid
2. disappointingly	☐ nice
3. connection	☐ small
4. sense	☐ vanish
5. help	☐ tied
6. disappear	☐ association
7. bound	☐ meaning
8. pleasant	☐ flat
9. apartment	☐ frustratingly

The European continent was not safe from the Phantom's greedy clutches either. In Germany, the test driver of a top secret automobile prototype simply drove off the test course onto a nearby motorway. The real test driver was found well bound in a bathroom. The prototype's manufacturers assume that the Phantom sold the prototype and its improvements in Asia for millions, where a cheap copy was produced.
One would think that such a successful criminal would retire with his money. But, if the Phantom was willing to go to such lengths

to get his hands on a piece of paper, then it must be something big. The inspector's stomach churned nervously at the thought of it.

ÜBUNG 184 !

Übung 184: Lesen Sie weiter und unterstreichen Sie das richtige Wort!

Elvira Elliot (1.) sped/drove slowly through the rolling hills.
It only took two telephone calls to find the (2.) future/previous (3.) mother/owner of the Ploughbottom painting. Hudson was right. Until a few (4.) weeks/minutes ago, the painting had belonged to the family. However, after the last Lord Ploughbottom died, impoverished and without any heirs, the executor of the estate decided to sell all of the Ploughbottom's (5.) cars/property.
The (6.) estate/flat in the outskirts of London was up for sale as well as the entire inventory.
Mr Blighton had purchased the painting at the estate.
Elvira pulled into the (7.) lake/drive. She was (8.) astonished/bored.

The building, at least the outside, was flawless. This was not untypical for modern British nobility – keep the outside looking good, while inside the bankruptcy administrator was valuing the silver.
"I'm going to have a look at your old house, my lord," said Elvira to the painting of Lord Ploughbottom that was leaning against the back seat. She had taken it with her, so that she could bring it back to the gallery on her way home. But that could wait.
Elvira went to the door and searched in vain for a doorbell. Instead she found an old-fashioned door knocker made of copper, in the shape of two dice.

Übung 185: Übersetzen Sie ins Englische, um das Geheimwort zu enträtseln!

1. Kupfer _ _ _ _ □ _
2. makellos _ □ _ _ _ _ _ _
3. vergeblich □ _ _ _ _ _
4. Erbe _ _ □ _
5. bankrott _ _ _ _ □ _ _ _
6. Familiensitz _ _ _ □ _ _

Lösung: _ _ _ _ _ _

How fitting, thought Elvira as she knocked twice against the old wooden door.

Seconds later, a pale, old man with a large moustache opened the door.

He's trying to give his boring, bookkeeping face some distinction with that moustache, thought Elvira, but he failed.

The man's face was so plain and ordinary as to be forgot within five minutes.

"What can I do for you?" the man asked.

"Hello. My name is Elvira Elliot. I called earlier."

"Of course, Miss Elliot. You wanted to view the remaining valuables that are for sale, right?"

Elvira nodded. She hadn't told the man that she was an insurance agent and was working on a case with Scotland Yard. Why make things unnecessarily complicated?

The man motioned her to come in.

“My name is Walter Nigma. I’m the executor of the Ploughbottom estate. There isn’t much left, I’m afraid. Most of the valuable items have already been sold.”

Übung 186: Übersetzen Sie ins Englische!

1. Ich werde die alten Gemälde überprüfen.

---

2. Er spazierte aus der Bank.

---

3. Miss Paddington hatte einen angenehmen Tag.

---

4. Der echte Arzt wurde an einen Stuhl gefesselt aufgefunden.

---

5. Wann wird er sich zur Ruhe setzen?

---

6. Dies war typisch für Versicherungsagenten.

“Oh, um, that’s all right. I am only a historian looking for interesting sources,” Elvira lied.
“I see,” answered Nigma and glanced at Elvira with his expressionless face.

Übung 187: Welcher Satz ist die richtige Übersetzung?

1. Das Gemälde lehnte gegen die Wand.
   a) ☐ The painting is leaning against the wall.
   b) ☐ The painting leaned from the wall.
   c) ☐ The painting leaned against the wall.

2. Sie entdeckte eine alte Schatzkiste.
   a) ☐ She finded an old treasure chest.
   b) ☐ She found an old treasure chest.
   c) ☐ She finds an old treasure chest.

3. In 5 Minuten wird Hudson dieses Gesicht vergessen.
   a) ☐ Hudson will forget this face in 5 minutes.
   b) ☐ Since 5 minutes Hudson forgets his face.
   c) ☐ Hudson is forgetting this face in 5 minutes.

4. Ich habe Ihnen diese Woche schon geschrieben.
   a) ☐ I was writing you already during the week.
   b) ☐ I will write you already this week.
   c) ☐ I already wrote to you this week.

5. Alles wird morgen verkauft.
   a) ☐ Everything will be sold tomorrow.
   b) ☐ Tomorrow everything will be selled.
   c) ☐ Everything is selling tomorrow.

"Please come in," he said and ushered her into the house. He held the door open for Elvira.

In the large hall, several tables had been set up crammed with a couple of sculptures, yellowed books and porcelain dishes.

Übung 188: Setzen Sie ein sinnvolles Synonym ein!

"It does look rather (1. bare) ________," said Elvira, attempting to hide her disappointment. How among these pitiful remnants was she to find a (2. hint) ____________ about the painting?

Mr Nigma said nothing.

"How did the Ploughbottoms become so (3. without money) ____ __________?" asked Elvira, hoping that Nigma knew something about the family history that could give her a valuable clue.

The executor was not very talkative.

"Gambling," was all he said. "It ran in the family like an addiction. The Ploughbottoms were (4. always) ________________ trying to gamble away their (5. possessions) ______________."

Elvira sighed.

"It looks like they were successful."

"What do you mean?" asked Nigma.

Elvira shook her head. "Nothing. Do you mind if I look around?"

"Not at all."

One could hardly (6. notice) ____________ the shake of his head.

"Look around. I will be in the salon next door. I have to make some calculations about the sale value of the property."

"Have fun," said Elvira and smiled at the executor.
Elvira went to the tables and examined the family property. As an insurance agent, she knew a bit about antiques – these things only had sentimental value.
Elvira ran her finger over a small statue of Fortuna, the goddess of luck. Obviously, she had not aided the Ploughbottoms in their gambling addiction.
Next to the statue were a pile of old books. Elvira took the topmost and dusted off the cover: *Calculation of Probability for Gambling and Roulette, London 1867* was the title.
Obviously books promising a failsafe strategy for roulette went way back.
Elvira was just about to return the book to the pile, when she noticed the smaller one that had lain beneath it.

Übung 189: Setzen Sie die Sätze ins Passiv!

1. Hudson found the clue in the painting.

____

2. The Phantom steered the car.

____

3. The phoney bank director took the money.

____

4. Mr Nigma takes care of the Ploughbottom estate.

____

5. Elvira picked up the book.

It was bound in thick, dark leather printed with gold letters, whose glitter had faded.
Elvira gasped. “This looks very promising,” she whispered to herself.
On the book was printed *The Diary of Lord Ploughbottom*. Her fingers trembled with excitement as Elvira opened the book. If there wasn’t a clue to the painting here, then where else?

ÜBUNG 190

Übung 190: Wie heißt das Wort auf Deutsch?

1. executor ______
2. tremble ______
3. gambling ______
4. occasion ______
5. bad luck ______
6. addiction ______
7. cover ______
8. diary ______
9. handwriting ______
10. fade ______

The yellowing pages were filled with a small but elegant handwriting. Elvira sighed. It would take days to read the diary. If need be, she could surely buy the book for a few pounds from Mr Nigma, so that she could read it at home.

But it wouldn't hurt to take a little peek at it now.

Elvira skimmed over the pages. Lord Ploughbottom must have really been a passionate gambler. Most of his diary entries were devoted to various bets and games.

It's amazing that the Ploughbottoms didn't go bankrupt sooner, thought Elvira. The goddess of luck, still standing nearby, really didn't seem to have helped them much.

According to the diary entries, Lord Ploughbottom more often lost at gambling than he won.

"Well, maybe he was lucky in love," murmured Elvira, shaking her head. She decided to hurry things up by turning to the last page.

Übung 191: Welche Wörter stehen in Beziehung zueinander?

1. gambling	☐ source
2. sports car	☐ cover
3. family	☐ religion
4. painting	☐ entry
5. historian	☐ secretary
6. goddess	☐ money
7. diary	☐ heir
8. book	☐ Impressionism
9. furniture	☐ tyre

The entries ended abruptly on the 28th of March, 1697. The writing of the last entries was shaky, as if it cost the writer a great

effort to put the words on paper. Elvira deciphered the last sentence: *"I feel the consumption taking over my body, yet I will go peacefully from this world ..."*
The diary ended there.

ÜBUNG 192 !

Übung 192: Unterstreichen Sie die Antworten auf folgende Fragen im Text!

1. What did Lord Ploughbottom die of?
2. What indicated that the lord was excited in an earlier diary entry?
3. Why did Lord Ploughbottom think he would win that night?
4. What piece of paper would determine who owned the island?
5. What was the name of the island?

Poor man, thought Elvira. He, like many of his contemporaries, had fallen victim to tuberculosis. But that didn't solve the mystery. Elvira went back a few pages. The handwriting was different, not so shaky, as if the lord had written in great agitation.
Elvira bent over the yellow pages, glanced over the entries and gasped.
She felt her heart beating faster. It couldn't possibly be true.
Elvira reached into her purse and grabbed her mobile phone. She pounded in Hudson's office phone number.
"James," she cried, without waiting to say hello, "I think I know what was in the back of the painting. I have Lord Ploughbottom's diary here. Are you sitting down? I'll read it to you:

In spite of my increasing weakness, I will meet again with Lord Elword this evening to play at dice. For three weeks, Lord Elword

has beaten me. According to the rules of probability, luck must be on my side tonight. Since money is tight, I will bet part of the family estate – a remote piece of land of some value. I will issue a debt certificate to be given to the mayor of the island, upon which, the island will fall into possession of the certificate holder.
I hope my ancestors forgive me for betting old family property, but I am sure that I will be lucky tonight. Besides, the Isle of Man was always too draughty for me."

Übung 193: Ist das Wort richtig übersetzt?
Markieren Sie: richtig ✓ oder falsch –?

1. consumption/Krebs
2. mobile phone/Handy
3. shorten/verlängern
4. abruptly/plötzlich
5. shaky/fest
6. riddle/Rätsel
7. skim/überfliegen
8. greet/verabschieden
9. probability/Wahrscheinlichkeit
10. debt/Schuld
11. dope/Panik

Elvira still couldn't believe it, even though she had already read the entry three times. Hudson was also silent on the other end.
"Did you hear that, James? Lord Ploughbottom bet the Isle of Man in a game of dice. The document hidden in the back of the portrait is the debt certificate. Whoever has this, just has to present it to the

Isle's mayor and the entire island is his! It's crazy, isn't it, James?" The mobile phone was silent. Either the inspector was speechless, or the connection had been terminated. Elvira looked at her display.

No reception appeared. Hopefully James had heard the most important part. She would drive immediately to Scotland Yard. She and Hudson had to stop the Phantom from reaching the Isle of Man with the debt certificate.

Then she realised that she couldn't just take the diary with her. She quickly went to the salon and quietly opened the door.

! ÜBUNG 194

Übung 194: Setzen Sie das richtige Verb in der korrekten Form ein!
(present, take over, support, grab, bet, devote, beat, forgive, lose)

1. He always __________ at dice.
2. Miss Paddington __________ Hudson yesterday at cards.
3. Can you __________ me for losing the estate?
4. He will __________ all his time to solving the case.
5. The Phantom wants to __________ the Isle of Man.
6. Last night, he __________ two horses in the dice game.
7. Elvira __________ Scotland Yard with art thefts.
8. The ghost __________ Hudson from behind.
9. If he __________ the certificate to the mayor, the property is his.

"Mr Nigma?" she called softly.

No one answered. The salon was empty. Elvira shrugged her shoulders and shut the door.

What can I do? she thought. She could always call the executor from the car and tell him that she had taken the diary.
Elvira raced through the main entrance, threw open the house door and dashed to her car.
The portrait of Lord Ploughbottom was still in the passenger's seat.

Übung 195: Wählen Sie die richtige Präposition!

ÜBUNG 195 !

1. _____ three weeks now, Lord Elword has beaten me.

a) ☐ In b) ☐ For c) ☐ Of

2. Lord Ploughbottom is _____ debt.

a) ☐ in b) ☐ on c) ☐ through

3. Hudson will bet _____ the black horse.

a) ☐ to b) ☐ in c) ☐ on

4. Present the certificate _____ the mayor and its yours.

a) ☐ to b) ☐ at c) ☐ against

5. Elvira looked _____ her rear view mirror.

a) ☐ through b) ☐ upon c) ☐ in

6. "That was silly _____ you," she murmured.

a) ☐ from b) ☐ of c) ☐ with

"That was really reckless of you, my dear lord, betting an entire island," she said as she moved to start the car. Suddenly, she noticed something moving in the rear view mirror. She whirled around in shock. In the back seat sat Mr Nigma with a smile on his face.

Übung 196: Bilden Sie Wörter aus dem Buchstabenchaos!

His smile was treacherous, not at all fitting with the 1. vonseeac-tivr __________ (konservativ) bookeeper image.

"I'm sorry, if I've frightened you my 2. seadrte __________ (Beste)," said Nigma with a deep, sonorous voice. "But I'm afraid I just can't part with that diary so easily."

With lightning 3. espde __________ (Geschwindigkeit), the man pulled the 4. soutmchea __________ (Schnurrbart) off his face. A few pieces of 5. ugle __________ (Klebstoff) stuck on the fake moustache.

"I'm sorry, but I had to get rid of that troublesome thing. It 6. htci-se __________ (juckt). I hate to use disguises with facial hair."

"D-disguises," stuttered Elvira as she stared into the stranger's eyes. They were no longer pale blue, but deep brown.

He had obviously worn contact lenses before. "You mean, you're not Mr Nigma. You're …"

The man smiled.

"Absolutely right. The Phantom. We had the pleasure of meeting already, when I was Mr Bixby. What won't one do in order to possess one little island. I assure you that what I must now do also brings me no pleasure."

Elvira's eyes widened.

"What are you going to do?" she cried and tried to open her door.

But the Phantom was faster and pressed a foul smelling handkerchief against her nose and mouth.

Chloroform rushed into her head.

She tried to tear his hand away from her face, but it was too late.

Darkness closed in around her.

Inspector Hudson pressed the receiver against his ear.

"Elvira," he called, "are you still there?"

But the line was quiet. The connection had been bad the whole time.

But Elvira's discovery was unbelievable. The Isle of Man!

No wonder the Phantom was so obsessed with getting a hold of the debt certificate.

The inspector thought it over.

Übung 197: Bilden Sie sinnvolle Sätze!

1. really Phantom Mr Nigma the be out turned to

____

2. was be found to salon the one in No

____

3. unbelievable The discovery be appeared to

____

4. barely could her understand Hudson

5. dead mobile The went phone all sudden a of

6. unconscious made drugs Elvira The

The Isle of Man lies in the Irish Sea, half way between England and Ireland. Unlike England, this tiny island was never conquered by the Romans or the Normans and first became part of the British Empire in the 14th century.
The inspector opened his Internet connection and called up the CIA World-Factbook site, a public source from his colleagues in the American secret service.
Seconds later, a drawing of the island appeared on his screen. The island was 33 miles long, 13 miles wide and had a population of 74,000. He remembered it as being a very beautiful island.

ÜBUNG 198 !

Übung 198: Setzen Sie die Steigerungsform des Adjektivs ein!

1. He can draw ________________ (expressive) than she can.
2. Elvira is ________________ (young) than Miss Paddington.
3. The man with the scar was ____________ (evil) than the other.
4. Sir Reginald feels ____________ (bad) than Hudson.
5. That was the ____________ (good) cup of tea I've ever had.
6. Lord Elword is ____________ (rich) than Lord Ploughbottom.

7. It was the ___________ (bad) day of Hudson's life.

8. Miss Paddington is ___________ (funny) than Hudson.

9. Elvira is ___________ (tired) than Mr Blighton.

10. Madrid is ___________ (sunny) than London.

Now Hudson really had to sit down. If the debt certificate was valid, then the island was certainly worth millions of millions of pounds, if a value could be placed on it at all. The Phantom could not be allowed to reach the island.

The inspector tried to reach Elvira again. Then he dialled an internal number.

"Is this the dispatch office? I need a car to take me to Liverpool. And book me on a ferry to the Isle of Man."

Elvira awoke with a furry tongue. She needed a few moments to realise that her arms were tied behind her back. Her feet were also tied together with a thick rope.

The young lady let loose a very unladylike curse and looked around. She was lying on a straw covered floor in a large wooden building. Probably a stable somewhere behind the estate.

Übung 199: Welches Wort ist das „schwarze Schaf"?

1. eyes, nose, jacket, foot ___________

2. car, ferry, rowing boat, yacht ___________

3. wood, iron, rubber, steel ___________

4. television, telephone, letter, e-mail ____________

5. paper, pen, kettle, pencil ____________

Elvira briefly considered calling for help, but decided not to. Apart from herself and the phoney executor, there seemed to be no-one on the estate. Besides, a cry for help would alert the Phantom – if he was still there.
Most likely, the master of disguise was already on his way to make good on the debt certificate and to take possession of the island.

ÜBUNG 200 !

Übung 200: Setzen Sie das richtige englische Verb ein!

Elvira needed something to (1. schneiden) ________________ her bonds. She looked around.

The stable was cleared out. Everything pointed or sharp had already been (2. entfernen) ___________.

With some effort, she could (3. spüren) ___________ the pockets of her suit. She groaned. As far as she knew, all she had in them was a bag of peppermint candies and a lighter.

She (4. fallen) ___________ back in the straw with a disappointed sigh. Then (5. kommen) _____________ a burning idea, literally: She could (6. brennen) ___________ through the bonds!

Elvira struggled to sit up and (7. verdrehen) ____________ her arms to reach the lighter. She had the feeling that an enormous amount of time had (8. vorbeigehen) ____________ before she was finally able to get the lighter out.

But at last she had it in her hand. She crawled away from the pile of straw, as she didn't want to set the whole stable on fire.

When she was far enough away, she positioned the lighter in the right spot behind her back. She searched for the flint and lit. She felt the heat from the small flame.

Now she had to be careful that the flame hit the rope and not her own hand. A few seconds later, a small cloud of smoke rose from behind her. Elvira put out the flame and waited a few seconds. She wanted to carefully melt the rope, as long as her hand was still in it. She repeated the process.

A few minutes later it happened. With a snap the last threads of the rope broke.

Elvira's hands were free. She quietly rejoiced and rubbed her aching wrists. After a few minutes, she had also undone the ropes around her ankles.

Elvira got up and carefully opened the stable door. It was slowly getting dark outside. Cautiously, she crept towards her sports car, still standing in front of the house.

The painting of the lord and his diary were still on the back seat. Elvira jumped in the car and sped away.

If she was right about Hudson, he would already be on his way to the Isle of Man to stop the Phantom.

And she would help him. That was for sure.

Übung 201: Wie lautet das Wort auf Englisch?

1. pelzig ______________
2. Geschmack ______________
3. Handgelenk ______________
4. Pferdestall ______________
5. Gegenstand ______________
6. Bonbon ______________
7. Seil ______________
8. Faust ______________
9. Feuerzeug ______________
10. Prozedur ______________

The inspector stood on the deck of the ferry gazing at the silhouette of Liverpool. A few hours ago, he left London in a flurry to get a seat on the 'Pride of the Sea', that was to take him to the Isle of Man. In the meantime, he had repeatedly tried to contact Elvira on her mobile phone, but to no avail.

Übung 202: Was wird beschrieben?

1. The room where you can dance.

____

2. A piece of furniture that you sit on in the bar.

____

3. The room where meetings take place.

4. A large piece of furniture that several people can sit on.

5. The room where people sit together to talk or watch television.

6. A house where pictures are sold.

7. A place where you train your muscles.

8. An appliance used for cooking and baking.

9. An appliance with a tap used to wash your hands or dishes.

10. A piece of furniture with a door where you can keep your clothes.

The wail of the ship's sirens signalled that the ship was ready to depart. The inspector patted the inside pocket of his jacket.
Sir Reginald has insisted on Hudson carrying a firearm. After all, one had to assume that the Phantom was also on his way to the island's capital, Douglas.

According to what Elvira had read out of the diary, the Phantom had to present the debt certificate to the mayor of the capital in person.
Hudson had taken precautions that would throw cold water on the master criminal's plans.

ÜBUNG 203

Übung 203: Gibt der Satz den richtigen Sachverhalt wieder? Markieren Sie: richtig ✓ oder falsch –?

1. The meeting at the estate was the first time Elvira and the Phantom had seen each other.
2. The Phantom's real eye colour is brown.
3. The Phantom used carbon monoxide to make Elvira unconscious.
4. The capital of the Isle of Man is Dublin.
5. The inspector used the Internet to research.
6. The island is worth a great deal of money.
7. Hudson plans to take the ferry from Brighton.
8. Elvira burned through the ropes to free herself.
9. The Phantom had taken her car, the diary and the painting when he left the estate.

The inspector smiled grimly as he watched several sailors loosen the ropes. Too bad Elvira couldn't be here, he thought.
At that moment, a familiar figure dashed onto the dock.
Inspector Hudson couldn't believe his eyes. It was Elvira Elliot running onto the ferry, with billowing hair and wild gestures.
Hudson moved quickly towards her. She was holding onto the railing and panting.
"My goodness, Elvira, did you run all the way here from London?"

"It feels like it, James. You have no idea what has happened to me since I last called. The Phantom kidnapped me, but I was able to get away."

Übung 204: Finden Sie das Lösungswort!

1. Hauptstadt _ _ ☐ _ _ _ _

2. sich beeilen ☐ _ _ _ _

3. Matrose _ ☐ _ _ _ _

4. entführen _ _ _ ☐ _ _

5. hecheln _ _ _ ☐

6. Anlegesteg _ ☐ _ _

7. Schusswaffe _ _ _ _ _ _ ☐

Lösung: _ _ _ _ _ _ _

Hudson looked at Elvira with concern.
"Oh my, Elvira. Are you all right? Did you get hurt?"
Elvira shook her head.
"Don't worry, James. It takes more than a faceless phantom to get rid of Elvira Elliot. But I'll tell you everything later. I want to go to my cabin and take a shower. Luckily I was able to use my mobile to book a cabin on the way here."
Hudson nodded.
"Of course, Elvira. Freshen up and get some rest. You can tell me

the whole story over dinner. We won't reach the Isle of Man until tomorrow morning anyway."

"Dinner sounds great, James."

With these words, Elvira disappeared into the ferry's interior. The inspector watched her go with admiration. What a woman!

Übung 205: Unterstreichen Sie das richtige Wort!

Two hours later, Elvira and Hudson were already sitting over their dessert. Elvira had bought a new (1.) sloppy/elegant dress on board. An observer looking at her and the inspector could (2.) think/know that they were two tourists on a (3.) business/holiday cruise.

But the topic of (4.) dialogue/conversation was anything but trivial. Elvira recounted her run-in with the Phantom alias Mr Nigma.

"My (5.) compliments/scorn, Elvira," said Hudson, taking a sip of espresso. "You really tricked the Phantom. But we have to be on our guard. The Phantom will also be on his (6.) way/road to Douglas to give the mayor the debt certificate. He could be anywhere, disguised as anyone."

Both of them started as a man (7.) left/approached their table. It was just the steward bringing them their bill with a (8.) rude/polite nod. Could he be the Phantom?

Everything was possible, but here in the (9.) full/empty dining room they felt safe.

Hudson reached for his (10.) handbag/wallet and handed the waiter a few banknotes.

"You don't mind if I pay, Elvira?" he asked.

"That's kind of you. I hope you can put it on your expense account."

"I'm afraid my expense account at Scotland Yard wouldn't even cover an espresso, not to mention this delicious meal. My compliments to the cook," said Hudson and gave a friendly glance to the waiter.

Elvira and Hudson stood up.

"Will you join me for a stroll on the deck, Elvira?" Hudson asked expectantly.

"A bit of exercise after dinner would do me good."

Elvira smiled and took his arm. "With pleasure, James."

Übung 206: Welche Worte haben dieselbe Bedeutung?

1.	tasty	☐ indicate
2.	trick	☐ eternal
3.	concerned	☐ relax
4.	tell	☐ delicious
5.	rest	☐ delay
6.	admiration	☐ outline
7.	signal	☐ cheat
8.	gun	☐ distant
9.	precaution	☐ worried
10.	believe	☐ respect
11.	silhouette	☐ recount
12.	leave	☐ preventative measures
13.	endless	☐ firearm
14.	far	☐ depart
15.	wait	☐ trust

"Do you think we will get there before the Phantom does, James?" asked Elvira worriedly. Hudson sighed.

"I hope so, Elvira. In any case, I have taken precautions to ensure the Phantom can't redeem the debt certificate. I shudder to think about what would happen if the entire Isle of Man were in the possession of a criminal."

Elvira looked at the inspector questioningly.

"What is the bastard thinking? I mean, as soon as he exposes himself by trying to redeem the certificate, you or the local authorities can arrest him!"

The inspector sighed.

"On what grounds? Scotland Yard and Interpol suspect that the Phantom is behind dozens of crimes, but we can't prove anything. We have no concrete evidence that the Phantom stole the portrait of Lord Ploughbottom. Or that he attacked you on the Ploughbottom estate. Anyone could have disguised themselves as the executor. That's what the Phantom would argue. All he needs to do is stroll into the town hall in any disguise he chooses and present the certificate. It's not a crime to run around in a disguise."

ÜBUNG 207 !

Übung 207: Übersetzen Sie den Satz ins Englische!

1. Elvira wollte ihm das Tagebuch persönlich vorlesen.

2. Die Matrosen stehen auf dem Anlegesteg.

3. Wirst du den ganzen Weg nach Hause zu Fuß gehen?

4. Hudson benutzte sein Handy, um eine Fahrkarte zu buchen.

5. Der Gefangene wird in den Gerichtssaal geleitet.

6. Der Kellner wird die Nachspeise auftragen.

Elvira looked gravely at James.

"I never thought of it that way. But you're right. Even if we could prove the Phantom stole the portrait, he would spend maybe a year in jail, and then come out as one of the world's richest men. Theoretically, he could declare the island as his private property and create his own country."

"I'd rather not think about it. Let's enjoy this lovely evening at sea."

Übung 208: Welche Antwort passt zur Frage?

1. What are you reading?
   - a) ☐ A song by the Beatles.
   - b) ☐ A ballet with Baryshnikov.
   - c) ☐ A poem by John Donne.

2. What would you like to have for lunch?
   - a) ☐ I will have a traditional English breakfast.
   - b) ☐ Ice cream.
   - c) ☐ I would like a tuna salad sandwich.

3. Why are you on the ferry to the Isle of Man?
   a) ☐ I want to see Buckingham Palace.
   b) ☐ I have business there.
   c) ☐ I want to go to Cornwall.

4. Where are you going on holiday?
   a) ☐ We are going to Thailand.
   b) ☐ We are going to the bank.
   c) ☐ We are going to work in Bangkok.

5. What is your favourite film?
   a) ☐ *The Magic Flute.*
   b) ☐ *Four Weddings and a Funeral.*
   c) ☐ The *Mona Lisa.*

Hudson and Elvira took in the fresh night air.
The stars shone over the Irish Sea, and the British flag waved in the breeze on the ship's bow.
"What a beautiful night," said Hudson softly. "A night like this could make you forget crime altogether."
Before Elvira could answer, a shadow appeared out of the darkness.

! ÜBUNG 209

Übung 209: Setzen Sie das richtige Pronomen ein!

"But crime doesn't forget 1. ____________!" the shadow shouted.

Hudson and Elvira took a step backwards, shocked.

In front of 2. ____________ was a broad-shouldered sailor with a small club in 3. __________ paws.

The inspector instinctively reached for the pistol in his pocket, but the stranger was quicker. Before 4. __________ could pull his gun, the club came crashing down.

The inspector managed to avoid the treacherous blow with a clever step aside.

The sailor only grunted and got ready to strike again.

Elvira looked around 5. _____________.

At this late hour, 6. __________________ were alone on deck.

Elvira knew, that if 7. _____________ tried to call for help, the drone of the ship's engines would drown 8. ____________ voice.

The sailor aimed his club at the inspector again. Hudson groaned in pain as the club hit his arm, but it was still better then getting a blow on the head.

Hudson shrank backwards, letting down his guard for a fraction of a second.

The attacker didn't need any more. He rushed forward and grabbed the inspector's throat.

The man was amazingly strong, but he hadn't counted on Elvira Elliot.

She took her handbag and sent it crashing down on the sailor's head several times.

More surprised than hurt, the sailor whipped his head around and stared at Elvira in astonishment.

ÜBUNG 210!

Übung 210: Bilden Sie sinnvolle Wörter aus dem Buchstabenchaos!

1. SPWA (Pranken) ____________________
2. CRAGE (Anmut) ____________________
3. ACBKRWASD (rückwärts) ____________________
4. CELEADR (erklären) ____________________
5. PTMTDEE (versucht) ____________________
6. SGGLETRU (Kampf) ____________________
7. BLUC (Knüppel) ____________________
8. ASRNRGTE (Fremde) ____________________
9. DREEME (einlösen) ____________________
10. TRARES (verhaften) ____________________

Hudson took advantage of this distraction to give the sailor a punch in the stomach, but the guy was really muscular.

At least the punch made the sailor let go of Hudson's throat.

"What the …," moaned the sailor, as he tried to stand upright.

A fraction of a second later, Elvira's handbag slammed against the sailor's nose.

The sailor groaned again, looked at Hudson and Elvira undecidedly, and then stormed away.

Elvira wanted to run after him, but Hudson held her back.

"Wait. By the time we catch up with him inside the ship, he will have already slipped into a new disguise."

Übung 211: Setzen Sie jeweils das erste Wort in den Genitiv!

ÜBUNG 211 !

1. Elvira/handbag ______________________
2. men/suits ______________________
3. inspectors/offices ______________________
4. James/health ______________________
5. children/stories ______________________
6. thieves/crimes ______________________
7. cell/bars ______________________

Elvira sighed.

The inspector brought Elvira to her cabin and waited until he heard her lock the door from the inside. Then he went to his own cabin and got ready for bed.

But even with the peaceful rocking of the waves, it took a long time before Hudson fell asleep.

There was something fishy about the attack by the sailor.

Übung 212: Beantworten Sie die Fragen zum Text!

ÜBUNG 212 !

1. What was the name of the ferry Hudson took from Liverpool?

____

2. Was he able to reach Elvira on her mobile again?

____

3. What did the inspector wish for that immediately came true?

4. What did Elvira want to do as soon as she was on the ship?

Inspector Hudson awoke before his little travel alarm clock rang. The weather had obviously got worse, and the ferry rocked between the waves.
Luckily, Hudson was not prone to seasickness.
Before he left his cabin to get Elvira for breakfast, he took another look at the display on his mobile. He had been trying to reach Sir Reginald to report in since their departure, but clearly there was no reception here on the high sea.
Hudson sighed, but wasn't too upset. As far as he knew, the Isle of Man had been selected as a test region for the new UMTS mobile network a few months ago. There shouldn't be a problem connecting with the mainland.
Still on his guard, Hudson left his cabin and reached Elvira's in a few steps.
Hudson smiled to himself as he knocked on Elvira's door.

ÜBUNG 213 !

Übung 213: Wie heißt die Redewendung auf Deutsch?

1. It can wait.	☐ Liebhaberwert
2. once in a while	☐ im wahrsten Sinne des Wortes
3. go to great lengths	☐ die Suppe versalzen
4. sentimental value	☐ ab und zu
5. go way back	☐ gewaltige Anstrengungen unternehmen

6. literally	☐	in der Familie liegen
7. throw cold water on	☐	Es hat Zeit.
8. run in the family	☐	eine lange Geschichte haben
9. knock on wood	☐	wie ein Vogel im Käfig
10. like a bird in the cage	☐	auf Holz klopfen

Elvira opened the door with a smile. She, too, seemed to be unaffected by the rough sea.

"Good morning, Elvira. Did you sleep well? All ready for the big day?"

"And how!" answered Elvira. "The hunt for the Phantom can start right now. The ugly ghost should be prepared for a little trouble."

Hudson held the door open for Elvira.

She locked her cabin door behind her and followed the inspector into the dining room. The stormy sea had kept most of the other passengers from breakfast. Hudson and Elvira chose one of the many free spots near the window.

While they drank their tea, they watched the waves spew their foam against the windows.

Übung 214: Ersetzen Sie die unterstrichenen Begriffe durch ein passenderes Wort!

! ÜBUNG 214

Elvira glanced at the inspector over the edge of her teacup.

"Do you think we will catch the Phantom before it is too early

1. ________________?"

"I want 2. ________________ so, Elvira. In any way 3. __________,

I've taken precautions, so that the Phantom, in whatever disguise he may appear, doesn't make it to the lawyer 4. ________________. I've alerted the local police, to guard the mayor, Mr Manxon, around the clock. And the bonus 5. _____________ certificate is only valid if presented in person."

Elvira smiled dissatisfied 6. ________________.

"That should be too much 7. _____________ to stop the Phantom. And we still have enough time to look for and apprehend the villain."

"I hope so, my dear. But I have a good 8. ________________ feeling, that the Phantom still has a trump to play."

An hour later, the 'Pride of the Sea' laid anchor at the Isle of Man. Dark clouds were appearing on the horizon. Hudson didn't believe in omens, but the weather seemed to sense that something evil was afoot.
Hudson and Elvira were greeted by a young police officer.
"You must be Inspector Hudson and Miss Elliot," said the young man. "It's my job to bring you to city hall immediately."
Inspector Hudson shook the policeman's hand and looked at him sceptically.
"Very kind of you, but can I see your badge? Not to be rude …"

Übung 215: Wie heißt der englische idiomatische Ausdruck?

1. improvisieren	☐	cost an arm and a leg
2. todsicher	☐	put oneself out
3. Glück haben	☐	sold up the river
4. zufällig	☐	play it by ear
5. chaotisch	☐	get lucky
6. extrem teuer sein	☐	at sixes and sevens
7. Umstände machen	☐	by chance
8. betrogen	☐	not my cup of tea
9. nicht mein Fall	☐	failsafe

"No problem, sir. My department already warned me that you would be suspicious, but I have no idea what this is all about."
Hudson nodded. It was probable that the police in the lower ranks only received the information that was absolutely necessary, in order to avoid panic. After all, the island was about to be taken possession of by an unscrupulous criminal.
The inspector nodded at the police officer and gave him back his badge.

Übung 216: Welche Wörter haben die gegenteilige Bedeutung?

1. villain	☐	firm
2. unscrupulous	☐	slow
3. asleep	☐	uneven
4. rapid	☐	hero
5. muscular	☐	carefree
6. undecided	☐	awake

7. restrain	☐	stormy
8. smooth	☐	flabby
9. tranquil	☐	moral
10. worried	☐	release

"Everything is OK, officer. Please bring us to city hall as quickly as possible."

"Everything is working out splendidly," Elvira remarked and looked out of the window. The first rain drops dashed against the glass.

"Wait and see," murmured the inspector, "… wait and see."

Übung 217: Setzen Sie die Sätze ins Aktiv!

1. Elvira was viciously attacked by Mr Nigma.

____

2. The debt certificate was possessed by the Phantom.

____

3. The gun was carried by Hudson.

____

4. Elvira was drugged by an unknown man.

____

5. Elvira's car is driven by Miss Paddington.

____

6. The beer will be drunk by Matches Marconi in the dive.

---

7. By whom will the letter be written?

A few minutes later, the police car stopped in front of the Douglas city hall. Hudson and Elvira got out. In spite of the increasing rain, they took a few moments to admire the Victorian building.
"Quite a beautiful building," observed the inspector. "What a pity that it should fall into the Phantom's hands."

Übung 218: Welche ist die richtige Übersetzung?

ÜBUNG 218 !

1. Hudson blickt über die Reling.
   a) ☐ Hudson leaned over the railing.
   b) ☐ Hudson looked over the railing.
   c) ☐ Hudson looked at the railing.

2. Es wird ein stürmischer Tag auf dem Meer sein.
   a) ☐ It will be a stormy day at sea.
   b) ☐ It was a stormy day in the sea.
   c) ☐ It will be a stormy day on top of the sea.

3. Die meisten Passagiere vermeiden das Frühstück.
   a) ☐ Most passengers allowed breakfast.
   b) ☐ Most passengers avoided breakfast.
   c) ☐ Most passengers avoid breakfast.

4. Sicherheitsvorkehrungen werden getroffen.
   a) ☐ Secure measures are taken.
   b) ☐ Security precautions will be taken.
   c) ☐ Security turns will be taken.

5. Er soll den Bürgermeister nie erreichen.
   a) ☐ He will never reach the mayor.
   b) ☐ He should never reach the mayor.
   c) ☐ He could never reach the mayor.

"But we're here to stop that, aren't we, James?" replied Elvira. Hudson nodded. They followed the young policeman, who led them through the imposing building to the mayor's office.
Two security guards were posted in front of the door. They nodded at Inspector Hudson and Elvira and opened the large wooden door. A large, jovial looking man stood up from his desk and approached them.

Übung 219: Bilden Sie Wörter aus dem Buchstabenchaos!

He was clearly of Irish ancestry. On his head, raged red-blond

1. surcl ________________ (Locken) that could not be tamed by a

2. obcm ________________ (Kamm).

"Miss Elliot and Mr Hudson from Scotland Yard," he cried with

visible 3. fereli ________________ (Erleichterung), "I'm 4. yphap

________________ (glücklich) that you're here to catch this

Phantom. Your boss told me the 5. ienret ____________

(ganze) story. I've been afraid to leave my office ever since."

The insurance agent reached into her handbag and pulled something out.
"Don't worry. The game is up. You can go where you like. The fact is, that I will even have to ask that you leave *my* office immediately!"
The inspector's eyes widened. Before he could say or do anything, Elvira had pressed a yellowed piece of paper into the hands of the speechless mayor.
Lord Ploughbottom's debt certificate!
"Elvira, what …?" stammered Hudson. But Elvira simply smiled coldly at him.

Übung 220: Unterstreichen Sie das richtige Verb! Achten Sie dabei auf die Situationshinweise!

1. Can/May you speak English? (Fähigkeit)
2. May/Shall I accompany you on the case? (Bitte um Erlaubnis)
3. Shall/Can we go to the cinema? (Vorschlag)
4. You should/may call your mother more often. (Verpflichtung)
5. He may/can come tonight. (Wahrscheinlichkeit)
6. He shall/should leave for Douglas tomorrow. (Zukunft)
7. They should/can arrive around 7 o'clock. (Schätzung)
8. They may/can not smoke here. (Verbot)
9. Can/May you pass the butter? (Bitte)
10. Should/Shall we go? (Frage nach einer Meinung)

"Thank you, inspector, for leading me directly to Mr Manxon. Without your help, I would have had a much harder time reaching him," said Elvira, with a voice that didn't sound like her.

Hudson involuntarily took a step back.

"You're … the Phantom!"

"Of course," answered Elvira. "Who else?"

The inspector became dizzy.

It all seemed to add up! He should have realised it earlier. The phoney 'Elvira' had said that she had booked a cabin using her mobile phone, yet the inspector had tried to call her at least half-a-dozen times on her mobile. Also, the sailor last night had reacted to Elvira's attack with shock, probably because the Phantom himself had ordered the attack on Hudson.

ÜBUNG 221

Übung 221: Ist das Idiom richtig übersetzt worden? Markieren Sie: richtig ✓ oder falsch –?

1. believe one's eyes/seinen Augen nicht trauen
2. to be on one's guard/locker sein
3. fishy/verdächtig
4. still have a trump to play/nichts mehr machen können
5. have a hard time/es schwer haben
6. to beat around the bush/Tacheles reden
7. to be on the go/auf Achse
8. to jump the gun/bedacht handeln
9. Hold your horses!/Bleib cool!
10. out-fox/täuschen

Hudson was *supposed* to believe that the Phantom was disguised as the sailor – in order to divert suspicion from the phoney Elvira!

The Phantom pulled a lifelike latex mask from his face and threw it on the floor.
The man behind the mask was about 35 years old, with short, dark hair. He was good looking, except for the long scar that ran across his face.
"Y-you'll never get away with that," stuttered Hudson as he instinctively reached for his weapon.
The Phantom only stared at him with pity.
"Forget your weapon. You are on my land, and you have no proof against me. And now, get out of my office before I have you thrown out!"
The inspector shrank back.

Übung 222: Beantworten Sie die Fragen zum Text!

ÜBUNG 222 !

1. What did Hudson notice about his mobile phone while at sea?

____

2. Why did many of the passengers not come to breakfast?

____

3. Why was the inspector not sure that his security precautions were enough?

____

4. What were these precautions?

____

5. Who did the Phantom disguise himself as?

____

Elvira Elliot – the real Elvira Elliot – sat in her sports car and dialled the inspector's number for the hundredth time.

Ever since she just missed the ferry, she had been trying desperately to contact Hudson.

Elvira stared at the painting of the smiling Lord Ploughbottom on her back seat.

Finally, a dial tone.

A few hundred miles away, Hudson's phone started ringing in his jacket pocket.

The Phantom raised an eyebrow.

"Don't hesitate to answer it, inspector," he said. "I don't want to be rude. Finish your call and leave my office, and my island!"

Then he smiled. "I hope it isn't your boss asking for an update."

Übung 223: Übersetzen Sie die Sätze ins Englische!

1. Das Gespräch war alles andere als lustig.

2. Im Moment nähert er sich langsam dem Tisch.

3. Wo kann ich diesen Coupon einlösen?

4. Jemand trat aus dem Schatten hervor.

5. Hudson wird die Ablenkung zum eigenen Vorteil nutzen.

6. Wir werden ihn nie einholen!

7. Er ist französischer Abstammung.

Hudson pressed the phone to his ear. It wasn't Sir Reginald. It was Elvira, the real Elvira.
"James! At last! You'll never believe what happened to me!"
"Elvira …"
"Listen to me, James. I solved the case. Do you remember the portrait of Lord Ploughbottom? It shows him smiling with a pair of dice in his hand. Both dice are showing a six! He hit the jackpot, so to say!"
"Elvira, what?"

Übung 224: Bilden Sie sinnvolle Sätze!

1. rocked waves the ferry The

2. clouds the gathered sky in Storm

3. Elvira The Elliot the presented letter phoney

4. with Are familiar the you Picasso of works?

5. full Sir a Reginald wants report

____

6. scar The was good-looking had Phantom but a

____

"No wait! That gave me an idea. I read Lord Ploughbottom's diary again. James, the Ploughbottoms were losers addicted to gambling. That's why we never thought that they could ever be lucky! Of course, Lord Ploughbottom bet the Isle of Man. But this time, James, this time he won!"

The inspector couldn't believe his ears.

"Won," he repeated. "You mean …"

"Lord Ploughbottom diced with his friend Lord Elword for the island – and won the game. On this evening, by the way of exception, it wasn't Ploughbottom who lost a fortune, but Elword. The debt certificate is totally worthless!"

The inspector glanced at the Phantom, who stood frozen behind the mayor's desk.

The word 'won' had not escaped him.

ÜBUNG 225 !

Übung 225: Wie heißt das Wort auf Deutsch?

1.	fortune	☐	falsch
2.	prevent	☐	Freizeichen
3.	ancestry	☐	verhindern
4.	baffled	☐	Volltreffer
5.	involuntarily	☐	würfeln

6.	phony	☐ Bescheinigung
7.	instigate	☐ Ausnahme
8.	life-like	☐ süchtig
9.	pity	☐ Tagebuch
10.	territory	☐ Mitleid
11.	barely	☐ Vermögen
12.	desperately	☐ Bericht
13.	dial tone	☐ kaum
14.	report	☐ Abstammung
15.	jackpot	☐ verzweifelt
16.	diary	☐ unwillkürlich
17.	addicted	☐ anstiften
18.	dice	☐ Boden
19.	certificate	☐ lebensecht
20.	exception	☐ verdutzt

"Thank you, Elvira. I'll call you back," said the inspector. And before Elvira had a chance to protest, Hudson hung up.

The confidence had vanished from the criminal's face. He went pale.

"I think you know what that telephone call was about, old boy. I arrest you for attempted fraud!"

The Phantom shrank back.

"That is ridiculous! You … you have no proof."

Hudson smiled.

"Well, you did try to take possession of an island using a worthless piece of paper. I'm sure that when we have a quiet moment to take your fingerprints, other crimes can be proved against you."

ÜBUNG 226 !

Übung 226: Welches Wort ist das „schwarze Schaf"?

1. nail, sunshine, thunder, storm ____________________
2. guard, security, lock, access ____________________
3. tree, wood, rose, oak ____________________
4. thriller, sonata, soap opera, quiz show ____________________
5. parody, satire, fantasy, power ____________________
6. dismiss, sack, promote, give notice ____________________
7. detached house, semi-detached house, terraced house, staircase ____________________

Hudson approached the Phantom with quick steps. Mr Manxon also rushed toward him. As the two men cornered him, the Phantom took a step back against the wall. He pressed against an ornate stained glass window with the crest of the Isle on it.

ÜBUNG 227 !

Übung 227: Setzen Sie das richtige Verb in der korrekten Form ein!

Hudson (1. ziehen) ____________ his weapon and took another step towards the Phantom.

"It's not over yet, Hudson," he (2. fauchen) ________________.

"We will see each other again. From now on, you'll never be able to (3. vertrauen) ____________ anyone!"

With this threat, the Phantom (4. drehen) ____________ his back to the inspector and (5. springen) ____________ out the window.

Coloured shards of glass (6. fliegen) ____________ through the room.

Hudson and the mayor protected their eyes and raced to the broken window.
The Phantom had vanished.
"Damn!" said the inspector.
"Don't make such a big deal about it, inspector. You saved the Isle of Man and its inhabitants from the clutches of a criminal. That is the most important thing!"
Hudson nodded.
"You're right, mayor. For now, we can be happy with the results. But one thing makes me nervous."
"Do you mean the Phantom's threats?" asked the mayor worriedly.
Hudson smiled.
"No, I can live with that. The bigger problem is that I have to confess to Elvira Elliot that I actually confused the Phantom with her …"

THE END

Abschlusstest

Übung 1: Nennen Sie ein Synonym für die folgenden Wörter!

1. criminal ____________________
2. picture ____________________
3. tunnel ____________________
4. phoney ____________________
5. shout ____________________
6. phantom ____________________
7. risky ____________________
8. safety ____________________
9. astonishing ____________________
10. nice ____________________

Übung 2: Setzen Sie das Verb in der korrekten Form ein!

1. Hudson could not (htcca) __________ the Phantom.
2. Yesterday, Miss Paddington (kema) __________ tea for Elvira.
3. Tomorrow, Sir Reginald (eavel) __________ for Leeds.
4. Hudson (lelt) __________ me two days ago.
5. (Mya) __________ I borrow your car?

6. Hudson (ntozie) __________ the thief five minutes ago.

7. Lord Ploughbottom (csrbbile) _________ in his diary every day.

8. Who has (skpea) __________ well about London?

9. In two weeks, I (tsrat) ________________ reading "The Hound of the Baskervilles".

10. Last year, we (vertal) __________ to the Provence on holiday.

Übung 3: Setzen Sie die Sätze vom Passiv ins Aktiv und umgekehrt!

1. Elvira eats the biscuit.

____

2. The Isle of Man was saved by Inspector Hudson.

____

3. The painting was copied by Jimmy Coltrane.

____

4. Who booked the ticket for the ferry?

____

5. Elvira filled her car with petrol.

____

6. The novel was read by Miss Paddington.

____

Übung 4: Wählen Sie den passenden Ausdruck für die jeweilige Situation!

1. You meet someone in the morning.
   a) ☐ Nice tomorrow.
   b) ☐ Good early day.
   c) ☐ Good morning.

2. Someone invites you to dinner and you can't go.
   a) ☐ I'm sorry but I have another engagement.
   b) ☐ Thanks, I would love to come.
   c) ☐ No, I don't want to come.

3. You like your friend's new dress.
   a) ☐ That's a hideous dress you have on.
   b) ☐ That's a lovely dress you have on.
   c) ☐ That's a strange dress you have on.

Übung 5: Ist der Satz richtig übersetzt?
Markieren Sie: richtig ✓ oder falsch –?

1. Miss Paddington fährt jeden Tag mit dem Bus./Miss Paddington takes the bus every day.
2. Hudson arbeitet bei Scotland Yard seit 5 Jahren./Hudson works for Scotland Yard since 5 years.
3. Ich mache kein Geschäfte mit Gaunern./I don't make business with thieves.
4. Das Phantom könnte zurückkehren./The Phantom could return.
5. Elvira kann Französisch und Spanisch./Elvira can French and Spanish.

Übung 6: Ordnen Sie die Wörter den richtigen Überbegriffen zu!

a) to brake
b) chancellor
c) cancer
d) humanism
e) exhibition
f) deaf
g) harp
h) density
i) fuel
j) instalment
k) to purchase
l) exhausted
m) prehistoric
n) data processing
o) sculpture
p) surgeon

1. Wirtschaft ______________________________

2. Technik ______________________________

3. Kunst/Musik ______________________________

4. Geschichte/Politik ______________________________

5. Medizin ______________________________

Übung 7: Wie lautet die Übersetzung?

1. Steuern hinterziehen	☐	reorganize
2. eine Rechnung stellen	☐	compensation claim
3. Überstunden machen	☐	render an account
4. umorganisieren	☐	work overtime
5. Schadenersatz	☐	avoid tax
6. das neueste Modell	☐	trademark
7. Markenzeichen	☐	the latest model
8. eine Rechnung begleichen	☐	settle a bill

Lösungen Abschlusstest

Übung 1: 1. crook 2. portrait, painting 3. chute 4. fake 5. yell, scream 6. ghost 7. dangerous 8. security 9. amazing 10. pleasant

Übung 2: 1. catch 2. made 3. leaves, will leave 4. told 5. May 6. notized 7. scribbled 8. spoken 9. will start 10. travelled

Übung 3: 1. The biscuit is eaten by Elvira. 2. Inspector Hudson saved the Isle of Man. 3. Jimmy Coltrane copied the painting. 4. By whom was the ticket for the ferry booked? 5. The car was filled with petrol by Elvira. 6. Miss Paddington read the novel.

Übung 4: 1. c 2. a 3. b

Übung 5: 1. richtig 2. falsch 3. falsch 4. richtig 5. falsch

Übung 6: 1. a, j, k 2. h, i, n 3. e, g, o 4. b, d, m 5. c, f, l, p

Übung 7: 1. avoid tax 2. render an account 3. work overtime 4. reorganize 5. compensation claim 6. the latest model 7. trademark 8. settle a bill

Lernkrimi Englisch

DAS RÄTSEL DER MUMIE

Compact Verlag

Lernkrimi Englisch Grammatik

Inhalt

Story

Im Londoner British Museum wurde auf unerklärliche Weise eine wertvolle Mumie gestohlen!
Inspector Hudson geht auf die Suche nach dem Täter und gerät in einen Kriminalfall, der zunehmend mysteriöser wird …
Wer könnte ein Motiv haben, eine fünftausend Jahre alte Mumie zu stehlen? Ist der Fluch des Pharao nur ein Aberglaube? Wird dieser geheimnisvolle Fall noch ein weiteres Menschenleben fordern?
Nach und nach gelingt es Inspector Hudson, Licht in das Dunkel des Unerklärlichen zu bringen …

The Mystery of the Mummy

Inspector James Hudson loved the soft noises that penetrated his flat on Baker Street early in the morning. Especially when he had a day off work, which rarely happened. How often had his housekeeper, Miss Paddington, insisted that he use up some of his overtime and stay at home in the morning. Usually at this time, he would have already been in his small office at Scotland Yard for quite a while, answering urgent phone-calls, interrogating witnesses or examining crime sites. However, today was different.

Übung 228: Unterstreichen Sie die regelmäßigen Verben im Simple Past!

James sighed deeply and closed his eyes, while he let himself sink down in his armchair. He could feel the calmness rubbing off on him. Still, he could not simply turn off his detective instincts. Breathing slowly and calmly, he listened to the tranquillity and tried to identify the noises which could be heard every so often. This was a relaxation exercise for him and at the same time concentration training.

To begin with, there was the old grandfather clock in the corner of the living room. Its steady ticking was like a heartbeat in the stillness. Or perhaps like a calming rhythm giving order to all the noises.

Suddenly James jumped, without opening his eyes. While the clock's ticking was a steady rhythm, from the kitchen came a crashing sound followed by Miss Paddington's curses. His housekeeper had probably dropped a pot or something. The inspector grinned at the old lady's curses, which were anything but ladylike, and continued his concentration exercise. Until this moment it had been quite simple.

A patter on the windowpane suggested it had begun to rain. Nothing unusual in London at this time of the year.

Or at any other time of the year …

ÜBUNG 229 !

Übung 229: Setzen Sie die Verben ins Simple Past!

Mr Hudson (1. to smile) _______________ to himself as he (2. to wait) _______________ for the next noise. The clock struck eight. Aaand … there it was. A muffled thump on the door.

Mr Hudson's smile widened.

Every time it (3. to rain) _________________, the paperboy, Tim, (4. not to do) ____________________ bother to put the London Times in the post box. He simply threw it in front of the house door, where this respectable printed newspaper soaked up the rain, if Miss Paddington did not quickly bring it in.

James Hudson could already hear his housekeeper as she (5. to grumble) _______________ when she (6. to go) _______________ to open the door cursing the paperboy. However, the squeaking of a rusty bicycle chain told him that Tim (7. to be) _______________ already well on his way and probably ignoring the elderly lady completely.

Mr Hudson still (8. to think) _______ everything was proceeding as usual, when he was puzzled by yet another noise: despite the pattering rain, it took Miss Paddington a few seconds to close the door behind her. That could only mean one thing. She must have been startled by the headlines on the first page of the Times. James (9. to frown) ________________. Miss Paddington had been his housekeeper for many years now. He knew the determined old lady was not easily shaken. And that meant only one thing. Hudson sighed again, opened his eyes and waited.

A minute later Miss Paddington (10. to enter) _______________ the living room. She was holding a silver tray on which there were a steaming teapot of tea, a couple of slices of bread, some marmalade – and the slightly wet morning edition of the London Times.

"Good morning, Mr Hudson," she said with slight disapproval in her voice. "On your day off, you could have slept in, you know?"

James (11. to laugh) ________________. "It's not that easy to change one's habits, my dear Miss Paddington."

"You work too hard," (12. to answer) ____________ Miss Paddington in a slightly disapproving tone of voice.

"Well, crime does not sleep either, Miss Paddington," (13. to reply) ______________ James and pointed at the newspaper.

"So, what new crime is about to spoil my day off work – apart from the weather?"
Miss Paddington gasped in surprise and placed the tray on the small coffee table near the armchair.

ÜBUNG 230

Übung 230: Welches Wort ist das „schwarze Schaf"?

1. my, your, his, walk, her __________
2. in, by, from, yesterday, for __________
3. enter, house, do, dream, dance __________
4. crime, theft, robbery, search __________
5. wet, hot, book, rainy __________
6. he, they, it, man __________
7. happily, awfully, dry, well __________
8. silence, tranquillity, calm, noise __________

"H-How did you know that again, James?"
Miss Paddington always tended to call her young employer by his first name, when she was surprised. And this was obviously the case. James poured himself a cup of tea and smiled. "I heard you wait a second longer before bringing in the newspaper. And I deduced that you were alarmed by the headlines. And since you are not easy to alarm, that can only mean two things: either the Queen of England has run away with a stableman –"
"Heaven forbid!" exclaimed Miss Paddington. "That is not a thing to joke about!"

"– or," continued Mr Hudson, "an unusual crime has been committed, which must be in my field of activity."
Miss Paddington shook her head in admiration. "Thank God for the latter, sir." Miss Paddington, an enthusiastic reader of crime novels and a hobby detective herself, was fascinated each time by the inspector's powers of deduction. Sometimes James believed that his housekeeper had adopted him on the spot only to have a real criminal investigator in the family.
"Let's see," said James as he picked up the newspaper from the tray. What he read on the first page was indeed unusual. So unusual he had to read the short sentence twice, to make sure he had not misunderstood it.
'SHOCKING MUMMY THEFT AT BRITISH MUSEUM' glared the headlines on the wet newspaper's first page.
"Who on earth would steal a mummy," asked Miss Paddington shaking her head.

Übung 231: Beantworten Sie die folgenden Fragen zum Text im Präsens!

ÜBUNG 231 !

1. Where does Mr Hudson live?

____

2. Who is Miss Paddington?

____

3. What noises can Mr Hudson hear?

____

4. What does Mr Hudson have for breakfast?

---

5. Which newspaper does Mr Hudson read?

"I have no idea," replied Hudson, "but I'm afraid it will be my job to find that out." He glanced at the old grandfather clock. It was 8.14. He took a quick gulp of his tea, stood up and went to the phone in the corridor and waited.

ÜBUNG 232

Übung 232: Unterstreichen Sie die unregelmäßigen Verben im Simple Past und überlegen Sie sich die Stammform!

Hudson did not have to wait for long. After two or three minutes the old-fashioned phone rang. Miss Paddington let out a loud, very audible sigh. She had a feeling that the inspector's day off was over. James let the phone ring twice – he thought it was impolite to pick up the receiver after the first ring – before answering.
"Good morning, Sir Reginald," said Hudson politely. The inspector knew that only one person could be on the other end of the line.

His superior at the Scotland Yard, Sir Reginald.
Although James Hudson was only an ordinary inspector at Scotland Yard, his advice was always needed for mysterious and unusual crimes. Normal cases such as bank robberies, or a basic crime of violence had not been in his field of activity for years. Every time anything bizarre happened, the case was assigned to him.
And without any doubt the case of the missing mummy would end up on Hudson's desk.

If this theft had made it to the first page of the Times, then with all probability there was already a crowd of reporters in his senior's office.

"Hudson!" barked Sir Reginald down the receiver. "I need you here!" Sir Reginald did not bother to return Hudson's greeting. If James was a tracker dog, then Sir Reginald was a bulldog! Tranquil and friendly when left alone, but snappish when someone treads on his toes.

Hudson smiled slightly as he remembered that Sir Reginald even looked a little like a bulldog.

Übung 233: Übersetzen Sie und enträtseln Sie das Lösungswort!

1. Hinweis ☐ _ _ _
2. Raub _ _ _ _ _ ☐ _
3. herausfinden _ ☐ _ _   _ _ _
4. Mord ☐ _ _ _ _ _
5. Polizei _ _ _ _ _ ☐

Lösung: _ _ _ _ _

"Hudson, I have a pack of journalists on my back who want to know something about the case of the missing mummy. I only read about it this morning in the newspaper. Good heavens, who would be stupid enough to steal a mummy?!"

"No idea, sir," replied Hudson smiling. "But I have a feeling you want me to find that out."

"Anyhow!" barked Sir Reginald. "Go to the museum at once, so that I can at least tell these nosy-parkers and stupid reporters that

I've put my best man on this difficult and mysterious job." "Very flattering, sir," said Hudson, "but may I just remind you that today's my day off?"

"Never mind. We'll talk about that later." Having said that, Sir Reginald abruptly rang off.

Hudson smiled. Any other reaction would have surprised him. To be honest with himself, he was actually very pleased about the new unexpected assignment. A day off with nothing to do could be nerve-racking. And the case of the missing mummy sounded interesting indeed. Sir Reginald had a point: what idiot would steal a mummy thousands of years old and, above all, why?

Well, he would find that out.

Übung 234: Setzen Sie den richtigen Artikel ein!
*(**a**, **an**, **the** oder nichts)*

1. Last night ____________ mummy was stolen from ________ British Museum.
2. Mr Hudson lives in ____________ big flat downtown.
3. ____________ elderly couple was crossing the road when ____________ police car drove by.
4. How much is the ticket for the museum? Fifteen pounds ____________ day.
5. How often does Miss Paddignton watch the news? Once ____________ hour.
6. ____________ fear is horrible.

7. I read __________ headlines __________ minute ago.

8. __________ English love drinking tea.

Whistling happily, he walked into the kitchen where Miss Paddington was busy again with her pots and pans. She observed the inspector's smile suspiciously.
"My dear Miss Paddington," said Hudson and prepared himself for trouble, "I'm afraid my day off work has come to an end. Sir Reginald needs me."
Miss Paddington banged a pan on the stove. "My dear Mr Hudson," she said reprovingly, "you specifically promised me that you would rest today. After the case of the Tower Bridge ghost you certainly have earned the right to a break."
Hudson shuddered at the thought of that crime. He had closed the case only a week before – and he had almost lost his life.
"Nothing comforts me more, Miss Paddington, than a little mystery which needs to be solved. And besides, nothing much can happen to anyone looking for a five-thousand-year old mummy," chuckled the inspector.
But how wrong he was indeed!

Übung 235: Wie lautet der Plural dieser Wörter?

1. newspaper __________

2. thief __________

3. woman __________

4. man __________

5. potato ______________

6. mouse ______________

7. knife ______________

8. ox ______________

9. fox ______________

10. lobby ______________

A few minutes later, Mr Hudson was dressed according to the weather. He said goodbye to Miss Paddington and got into his car. The Bentley's engine spluttered protestingly as he turned the ignition key. Such an old car felt the weather just like any human would.

At last, after three more attempts the engine started. Rattling loudly the heavy car jerked forward through the rainy streets.

Hudson had been driving the car for many years and still managed to create a sensation. When passers-by on the street saw this type of precious car, they all expected a smooth moving car with a purring engine. But a Bentley, too, grows old sooner or later and shares the same destiny as any other automobile. The engine rattled, the exhaust pipe emanated strange noises and rust stains were becoming visible.

Such old Bentleys were not often seen around. Probably because people who could afford a luxury car, could also afford a new luxury car.

The inspector didn't care. He liked the comfortable seats and its steady hold on the road. He would never ever have exchanged it for a smaller Japanese car. At the most, for a new limousine, but of course he couldn't afford that with his small inspector's income.

Übung 236: Stellen Sie zu den Antworten die richtigen Fragen! Verwenden Sie folgende Wörter: ***what, where, how, whose, when, why, how much/many/often***

1. Mr Hudson lives in Baker Street.

2. He goes to work by car.

3. That's his car.

4. It's a Bentley.

5. He reads the newspaper every morning.

6. The museum closes at five o'clock.

7. She's his housekeeper.

8. It's about a missing mummy.

9. Six pounds.

10. He closed his last case a week before.

____

11. Because it has a comfortable seat and holds the road well.

____

Perhaps he could turn a couple of his cases into detective books and earn a lot of money. If only he didn't hate detective books so much. He was so deep in thought that he did not notice a small red sports car following him through the streets of London.
When Hudson arrived at the museum there was already a lot of excitement. The main entrance was surrounded by a large crowd of photographers and reporters.

ÜBUNG 237

Übung 237: Ordnen Sie die Buchstaben zu einem sinnvollen Wort!

It was useless to try and enter the museum through the main door, so the inspector drove his car around the (1. giinulbd) ______________.

A few minutes later Hudson had found what he was looking for. An unguarded warehouse (2. rentncae) ______________. He parked his car near the entrance and got out. Cold (3. inar) ______________ hit his face, but, like all Londoners, he was accustomed to it. Undisturbed, he went inside the (4. eummus) ______________.

After going through a couple of rather uninviting storage rooms, he came to the actual display rooms.

Although time was pressing, James (5. ppedsto) ______________ for a few seconds and breathed in deeply. He loved the (6. emsll) ______________ of these ancient rooms. As a school kid he had come here on class outings to (7. idscorve) ______________ the world.

The world's most important ancient civilizations were put on display here, such as ancient Greece, the Romans or the South American Incas. And of course the Egyptians. Hudson cleared his throat and set to his task once again. A blue arrow pointed in the direction of the Egyptian area of the museum. With nearly child-like joy James Hudson ran up the steps to the first floor where some irreplaceable relics from ancient Egypt were displayed. He did not need to follow the blue arrow as he remembered his way very well.

Übung 238: Welche Synonyme gehören zusammen? Setzen Sie die richtige Nummer in das Kästchen!

1. display	☐ rob
2. see	☐ gather evidence
3. find out	☐ do
4. make	☐ catch
5. help	☐ run away
6. investigate	☐ exhibit
7. arrest	☐ look
8. escape	☐ discover
9. steal	☐ assist

Because of the shocking theft, the museum was closed to the public. Hudson's steps echoed in the silence until he finally reached the 'Egyptian Hall'.
And here the silence was broken. The room was swarming with numerous policemen in plain clothes and in uniforms, taking photos and finger prints as well as measurements. Hudson was pleased. He loved the precision and devotion with which the policemen investigated the scene of a crime. Each little clue was carefully gathered. And in the end one had many pieces of a puzzle, which could be put together to solve the case.
"May I help you, sir?" a voiced asked behind him. It was more of a reproach than a question.
Hudson turned around and faced a grim bobby with an enormous moustache who was glaring at him.
"You certainly may, constable," said Hudson politely, "by telling me what precisely happened here."
"That has nothing to do with you, sir," answered the policeman. "This is the scene of a crime and the museum is closed to the public today."
"That's bad enough," said Hudson, "I'm sure many school classes will be standing outside in the rain very disappointed."
The constable looked confused.

ÜBUNG 239 !

Übung 239: Wie heißt das Simple Past der folgenden unregelmäßigen Verben?

1. catch ______________
2. steal ______________
3. know ______________

4. shake ____________________

5. bring ____________________

6. see ____________________

7. come ____________________

8. go ____________________

9. begin ____________________

10. win ____________________

11. sleep ____________________

12. take ____________________

13. can ____________________

14. eat ____________________

15. have ____________________

"Anyway, I'm Inspector James Hudson from Scotland Yard. Sir Reginald has assigned me to this case."

The look on the constable's face became friendlier on the spot. "Oh, I'm so terribly sorry, sir. How was I to know that? I was not informed that someone from Scotland Yard was coming."

"Don't worry, old friend," replied Hudson. "I took the liberty of letting myself in."

The policeman's face had an enquiring expression.

"Oh, forget it," said Hudson quickly. He did not wish to confuse the man unnecessarily. "So where was our dead man kidnapped?"

"The mummy, I mean. Where was it stolen?" Inspector Hudson explained himself.

Übung 240: Lesen Sie weiter und unterstreichen Sie die Substantive!

"Hmm, I understand. Please follow me. I'll take you there."
Hudson followed the constable across the large room. On his way to the site of the crime, Hudson looked around. The pieces exhibited had not changed much since his childhood. As the Egyptian empire had ceased to exist thousands of years ago. In the meantime there had not been many new findings. And when new relics were found, most of them stayed in Egypt where they belonged.

As a child Hudson had already wondered what the British would think if, all of a sudden, Egyptians were to make an expedition to their country to break into ancient Celtic tombs and take the treasures back with them. Here in the British Museum the treasures and relics would at least be looked after carefully.
Well, that's what he thought until the constable led him to a shattered display case. The glass box in which the mummy had been propped up was about two metres high and a metre wide. The front panel had been smashed. Inside glass splinters shone like small diamonds under the electric light from the ceiling.

Übung 241: Geben Sie die verneinte Form an!

1. I am ____________________
2. We are ____________________
3. He was ____________________
4. I will ____________________
5. I did ____________________

6. She can ______________

7. He stole ______________

8. You have stolen ______________

9. I've got ______________

10. He steals ______________

11. You dream ______________

"How awful!" exclaimed Hudson.
The constable added, "Who would do anything like this?"
"That," said Hudson for the second time that day, "is what I intend to find out. Have you found any clues?"
The constable shook his head.
"The thief obviously got into the museum without breaking anything. The burglar alarm was not activated. Whoever entered the building, came here directly, broke open the display case and walked off with the mummy."

Übung 242: Setzen Sie das passende Synonym ein:
(scene, recalled, grin, brusque, enquired, criminal, surprised)

"Mmm, that means the (1. culprit) __________ had access to the building. Perhaps even a key!"

"Maybe there isn't a culprit," said a (2. gruff) ______________ voice next to them. Hudson and the constable looked around (3. startled) __________.

ÜBUNG 242 !

Behind them stood a sour-looking man in grey overalls. He was holding a broom in his hand. A cigar hung out of the corner of his mouth, leaving ash all around the crime (4. site) ______________. Hudson could not avoid a (5. smile) ________________. If he (6. remembered) ___________ rightly, that was the same caretaker who told them off when, as kids, they had run through the entrance or had talked too loudly.

"What do you mean by that, sir?" (7. asked) _____________ the constable. "And please be careful, the forensic check is still not finished!"

"Grrrr," grunted the caretaker and, shaking his head in the direction of the smashed glass, said, "Tut-Enk-Ra's mummy was in there. The sun king."

"Yes?" said Hudson curiously.

"Well, there are many stories about the old man, you know. When he was alive, he laid a curse on anyone who disturbed his deathbed. And, indeed, it appears that there were numerous mysterious deaths among the people who took part in the excavations."

"How interesting," said Hudson, lost in thought. "And what would your conclusion be, sir?"

The caretaker let out a thick puff of smoke. The constable coughed loudly.

"I think the mummy might have simply walked out of his display case of his own accord. You know, to take revenge on the descendants of the expeditionists, or the likes."

"You watch too many movies," interrupted the constable.

"What rubbish!"
Hudson nodded.
"I have to agree with the constable on one point."
Hudson pointed at the glass splinters inside the broken glass case.

Übung 243: Bilden Sie die fehlenden Formen!

	Infinitiv	Past	Past Participle
1.	lose	______	______
2.	______	rang	______
3.	______	______	thought
4.	wake	______	______
5.	______	spoke	______
6.	______	______	stolen
7.	shoot	______	______
8.	______	______	sat
9.	pay	______	______
10.	______	hit	______
11.	teach	______	______

"If the mummy had really walked out on his own, the glass splinters would be all around the display case. Instead they're inside. That means the glass panel was smashed in from the outside."
The caretaker shrugged his shoulders. "Perhaps the mummy had an accomplice."

"I rather think," laughed Hudson, "that Prince Tut-Enk-Ra did not leave his glass home of his own free will."
"Well, whatever," growled the caretaker, holding his broom, "I have to tidy up the whole mess."
"Don't you dare!" cried the constable. "You can't simply sweep away the clues. Take your broom away!"
The caretaker growled at the policeman. And Hudson had to come between them before it turned into a serious fight.
He laid his hand on the caretaker's shoulder.
"Tell me," he asked, "isn't there a surveillance system here?"
"Do you mean a video camera?"
"Exactly."
"Sure," replied the caretaker, "here everything is state-of-the-art. Do you think the thief was filmed while he stole the mummy?"
"That won't be difficult to find out. All we need to do is look at last night's tapes. Please take me to the security guards' room."
"Certainly," grunted the caretaker.
Hudson followed the grumbling old man and, turning towards the constable, said "And leave everything in order when you have finished here, OK, constable?"
The policeman nearly saluted him. "Yes, sir inspector!"

ÜBUNG 244 !

Übung 244: Sind die folgenden Sätze inhaltlich richtig oder falsch? Markieren Sie: richtig ✔ falsch –

1. The policeman and the caretaker had a fist fight.
2. The mummy was lying in his display case.
3. State-of-the-art means the current stage of development of a practical or technological subject.
4. The alarm was activated when the thief entered the museum.

5. Some of the people who dug up Tut-Enk-Ra's grave died.
6. The mummy's display case was made of iron.
7. The caretaker swept away the clues with his broom.

Ten minutes later, Inspector Hudson was sitting in a room with very futuristic equipment. On the one wall over a dozen monitors were flickering and surveying all the museum's rooms. As the British Museum was still closed, the Egyptian area was the only place where any activity was going on. Hudson could see that the policemen were slowly packing away their instruments and cameras. The forensic test was nearly over.

"Could we watch all the tapes videoed last night?" Mr Hudson asked the man at the control desk.

"Of course …" said the technician and pressed a few buttons.

He seemed rather excited at the idea of helping Scotland Yard in an investigation. His job was probably normally dead boring.

Hudson concentrated on the monitor in front of him. The Egyptian hall could clearly be seen, filmed by a camera on the white ceiling.

*Übung 245 : Setzen Sie **a/an** oder **some** ein!*

1. _______ alibi 2. _______ tree 3. _______ money 4. _______ tomato 5. _________ job 6. ________ music 7. ________ apple 8. _______ work 9. _______ investigation 10. _______ evidence 11. _______ information

The camera moved around the room and also videoed the display case with the mummy. The shrouded corpse of Tut-Enk-Ra stood

unmoving, just as it had been doing so for thousands of years.
"Shall I wind the tape forward?" asked the technician.
Hudson did not really feel like watching the nightly happenings of the museum hall in real time.
"Yes, if possible," he said.
"No problem."
The technician pressed another couple of buttons and the recording started to move wildly across the screen.
"I can wind it forward even faster, if you wish, sir," said the technician.
"That'll do," replied Hudson.
He was already getting dizzy.
He concentrated carefully on the screen. The camera moved from left to right and back again at the speed of lightning.
Again and again.
Nothing.

ÜBUNG 246 !

Übung 246: Welche Gegenteile gehören zusammen? Schreiben Sie die Nummer in das richtige Kästchen!

1. reply	☐ dry
2. rainy	☐ start
3. speak	☐ happy
4. yes	☐ hot
5. finish	☐ healthy
6. sad	☐ calm
7. cold	☐ listen
8. panic	☐ ask
9. sick	☐ no

Suddenly Hudson thought he saw something like a shadow flash across the picture.
"Stop the tape!" he ordered.
The technician had also noticed it, because at that exact moment he pressed the 'pause' button.
The picture froze.
Both men bent forward and were hypnotized by the screen.
No doubt about it, the silhouette of a man moved towards the mummy's glass case. He was holding a long object in his hand.
An iron bar.
"Please play the tape at a normal speed."
The technician pressed a button. The frozen picture started moving again. The man took a few steps towards the glass case. He was wearing some black overalls and his whole face, except for his eyes, was covered by a cloth.

Übung 247: Lesen Sie weiter und setzen Sie die richtigen Präpositionen in die Lücken ein!

Whoever it was, he knew he was being watched 1. _______ a camera. Hudson also noticed something else. At first he thought it was some kind of a disturbance 2. _______ the screen, but, looking 3. _______ it for the second time, he was absolutely sure: the man limped. He dragged his left leg only very slightly, but once detected, the limp could not be ignored.

Hudson made a mental note. The limp was not a breakthrough, but

perhaps a first and important clue which helps to find the mean thief. On the monitor the man had now reached the showcase. He lifted the iron bar and without hesitating smashed the glass. On the mute videotape, the breaking glass could not be heard. Hudson and the technician watched as the man carefully took the mummy out 4. _______ the glass box and carried it away. The camera moved again and once it had focussed 5. _______ the showcase again, both the man and the mummy had disappeared.
"Well we've just caught the thief red-handed on film and still haven't made any progress," said Hudson 6. _______ a sigh.
"Please send the tape to Scotland Yard," he told the technician. "The guys 7. _______ the technical department might be able to find out something else about the thief."

Puzzled, Hudson stood up and went to the door.
"Oh, by the way," he said, "is there any such thing as a list with all the people who have a key to the museum?"
"An access card," corrected the technician.
"A what?" asked Hudson.
"An electronic access card. A bit like a credit card, sir. Only this card opens the doors to the museum. Normal keys are nowhere near as safe. If you have a moment, I'd be happy to print you a list with all the names."
Hudson sighed.
It did not sound as if the list would be very short.

A quarter of an hour later, Hudson got into his Bentley. On the passenger's seat lay a sheet of paper with the names of two dozen card possessors.

Übung 248: Übersetzen Sie folgende Sätze!

1. Inspector Hudson liebte die leisen Geräusche.

2. James ließ das Telefon zweimal klingeln.

3. Er las die Titelseite nochmals.

4. Eine Minute später trat Miss Paddington ins Wohnzimmer.

5. Der Constable blickte ihn verwirrt an.

6. Vielleicht hatte die Mumie einen Komplizen.

7. Hudson konzentrierte sich auf den Bildschirm.

Things had started well.
Inspector Hudson drove his car through the centre of London.

Luckily it was late morning and the first rush hour was over. This is where, in the early morning hours, cars drove bumper to bumper. But now Hudson had a clear road.
Actually, after visiting the museum, he had intended to go to Scotland Yard. But then he had noticed the red sports car that had been following him for at least a quarter of an hour.
Of course it could have been a coincidence, but Hudson had been working for Scotland Yard too long to believe in coincidences.

! ÜBUNG 249

Übung 249: Setzen Sie ***any*** *oder* ***some*** *ein!*

1. Mr Hudson hasn't collected ______ evidence on the case yet.
2. Miss Paddington bought _______ tea, but the grocer didn't have _______ bread.
3. I don't have _______ free time today. Sorry.
4. I haven't got _______ paper.
5. Would you like _______ milk?
6. Yes thank you. I would love _______.
7. I don't have _______ money in my purse.

"Let's see, my little friend," murmured Hudson, "who we are dealing with."
The inspector pressed his foot on the accelerator. The old Bentley protested – it was not accustomed to this treatment – and jerked forward.
Hudson drove elegantly through an orange traffic light – and did

not believe his eyes. Although Hudson himself had gone through the orange traffic light, the sports car's engine roared and the car, too, raced through the busy intersection.

Cars hooted and shocked drivers cursed the person of the sports car. Whoever was driving that car, Hudson thought to himself, really had good nerves.

An accident could have easily happened.

The sports car – an expensive European make that Hudson didn't know – was driven by either a madman or a reporter hoping to get a headline for some tabloid newspaper.

"If you continue driving like that," murmured Hudson to himself, "you'll end up writing your story in prison or in hospital."

The inspector spun the steering wheel around and turned suddenly into a side-street. The sports car followed him with a screeching of wheels. A couple of pedestrians jumped aside in panic.

The inspector shook his head.

Such a wild chase was fun all right, but it put innocent passers-by in danger.

Übung 250: Wie lauten die Sätze? Passen Sie auf die Adverbien auf!

! ÜBUNG 250

1. you the Do go to often museum?

____

2. because never drink I don't tea I it like

____

3. never Hudson for is work late

____

4. housekeeper watches My always evening in the news the

____

5. inspector has The rarely a off day

____

6. The suddenly car braked old

____

7. cars The at loudly the hooted pedestrians

____

He looked at the road ahead and saw the large luminous sign of a parking garage. He turned the headlights on and followed the winding way up.
The sports car was close behind and – believe it or not – even flashed its lights at Hudson.
Only a reporter could have had such a courage, or perhaps someone even worse.
Hudson drove his Bentley to the topmost floor of the parking space, steered it into a free parking place and turned the engine off.

ÜBUNG 251 !

Übung 251: Unterstreichen Sie die Adverbien!

Behind him the sportscar's engine roared. Wheels screeched and the car braked violently as it pulled into the parking space next to the Bentley.
The inspector got out.
The door of the sports car also opened. The first thing Hudson saw was a short, red mop of hair.

“Do you buy your cars to match your hair colour, Elvira?” asked the inspector.
“James, my goodness, you drive like lightning. One could get the impression that you were trying to get rid of me.”
“Tut, tut,” replied Hudson, “what makes you think that? Only because you have the habit of putting your nose into my investigations and putting me into tricky situations?”
Elvira Elliot was a young woman in her thirties and by trade an insurance agent for an important insurance company in London. Similarly to Hudson at the Yard, Miss Elliot was always assigned to the unsolvable cases. More than once she had prevented her company from paying costly damages, because she had recovered stolen or missing valuable goods. And she was obviously very well paid for her services, thought the inspector looking at the brand new sports car. Elvira noticed this.
“Do you like it?” she asked proudly and snobbishly at the same time.

“I bought it during my last holiday in Europe.”
“Mmm,” answered the inspector and had to admit to himself that he was starting to sound like the grumpy caretaker at the museum. Actually, he liked Elvira a lot – although he would never have admitted it.

*Übung 252: Setzen Sie die richtige Präposition **at**, **in** oder **on** ein!*

1. ________ six o’clock
2. ________ Saturday
3. ________ Christmas

4. ________ 1998

5. ________ the morning

6. ________ night

7. ________ midday

8. ________ dusk

9. ________ Easter Sunday

10. ________ winter

11. ________ October

12. ________ the airport

Unlike him, Elvira was a nervous person who drew conclusions too quickly and was inclined to take hasty decisions.
Although apparently with good results.
“Come on. Don’t pull such a face, James,” Elvira said laughing.
“I had a feeling you would take on the case of the stolen mummy and I’ve been following you since you left your house this morning. I’m very interested in this case, perhaps we could work together again this time.”
The inspector shook his head.
“No chance,” he said quickly. “Last time we worked together I nearly lost my job.”
Elvira bowed her head and then looked at Hudson with big eyes.
“Was it that bad? Don’t you like me at all, James. Not even a teeny weeny bit?”
“That has nothing to do with it,” replied Hudson, blushing.
“Our investigative methods are simply different.”

"And that is exactly why we complement one another so well," cried Elvira. "Come on!"
The inspector shook his head, although he was not as convinced as a minute before.
"What interest do you have in this case?" he asked. "Why are you interested in a three-thousand-year-old mummy? I thought you liked crispy young men?"
"Not only," replied Elvira looking at the inspector meaningfully. "I'm also interested in ancient Egyptian princes, when they're worth a couple of million pounds."
Hudson swallowed hard.

Übung 253: Adverb und Adjektiv bedeuten nicht dasselbe! Ordnen Sie die Übersetzungen richtig zu: ***gesund, gerade, nur, ziemlich, einzig, gut, gerecht, hübsch***

ÜBUNG 253 !

1. well ______________________
2. pretty ______________________
3. only ______________________
4. just ______________________

James Hudson looked at Elvira Elliot over the edge of his tea cup. After the little hunt and the conversation in the parking garage, both had gone to a small café – Hudson had insisted on taking the Bentley – where they had been talking now for over a quarter of an hour.
Elvira waved her hand at the waiter to order her second coffee.
No wonder, the woman was always so overexcited, Hudson thought to himself as he sipped his Earl Grey tea.

Übung 254: Setzen Sie die Verben ins Present Perfect!

1. catch ____________
2. know ____________
3. shake ____________
4. bring ____________
5. see ____________
6. come ____________
7. go ____________
8. begin ____________
9. win ____________
10. sleep ____________
11. take ____________
12. can ____________

"So," he asked Elvira, once her coffee had been served, "what makes you think the mummy is worth a couple of million pounds? I mean, I know its archaeological worth is inestimable. But I don't believe the British Museum would have insured it for that much."
Elvira took a sip of coffee and smiled like a sphinx.
"Strictly speaking, it's not just about the mummy," she admitted smiling. "This old prince Tut-Enk-Rap –"
"Tut-Enk-Ra," corrected Hudson.
"– this old friend wasn't actually insured for much. Who would have dreamt that a mummy could be stolen. I really mean, a shrouded corpse is not exactly the kind of thing someone puts in

his front garden to enjoy a romantic summer evening."
Hudson nodded. The motive would be an important clue as to who the thief was; it certainly wasn't a common burglar.
"In other words," Elvira continued, "the insurance premium is hardly worth mentioning. Peanuts, so to say."
Hudson shook his head. When someone like Elvira spoke of peanuts, then it usually implied more money than he would ever earn at the Yard.

Übung 255: Unterstreichen Sie die richtige Form des Präsens!

1. Mr Hudson always works/is working overtime.
2. It rains/It's raining at the moment.
3. Hudson lives/is living in London.
4. What does Mr Hudson drink/is Mr Hudson drinking at the moment?
5. He looks/is looking for clues.
6. Miss Paddington brings/is bringing Mr Hudson breakfast every morning.
7. Hudson thinks/is thinking Elvira jumps to conclusions.

"Then why are you so interested, Elvira? Is business so bad, you are now chasing the small fish? Perhaps you shouldn't go on holiday so often and bring back little cars as souvenirs."
Elvira laughed, eyes flashing.
"Since when have you become so sarcastic, dear James. I like it."
She took another sip of coffee. Hudson noticed that the cup was already empty again.
"Don't look so surprised, James. Coffee increases your ability to concentrate and makes you happy. With this weather I need it."

ÜBUNG 256 !

Übung 256: Setzen Sie die fehlenden Wörter ein!
(meeting, tip, parties, over, impatiently, drizzling, throat)

The inspector quickly looked outside. It was 1. ________________ and drops of rain were running down the window pane.

His attention was diverted for a couple of seconds, then he concentrated on Elvira again. Actually he was enjoying this cosy little 2. ________________ with the pretty insurance agent, but after all he did have a case to solve. Sir Reginald was probably waiting 3. ________________.

"So Elvira, why are you interested in the case? So much so, that you are ready to sit with me in a boring cafè, instead of enjoying yourself at one of those high-society 4. ________________ with the rich and beautiful?"

"Oh, actually I quite like sitting here with you!" replied Elvira and looked Hudson in the eyes. She burst out laughing when his ears turned red.

Then she cleared her 5. ________________ and became serious.

"Do you know, James, that the mummy theft is only the 6. ________________ of the iceberg. For the last two months ancient Egyptian objects have been disappearing all 7. ________________ England and even in Europe and the States."

The inspector became very attentive … "Disappearing?"

"Yes, they have been reported as stolen. Look here," said Elvira and glanced at Hudson with wide opened eyes.

Übung 257: Welcher Satz enthält die richtige Zeitform? Kreuzen Sie an!

ÜBUNG 257 !

1. Mr Hudson kennt Miss Paddington seit vielen Jahren.
   a) ☐ Mr Hudson knows Miss Paddington for many years.
   b) ☐ Mr Hudson has known Miss Paddington many years.
   c) ☐ Mr Hudson has known Miss Paddington for many years.

2. Ich habe viele Länder in meinem Leben besucht.
   a) ☐ I has been to many countries in my life.
   b) ☐ I have been to many countries in my life.
   c) ☐ I went to many countries in my life.

3. Was hast du gestern Abend gemacht?
   a) ☐ What do you do last night?
   b) ☐ What have you done last night?
   c) ☐ What did you do last night?

4. Ich sah Ihre Anzeige in der Zeitung.
   a) ☐ I have seen your advertisement in the newspaper.
   b) ☐ I sawn your advertisement in the newspaper.
   c) ☐ I saw your advertisement in the newspaper.

5. Mr Hudson wohnt seit 1990 in der Baker Street.
   a) ☐ Mr Hudson has lived in Baker Street since 1990.
   b) ☐ Mr Hudson is living in Baker Street since 1990.
   c) ☐ Mr Baker lives in Baker Street since 1990.

6. Hudson hat Griechenland vor 2 Jahren besucht.
   a) ☐ He was in Greece since two years.
   b) ☐ He went to Greece two years ago.
   c) ☐ He has been to Greece two years ago.

Elvira rummaged in her fashionable bag, which without doubt had cost most of Hudson's monthly salary. On the front of it, shone the name of a designer in golden letters, which Hudson could not even pronounce.
At long last, Elvira took a piece of paper out of her bag and unfolded it carefully. "This is a list of the Egyptian artifacts that have been stolen over the last few months."
Hudson bent over and looked at the list.
A broker in Soho had had a golden statue of the cat goddess stolen. A widow in Switzerland had informed the police that a golden sceptre of an Egyptian prince had gone missing. An American film producer, whose name Hudson had vaguely heard of, had been robbed of an Egyptian death mask.
And that was only the beginning of the list.

ÜBUNG 258 !

Übung 258: Übersetzen Sie die Sätze im Konditional!

1. Er würde es nie zugeben, dass er Elvira mochte.

____

2. Das Tatmotiv würde Hudson einen Hinweis auf den Dieb geben.

____

3. Inspector Hudson würde stolz auf sie sein.

____

4. Er würde herausfinden, wer die Mumie gestohlen hat.

____

5. Es war mehr Geld, als er jemals beim Yard verdienen würde.

____

6. Er würde mit ihr zusammenarbeiten.

____

7. Aber Sir Reginald würde nie etwas davon erfahren.

____

"Astonishing," murmured Hudson. "A serial thief, who only steals Egyptian antiquities."
"Exactly. And many of them were insured by my company."
"And you think the same thief stole the mummy from the museum?"
"I'm convinced of it, James."
"And why do you think that precisely the mummy theft will lead us to the criminal?"
"It's very simple, James," smiled Elvira, "because you have been assigned to the case."

Übung 259: Geben Sie den Komparativ und den Superlativ der folgenden Adjektive an!

ÜBUNG 259!

1. happy ______________ ______________

2. good ______________ ______________

3. young ______________ ______________

4. beautiful ______________ ______________

5. bad ______________ ______________

6. comfortable ______________ ______________

7. busy ______________ ______________

8. patient ______________ ______________

9. polite ______________ ______________

10. far ______________ ______________

James Hudson could not help but feel flattered.
Perhaps that was the reason, he took a list out of his pocket, although it went strictly against the rules.
"Today I was given this list," said Hudson and showed Elvira the printed sheet.
"It looks like the thief sneaked into the museum without having to force open a door. Therefore it is obvious that he or she had a key … an 'access card'. This is a list of the people who have such a card. From the caretaker to the museum manager."
"But there are dozens!" gasped Elvira.
Hudson nodded his head frustrated.
"I'm afraid so. And any one of them could be the thief. Apart from the fact that one of these cards might have been stolen. However, today I saw the surveillance video of the theft and –"
"A video? That means the thief was filmed?" Elvira interrupted him. Hudson nodded.
"Yes and no. He was unrecognizable. But he was so sure of himself in the museum room, that he must have known the museum inside out."

Übung 260: Vervollständigen Sie die Sätze mit
anything, nothing, nobody, anywhere, anybody!

1. I don't want ____________ to drink. I'm not thirsty.
2. The museum was completely empty. ____________ was in it.
3. What did you buy? ____________. There wasn't ____________ I liked.
4. Have you seen my watch? I can't find it ____________.
5. There was complete silence in the room. ____________ said ____________.
6. She told ____________ about her plans.
7. She wasn't afraid of ____________.

"Well," sighed Elvira, "that reduces the number of suspects to a couple of dozen."
"Police work is hard work," said Hudson nearly joyfully. With a list full of suspects he was right in his element.

Übung 261: Unterstreichen Sie Hudsons Gedanken!

"I have a proposal. Why don't you check if the stolen goods on your list have anything in common. And I'll deal with my list."
"Does that mean we're working together, James?"
Her face broke into a wide smile.
Well, what should he do, thought Hudson. After all, if it hadn't been for Elvira, he might never have heard about the other thefts.

It was only fair to let her take part in the investigation.
Sir Reginald must never know of it, though.
"Sure, as long as you don't get in my way, Elvira."
"Fantastic!" shouted Elvira for joy.
"If you can excuse me, I have to go to my office and report to Sir Reginald."
"Of course, James. Give my regards to the old bulldog."
James could not stop himself from smiling, as he looked around for the waiter.
"Leave it, James," said Elvira. "Your tea's on me. I wanted to order something else anyway."
"Thanks for the invitation, Elvira."
"You're welcome, James. Here's to our collaboration."
"Yes, … our collaboration," replied James.
Hopefully he would not regret this decision. He stood up and went towards the door.

The cold drizzle hit his face.
Behind him he heard Elvira ordering yet another coffee.
Hudson drove his Bentley into the parking place behind the building of New Scotland Yard. He made sure that he had put away the list of card holders. Then he went into the building through the back entrance. He took the lift up to the third floor where Sir Reginald had his office.
He went down the passageway and straightened his tie before knocking on the door.
Instead of the expected 'come in', the door was torn open. Sir Reginald stood before him panting like a bulldog in a tweed jacket.
"Hudson," he growled, "there you are at last. I've been trying to get hold of you the whole morning. Sooner or later you'll have to get a mobile phone!"

Übung 262: Welche Gegenteile gehören zusammen? Setzen Sie die richtige Nummer ein!

1. straight	☐ boiling
2. back	☐ poor
3. wealthy	☐ reserved
4. young	☐ crooked
5. freezing	☐ lazy
6. hard-working	☐ cry
7. laugh	☐ elderly
8. outgoing	☐ front
9. black	☐ decrease
10. grow	☐ angel
11. tumult	☐ often
12. devil	☐ identical
13. broken	☐ intact
14. diverse	☐ white
15. seldom	☐ calm

God forbid, thought Hudson and followed his superior with surprise.
“What’s wrong, Sir Reginald?” he enquired.
“What’s wrong. Hell’s broken loose! And all because of a damned mummy!”
Hudson followed the man in a hurry. Both came to a room with a large door.
‘Conference room’ were the words written over it.
“In the conference room, sir?” asked Hudson surprised. “Have we set up a special investigation panel?”
“Special investigation panel,” growled Sir Reginald. “I suppose you could also call it that.”

ÜBUNG 263 !

Übung 263: Welches Wort gehört in die Lücke!
(charge, manslaughter, sentence, defence, guilty, killed, stole)

1. You'll be OK. Get a good ____________ lawyer.
2. If the police arrest you they ____________ you with a crime.
3. The charge of murder was reduced to ____________.
4. Because of good behaviour their ____________ was reduced by a year and a half.
5. The thief ____________ the Crown Jewels from the Tower Bridge.
6. She __________ her husband with a knife while he was asleep.
7. The court found him ____________ of murder.

Sir Reginald opened the door and nearly pushed Hudson into the room.
The inspector closed his eyes blindly. He was greeted by a storm of flashes. At least two dozen reporters jumped up from their places armed with cameras and notebooks.
Sir Reginald pulled poor Hudson to the speaker's desk.
"Our special investigator, Inspector James Hudson, is at your disposal for any questions, ladies and gentlemen. Fire away!"
Another series of flashes was followed by a confused wave of questions.
"Good luck, my friend!" Sir Reginald growled in Hudson's ear. And then he took off hurriedly towards the door.
"Are you already on the tracks of the mummy thief?" asked a fat reporter with a sweaty shirt.

"Do you think Tut-Enk-Ra's curse has anything to do with this?" shouted a lady with pink make-up.
"Is it all a publicity gag by the British Museum?" asked a thin man who obviously wrote for a serious newspaper.
The inspector swallowed.
"Hmm, please one after the other, ladies and gentlemen. I'll answer all your questions one after the other if possible."

Übung 264: Unterstreichen Sie die Verben im Past Perfect und Past Perfect Continuous!

A pimply young man with a "Star-Trek" T-shirt waved wildly in the air with his pencil.
"Does the mummy theft have anything to do with the latest corn circle sightings?" he asked in a shrill voice.
Inspector Hudson sighed and wished he had not answered the phone that morning.
It was a nightmare.

The dead silence around Elvira was driving her mad.
She had been sitting in this boring library for an hour studying all types of books on Egyptian art.
She had laid down the list of all the stolen relics next to the pile of books. She had been busy for the last hour gathering information and analysing the story of each piece.
If it carried on like this she would soon be able to take part in a quiz transmission on Egyptian culture. And there were still a lot of empty spaces on her list.
She still hadn't come across anything important. The stolen pieces were more or less valuable; some of the policy holders had

cheated a little on the value of their items. The company would be glad about that, but all in all, this terribly boring research had not led her anywhere.
The next item on her list was a scarab pendant which had been stolen from an opera singer.

ÜBUNG 265

*Übung 265: In welchem der folgenden Sätze muss ein Artikel stehen? (**the**, **a**, **an** oder nichts)*

1. Elvira is going on __________ holiday.
2. The police are still looking for __________ evidence.
3. This fingerprint is __________ proof that he did it.
4. Mr Hudson lives in __________ city of London.
5. Miss Paddington goes to __________ church on Sunday.
6. Lord Winterbutton is __________ member of the 'Egyptian Society'.
7. James is looking forward to seeing __________ good old Elvira again.

Elvira turned over the pages of the next volume and followed the index at the end of the book with her forefinger.
The pendant – a copy of a dung-beetle, revolting – was actually described in the book.
Bored to tears, the insurance agent skimmed through all the information she could find about the relic.
Age, function, estimated value, site of finding.
Blah, blah, blah.

Suddenly, she stopped short, and turned back the page.
These Egyptian names were real tongue twisters, but she had not been mistaken. Elvira picked up her list. For each stolen relic she had taken notes which she was comparing.
… it was right …
She closed the thick volume triumphantly.
A loud thump resounded through the library. A few visitors looked at her irritated. But Elvira took no notice whatsoever.
Inspector Hudson would be proud of her.
Regardless of the fact she was in a library, she picked up her mobile to phone him.
Then she remembered that the charming, old-fashioned man did not own one.
Elvira folded up her list and left the library without putting away the books she had consulted.
An elderly lady at a table nearby shook her head.

Übung 266: Beantworten Sie die Fragen zum Text!

ÜBUNG 266 !

1. Why had Sir Reginald been looking for Hudson all morning?

___

___

2. What was Elvira doing at the library?

___

___

3. Why do you think Hudson does not own a mobile phone?

___

___

James Hudson sat exhausted in his office. He felt as if he had just fought with a pack of hyenas. What had happened to the good old British press?

The reporters had tortured him for two hours with stupid questions. Two hours which he could have easily made better use of, if he had looked for clues.

Übung 267: Verbinden Sie die Bezeichnung der Tierarten mit dem richtigen 'collective noun'! Setzen Sie die Ziffer in das Kästchen!

1. swarm	☐ hyenas
2. pack	☐ geese
3. flight	☐ wolves
4. herd	☐ fish
5. pack	☐ birds
6. school	☐ bees
7. gaggle	☐ cattle

He was frustrated as he looked at the list of card owners who had free access to the British Museum. The list ranged from 'A' for Atwood, animal embalmer, to 'Z' such as Zin-Yang Wo, caretaker of the Chinese section.

Hopefully Elvira was having more luck, thought the inspector to himself.

And she was!

At that very moment the door opened and Elvira Elliot walked into the room, naturally without knocking.

"Elvira," exclaimed Hudson, "I was just thinking of you at the moment!"

"How nice, I'm happy to hear that," she laughed.

"I've had a terrible morning," sighed Hudson thinking of the frightfully noisy reporters.
"Oh, so have I," said Elvira recalling the terribly boring and silent library.
"Anyway," she continued, "I've come across something very interesting."
"Fire away!" said the inspector looking curiously at the scribbled piece of paper that Elvira was waving in the air.
Elvira looked around Hudson's tiny little office and sceptically observed the bare walls and the miserable cactuses, growing on the window sill.

Übung 268: Setzen Sie die Verben in der richtigen Zeitform ein!

Then she (1. pull) ______ up a chair and (2. sit) ______ next to Hudson.

The inspector (3. can) __________ smell her fruity perfume. He had to ask her what it was when the opportunity came up. In all probability it had an exotic name and (4. be) ______________ very expensive.

Then his attention focussed once more on important things. Elvira moved a couple of files aside and smoothed the sheet of paper on the desk.

"Well," she began, "I spent hours looking for information concerning the stolen Egyptian items. It was so boring.

But while I (5. do) ____________________ it I (6. come across) __________ something very interesting."

The inspector looked at her in suspense.

Elvira (7. take) _______ a long pause. She seemed to be enjoying the suspense.

"Over the last few months, various Egyptian relics (8. steal + passive) __________________________________ all over the world.

In England, Europe, the USA and even in Australia. And this list only contains the items which were reported missing."
"And?" asked Hudson impatiently.
"All the stolen objects have one thing in common. Not only did they all come from the same dynasty, but they were also all found in the same tomb chamber. And guess which one?"
Hudson hardly needed to guess.
"In Tut-Ench-Ra's tomb chamber!" he exclaimed.
"In the last resting place of the prince, whose mummy was removed last night. Exactly."
Hudson fell back in his chair.
That was more than a mere coincidence. Someone was after the ancient tomb treasures that were meant to accompany the prince on his journey to the other world. And had then taken the good old boy too.
Strange, very strange indeed!
All the more of a case for him.
He could feel his hunting fever rising. But he had to control it. This case, like any other, needed presence of mind and cool deduction.

Übung 269: Bilden Sie Sätze mit dem Komparativ!

Beispiel: The Thames/The Nile
The Nile is longer than the Thames.

1. Bentley/Ford (expensive)

____

2. clock/watch (big)

____

3. pyramid/sphinx (high)

____

4. village/town (large)

____

5. pond/lake (deep)

____

6. bush/tree (tall)

____

7. England/Germany (big)

____

Elvira looked at him expectantly.
"Fantastic work, Elvira. Absolutely super," said Hudson and proudly looked at her.
The insurance agent laughed happily.

"But what do we do now?" she asked.
"Good question," replied Hudson.
He meditated. If the thief was so interested in the old Egyptian prince, the mummy must have had something interesting itself. They needed more information. And this is why they had – and Scotland Yard had – a very good source of information.
The Internet.
"Let's see if the Web knows anything about our prince," said Hudson turning on the computer.
Of course, it wasn't the latest version, and the old box needed a few minutes before the homepage was loaded.
In the meantime, Hudson had had enough time to brew some tea and offer Elvira a cup.

ÜBUNG 270 !

Übung 270: Setzen Sie die Präpositionen ein!

1. The thief broke __________ the building and stole the painting.
2. While surfing on the Web, I came __________ some interesting information.
3. It didn't take him long to find __________ who the thief was.
4. Somebody was __________ all the relics found in the tomb.
5. The police are looking __________ a man with a limp.
6. Take good care __________ yourself!
7. Elvira has decided to give __________ drinking coffee.

The young woman was so excited, that she even gulped down the tea, without asking for coffee.

"I would never have thought you could use the Internet, James," she said dryly. "Isn't it too modern for you?"
"Well, I must admit that, at first, I was a bit at loss with it, but since then it has become an irreplaceable source of information for me."
Actually the inspector enjoyed surfing on the Web in his little free time, searching for up-to-date news on criminal investigation or reading reports on historical cases.
The computer's modem made a shrill noise and the connection had been made. Hudson had requested a permanent line months before, but the bureaucracy at the Yard was as slow as any other authority.
Especially when it meant spending money.
Hudson thought quickly and typed the name of Tut-Enk-Ra in the search bar of a search engine.
Both looked curiously at the screen.
Only seconds later a very long list with texts and websites containing the name of the prince appeared.
"Oh dear," cried Elvira. "Another endless list."

Übung 271: Schreiben Sie die Zahlen in Buchstaben!

1. 26 ____________________
2. 2nd ____________________
3. 1st ____________________
4. 30th ____________________
5. $^1/_2$ ____________________
6. 1933 ____________________

7. 853000 ________________________

8. 5.78 ________________________

9. $^{3}/_{4}$ ________________________

"Don't worry, Elvira. It looks worse than it actually is."
In fact, many entries were only references to online editions of various newspapers which contained articles on the missing mummy.
A quarter of an hour and two cups of tea later, Hudson and Elvira had found a very interesting source. It was the homepage of the 'Egyptian Society', of an exclusive London-based club, founded by the descendants of the members of old expeditions and Egyptologists.

ÜBUNG 272 !

Übung 272: Unterstreichen Sie all die Verben, die mit dem Sprechen zu tun haben!

"What a club of old gentlemen," murmured Elvira, when she saw a group photo of the club members. "And in all probability women aren't even allowed in the club."
"Ah, how peaceful it must be," said the inspector jokingly.
"James!" exclaimed Elvira laughing and threatened him with a rolled up file.
"I'm sorry, Elvira. But this 'Egyptian Society' looks to me like a very conservative hangout. And look here – there's a link to information concerning Tut-Enk-Ra!"
"Click it!" cried Elvira very excited.
The inspector moved the cursor on the name of the old Pharaoh and pressed the mouse button. Seconds later a new page opened.

A scanned, yellowed photo was displayed. It showed a man in his thirties, standing proudly in front of the entrance to an Egyptian tomb chamber.

The large metal door behind him had been broken open with rudimentary tools. The methods used by archaeologists then were rather basic, thought Hudson.

"Who is this good-looking chap?" asked Elvira.

Hudson read the caption underneath.

"Lord Douglas Winterbutton, discoverer of Tut-Enk-Ra's tomb chamber, 1903"

By the looks of it, the lord had not hesitated at all before breaking into the Pharaoh's tomb.

"Rather extreme. But the fellow isn't bad looking at all."

Hudson had to admit that Lord Winterbutton had a really attractive face. If he had not been an archaeologist, he could have easily made a career as a film star. But that was not fitting for a lord. Not in those days.

Übung 273: Welche Wörter gehören in die Lücke?
(still, yet, any more/any longer, no longer)

1. It's 10 pm and Hudson is ____________ at work.
2. Has it stopped drizzling ____________?
3. She ____________ hasn't written to me.
4. Mr Johnson doesn't work here __________. He left a week ago.
5. He has been promoted. He is ____________ an inspector.
6. Harry lost his job last year and he is __________ unemployed.

Hudson cleared his throat and read the short text under the photo out loud.

"After the expedition was nearly declared a fiasco, Lord Douglas Winterbutton discovered by chance in 1903 the long sought tomb of the Pharaoh Tut-Enk-Ra.
Most of the relics found inside the chamber are privately owned, mainly by the Winterbutton family.
The mummy of the Pharaoh was soon donated to the British Museum."

"How generous," sneered Elvira. "They took the treasures home and donated the plundered mummy to the British Museum in London."
Hudson nodded. "That's how things went then. The British Empire considered nearly the whole world as its treasure chamber. Thank goodness things have changed since then."
"Yes, and …," Elvira wanted to add her opinion, but she noticed that Hudson was too busy reading her list.
"What are you looking for, James?" she asked.
James answered without looking up.
"Please see if Lord Winterbutton is on my list," said Hudson with a thoughtful glance."
"Sure," Elvira replied and skimmed through the list.
"Yes, here he is," she said a few seconds later. "Lord Stephen Winterbutton is a member of the museum's board of directors and has an access card."
"Interesting," murmured Hudson. "And … you're sure, he's not on your list."
Elvira looked at him questioningly.

Übung 274: Welches Verb gehört zu welchem Objekt? Setzen Sie die richtige Ziffer ein!

ÜBUNG 274 !

1.	fill in	☐ clothes in a shop
2.	put away	☐ children
3.	sort out	☐ information
4.	find out	☐ a new idea
5.	try on	☐ a mess
6.	try out	☐ clothes in a cupboard
7.	bring up	☐ a form
8.	take back	☐ a meeting to another time
9.	put off	☐ something you don't want
10.	clear up	☐ a fire
11.	put out	☐ a problem

"That could mean, my dear, that we have our first lead."
Elvira shrugged her shoulders.
"I don't understand. There's nothing concerning Lord Winterbutton."

Übung 275: Lesen Sie weiter und finden Sie ein sinnvolles Synonym!

ÜBUNG 275 !

"Exactly," (1. smiled) ___________ Hudson. "Just think. All the stolen items come from Tut-Enk-Ra's death chamber. According to the Internet, Lord Winterbutton (2. owns) ___________ one of the largest collections of the Pharaoh's (3. antiquities) ___________."
"And … yet, none of his items have been reported missing,"

exclaimed Elvira pensively. "Are you sure?"

"Yes. If the thief is only after treasures from Tut-Enk-Ra's (4. tomb) ________________, then you'd think that he would have raided the largest existing collection."

"Perhaps the (5. aristocrat's) ______________________ house is too well secured," suggested Elvira. "Or the thief is keeping the best items for last."

Hudson rubbed his chin thoughtfully. "But there is another possibility. Lord Winterbutton is after all one of the people who have an access card. And therefore is also a suspect. Of course it could all be a (6. coincidence) ____________ – but I don't believe in coincidences. Not in such big ones, anyway."

Elvira (7. exhaled) ____________ sharply.

"Do you mean that Lord Winterbutton has set his heart on completing his collection? Legally or illegally?"

Hudson shrugged his shoulders.

"Maybe, Elvira. There's no proof, but Lord Winterbutton is certainly at the top of the list of the people whom we need to speak to."

"Another list," sighed Elvira. However, she could not hide her thirst for action.

Inspector Hudson picked up the phone and dialled the information number to get Lord Winterbutton's number.

The aristocrat lived in a villa not far from the old and famous Tower of London.

Übung 276: Welche Relativpronomen gehören in die Lücke? Oder bleiben Lücken leer?

1. I received a phone-call this morning __________ really upset me.
2. I recently visited the town __________ Al Capone was born.
3. Apparently she'd lost all her money gambling, __________ really annoyed him.
4. The people __________ used to live next-door have moved to Scotland.
5. Tom, ______________ parents live in London, is Hudson's colleague.
6. She told me a story __________ I found hard to believe.
7. The year __________ I was born, man went to the moon.
8. Miss Paddington cooked a meal __________ tasted delicious.

Hudson took down the number and dialled it, without taking any notice of Elvira who was amused by the old-fashioned telephone. It rang at least a dozen times, before someone picked up the receiver.

A nasal voice answered.

"Lord Winterbutton's residence."

The inspector smiled. He would have been surprised if the lord had answered the phone personally.

"Good afternoon," he said, "I would like to speak to Lord Winterbutton. My name is Inspector James Hudson from Scotland Yard."

Übung 277: Hat das englische Idiom wirklich die gleiche Bedeutung? Markieren Sie: richtig ✓ falsch –

1. to ape someone – jemanden nachäffen
2. to swallow the bitter pill – in den sauren Apfel beißen
3. to have a bee in one's bonnet – eine Eselsbrücke bauen
4. to be on tenterhooks – gespannt sein
5. to be hot on someone's trail – Blut und Wasser schwitzen
6. to be after something – es auf etwas abgesehen haben
7. the last resting place – die letzte Ruhestätte

At the other end there was a small pause. That was not unusual. Most people were surprised when an officer from the legendary London Metropolitan Police phoned them.

"May I hear why?" asked the voice at the other end at last.

"I would like to tell Lord Winterbutton personally. Is he available?"

"I'm sorry, sir. But the lord is in a club at the moment, in London City."

"Oh, and what club would that be, may I ask?"

The voice at the other end answered: "Lord Winterbutton is at the Egyptian Society at the moment. Shall I give him a message when he comes home, sir?"

"That won't be necessary," replied Hudson. "I think we'll look for Lord Winterbutton at the club. May I ask with whom I have had the pleasure of speaking?"

"Of course, sir. My name is George and I'm Lord Winterbutton's butler."

"I thought so. Have a good day, sir."

Hudson put the receiver down. Elvira had listened to the conversation on the loudspeaker. She threw back her head and held her nose, so that her voice sounded like the nasal sound of the butler's. "I'm George the butler of the lord!" She had to laugh. "Oh dear, what a snob."

Übung 278: Geben Sie die richtigen Verbformen (im Passiv oder Aktiv) an!

New York police (1. announce) ____________ just ____________ that five paintings by Picasso (2. steal) ____________ from the Guggenheim Museum. The paintings (3. value) ____________ by experts at 5 million dollars. Police believe that they (4. take) ____________ early on Saturday evening, but for some reason the museums burglar alarm (5. not go off) ____________________. And the theft (6. not discover) ________________________ until Monday morning. No clues (7. find) ________________________ so far at the scene of the crime.

Hudson grinned and went to get his coat.
"Are you ready, Elvira? In all probability, the butler will have already informed his employer that Scotland Yard wants to speak to him. That is if the club allows modern means of communication like telephones."
But Elvira was looking at the computer screen.
She had found another interesting link on the homepage of the Egyptian Society.

Übung 279: Wählen Sie die richtige Form aus und kreuzen Sie sie an!

1. Hudson stopped
   a) ☐ to drink coffee when he was 30.
   b) ☐ drink coffee when he was 30.
   c) ☐ drinking coffee when he was 30.

2. Elvira and Hudson stopped
   a) ☐ having coffee in the café.
   b) ☐ to have coffee in the café.
   c) ☐ for having coffee in the café.

3. He tried
   a) ☐ to tell her the truth about the murder.
   b) ☐ to say her the truth about the murder.
   c) ☐ tell her truth about the murder.

4. The police let him
   a) ☐ to go after interrogating him.
   b) ☐ go after interrogating him.
   c) ☐ going after interrogating him.

5. She couldn't
   a) ☐ helping him on the case.
   b) ☐ help him on the case.
   c) ☐ to help him on the case.

6. Hudson enjoyed
   a) ☐ to work for Scotland Yard.
   b) ☐ work for Scotland Yard.
   c) ☐ working for Scotland Yard.

7. Elvira said she wouldn't mind
   a) ☐ to stay in the car.
   b) ☐ staying in the car.
   c) ☐ stay in the car.

"Just a second, James. This could be very interesting. I'll just print it out quickly, if you don't mind. Since I'm not allowed to enter this boring club, I need something to read to kill time."
Elvira pressed the mouse button and the printer in the corner of the office began to rattle.
The doorkeeper of the 'Egyptian Society' was not particularly impressed by the Bentley's arrival in front of the club. Of course, during his years as a porter he had seen many Bentleys park there, but none of them had been as old as this one.

Übung 280: Unterstreichen Sie die direkte Rede!

Inspector Hudson rolled down the window and smiled when he saw the porter's startled look.
"Good afternoon, old chap," he called, "where can I park my car, please?"
The porter had quickly recovered.
"I'm sorry sir, the club and its parking places are for members only."
"Arrogant pig!" whispered Elvira from the passenger seat. Hudson ignored her comment. He reached into the pocket of his coat and took out his official badge.
"I don't have a member's card, but perhaps this will open the door to your respectable rooms."
The porter swallowed hard.

"Scotland Yard? I'm very sorry, sir. I didn't know. You may park directly behind the building in the guests' parking place."
The inspector thanked the man and drove his car around the old Victorian building.
As promised, the building's courtyard housed a row of wide parking places for guests. Obviously most of the visitors came in wide limousines.
"Now, Elvira," said Hudson regretfully, "I'm afraid the authority of my badge is not enough to get you into the club as well."

Übung 281: Verwandeln Sie die Sätze in die indirekte Rede!

1. "Where can I park my car, please?" James asked where ______

   ____.

2. "I don't have a member's card." James said ______________

   ____.

3. "Perhaps my badge will let me in." James said ____________

   ____.

4. "You may park behind the building." The porter said _______

   ____.

5. "I'll read Lord Winterbutton's diary." Elvira said _________

   ____.

6. "You promised to rest, James." Miss Paddington said ______

   ____.

7. “What are you looking for James?” Elvira asked James ______ ____.

Elvira shook her head.
“You must know that clubs which forbid women to enter are against the law, Mr Inspector?” she said smiling.
Hudson frowned. He believed he had just been informed of a relatively new constitutional ruling.
“Perhaps,” he said all the same, “there’s no point in getting the gentlemen angry. It would be much wiser if you simply waited for me in the car. It won’t take long.”
“Of course, James,” replied Elvira, “go alone. You’re right. Anyway, I brought myself something to read.”
The insurance agent picked up her hand bag where she had put the printed pages. Inspector Hudson said good-bye and got out the old Bentley.

Übung 282: Welches Wort passt in die Lücke?
(alibi, clue, evidence, red herring, inspector, suspects, witness)

1. A ____________ is something that helps to solve a mystery or problem.
2. A ____________ is a false lead that throws the investigator off track.
3. An ____________ is the proof of an accused person of not having been at the scene of crime.

4. A ___________ is a person who has personal knowledge about the crime.
5. An ___________ is an investigator or detective.
6. ___________ is something that tends to prove who committed the crime.
7. ___________ are people who appear to have a motive to have committed the crime.

Elvira sighed and took the printed Internet pages out of her bag. They were the facsimile of the diary of Sir Douglas Winterbutton, the discoverer of Tut-Enk-Ra's grave. She began reading the elegantly written daily entries. After a few minutes she had forgotten the rain pattering on the Bentley's windscreen.

! ÜBUNG 283

Übung 283: Unterstreichen Sie die Synonyme der Wörter in Klammern! ***(surrender, fantasy, morale, hint, caught, puzzled, drugs, doubters)***

12th July 1903
"The heat is unbearable. I would do anything for a few drops of cool, English rain. We have been crossing the desert for days now, without even a trace of Tut-Enk-Ra's pyramid.
I'm starting to believe that the sceptics in London were right and that this mysterious Pharaoh is only a product of the imagination, a legend. A couple of the expedition members are already insisting we give up the search. But I don't want to give up yet."

13th July 1903
"The troop's spirits are getting lower and lower. Two of the carriers have picked up an unknown fever. Doctor Fauntleroy, the expedition's physician, is perplexed. None of the medication seems to be helping.
And I myself feel like giving up. But I do not want to give the sceptics in London that satisfaction."

14th July 1903
"What a day!
This morning, Achmed, our guide, came across a strange, pointed stone in the middle of the desert. At first, we did not give the finding much importance, but then my curiosity took over. I made the men dig up the stone, which to our surprise took longer and longer.
And then I realized that it wasn't just a stone in the desert, but the broken tip of a small pyramid, which had been covered by desert sand over the centuries.
Tut-Enk-Ra's Pyramid.
I've found it!"

Übung 284: Setzen Sie ***been*** *oder* ***gone*** *in die Lücke ein!*

1. "Where's Hudson?" "He's ___________ into the club."
2. Where has Elvira ___________ – she's so brown?
3. I've never ___________ to London, but I'd like to go.
4. "Are you going to the cinema this afternoon?" "No, I've already ___________."

5. "Where's Tom these days?" "Didn't you know? He's ______ ________ to another company."

6. "When's your holiday Elvira?" "I've already ______________. I went to Europe."

7. "Can I speak to Lord Winterbutton, please?" "I'm afraid he's ___________ to the club. Can I take a message?"

15th July 1903

"It is very difficult for me to write. My hands are trembling for excitement and also because of the unknown fever which I have also caught.

But that doesn't matter now. This afternoon we found the entrance to the inside of the pyramid. A narrow passageway leads directly to the tomb which is closed by a metal door. The door is covered in hieroglyphs. But, luckily, our guide was able to decipher some of them.

It seems to be a warning. Whoever disturbs the Pharaoh's last resting place shall be put under a curse, which will afflict his children and his children's children.

What nonsense.

Naturally I broke down the door immediately. And I did not allow anyone to enter the grave before me.

Incredible treasures glowed in the light of my torch. I shall pack them up carefully and ship them to London.

My return home will be triumphant!

I can hardly wait to embrace my beloved Mary and to cover her with the ancient treasures like a queen!

But now I have to end today's entry. The doctor ordered me to rest, so that I may recover from the fever.
Tomorrow's another day."

Übung 285: Bilden Sie mit Hilfe eines Partizips aus zwei Sätzen einen!

ÜBUNG 285 !

1. I heard her. She whispered all through the night.
I heard her whispering all through the night.

2. Hudson sits in his bureau. He listens to the radio.

____

3. Elvira finds out a lot. She reads the books.

____

4. Miss Paddington came into the kitchen. She wanted to cook for dinner.

____

5. The man walks away. He looks a little pale.

____

Elvira put down the last page of the diary. What a story.
In the meantime, Inspector Hudson had entered the time-honoured rooms of the 'Egyptian Society'.
The distinct smell of leather chairs, old books and pipe smoke hit him.
This club was the quintessence of English tradition.
Hudson went into the entrance hall.

He was immediately greeted by a butler, who managed to cover the distance between them in record time.
"Can I help you?" he asked.
"Yes, actually," answered Hudson. "My name is Hudson, from Scotland Yard. I would like to speak to Lord Winterbutton."
"Of course, sir. But I'm not sure he's here. Please follow me to the club room."

ÜBUNG 286 !

Übung 286: Unterstreichen Sie alle Präpositionen mit lokaler Bedeutung!

"Thank you," replied Hudson and followed the uniformed man. The entrance hall had been impressing enough, but this room was even more luxurious. An enormous Indian carpet stretched from one end of the room to the other. The walls were covered with oak book shelves holding without doubt thousands of books.
Hudson had seen city libraries with less volumes. All around the room there were very old and terribly comfortable-looking leather armchairs. Next to each one was a small table where an ashtray or a glass of sherry could be placed.
And despite the early hour, the club was already frequented by quite a few members.
There were thick clouds of smoke in the air.
A few visitors were sitting in the armchairs reading the newspaper, others were reading books or conversing in hushed tones.
Once in a while a hearty laugh rang through the room.

The butler asked Inspector Hudson to wait a moment.
Then he left to search for Lord Winterbutton.
Hudson watched amused as the butler carefully peered over

the armrests of the chairs to see who was behind the newspaper. He did not want to disturb the guests in any way.
Eventually he came back.
"I'm sorry sir. But it looks as if Lord Winterbutton is not present."
He looked as if he considered the circumstance as a personal defeat.

Übung 287: Unterstreichen Sie das passende Wort!

ÜBUNG 287 !

1. He wasted/earned all his money betting on the horses.
2. Elvira is very hard up/well-off. She's just bought herself a sports car.
3. If only Lord Winterbutton had left him something in his will/savings.
4. His grandfather keeps all his money in a cash dispenser/safe under the bed.
5. Hudson's salary/wages is paid into his bank account every month.
6. A penny is an English coin/currency.
7. I'm bankrupt/broke. Can you lend me a couple of pounds until the end of the month.

"Don't worry," said Hudson and was about to leave when an elderly man came up to him.
"Are you looking for the young Lord Winterbutton?" asked the man in a croaking voice.
Hudson looked at the old man. He was haggard and had a very pronounced hooked nose. A few wisps of white hair lay in a disorderly manner on an otherwise bald head. The man was so curved, he reminded Hudson of a giant question mark on legs.
"Well, yes," replied Hudson a little surprised.

The butler left with a slight bow. Hudson had a feeling that he was in a hurry to get away.

ÜBUNG 288 !

Übung 288: Verwandeln Sie das Adjektiv in ein Adverb!

1. perfect ____________________
2. careful ____________________
3. heavy ____________________
4. good ____________________
5. fast ____________________
6. hard ____________________
7. late ____________________

"Yes, the fellow is no longer here," the old man croaked.
"Yes, the butler has already told me so. I'll try coming again when Winterbutton is here."
"Good idea," said the old man, "but don't wait too long before paying him a visit, ha ha."
The old man's laugh sounded more like a crow.
Hudson frowned. "What do you mean by that?"
"Well," answered the old man with a nearly sorrowful gesture, "it's nearly Stephen's birthday. He's turning thirty-three, poor fellow."
Hudson shook his head irritated.
"I don't quite understand, Mister –?"
"Cornwall," said the man, "Ebenezer Cornwall."
Hudson shook the man's hand. His skin was very thin, but his handshake was surprisingly strong.

"Pleased to meet you, sir. My name is James Hudson, from Scotland Yard."
Mr Cornwall smiled.

Übung 289: Finden Sie das Gegenteil für die Wörter in Klammern!

"I see. From Scotland Yard. Stephen hasn't been up to mischief, has he. If you want to charge him with (1. nothing) __________, then you'd better (2. take your time) __________."

Mr Cornwall laughed in his ugly way again. A few of the other guests turned around surprised. The old man did not seem to notice. Another allusion, thought Hudson. What did this all mean.

It would be (3. worst) __________ to be (4. indirect) __________ __________ with the old man and ask him what he meant.

"Sir, would you be (5. rude) ______________ enough to tell me exactly what you mean?"

Mr Cornwall studied Hudson.

"You don't know anything, do you?"

Then he said: "Ah, how could you? Here at the club everyone has heard the story. And I leave this place so (6. often) __________, I sometimes forget there's a (7. unreal) ______________ world (8. inside) __________ with cable TV, notebooks, satellites and those small, cordless phones, uhhm, what are they called …?"

"Mobile phones," said Hudson laughing at the old man.

"Yes of course. Those little pests."

The inspector nodded in (9. disagreement) __________. "I have to agree with you there. But you were telling me about what you meant with …"

The old man (10. put down) __________ his bushy eyebrows. "Was I? Oh yes. I go off track sometimes."

Hudson sighed. He hoped he would never need Mr Cornwall as a witness.
Mr Cornwall pointed at two free armchairs next to each other in the corner of the room.
"Let's sit down," he said, "my rheumatism is giving me trouble."
Hudson followed the old man to the armchairs, which not only looked comfortable.

! ÜBUNG 290

Übung 290: Setzen Sie das richtige Adverb/Adjektiv in die Lücke ein! ***(hard, hardly, late, lately, good, well)***

1. Your writing is terrible. I can __________ read it.
2. Elvira works very __________.
3. How much did she eat? __________ anything.
4. She speaks English very __________.

5. The company's financial situation is not very ____________ at the moment.

6. Have you seen Tom ____________?

7. I think he was fired because he was always ________ for work.

Mr Cornwall waved at the butler. A few seconds later he brought a decanter of sherry and two glasses. Mr Cornwall obviously ordered this often.
The old man poured himself a glass and sipped it with pleasure.
"Ah, this invigorates heart and soul. Help yourself to one, old friend."
Hudson refused politely.
"No, thank you. It's a bit too early for me. No alcohol before sunset."
The old man replied: "Does that mean you stay thirsty in the summer?"
The inspector looked at his watch meaningfully. Elvira was still waiting outside in the car. And patience was not a virtue she possessed.
Hudson was afraid she would burst into the club any moment.
Mr Cornwall saw him do this and laughed.

Übung 291: Übersetzen Sie folgende Sätze!

ÜBUNG 291 !

1. Inzwischen hatte Hudson genug Zeit gehabt, um einen Tee zu kochen und Elvira eine Tasse zu servieren.

____

____

2. Lord Douglas Winterbutton entdeckte im Juli 1903 durch einen Zufall die Grabkammer des Pharaos Tut-Ench-Ra.

3. Es läutete mindestens ein Dutzend Mal, bevor jemand am anderen Ende der Leitung abhob.

4. Inspector Hudson verabschiedete sich und stieg aus dem Wagen.

5. Ein paar der anderen Gäste blickten sich überrascht um.

6. Mister Cornwall deutete auf zwei freie Sessel, die in einer Ecke des Saales beieinander standen.

7. Geduld war eine Tugend, die Elvira ganz sicher nicht besaß.

“I see. You’re in a hurry. Of course. Can’t keep crime waiting, can you? So what was I saying?”
“I’m not sure,” answered Hudson patiently, “but you made some allusions in which you said that Lord Winterbutton might pass away soon.”
“Oh yes.” The old man seemed nearly pleased. He probably didn’t find that many people to talk to at the club.
Then he cleared his throat and looked ahead to concentrate.
Hopefully, he wouldn’t start from Adam and Eve thought Hudson.
He thought of Elvira again sitting in the car.

Übung 292: Unterstreichen Sie die Verben!

“It all began in the summer of 1903,” started Mr Cornwall. “At that time the British Empire was world power. Lord Douglas Winterbutton was heading an expedition which aimed at finding the grave of the legendary Tut-Enk-Ra. Nobody knew for sure then if the Pharaoh really had existed or if he was just a myth.
Many of his contemporaries thought he was a crazy man who would only obtain one thing with the expedition: to squander his family’s considerable patrimony. And many regarded him as an irresponsible, since he was married to a beautiful woman who was expecting his child.
But the lord was very stubborn and took the chance. Such an expedition was a real adventure in those days. All the equipment had to be transported on camels and there were no satellite photos of the desert to help archaeologists find the tombs.

Anyhow, the expedition seemed to be an absolute fiasco. Winterbutton was on the point of becoming the laughingstock of the

aristocracy, because he was chasing a ghost through the desert. But perhaps you already know how it ended. After many weeks the lord discovered the pyramid by chance.
Rash as he was, he broke down the door there and then. He ignored the curse that Tut-Enk-Ra was supposed to have made. Anyone who disturbed the Pharaoh's tomb would have to pay dearly for it. And so would his descendants."
"A veritable biblical curse," added Inspector Hudson.
"In any case. Foolish superstition, is what we'd call it today. And that's what Lord Winterbutton also thought. He had the whole tomb emptied and took the cache to his estate in England. Of course, that wasn't completely legal. But those were turbulent times and people had other things to worry about.
The Winterbutton family were anything but hard up and the little Egyptian adventure had not increased family's wealth particularly. At the time the Winterbuttons were one of the richest families in the country. Only later during the First World War were they forced to sell a few Egyptian relics to collectors from all over the world.
What a pity that Douglas Winterbutton did not benefit from it," said Mr Cornwall.

! ÜBUNG 293

Übung 293: Welches Wort ist das „schwarze Schaf"?

1. disease, fever, hunger, illness ______________
2. son, grandson, aunt, friend ______________
3. throat, dizzy, forehead, eyebrow ______________
4. whirlwind, tornado, hurricane, widow ______________

5. crow, penguin, sparrow, seagull ____________________

6. bumper, review mirror, dashboard, dish ____________________

7. story, narration, author, fable ____________________

The old man cleared his throat and sipped some sherry.
"Excuse me, my throat is dry from this dusty story."
Mr Cornwall cleared his throat again and continued his narration. Or rather he wanted to continue but apparently had lost the thread.
"Hmm, where was I?" he asked the inspector.
"You were saying that Lord Winterbutton did not benefit from the treasures he found."
"That's right. It appears that Tut-Enk-Ra's curse was more than a trick to mislead superstitious tomb raiders. Shortly after opening the Pharaoh's tomb, Lord Winterbutton caught a mysterious fever which got worse every day. The expedition's doctor was powerless. Soon the aristocrat was but a shadow of his former self and he died during the journey home. Exactly on his thirty-third birthday. A few months later his widow bore a son who would never see his father."
The inspector nodded.

Übung 294: Welche Sätze sind richtig?
Markieren Sie: richtig ✓ falsch –

ÜBUNG 294 !

1. When Hudson entered the club a few visitors were sitting on stools speaking very loudly.
2. The descendants of Lord Winterbutton were his grandfather and his great grandfather.
3. Lord Winterbutton nearly gave up his search for the pyramid.

4. The expeditioners saw a cave in the desert which turned out to be the tomb.
5. The Winterbutton family was wealthy.
6. Lord Winterbutton entered the tomb after his helpers.
7. Hudson did not believe in the curse.

"What a tragic story, but surely a coincidence. In all likelihood, the lord had caught a tropical disease which would have killed him – with or without the curse."
The old man gave Hudson a penetrating look.
"It's possible, my friend, possible. But how do you explain then that his son, too, died on his thirty-third birthday and thirty-three years later his grandson?"
Hudson looked at the man silently. That was a very strong coincidence. And as he had told Elvira earlier on, he did not believe in coincidences. But, that would imply that he believed in a curse made thousands of years before by the Pharaoh.
And this thought pleased him even less.

ÜBUNG 295 !

Übung 295: Setzen Sie die Verben in der passenden Form (first conditional) ein!

1. If you (not live) *did not live* so far away, we *would visit* you more often.
2. Sir Arthur (not be) ____________ so fat, if he (eat) ____________ less.
3. If Hudson (not have to work) ____________ tomorrow, he (can

meet) ____________ Elvira.

4. This coffee (taste) ____________ better, if it (have) ____________ more sugar.

5. Hudson (know) ____________ who the thief is, if he (have) ____________ more clues.

6. If I (be) __________ rich, I (live) __________ near Hyde Park.

7. Hudson (buy) ____________ a new Bentley, if he (earn) ____________ more money.

8. If you (listen) ______________ to me, you (make) ______________ no mistakes.

Inspector Hudson thanked Mr Cornwall and stood up.
He noticed that he was a little dizzy, although he had not even touched the sherry.
Should he believe the old man's story? How could one Winterbutton die after the other on their thirty-third birthday because of a Pharaoh's curse? Or was there another darker explanation?
"Hmm," there was a little cough behind him, "excuse me, but I could not help overhearing your conversation."
Hudson turned around. A small rounded man in a dark suit stood before him. His jacket looked very expensive, but it pulled very dangerously across his big belly.
"Yes?" answered Hudson curiously. He had been so involved in Mr Cornwall's narration that he had not noticed the man at all. With his short legs and beak nose, the stranger reminded him of a penguin.

Übung 296: Steigern Sie die folgenden Adjektive!

1.	big	______	______
2.	nervous	______	______
3.	thirsty	______	______
4.	polite	______	______
5.	much	______	______
6.	good	______	______
7.	quiet	______	______
8.	far	______	______
9.	lucky	______	______
10.	careful	______	______

"My name is Arthur Cobblepot. Sir Arthur Cobblepot."
The man meaningfully stressed the word sir.
"I am, by the way, the Winterbutton family's lawyer. We have been representing the Winterbuttons for generations. May I ask why you are so interested in our client's story?"
"My name is James Hudson. Inspector James Hudson, from Scotland Yard. As you probably already know, this morning Tut-Enk-Ra's mummy was found missing from the British Museum. And as I have just found out, there is a special link between the Winterbutton family and the mummy."
Cobblepot nodded. "Yes, a tragic old story, in fact. But you can't really see a connection between the missing mummy and my client, Lord Stephen Winterbutton?"

The lawyer's question sounded more like a threat than a simple enquiry. Hudson jerked.

*Übung 297: Formulieren Sie Sätze mit dem Verb **wish**!*

1. Elvira can't give up drinking coffee. She wishes

   she could stop.

2. Hudson isn't here (and I need him). I wish

   ____

3. I live in London (and I hate London). I wish

   ____

4. Hudson has an old Bentley. He wishes

   ____

5. Lord Winterbutton is turning thirty-three soon. He wishes

   ____

6. Sir Cobblepot is short and fat. He wishes

   ____

7. I wish I (know) ______________ how this book ends.

"Of course not," said the inspector. "But, after all, many of Tut-Enk-Ra's relics are owned by the Winterbuttons. Therefore I would like to consult Lord Winterbutton, for his expert advice."
The lawyer gave Hudson a penetrating look with his bird eyes.
"I see. I'm not sure if it is the right time. Lord Stephen is not

feeling very well at the moment. I saw him a little while ago and he looked rather unwell."

A croaking laugh came from the leather armchair next to Hudson. Mr Cornwall was watching the lawyer.

"He isn't feeling well, is he? So soon before his thirty-third birthday? What a coincidence. I told you inspector!"

Sir Arthur looked at the old man annoyed. "Please mind your own business, Cornwall. You should be ashamed of yourself for telling such old wives' tales."

For a moment Hudson feared the two men would fly at each other. The old crow against the fat penguin. What a scene. But the old man's reaction was only to laugh and to sip his sherry.

The lawyer shook his head, took a business card out of his pocket and gave it to the inspector.

ÜBUNG 298 !

Übung 298: Welches Wort hat die stärkere Bedeutung? Kreuzen Sie an!

1.	☐ angry	☐ annoyed
2.	☐ smile	☐ beam
3.	☐ hot	☐ boiling
4.	☐ exhausted	☐ tired
5.	☐ speak	☐ shout
6.	☐ terrified	☐ afraid
7.	☐ discuss	☐ argue

"Here is my card. As I said, my family's firm represents the Winterbuttons in all legal matters. Furthermore we are also their estate administrators. If you want to speak to Lord Winterbutton, I have to ask you to contact me first."

"Of course sir. I'll contact you in the next few days."
"Thank you, inspector, and have a nice day."
Having said this, Sir Arthur turned and left the room.
He waggled just like a penguin, thought Hudson amused.
But his smile did not last long. Hudson recalled what Cobblepot had said: it seemed that the present Lord Winterbutton was also ill. Shortly before his thirty-third birthday.
The whole story was becoming more and more mysterious.

Miss Paddington put a steaming cup of tea on the table in front of Hudson. "Thanks a lot," said Hudson smiling.
"You looked exhausted, James," said Miss Paddington, "a nice cup of Earl Grey is just what you need."
Hudson nodded. He really was tired. His planned 'day off' had turned out to be the most tiring day of the week. After his conversation with Cobblepot and Mr Cornwall, he had gone back to his car where Elvira was waiting impatiently. Last of all, he had accompanied the young insurance agent home. On the way there, the two had exchanged their stories. Elvira told Hudson of the former Lord Winterbutton's diary and Hudson completed the story with the information he had gathered from Mr Cornwall. Then he had left Elvira at her flat and had gone immediately home.

Übung 299: Finden und unterstreichen Sie die Synonyme der Wörter in Klammern! ***(thin, smiling, appreciatively, lounge, start again, presently, hollow)***

ÜBUNG 299 !

He had worked enough for today.
"Shall I prepare you a couple of sandwiches, James?" asked Miss Paddington. "You probably haven't eaten anything the whole day.

You'll become skin and bones."
James thought about it. He had, in fact, forgotten to eat today. And only now that Miss Paddington had mentioned it, did he feel how empty his stomach was.
"Oh that would be so nice of you, my dear," he said gratefully.
Beaming, his housekeeper left the living room. Before long he heard the lady pottering about in the kitchen. He closed his eyes sleepily. And relaxing his shoulders, resumed the game he had been playing in the early morning.

He tried to guess what Miss Paddington was doing from the noises she made. A soft plucking noise indicated that she was preparing the lettuce leaves. Then there was the banging of the bread box, followed by the rhythmic noise of a knife-blade on wood. She was probably slicing the onions or tomatoes. Hudson's mouth watered. At least the day would have a peaceful finale. He breathed in deeply and felt pleasantly tired. But, then the doorbell rang. Hudson jumped out of his chair. In the kitchen Miss Paddington dropped the knife from the fright she got. "Who can it be so late in the evening?" she called. "People simply don't have good manners any more!" The inspector took a deep breath while Miss Paddington went to the door.

ÜBUNG 300 !

Übung 300: Verbinden Sie die Wörter, um Komposita zu bilden! Setzen Sie die richtige Ziffer ein!

1. driving	☐ estate
2. steering	☐ glasses
3. insurance	☐ card
4. air	☐ licence
5. birthday	☐ lights

6. motor	☐ agent
7. country	☐ port
8. sun	☐ way
9. head	☐ wheel

"It is not good manners to ring on somebody's door so late!" he heard her say in the entrance.
But then her tone changed and became friendlier all of a sudden.
"Oh it's you. That's another matter. Please come in deary!"
The inspector was curious. "It's you"? "Deary"?
Who could it be?
A few seconds later his question was answered.
Elvira Elliot stormed into the room, as excited and animated as usual.

Übung 301: Übersetzen Sie die Sätze!
Achten Sie dabei auf die Modalverben!

1. Er musste ziemlich oft ins Ausland fahren.

____

2. Die Familie Winterbutton hatte Pech gehabt.

____

3. Der Dieb muss es getan haben.

____

4. Hudson darf im Dienst nicht trinken.

____

"James!" she shouted, without bothering to say hello. "Are you ready?"
"Ready? For what? And a good evening to you too!"
Elvira waved her hand.
"OK, OK, good evening. Come on, it's already late."
The inspector shook his head.
"But, what is wrong?"
"Well, you don't want to idle away the evening, do you? While the mummy is up to its tricks. Or at least its curse is. I thought we could go to Lord Winterbutton and see how the fellow is."
"At this hour?" asked Hudson. "By the time we get there it'll be midnight!"
"All the better," replied Elvira. "Surprise visits have the best results."
The inspector rolled his eyes and sighed. It was no good contradicting Elvira. It would be like trying to stop a whirlwind. James got up from his armchair and went to get his coat.

ÜBUNG 302 !

Übung 302: Unterstreichen Sie Adverbien and Adjektive!

Inspector Hudson fastened his seat-belt carefully.
Elvira raced through the bends on the country road, without ever taking her foot off the accelerator. The centrifugal force pushed Hudson against the passenger's door. It was like being on a roller coaster.
"Could you please drive a little more slowly, Elvira?" he said gruffly.
Elvira shook her head. "I'm not a fast driver, James, but a sporty one."
"Then please be unsporty."

The insurance agent laughed and changed into a slower gear.
"As you wish, James."
The inspector breathed out. Luckily Winterbutton's estate was not far away and they would probably get there safe and sound. Elvira had chosen the wrong profession. She should have been a racing driver. She took the next curve at a more moderate pace.
"Do you really believe there's a curse, James?" she asked, looking at him curiously. Hudson pointed at the road.
"I would appreciate it if you kept your eyes on the road. And no, I don't believe in supernatural curses, black magic and the likes."

Übung 303: Setzen Sie die Verben in der passenden Verbform ein.

ÜBUNG 303

1. If Hudson *had known* Sir Reginald was on the phone, he (not answer) ________________.
2. If Elvira (not drive) ________________ so fast, Hudson (not get) ________________ car sick.
3. If Lord Winterbutton (give) ________________ them an appointment, they (not go) ________________ to his home so late.
4. If Sir Douglas Winterbutton (be) ________________ poor, he (not go) ________________ on the expedition.
5. If Elvira (not follow) ________________ Hudson, he (not find out) ________________ about the other thefts.

6. If Sir Douglas Winterbutton (not go) ________________ to the desert, he (not die) ________________ of a fever.

"But it can't be a coincidence that all the Winterbuttons die on their thirty-third birthday. There must be something behind it all."
"Exactly," agreed Hudson. "Something we are going to find out!"
"Perhaps Lord Winterbutton can help us."
"That's if he lets us in at this time of the night," replied the inspector and looked at the digital clock on the dashboard. It was already 11 o'clock.
"Oh, I'm sure he will," said Elvira in a strange undertone. She had something in her mind, thought Hudson to himself, and I don't want to know what it is.
"Tell me Elvira, do you have the pages from the diary with you?" he asked.
Elvira nodded.
"Yes, in the glove compartment."
Hudson opened the glove compartment and took the pages out.
"Will it bother your driving if I switch the light on?"
"Not at all. The road is straight from here on."
Hudson switched on the small light on the car ceiling and began to read.

ÜBUNG 304 !

Übung 304: Übersetzen Sie und tragen Sie den richtigen Buchstaben ein! Wie lautet das Lösungswort?

1. ruinieren _ _ ☐ _

2. Prinz _ _ _ ☐ _ _

3. Gewalt □ _ _ _ _ _ _ _

4. Landsitz _ _ _ _ _ □

5. Verdächtiger _ _ □ _ _ _ _

6. Grab □ _ _ _

7. Zufall _ _ □ _ _ _ _ _ _ _ _

8. vernehmen _ _ _ _ _ _ _ _ □ _ _

9. Zeitungsjunge _ □ _ _ _ _ _ _

10. Nachkomme _ _ _ _ _ _ _ _ _ □

11. sterben _ □ _

12. Sprache _ □ _ _ _ _

13. Schmerz _ _ _ □

Lösung: _ _ _ _ _ _ _ _ _ _ _ _ _ _ _

Elvira had told him what she had read in the diary, but one thing had puzzled him. He soon found what he was looking for. Elvira was curious.

"So, James?"

James pointed at the road.

"I'll tell you as soon as you look at the road."

The inspector referred to a passage from the diary.

"Here it is. On the 13th of July Lord Winterbutton wrote about two carriers catching an unknown fever which the expedition's doctor could not cure."

"Yes, and?" asked Elvira, this time without taking her eyes off the road.

Übung 305: Setzen Sie die folgenden Wörter in die Lücke:
much, many, a lot, a lot of

1. When Lord Winterbutton caught the fever there wasn't _____ ______ his doctor could do.
2. __________ people believed that the family was under a curse.
3. Hudson has __________ work to catch up on.
4. __________ of his contemporaries thought he was a crazy man who would only obtain one thing with the expedition.
5. Hudson thought nothing __________ could happen to anyone looking for a five-thousand-year old mummy.
6. Miss Paddington had been his housekeeper for __________ years now.
7. Actually, Hudson liked Elvira __________.
8. Perhaps he could turn a couple of his cases into detective books and earn __________ money.
9. There's __________ to be done.

"And it was only a day later, on the 14th of July, that he came across the pyramid. Soon after that he fell ill, too. He probably had the same unknown fever that the carriers had."
Elvira nodded thoughtfully.
"You're right. But the carriers had the symptoms before they discovered the pyramid."

Übung 306: Setzen Sie die richtigen Konjunktionen ein!
(unless, only, but, before, too, then)

Hudson nodded.

"Supposing the cause of the fever was the same."

"… which is highly probable …"

"The mummy's curse had nothing to do with Lord Winterbutton's death. (1.) __________ the Pharaoh's curse started (2.) __________ Winterbutton disturbed his sleep."

"Exactly," agreed Hudson.

"(3.) __________ that doesn't explain the mysterious deaths of his son and his grandson exactly on their thirty-third birthday."

"We'll get to the bottom of that mystery, (4.) __________, Elvira." said Hudson optimistically.

The inspector sighed happily. That took a load off his mind. He would have found it difficult to come to terms with the possibility of a curse. Elvira slowed down and turned into a wide driveway which led to a country house. (5.) __________ the entrance hall and a room on the first floor had their lights on.

Elvira stopped the car next to a Jaguar parked in front of the entrance door.
"Here we are," she said, "and by the looks of it, Lord Winterbutton is here, too."

She got out of the car and looked at the residence.
Hudson did the same. The building was at least 200 years old and, even in the dark, it emanated an atmosphere of old upper-class wealth.
The two of them went to the entrance door.
Portal would have been a more appropriate term. And as could be expected, there was no ordinary door bell, but, instead, an old door-knocker in solid iron, in the shape of a sphinx's face.
Without hesitating Elvira grasped it and hammered energetically on the door.

! ÜBUNG 307

*Übung 307: Geben Sie die richtigen Formen von **to go** an!*

1. einfache Gegenwart: ____________
2. Verlaufsform der Gegenwart: ____________
3. Einfache Vergangenheit: *he went*
4. Vergangenheit mit "used to": ____________
5. Verlaufsform der Vergangenheit: ____________
6. present perfect: ____________
7. Verlaufsform des present perfect: ____________
8. Plusquamperfekt: ____________
9. Verlaufsform des Plusquamperfekts: *he had been going*
10. Zukunft mit "going to": ____________

11. Zukunft mit "will": ____________________

12. future perfect: ____________________

13. Verlaufsform des future perfect: ____________________

The knocks echoed through the dead silent house.
Despite the late hour, it took only a few seconds for some limping steps to be heard. A man in a butler's uniform opened the door. He looked about forty, had short, dark brown hair and a very striking face. And for a butler, who probably never carried anything heavier than a silver tray, he had surprisingly wide shoulders.
"Can I help you?" he asked.
Inspector Hudson was about to say something, but Elvira beat him to it.
"Good evening sir, we would like to speak to Lord Winterbutton."
"And may I ask who you are?" asked the butler without batting an eyelid.
Hudson cleared his throat.

Übung 308: Welche Synonyme gehören zusammen? Setzen Sie die richtige Ziffer ein!

ÜBUNG 308 !

1. ancient	☐ deceased
2. automobile	☐ ask
3. dead	☐ policeman
4. enquire	☐ car
5. cop	☐ bizarre
6. steal	☐ old
7. strange	☐ pinch
8. drink	☐ sip

"I think we spoke to each other on the phone. Inspector Hudson from Scotland Yard and Elvira Elliot. May we speak to the lord?"
The butler looked at them doubtfully.
Then he shook his head.
"I'm sorry, but Lord Winterbutton is not feeling very well. If you could leave your business cards, he will definitely get in touch with you."
Hudson sighed and gave the man his card and so did Elvira.
The butler took the cards and bade them a good night before shutting the door.
They could hear a bolt being slid into place.
"What an unfriendly man," said Elvira.

ÜBUNG 309 !

Übung 309: Setzen Sie die passende Verbform ein!

But James Hudson (1. not listen) ______________. He (2. to stare) ________________ at the closed door. Something about the butler (3. to ring) ____________ a bell. "James, (4. to be) ______________ everything all right?" asked Elvira. Hudson still (5. to take) ______________ no notice of her. He (6. to try) ______________ to concentrate on the butler.

Something wasn't right.

Then it struck like a bolt of lightning!

Of course!

It wasn't the butler's face which had caught his attention, but the sound of his footsteps as he (7. to come) ____________ to the door.

"The butler limps!" he exclaimed.

Elvira looked at him questioningly.

"Sorry?"

"Elvira, when the butler opened the door I heard his feet dragging."

Elvira still did not understand.

How could she? The inspector led her away from the door.

"I told you that I saw the surveillance tape at the museum this morning …"

"Yes?"

"Well the thief could not be identified, but he had a limp!"

"Like the butler!" cried Elvira excitedly. The inspector put his index finger to his lips. "Shhh!" he said as they returned to the car. "It could also be a coincidence, but there seem to be a few too many coincidences now. Lord Winterbutton is the grandson of the Tut-Enk-Ra's discoverer; he has access to the museum; he is the only person whose relics have not been stolen; and his butler limps just like the thief. I believe we are on the right track!"

"Great! At last, we are taking a step forward." Elvira started the engine and drove the car back on the country road.

Übung 310: Beantworten Sie die Fragen zum Text!

1. What made Hudson believe that the curse didn't have anything to do with Lord Douglas Winterbutton's death?

____

2. How many rooms in Lord Winterbutton's country estate had their lights on?

____

3. What made the butler seem to be a possible suspect?

____

4. What made Lord Winterbutton a very probable suspect?

____

____

5. Why didn't Lord Winterbutton speak to Hudson and Elvira?

____

But, to Hudson's great surprise, she stopped the car on the side of the road, switched off the engine and jumped out.

"Come on, James! We have no time to lose!"

The inspector looked at her inquiringly.

"What are you doing, Elvira?"

"Well what do you think? If his lordship won't receive us, then we'll invite ourselves in!"

Hudson could not believe his ears.

"D-do you want to break into the house?" he stuttered.

Elvira laughed. "Don't look so shocked. We'll just have a little look around. Come on!"

Without waiting for his answer, she disappeared into the darkness in the direction of the country house. The inspector sighed and followed her unwillingly. Perhaps, he could at least prevent her from getting into trouble.

"Elvira you can't do that," he whispered.

"Too late!"

Elvira Elliot had found an unfastened kitchen window at the back of the house and was pushing it open carefully.

Übung 311: Setzen Sie die richtige Person ein!
(he, she, Hudson, Elvira)

ÜBUNG 311 !

Before (1.) ________________ could do anything, (2.) ________________ had already slipped into the house. (3.) ________________ then stuck her head out of the window and grinned at him.

"Come in or do you want to take root there?"

(4.) ______________ sighed again. This was trespassing. And as an officer of law he was supposed to arrest Elvira not become her accomplice. But now it was too late.

(5.) ______________ looked around him – like a thief in the night – and climbed through the window.

Once inside, (6.) ______________ looked around.

The kitchen light was off, but the moonlight was streaming through the window. The room was larger than Hudson's lounge and furnished with ultramodern kitchen fittings.
"Not bad," whispered Elvira and slipped through the kitchen door. She cautiously looked towards the entrance hall beyond.

Übung 312: Finden Sie ein passendes Synonym für die Wörter in Klammern!

ÜBUNG 312 !

"Be careful you don't (1. run into) ________________ the butler, Elvira!" whispered Hudson.

"Don't worry. This isn't the first time I've done something like this," she whispered back.

The inspector (2. groaned softly) __________. He had feared that. He (3. followed) ________________ Elvira into the (4. enormous) ________________ entrance hall. He had seen station halls which were smaller. The wood-panelled walls held family portraits; proud aristocratic faces looked down at the inspector. Nearly disapprovingly as if they disapproved of him and Elvira trespassing in their home.

Elvira carefully opened a heavy oak door and (5. peered) ________________ into the room behind it. She saw a huge library with very old books and maps.

The next door opened into a drawing-room.

At the further end of the room there was an elegant bar in wood and in the (6. centre) __________________ an expensive billiard table.

The inspector picked up some courage and opened the next door himself. He looked into a large living room furnished with old leather armchairs and a heavy, tasteful oak table. In the corner stood an oak cupboard which probably elegantly hid a television. Hudson was absolutely sure the television only transmitted the BBC, that is, if it was ever used.

But something puzzled him. The rooms they had inspected so far, were elegantly furnished, but something in particular was missing. Hudson followed Elvira up a wide staircase to the first floor.
"Elvira," he whispered, "be careful. Remember, when we arrived, there was a light burning on the first floor. Somebody else apart from the butler is still awake!"
Elvira nodded. "Thank you for the warning, James. I'll be careful."
When they came to the top of the stairs, they saw a long, dark corridor. A dull light shone through the gap under the last door. Without hesitating or taking any notice of Hudson shaking his head, Elvira went towards it. Hushed voices could be heard in the room.

Übung 313: Finden und übersetzen Sie das bekannte Sprichwort, das sich im Text versteckt hat!

ÜBUNG 313 !

A man coughed. A second man spoke in an encouraging tone, but Hudson could not understand what was being said.
But he recognised the voice – he had already heard it before. Forgetting his caution, he bent over and looked through the keyhole, which, for an inspector from Scotland Yard, was disgraceful. But the end justifies the means.

"What can you see?" asked Elvira softly. But the inspector did not answer or turn away from the keyhole. He had to concentrate on what the two men were saying.
On a wide, untidy bed, lay a young-looking man in his thirties. It must have been the present Lord Winterbutton. His similarity with the portraits was unmistakable. The lord was talking to another man who sat next to the bed.
Hudson recognised the small round figure immediately.
It was Cobblepot, the Winterbuttons' lawyer.

ÜBUNG 314 !

Übung 314: Lesen Sie weiter und unterstreichen Sie die „phrasal verbs"!

Now that Hudson could read their lips, it was easier for him to make out what was being said. "Don't worry Lord Stephen," said Sir Cobblepot and patted the young man's hand.
Lord Stephen laughed gratefully.
"Thank you Arthur. I'm very grateful that you dropped in on the eve of my thirty-third birthday, the family's horror day."
The lord coughed, Cobblepot shook his head.
"But, Stephen. You can't really believe this nonsense about the mummy's curse. You simply have a touch of flu, which is no surprise with this weather. All the rest is a stupid coincidence. In a couple of days you'll be laughing about this, I promise you."
Lord Winterbutton shook his head.
"No, Arthur. I don't believe it's a coincidence. But I have taken certain precautions to calm down Tut-Enk-Ra. I hope the curse will have soon left my family for ever."
Cobblepot was taken aback by this remark. The inspector was also surprised. What did Lord Winterbutton mean?
"Anyway, Stephen," said Cobblepot taking a small glass bottle out of his pocket, "I've brought along a vitamin preparation.

A simple vegetable mixture. My family has had this mixture prepared with a special recipe for a hundred years. It did my grandfather and father a lot of good. You should take a spoonful before going to sleep."
Lord Winterbutton nodded gratefully.
"You are a true friend, Arthur. Thank you. I don't know what I would do without you."
Cobblepot replied, "Oh, nonsense, Stephen. The Cobblepots have

been your family's lawyers and estate administrators for over a 150 years. I have to go now Stephen. I'll come and visit you in the morning if you wish."

Lord Winterbutton raised himself from his pillows to shake Cobblepot's hand.

"That would be nice, Arthur. See you tomorrow - and could you please close the door after you? When I have a fever I'm very sensitive to any noise."

"Of course. Good night, Stephen."

The lawyer nodded at the young man and went towards the door. Inspector Hudson stood up quickly.

Übung 315: Formulieren Sie die Sätze im Passiv.

ÜBUNG 315 !

1. Somebody stole the mummy from the museum.

____

2. The police are conducting some forensic tests.

____

3. Hudson will have solved the case.

____

4. Winterbutton opened the tomb straight away.

____

5. The butler did not invite Elvira and Hudson.

____

____

"What's wrong?" asked Elvira.

"Shhh!" Hudson pulled her away from the door.

They tiptoed to a dark corner in the corridor and hid in the shadow of an old grandfather clock. Just in the nick of time … thought the inspector.

A few seconds later the door opened and Cobblepot came out. Even in the dim light Hudson could see the satisfied grin on the lawyer's penguin face.

Cobblepot waggled down the stairs to the entrance hall. And left the house.

"Who was that?" asked Elvira.

"Lord Winterbutton's lawyer," replied Hudson. "I met him today at the 'Egyptian Society'. A rather unpleasant fellow, but obviously a trusted friend of Lord Winterbutton."

Elvira frowned.

"And does he know anything about the mummy theft?"

! ÜBUNG 316

Übung 316: Wie lauten die Sätze richtig?

1. tiredly Lord Winterbutton himself raised his from pillows

2. thief into the broke The house

3. Before he dropped going home her off

4. is Hudson forward to looking day off his

5. Hudson the always assigned was cases difficult

____

6. into house the and broke stole some They portraits

____

7. he about know Does anything the mummy theft?

____

8. Egyptian is culture really interesting The

____

Hudson thought about it and shook his head.
"I don't think so," he answered. "Lord Winterbutton said something very strange about having taken measures against the curse … and Cobblepot seemed surprised about the fact."
"Taken measures against the curse?" repeated Elvira.
"What did he mean by that?"
Hudson frowned.
"I'm not sure, dear, but I have a suspicion. Did you notice anything strange in our little 'house visit'?"
Elvira looked at Hudson puzzled.
"No, what do you mean, James?"
"Well, do you remember that Lord Winterbutton – whether or not he has anything to do with the theft – owns the largest collection of Tut-Enk-Ra's relics?"
"Yes?"
"Elvira, apart from the door-knocker in the shape of a sphinx, there isn't one Egyptian relic to be seen in the whole house. The question is: Where did Lord Winterbutton hide his collection – and why on earth did he hide it?"

Übung 317: Lesen Sie weiter und korrigieren Sie die Wörter in Klammern!

Inspector Hudson and Elvira (1. quick) ________________ crept through the dark entrance hall. Luckily even the butler seemed to be asleep at this late hour and they were able to look around undisturbed.

"What are we looking for exactly?" asked Elvira.

The inspector looked around. He could be on the wrong track, but it was worth a try. For some reason or another, Lord Winterbutton (2. keeped) ________________ his Egyptian collection out of sight. And to hide such a large collection there was only one possibility: (3. it must being stored) ________________ in a cellar. And Hudson was sure that the old country house had a large underground vault.

"Let's look for it, Elvira!"

Hudson pointed to a wooden door in the entrance hall. It was smaller and less imposing (4. as) ________________ the other decorated oak doors which led to the drawing room and the lounge. (5. Without to wait) ________________ for Elvira to answer, Hudson went to the cellar door. It was not locked. A narrow, steep staircase lead down into the darkness. Directly (6. next the door)

_______________ was a switch, but the inspector did not want to risk turning the light on. (7. Lucky) _______________ Elvira had the solution.

Übung 318: Ordnen Sie die Satzhälften richtig zu! Tragen Sie die passende Ziffer in das Kästchen ein!

1. Elvira gave up smoking	☐ a) for years.
2. Elvira didn't give up smoking	☐ b) when Hudson first met her.
3. Elvira hadn't given up smoking	☐ c) years ago.
4. Elvira had given up smoking	☐ d) until she was 30.
5. Elvira had been trying to give up smoking	☐ e) by the time she was thirty.
6. Hudson didn't wait	☐ f) since 6 o'clock.
7. Hudson had been waiting	☐ g) until Elvira arrived.
8. Hudson was waiting here	☐ h) when Elvira finally arrived.
9. Hudson had been waiting an hour	☐ i) for long.
10. Hudson waited	☐ j) a minute ago.

ÜBUNG 318 !

She rummaged in her handbag and took out a flashlight. She was apparently prepared for everything. The inspector wondered how long she had been planning this unlawful entry.

But it was too late now to get cold feet. Hudson switched on the electric torch which had a surprisingly strong light. Hudson and Elvira went carefully down the stairs.
The temperature dropped after only a few steps.
"Brrr, it's cold down here," complained Elvira.
The inspector nodded. And by the looks of it, the cellar had been dug directly into the rock beneath the house.

ÜBUNG 319 !

Übung 319: Bilden Sie einen Relativsatz aus den zwei Sätzen!

1. This is the detective book. I was telling you about it.
   This is the detective book (which) I was telling you about.
2. Elvira is a friend. Hudson can always rely on her.

   ____
3. That's the man. The police were looking for him.

   ____
4. That is the mummy. The investigator is looking for it.

   ____
5. Sir Reginald is the boss. Hudson listens to him.

   ____
6. This is a clue. Hudson looked for it carefully.

   ____
7. That's his friend. He is sitting next to him.

   ____

They finally reached the actual cellar. The ceiling consisted of semi-arches. Hudson directed the electric torchlight throughout the enormous room. In the corners there was old furniture which had been carefully covered with sheets to avoid the dust. Looking at the silhouettes one could make out: various chairs, tables and cupboards.
"Wow," exclaimed Elvira, as she lifted a sheet and saw an old chest of drawers. "I know some antique dealers who would sell their grandmothers for such old antiques."
"Perhaps," replied Hudson, "but we're looking for much older items. Come Elvira."
The torch's light fell on another door which wasn't locked either. Hudson and Elvira went into the room on the other side carefully.
"Not bad," said Elvira and nodded approvingly.
Wooden wine racks stretched from one end of the cellar to another. There were no other doors.

Übung 320: Setzen Sie folgende Wörter in die Lücken!
(taste, size, torch, horizontally, label, trespassing)

"There must be at least a thousand bottles here," said Hudson and picked one up carefully. The 1. ______________ informed him that it was over 50 years old and therefore worth a fortune.

"It's nearly a pity to drink it," said Elvira. "The lord has good 2. ______________, but this is still not what we are looking for. And I can't see any other door. It looks like your instinct has let you down this time."

The inspector looked at the wine racks. Indeed, there were no other doors except for the one they had come through.

But something was wrong. Usually the cellar had the same surface area as the ground plan of the house. Considering the enormous 3. ________ of the house, the cellar should have been a lot bigger.

"Shouldn't we go back up?" asked Elvira at the door.

Hudson shook his head.

"I would like to look around a little longer," he answered.

"For me, we could open a bottle of wine and make ourselves comfortable," said Elvira laughing.

James shook his head.

"That way we could be charged with 4. __________ and burglary."

He looked carefully at the wine racks. The bottles lay 5. ______ ________ on the racks on all four walls.

Suddenly, the inspector directed his 6. _______________ onto the narrow side of the wine-vault.

"What have you seen?" cried Elvira.
"I don't know Elvira. But, look here at the wine rack."
Hudson went towards the wooden rack and Elvira followed him cautiously. The rack in front of them held dozens of bottles.
"Look at this," said Hudson pointing at the bottles.
"Yes," said Elvira. "There are a great deal of bottles like all the other racks."

Übung 321: Welche Gegenteile gehören zusammen? Setzen Sie die richtige Ziffer ein!

ÜBUNG 321 !

1. upright	☐ cry
2. right	☐ backwards
3. forwards	☐ horizontal
4. laugh	☐ wide
5. approve	☐ tiny
6. huge	☐ carelessly
7. carefully	☐ gradual
8. steep	☐ wrong
9. narrow	☐ disapprove

Smiling, Hudson replied, “Not exactly, Elvira. These bottles are vertical. All the other bottles are in a horizontal position.”
“You’re right!” exclaimed Elvira.
Then she picked up a vertical bottle and read the wine label.
“Mmmm, a 1999 Bordeaux,” she murmured. “Enjoyable, but nothing special. I sometimes use it to cook with.”
“It doesn’t have much to do with all these vintage wines. I wonder why Lord Winterbutton would store such an ordinary bottle of wine here, in a vertical position.”

Übung 322: Setzen Sie die Verben in der passenden Form (aktiv oder passiv) ein!

ÜBUNG 322 !

The insurance agent (1. put) ________________ the bottle back and (2. hold) ____________ the torch while Hudson tackled the rack. He gripped one side of the rack and pulled it.

And immediately the rack (3. give) ________________ way. It (4. swing) ____________ open to one side like a door.

"There you (5. be) ____________," (6. say) ____________ Hudson triumphantly. "Just like I thought. Another hidden vault!"

Elvira directed the torchlight in the room behind the door.

Both she and the inspector (7. freeze) ____________ with horror.

"Oh my God!" cried Elvira.

All of a sudden Hudson thought he (8. catapult) ______________ into another world. The torchlight no longer illuminated the dusty wine racks and antique furniture, but lit up an incredible splendour. Hudson (9. can) __________________ not believe his eyes. And hearing Elvira's surprised gasps, he concluded that she was also astounded. Instead of a wine cellar, they were faced by an Egyptian death chamber. The walls were inlaid with stone slabs which (10. decorate) ________________ with reliefs of Egyptian gods.

The floor was tiled with gold flagstones.
Two oversized falcon gods watched over both sides of the entrance. However, the real eye catcher of the chamber was an oblong pedestal decorated with precious stones on which a gold-plated sarcophagus reposed.
"Incredible!" was all Elvira could say, for once at loss for words.
"W-what on earth is this here, James?" she asked bewildered.

James too was incredulous. He had expected to find Lord Winterbutton's Egyptian collection, but not a private museum!
"I think this is an exact imitation of Tut-Enk-Ra's tomb. Constructed with the family's collection …"
"… and the relics stolen all over the world!"
Elvira pointed at a small statue of a sacred cat whose diamond eyes flashed sinisterly.
"This cat was in the list of stolen relics. And this necklace on the pedestal too."

Übung 323: Ergänzen Sie die Sätze mit dem passenden „question tag"!

ÜBUNG 323 !

1. "You'd love a cup of tea, James, *wouldn't you*?"

2. Elvira won't forget her list of suspects, ________________?

3. Let's go and visit Lord Winterbutton, ________________?

4. It's a bit too late, ________________?

5. Mr Cobblepot doesn't like Hudson, ________________?

6. Elvira should drive more carefully, ________________?

7. Drive more slowly, ________________?

8. I'm in trouble, ________________?

Hudson directed the torchlight on the pedestal. Indeed, there was a necklace near an empty, open sarcophagus.
"That is the mummy's jewellery, if I'm not mistaken," he said. "The question is – where's the mummy, Elvira?"
But the insurance agent was no longer standing next to Hudson

because she had gone deeper into the chamber, to have a close look at the precious antiquities.

"Incredible," she said once again. "I don't have my list with me, but I'm sure all the stolen relics from Tut-Enk-Ra's tomb are in this room. My company will be very happy."

Hudson nodded and followed Elvira into the tomb. He was happy for her. Her company would save millions of pounds and she would probably get a generous percentage as a reward.

But his task was not over yet. The stolen mummy was nowhere to be seen.

But it could not be far away.

ÜBUNG 324 !

Übung 324: Setzen Sie die richtige Form von ***will*** *oder* ***going to*** *in die Lücke ein!*

1. Miss Paddington says to Hudson: "I ________________ make myself a cup of tea. Do you want one?"
2. Hudson _________ write a report when he has solved the case.
3. Do you think Hudson ________________ find the thief?
4. Why don't you check if the stolen goods on your list have anything in common. And I __________________ deal with my list about the access cards.
5. Miss Paddington says to Hudson "If you don't eat more, you ________________ become skin and bones."
6. Hudson says "I (not) ________________ work today. I'm tired."

7. Hudson says “It’s hot in this room” and Miss Paddington answers “I ____________________ open the window.”
8. Hudson asks Elvira “Where ____________________ to spend your next holiday?”
9. There are some very black clouds in the sky. It ____________ ________ rain again.

Inspector Hudson took a step forward and nearly tripped over an uneven flagstone. He looked down. The golden tiles covering the floor were decorated with reliefs portraying various Egyptian gods, some of whom Hudson knew:
the sun god Horus with his falcon head, Bastet the cat goddess and the fertility god Osiris.

Übung 325: Welches Wort ist das „schwarze Schaf“?

1. onwards, forwards, towards, on ____________________
2. always, often, between, sometimes ____________________
3. have, would, should, must ____________________
4. heavy, weight, scale, width ____________________
5. death, after-life, depth, eternal repose ____________________
6. surprised, astounded, shocked, alive ____________________
7. trespass, break in, run away, burgle ____________________
8. suspect, criminal, offender, policeman ____________________

And Elvira herself stepped towards a tile depicting Anubis, the death god with a jackal head.
"Elvira!" cried Hudson. "Don't move!"
Elvira looked at him surprised. Her foot was suspended over the gold tile with Anubis.
"I've just thought of something," he said. "If this is a 1:1 reconstruction of the real chamber, then Lord Winterbutton might have also copied the deathtrap which was in the original tomb."
"Deathtrap?" gasped Elvira and looked down at the jackal-headed god at her feet.
"What an unpleasant god," she said.
"Not necessarily," explained Hudson. "Anubis only checked who deserved to be redeemed and who was to be sent to the underworld. And considering your dissipated lifestyle, I wouldn't step on it if I were you."
"Very funny, James," retorted Elvira. "But do you really believe that this flagstone will trigger a deathtrap?"

! ÜBUNG 326

*Übung 326: Schreiben Sie einen passenden Satz mit den Wörtern in Klammern! Nutzen Sie **might, must** oder **could**!*

1. Lord Winterbutton has got a cough. (might, bronchitis)

   He might have bronchitis.

2. He looks very miserable. (must, afraid, die)

   ____

3. He doesn't have any Egyptian relics in his house. (might, hide)

   ____

4. Hudson has been working all day. (must, deadline to meet)

____

5. Why are there two lights on in Lord Winterbutton's house? (could, be awake)

____

6. I wonder how the thief got into the museum? (must, use access card)

____

7. It's nearly midnight. (Lord Winterbutton, might, sleep)

____

8. All the Winterbuttons died on their thirty-third birthday. (must, be unlucky)

____

9. How did the burglar get into our apartment? (he could, use, fire escape)

____

The inspector kneeled down carefully next to the golden tile on the floor. In the torchlight it was easy to see that the grooves of the tile were wider than the bordering tiles.
"I'm nearly sure …," he answered thoughtfully. "It is likely that there is a spring mechanism beneath it, which is linked to a trap.

The ancient Egyptians knew how to protect their graves."
Suddenly a ceiling light was turned on. The light reflected itself a thousand times on the golden relics in the death chamber.

Übung 327: Ordnen Sie die Buchstaben zu einem sinnvollen Wort!

"Luckily my great-grandfather knew all the (1. rictks) ________!" cried a voice.

Inspector Hudson blinked in the dazzling light. He could just make out two figures standing at the entrance of the (2. mbot) ________. His eyes slowly became accustomed to the light and he recognised Winterbutton and his wide-shouldered (3. reltub) __________. Winterbutton looked even paler than he did in bed. He had to lean on the butler's shoulder. However, he still looked angrily at the two trespassers.

"May I ask with whom I have the unexpected pleasure?" asked the lord. Hudson assumed an official attitude and tried to inspire (4. uathroyit) ____________________, which was a little difficult considering he had been (5. ghtcau) _________________________ trespassing.

"I'm (6. rotcepsin) ________ James Hudson from Scotland Yard," he said and pointed to Elvira. "And my assistant Miss Elliot."

"Assistant, did I hear correctly?" whispered Elvira and gave him a little push.
"Not now, Elvira," whispered Hudson back and turned his attention to Lord Winterbutton.
"Please excuse our unconventional admission, but we suspected that you had something to do with the disappearance of the mummy, Lord Winterbutton."

Übung 328: Unterstreichen Sie die direkte Rede!

"With the disappearance of the mummy!" said Elvira angrily. "You mean with the theft of the Egyptian mummy, just like all the other thefts. Half the relics have been stolen from all around the world."
Lord Winterbutton sighed and looked guiltily at the floor.
"I'm afraid you're right, sir. But I had my good reasons."
Inspector Hudson shook his head. The young lord looked a picture of misery, but he was after all guilty of several thefts. And he had just confessed.
"And I have good reasons to arrest you, Lord Winterbutton!" said Hudson sternly. But Lord Winterbutton shook his head looking sadly.
"I'm very sorry, but I can't allow that. It would be my death sentence."

Then he nodded at his butler. Without hesitating the butler rushed forward. With three limping, but quick steps he reached the inspector and the insurance agent.
But he wasn't prepared for Elvira's belligerence. She suddenly pushed the surprised inspector aside and stood in the butler's way. The wide-shouldered man wanted to thrash Elvira, but she dodged

him and grabbed his wrist and whirled him over her shoulder onto the floor. The man hit the golden-tiled floor with a bang and lay there moaning.

Both Hudson and Lord Winterbutton had watched the scene with their mouths gaping. Elvira looked from one to another.

"And that'll be that!" she said.

Inspector Hudson swallowed. He was really glad Elvira was on his side.

"I'm sorry Lord Winterbutton, but I have to arrest you now. And your employee for attacking an officer on duty."

Lord Winterbutton became even paler. He took a few steps forward, then he had to hold onto the empty sarcophagus to avoid falling down.

! ÜBUNG 329

*Übung 329: Übersetzen Sie die Verben ins Englische! Wann kommt **oneself** hinzu?*

1. sich ändern ____________________
2. sich verletzen ____________________
3. sich fühlen ____________________
4. sich erinnern ____________________
5. sich amüsieren ____________________
6. auf sich achten ____________________

"No, inspector, you can't arrest me. It would be like killing me!" he cried. Inspector Hudson frowned.

“You said something like that before!” he said. “What do you mean?”
Hudson felt really sorry for the young man. Elvira, too, took a step forward to stop the aristocrat from falling.
The lord sighed.

Übung 330: Setzen Sie die richtige Präposition in die Lücke!

ÜBUNG 330

1. Are you afraid ______________ the dark cellar?
2. Who is responsible ______________ cleaning the museum?
3. London is famous ______________ the rain.
4. Lord Winterbutton should be ashamed ________ what he did.
5. What’s wrong ______________ Lord Winterbutton? He looks a little pale.
6. Elvira is excited ______________ finding the thief.
7. Hudson is not used ______________ relaxing in the morning.
8. Lord Winterbutton is grateful ______________ Hudson’s help.
9. Miss Paddington’s reaction ________ the news was surprise.
10. She was very shocked ______________ the news.
11. Hudson was suspicious ______________ the butler.
12. Elvira is very good ______________ her job.

“The curse of the mummy, inspector. Tut-Enk-Ra put a curse on my whole family because my great-grandfather disturbed his

eternal repose. And that is why I brought everything here. The Pharaoh's whole death chamber. Some of the relics here are a part of the family collection. My faithful butler stole the rest."
The lord pointed to his butler who still lay dazed on the floor.
"I'm ashamed of what I have done – but I had no other choice. My thirty-third birthday is just around the corner, and you can already see that I am unwell."
Suddenly the inspector understood what Lord Winterbutton had in mind.
"My God, Lord Winterbutton," he exclaimed, "you built an exact imitation of the death chamber in your cellar …"
"… so that the Pharaoh could have his peace back and take back the curse!" finished Elvira.
Winterbutton nodded.

ÜBUNG 331 !

Übung 331: Finden Sie die Nomen zu den Verben!

1. discuss ______________________
2. suspect ______________________
3. advise ______________________
4. exclaim ______________________
5. enquire ______________________
6. imitate ______________________
7. employ ______________________

"I'm very sorry I involved my butler in the thefts, but I could see no other way. Once I had all the treasures together again, the mummy was the only missing piece. I lent George, my butler, the access card to the British Museum and prepared the death chamber here in my cellar. Tonight I was going to put the prince back in his tomb and seal this room forever. But a while ago, after my lawyer had left, I heard your voices in the corridor. Because of the fever, my ears are very sensitive to noises."

Hudson nodded. He and Elvira had been very careless. Luckily the whole episode had ended without much harm being done.

"Lord Winterbutton," he said in a soothing tone, "I can assure you that the mummy's curse is just superstition. You are in no danger."

"I wouldn't be so sure of that," said a voice behind them.

Inspector Hudson turned around.

None of them had heard Arthur Cobblepot arrive.

The small fat man still reminded the inspector of a penguin. A penguin holding a pistol.

Übung 332: Übersetzen Sie die Wörter in Klammern!

"Arthur!" exclaimed Lord Winterbutton, shocked. "What are you doing? Why are you holding a gun?"

Cobblepot (1. grinste) ________________.

"Well, dear Stephen, because you were a naughty boy and didn't take your medicine, I'm forced to take drastic (2. Mittel) ________________."

"M-My medicine?" he (3. fragte) ________________, "I don't understand."

"I do!" exclaimed Hudson. "The so-called tonic is (4. Gift) ________________, isn't it, Cobblepot? How long have you been giving it to Lord Winterbutton?"

"Oh, for quite some time, inspector," answered the (5. Rechtsanwalt) ________________. "However, I was only following a family tradition." Cobblepot cackled.

Hudson took a deep breath. Now he understood what a horrible (6. Verbrechen) ________________ he and Elvira had come across. Only Lord Winterbutton did not seem to understand. Perhaps the shock was too much for him.

"What do you mean, Arthur?" he asked.

Cobblepot cackled again.

"Oh Stephen, you Winterbuttons have never been very (7. schlau) ________________. That's why my family had so little trouble gaining your (8. Vertrauen) ____________."

"Good Arthur Cobblepot tried to poison you, Stephen," interrupted Hudson, "just like his father poisoned your father, and his grandfather poisoned your grandfather. Not so Cobblepot?"

"Certainly," replied the lawyer proudly and waved his gun around. "As I said, it was a family tradition."

Lord Winterbutton went even paler. His world was going to pieces. "But why, Cobblepot?"

"It's very simple, dear Stephen – to profit from your family.

Übung 333: Unterstreichen Sie das richtige Modalverb!

1. You shouldn't/mustn't have any problem with the surveillance system.
2. You don't have to/mustn't wear wellingtons in the rain, but they keep your feet drier.
3. Hudson couldn't/wouldn't have a relaxing day off because Sir Reginald called him for a case.
4. Elvira's so stubborn. She can't/won't do what she is told.
5. Hudson was able to/could obtain a copy of the surveillance tape.
6. "You don't have to/mustn't say a word about working with me," said Hudson to Elvira.
7. Hudson should have obtained/had to obtain a search warrant to enter Lord Winterbutton's home, but Elvira was too impatient.

Everytime a Winterbutton died, my family took care of the inheritance and we kept a lot of the family's fortune. Two hundred thousand pounds here, a little property there – you have no idea, Stephen, how rich your family would be if we hadn't been your lawyers for such a long time."

"And the curse of the mummy?" asked Elvira.

She was also very shocked at the young lawyer's cold-bloodedness.

"All nonsense," replied Cobblepot. "After opening the tomb, the old Douglas Winterbutton died of a normal tropical fever. My grandfather took advantage of the legend to poison your grandfather thirty-three years later. Just like my father poisoned your father on his thirty-third birthday. And now it was my turn to get rid of you, Stephen, if only you hadn't had this foolish idea of stealing the mummy to put the curse to an end."

ÜBUNG 334 !

Übung 334: Welche Präposition muss in die Lücke?

1. daran denken	think *of*
2. unfähig sein zu …	be incapable ___
3. in der Angst leben, dass …	live in fear ___
4. glauben an …	believe ___
5. darauf bestehen, dass …	insist ___
6. schwierig finden zu …	have difficulty ___
7. sich interessieren für …	be interested ___
8. davon träumen zu …	dream ___

Cobblepot cackled again and pointed the gun at the lord.
"Well, I'll close you and the two nosy-parkers in this chamber. And nobody will ever see you again. Actually it'll be even better if you disappear without a trace, because as your estate administrator I'll have free disposition of your fortune."
However, when Cobblepot released the gun's safety catch, Hudson had had enough. He slowly walked towards the fraudulent lawyer. "That's enough Cobblepot," he said sternly. "You can't get away with this. Put down the gun."
Cobblepot pointed his gun at Hudson
"Don't come any closer," he threatened. "Or I'll pull the trigger!"

ÜBUNG 335 !

Übung 335: Verbinden Sie die zwei passenden Satzteile und setzen Sie die richtige Ziffer in das Kästchen!

1. I'm ashamed
2. Inspector Hudson
3. The main entrance
4. He seemed rather excited

5. The sports car
6. All the equipment
7. When they came

- ☐ at the idea of helping Scotland Yard in an investigation.
- ☐ of what I have done.
- ☐ was driven by either a madman or a reporter.
- ☐ to the top of the stairs, they saw a long, dark corridor.
- ☐ was surrounded by a large crowd of photographers.
- ☐ had to be transported on camels.
- ☐ took a step forward.

Hudson took a deep breath and took another step. Instinctively Cobblepot stepped backwards and aimed at Hudson's head.
"James!" screamed Elvira. "He'll shoot you!"
"Listen to your friend!" said Cobblepot while Hudson took yet another step forward.
Cobblepot took a step backwards. Then he screamed.
A gun shot rang through the tomb.

Übung 336: Beantworten Sie die folgenden Fragen zum Text!

! **ÜBUNG 336**

1. What did Hudson and Elvira find exactly?

____

2. What was missing in the death chamber?

____

3. What happened to the butler?

____

4. Why did the Cobblepots poison one Winterbutton after another?

____

5. What did Cobblepot want to do to Elvira and Hudson?

____

Inspector Hudson's plan had worked. He had imagined that Cobblepot would step backwards before pulling the trigger.
And so the killer lawyer stepped on the flagstone with the engraving of Anubis the death god.
And as the inspector had expected, the flagstone set off the trap. The flagstone gave way and Cobblepot fell into a hole. He instinctively pulled the trigger as he was falling, but the bullet flew harmlessly over Hudson's head.
Hudson, Elvira and Lord Winterbutton all ran to the edge of the narrow hole. The little fat man was wedged in the narrow, two metre deep hole. Unhurt but wailing.
"Get me out of here!" he cried. "I'm stuck."
Anger had given Lord Winterbutton's cheeks a bit of colour.
"You horrible man. You're lucky that I didn't make a real death trap. In the real tomb the hole was full of snakes.

! ÜBUNG 337

Übung 337: Setzen Sie die richtige Verbform ein!

The inspector couldn't help smiling.

"Tell us if there is an antidote against the poison you (1. give) ________________ poor Lord Winterbutton. Then we (2. pull) ________________ you out of the deathtrap."

Cobblepot shook his head in a panic.

"Lord Winterbutton (3. not need) ______________ an antidote. His body (4. eliminate) ______________ the poison on its own. I wanted to give the fatal dose tonight."

Lord Winterbutton sighed in relief. The prospect of (5. be) ______________ rid of the curse made him feel better already.

"Thank God," he coughed.

In that moment they (6. hear) ______________ the chimes of the grandfather clock in the corridor. It was midnight.

Lord Winterbutton (7. overjoy) ______________.

"12 o'clock. Today is my birthday. My thirty-third birthday!"

Hudson patted the young aristocrat on the shoulder.

"And you also (8. celebrate) ______________ your thirty-fourth birthday, Lord Winterbutton!" he said.

Elvira (9. go) ______________ up to the lord and gave him a kiss on the forehead.

"Happy birthday, dearie!" she said.

Inspector Hudson gratefully took the cup of steaming tea from the tray that Miss Paddington was holding.
Then he took a sip of the Earl Grey and leaned back in his armchair. It was nine o'clock in the morning and outside it was drizzling.

Übung 338: Übersetzen Sie die folgenden Sätze!

1. Elvira Elliot hatte ein halb geöffnetes Fenster gefunden und drückte es vorsichtig auf.

2. Langsam gewöhnten sich seine Augen an die Dunkelheit.

3. Er freute sich für die Versicherungsagentin, da ihre Auftraggeber Millionen von Pfund sparen würden.

4. Hudson traute seinen Augen nicht, denn was vor ihnen lag, war kein Keller, sondern eine ägyptische Totenkammer.

5. Zum Glück schien auch der Butler zu dieser späten Stunde bereits zu schlafen.

6. Es brannte Licht in einem der Stockwerke, so waren beide vorsichtig.

7. Trotz der späten Stunde dauerte es nur ein paar Sekunden, bis ein Mann in einer Butleruniform die Tür öffnete.

____

____

"And what will happen to Lord Winterbutton?" asked Miss Paddington nearly worried.
Hudson had got home very late. First they had pulled the trembling Sir Cobblepot out of the hole. Then Hudson had informed the police and had had to fill in several forms.
And lastly Elvira had insisted that they celebrate the day in one of those downtown cocktail bars in London.
And although the inspector had arrived home in the middle of the night, absolutely exhausted, Miss Paddington had obliged him to tell her the whole story of the case.
But at least he could catch up on his day off today.

Übung 339: Geben Sie die richtige Präposition nach dem Verb an!

ÜBUNG 339 !

1. They accused him _____ stealing the mummy from the museum.
2. Hudson prevented Lord Winterbutton ____________ being poisoned by Sir Cobblepot.
3. Hudson warned Elvira ___________ trespassing.
4. Lord Winterbutton apologised ___________ stealing the relics.
5. Hudson succeeded ___________ solving the case in 24 hours.
6. Elvira thanked Hudson __________ letting her work with him.

Hudson took another sip of tea and looked at the housekeeper.
"Well, he did after all involve his butler in numerous thefts. But it was in a way in self defence. I think both will get off with a short suspended sentence. Anyhow, both are very happy that the whole nightmare is over. The Winterbuttons have had to live long enough with the fear of the 'curse'."
"So the curse of the mummy was just hocus-pocus?" asked Miss Paddington.
Mr Hudson shook his head slowly.
"Well, no matter what people thought it was, two members of the Winterbutton family lost their lives because of the tomb desecration. So in a certain way, the curse did come true. And Stephen Winterbutton was the first one who wanted to give back the mummy its peace – and this had also saved his life. The British Museum has agreed to let the mummy be taken back to Egypt together with the relics owned by the Winterbutton family."

ÜBUNG 340 !

Übung 340: Geben Sie die richtigen Formen von ***to steal*** *an!*

1. einfache Gegenwart: *he steals*
2. Verlaufsform der Gegenwart: ____________
3. Einfache Vergangenheit: ____________
4. Vergangenheit mit "used to": ____________
5. Verlaufsform der Vergangenheit: ____________
6. present perfect: ____________
7. Verlaufsform des present perfect: *he has been stealing*

8. Plusquamperfekt: ____________________

9. Verlaufsform des Plusquamperfekts: ____________________

10. Zukunft mit “going to”: ____________________

11. Zukunft mit “will”: ____________________

12. future perfect: *he will have stolen*

13. Verlaufsform des future perfect: ____________________

Miss Paddington thought about it for a few seconds and then, once again, turned her attention to practical things.
“I’ll prepare you something for breakfast, James,” she said in a motherly tone. “You look hungry. Lean back and enjoy your day off at last.”
Then she went with determined steps towards the kitchen.
Inspector Hudson closed his eyes and sighed.
Outside the rain pattered on the window. In the kitchen Miss Paddington’s pots and pans banged. There was the usual thump outside the door when the newspaper was delivered.
Hudson did not even get a fright when the phone rang.
A few seconds later, Miss Paddington entered the room.
“It’s for you, Sir Reginald is on the phone. It’s about some magician who disappeared during a performance yesterday and hasn’t turned up since. Sir Reginald thinks it’s the right case for you.”
Hudson opened his eyes and took another sip of tea.
“Tell him I’m on my way,” he sighed.

THE END

Abschlusstest

Übung 1: Unterstreichen Sie die richtige Form des Präsens!

1. Hudson drinks/is drinking tea at the moment.
2. What is he doing/does he do today?
3. Elvira usually travels/is travelling by plane to Europe.
4. Hudson always knows/is knowing what to do.
5. He is looking/looks for clues.
6. It rains/is raining outside.

Übung 2: Schreiben Sie die Sätze im „first conditional“!

1. If the phone had not rung Inspector Hudson (enjoy) his day off.

   ____

2. Elvira (like) to work on the case with Hudson.

   ____

3. Sir Reginald (not put) anyone else in charge of the case.

   ____

*Übung 3: Verbinden Sie das **phrasal verb** mit der richtigen englischen Erklärung! Setzen Sie die Ziffer ein!*

1. to find out	☐	a) admit responsibility
2. to turn up	☐	b) not stay at home
3. to own up	☐	c) arrive uninvited
4. to go out	☐	d) wait
5. to hold on	☐	e) meet/find by chance
6. to come across	☐	f) discover

Übung 4: Schreiben Sie Datum und Uhrzeit aus!

1. 7. Januar 2003 ______________________________
2. 18.45 Uhr ______________________________
3. Morgen um 12.00 mittags ______________________________
4. Am fünften Mai ______________________________
5. Zehn Minuten vor sechs, heute Abend ______________________________
____
6. 1812 ______________________________

Übung 5: Welche Präpositionen passen?

1. ________ Christmas
2. ________ the world
3. ________ the beach
4. ________ the end
5. ________ a concert
6. ________ the phone
7. ________ the morning
8. ________ summer
9. ________ night

Übung 6: ***Some*** *oder* ***any, much*** *oder* ***many*** *oder* ***a lot of****?*

1. Hudson has brought ____________ friends to the Yard.
2. Elvira never gets ____________ information about James.
3. Is there ____________ tea left?
4. He hasn't got ____________ time?
5. Hudson did have ____________ trouble.
6. Elvira thinks she knows ____________ history.
7. Miss Paddington has got ____________ nice ideas.

Lösungen Abschlusstest

Übung 1: 1. is drinking 2. is he doing 3. travels 4. knows 5. is looking 6. is raining

Übung 2: 1. would have enjoyed 2. would like 3. wouldn't put

Übung 3: 1. f 2. c 3. a 4. b 5. d 6. e

Übung 4: 1. January the seventh two thousand and three 2. a quarter to seven 3. tomorrow at noon 4. on the fifth of May 5. ten minutes to six this evening 6. eighteen twelve

Übung 5: 1. at 2. in 3. on 4. in 5. at 6. on 7. in 8. in 9. at

Übung 6: 1. some 2. much 3. any 4. much 5. a lot of 6. a lot of 7. many

Lösungen

Übung 1: 1. midnight/midday 2. light/heavy 3. big/small 4. tall/short 5. beautiful/ugly 6. dark/light 7. evening/morning 8. thick/thin 9. clean/dirty 10. happy/sad
Übung 2: 1. b 2. a 3. a 4. b
Übung 3: 2. man 3. rose 4. hands 5. air 6. moonlight 7. pub 8. walk 9. night 10. park
Übung 4: 1. white 2. red 3. black 4. green 5. brown 6. grey 7. yellow 8. blue 9. Orange
Übung 5: 1. fish and chips 2. bread and butter 3. salt and pepper 4. night and day 5. black and white 6. up and down 7. brush and comb 8. husband and wife 9. brother and sister 10. son and daughter 11. work and play 12. fruit and vegetables 13. sun and rain 14. summer and winter 15. now and again
Übung 6: 2. inspector 3. pair 4. trousers 5. road worker 6. waistcoat 7. head 8. fashion
Übung 7: 1. cap 2. slippers 3. trousers 4. skirt 5. shorts 6. dress 7. shirt
Lösung: clothes
Übung 8: 1. tired 2. shocked 3. hate 4. driver 5. policeman 6. bank 7. busy 8. angry 9. glass
Übung 9: CDs, furniture, lamps, computer systems, fax machines
Übung 10: 1. clown 2. actor 3. juggler 4. fire-eater 5. mime artist 6. street entertainer 7. acrobat 8. animal trainer
Übung 11: 2. I'm afraid that the tourists will stay away. 3. It was a very good idea. 4. Let's stop and watch the mime artist. 5. A lot of tourists go to that restaurant.
Übung 12: 1. sighed 2. midday 3. narrow 4. Crowds 5. stopped 6. prices 7. difficult 8. easy 9. checked 10. wallet
Übung 13: 1. Yes, there were a lot of people at the market. 2. No, nobody stole it. 3. They were watching a mime artist. 4. Yes, he was very good. 5. Because the mime artist pretended to slip on a banana skin.
Übung 14: 1. for 2. out 3. towards 4. to 5. at 6. towards 7. off 8. at
Übung 15: 1. talk 2. park 3. cry 4. stylist 5. water 6. sweating 7. slow 8. throw 9. watch 10. ship
Übung 16: 1. richtig 2. richtig 3. falsch 4. richtig 5. falsch
Übung 17: 1. Hudson and Elvira were very surprised. 2. The man was riding a small bicycle. 3. The artist could not escape. 4. His friends tried to help him. 5. They ran very fast.
Übung 18: 1. thin 2. quickly 3. high 4. heavy 5. loud 6. late 7. ugly 8. young
Übung 19: 1. foot 2. chin 3. knee 4. gum 5. ear 6. eyebrow 7. ankle 8. stomach 9. lip 10. shoulder
Lösung: fingernail
Übung 20: 1. finger print 2. bus stop 3. alarm clock 4. phone call 5. washing machine 6. car park 7. sunglasses 8. mobile phone 9. sign post 10. traffic lights

Übung 21: 1. a 2. c 3. c 4. b 5. a
Übung 22: 2. hotel 3. station 4. post office 5. supermarket 6. theatre 7. restaurant 8. cinema 9. museum 10. town hall
Übung 23: 1. She went to the bathroom. 2. The woman took a shower. 3. All he wanted was to go home and go to bed. 4. Suddenly she turned around starting to sing a christmas song. 5. I live just around the corner.
Übung 24: 1. open/closed 2. interesting/boring 3. dangerous/harmless 4. pleasant/unpleasant 5. empty/full 6. high/low 7. lazy/hard-working 8. polite/rude 9. healthy/ill 10. nice/horrible
Übung 25: 1. Elvira asked her friends to come in. 2. They wondered what the noise could be. 3. She broke her leg and had to stay in bed. 4. Could you put these flowers in some water? 5. It is boring in hospital if you have nothing to do.
Übung 26: 1. cupboard 2. suddenly 3. boss 4. why 5. tie 6. pretty 7. astonishment 8. schoolgirl 9. knock 10. nurses
Übung 27: 1. say hello 2. watch television 3. pay a bill 4. make a phone call 5. give a present 6. read a book 7. brush one's teeth 8. do some work 9. drive a car 10. ride a bike
Übung 28: 1. b 2. b 3. a 4. b 5. a
Übung 29: 1. No, she doesn't. 2. He was hiding from the nurses. 3. He brought her some flowers. 4. She gave Elvira some detective stories. 5. Yes, he does.
Übung 30: 1. politics 2. sports 3. business 4. travel 5. current affairs 6. arts 7. education
Übung 31: figure, victims, person, madman, couple, stranger, villain, police, someone
Übung 32: 1. film 2. head 3. magazine 4. eyewitness 5. fat 6. hospital 7. healthy 8. relaxed 9. terrible 10. lift
Übung 33: 1. a 2. b 3. b 4. a 5. c
Übung 34: 1. elevator/lift 2. sketch/drawing 3. smile/grin 4. nonsense/rubbish 5. way out/exit 6. hurry/rush 7. wallet/purse 8. notice/catch sight of 9. discuss/talk about 10. surprise/astonishment
Übung 35: 1. home 2. policemen 3. room 4. pot of tea 5. housekeeper 6. steaming 7. cup 8. town
Übung 36: 1. plant 2. armchair 3. television 4. cushion 5. curtain 6. board games 7. carpet 8. bookcase 9. remote control 10. lamp Lösung: living room
Übung 37: 1. famous actor 2. horror movie 3. friendly smile 4. dangerous criminal 5. comfortable chair 6. good news 7. bright light 8. thick fog 9. close friend 10. fast car
Übung 38: 1. into 2. Half an hour ago 3. in front of 4. for 5. wife 6. every evening 7. change 8. bought 9. paid for 10. cheap
Übung 39: 1. c 2. b 3. b 4. b 5. a
Übung 40: 1. Where 2. Who 3. What 4. When 5. How 6. Why 7. Which 8. What 9. Who 10. Where
Übung 41: anser (answer), lorghter (laughter), theirselfes (themselves), breethed (breathed), closser (closer), lite (light), court (caught), waring (wearing), wurst

(worst), sranger's (stranger's)

Übung 42: 1. up 2. in 3. off 4. on 5. down 6. up 7. off 8. up 9. down 10. in

Übung 43: 1. telephone 2. sleep 3. vampire 4. kill 5. eyes 6. radio 7. clock 8. week

Übung 44: 1. dishonest 2. lucky 3. impatient 4. generous 5. stupid 6. foreign 7. thirsty 8. careful 9. shy 10. reliable

Übung 45: 1. There's nothing better than a nice cup of tea. 2. Hudson asked his housekeeper to help him. 3. Why does a vampire need to steal money? 4. Could you come into the office right away? 5. He put on his new blue suit and a tie.

Übung 46: 1. car and petrol 2. tea and sugar 3. shoes and socks 4. knife and fork 5. table and chair 6. computer and printer 7. airport and plane 8. cinema and film 9. theatre and play 10. bank and money

Übung 47: 1. Nobody 2. bankrupt 3. earned 4. lonely 5. life 6. years 7. strange 8. story 9. at night 10. traffic lights

Übung 48: 1. take 2. do 3. make 4. do 5. make 6. Take 7. make 8. make 9. do 10. take

Übung 49: 1. young 2. tall 3. long 4. sharp 5. crazy 6. angry 7. serious 8. sensational 9. frightened 10. surprised

Übung 50: 1. garlic 2. banana 3. onion 4. butter 5. grapes 6. lemon 7. raspberry 8. potato 9. honey 10. ice-cream

Übung 51: 1. He is an actor who played Dracula in the 1970s. 2. No, he doesn't. 3. He lives in a lonely house in the country. 4. No, there aren't. 5. No, they opened again last year. 6. He decides to go to Anvil Studios.

Übung 52: 1. entrance/exit 2. enormous/tiny 3. allowed/forbidden 4. famous/unknown 5. early/late 6. ceiling/floor 7. lazy/hard-working 8. formal/casual 9. unusual/ordinary 10. stop/start

Übung 53: 1. apart from 2. excellent 3. series 4. sale 5. shook 6. part with 7. What a pity 8. goodbye 9. Just a moment 10. made

Übung 54: 1. long 2. possibly 3. arrive 4. helpless 5. choke 6. shout 7. ordinary 8. gasp 9. grin 10. behind

Übung 55: 1. make a film 2. ask a question 3. knock on/at the door 4. solve a problem 5. wear clothes 6. tell a lie 7. deliver a message 8. smoke a pipe 9. pass a test 10. commit a crime

Übung 56: 1. b 2. b 3. a 4. a 5. b

Übung 57: 1. Not many people are swimming in the lake. 2. He works in a hospital. 3. She went to bed early. 4. I work as a gardener. 5. Be careful of the sharks.

Übung 58: 1. is 2. does 3. Are 4. did 5. Am 6. do 7. are 8. were 9. Was 10. did

Übung 59: 1. director 2. assistant 3. housekeeper 4. policeman 5. cameraman 6. porter 7. gardener 8. manager 9. vampire

Übung 60: 1. falsch 2. richtig 3. richtig 4. falsch 5. falsch 6. richtig

Übung 61: 1. didn't have a clue 2. key 3. playing the role 4. fantastic 5. imagine 6. cautious 7. idea 8. coach

Übung 62: 1. an 2. – 3. the/the 4. a 5. – 6. a 7. the/the 8. The 9. a 10. a
Übung 63: 1. Miss Paddington could not believe her eyes. 2. The actor pushed the inspector to the floor. 3. The director knew something about the vampire attacks. 4. I'd like to ask you a few questions. 5. Could you tell me where you were last night?
Übung 64: 1. surprising 2. surprised 3. interesting 4. exciting 5. tired 6. tiring 7. boring/interesting 8. excited 9. shocked 10. disappointing
Übung 65: 1. moon 2. earth 3. mountains 4. space 5. helmet 6. everyone 7. recording 8. baseball 9. hair 10. dust
Übung 66: 1. furious 2. moustache 3. destroy 4. apologise 5. earth 6. sky 7. library 8. post office 9. studio
Übung 67: buildings, billboards, neon signs, street lamp, dustbins, signpost, mail box, newspaper stand, taxi
Übung 68: 1. on 2. in 3. at 4. in 5. at 6. in 7. at/on 8. in 9. at 10. at
Übung 69: brige (bridge), wals (walls), live (life), roome (room), quitely (quietly), throow (through), eazy (easy), evry (every), nobodie (nobody)
Übung 70: 1. c 2. e 3. g 4. a 5. h 6. i 7. j 8. b 9. f 10. d
Übung 71: 1. It was about a submarine. 2. Yes, it did. 3. No, he was very quiet. 4. In a torpedo tube. 5. She hit him with her handbag.
Übung 72: 1. prison/jail 2. taxi/cab 3. lift/elevator 4. pavement/sidewalk 5. rubbish/garbage 6. petrol/gasoline 7. lorry/truck 8. motorway/freeway 9. holiday/vacation 10. flat/apartment
Übung 73: 1. what about 2. afford 3. have 4. shouldn't 5. sorrowfully 6. lose 7. his shoulders 8. nothing 9. Unless 10. pricked up
Übung 74: 1. mess 2. fun 3. bedroom 4. comfortable 5. plate 6. screen 7. kitchen 8. fascinate 9. freeze Lösung: submarine
Übung 75: 1. bathroom 2. pub 3. garage 4. cemetery 5. camping site 6. stadium 7. beach 8. forest 9. mountain 10. border
Übung 76: 1. b 2. c 3. b 4. a 5. a
Übung 77: 1. were 2. began 3. gave 4. left 5. went 6. was 7. smiled 8. lost 9. thought 10. came
Übung 78: 1. b 2. a 3. a 4. b
Übung 79: 1. laptop 2. printer 3. mobile 4. keyboard 5. modem 6. Internet 7. mouse 8. e-mail
Übung 80: 1. head 2. scream 3. everything 4. hide 5. blanket 6. quickly 7. patients 8. read 9. volume 10. cinema
Übung 81: 1. find out/discover 2. freeze/turn to ice 3. biography/life story 4. most famous/best known 5. switch off/turn off 6. close/shut 7. fan/admirer 8. scream/shriek 9. position/place 10. keen/eager
Übung 82: 1. He owes me some money. 2. My mobile phone rang and I answered it. 3. Take the money and put it in your pocket! 4. It's not worth waiting any longer.

5. We must find out about Basil Thornwood.
Übung 83: 1. in his heyday 2. over 3. for ages 4. retired from the public eye 5. make a comeback 6. wasn't successful 7. regretfully 8. nowadays
Übung 84: 1. attack/defend 2. country/city 3. question/answer 4. simple/complicated 5. public/private 6. alive/dead 7. past/future 8. hide/reveal 9. artificial/natural 10. brave/cowardly
Übung 85: 1. park a car 2. find the way 3. spend money 4. pour a drink 5. listen to the radio 6. hear a noise 7. make an appointment 8. dig a hole 9. remember someone's birthday 10. sign a letter
Übung 86: 1. outside 2. cigarette 3. clouds 4. customers 5. walked 6. followed 7. Excuse 8. afraid
Übung 87: 1. your 2. them 3. mine 4. her 5. our 6. their 7. his 8. me 9. him 10. my
Übung 88: 1. falsch 2. richtig 3. falsch 4. richtig 5. richtig 6. falsch
Übung 89: 1. retired 2. impressed 3. real 4. actually 5. open 6. Either 7. uninvited 8. won't
Übung 90: 1. bang 2. crash 3. ticking 4. hoot 5. squeak 6. yell 7. pop 8. clap
Übung 91: 1. hostess 2. waitress 3. policewoman 4. stewardess 5. actress 6. manageress 7. wife 8. niece 9. aunt 10. Mrs/Miss/Ms
Übung 92: 1. tightly 2. comfortable 3. tricks 4. underestimate 5. mind 6. dangerous 7. thoughts 8. discovered 9. narrow
Übung 93: 1. Basil Thornwood, by remote control. 2. In a film called 'Encounter with a Vampire'. 3. No, they don't. 4. There are small torches on the wall. 5. He falls through a trapdoor.
Übung 94: 1. deep 2. high 3. dangerously 4. heavily 5. well 6. patient 7. quiet 8. suddenly 9. angry 10. good
Übung 95: boring, beautiful, hungry, wonderful, nice, interesting, lonely, plastic
Übung 96: 1. a terrifying experience 2. a sigh of relief 3. a good idea 4. a narrow escape 5. a stroke of luck 6. a happy occasion 7. a terrible headache 8. a box of matches 9. a heavy rainfall 10. a bunch of flowers
Übung 97: 1. c 2. b 3. c 4. a 5. a
Übung 98: 1. The old man was obviously completely mad. 2. They were shocked when the vampire spoke. 3. Hudson wanted to arrest the old actor. 4. A loud laugh echoed through the huge hall. 5. It was amazing how fit the man was 6. The long cape fluttered around.
Übung 99: 1. nerve 2. feet 3. foot 4. nose 5. eye 6. skin and bones 7. arms 8. mouth
Übung 100: 1. madness 2. strength 3. push 4. foul 5. helpless 6. sharp 7. fatal
Übung 101: 1. fruit 2. eggs 3. menu 4. frying pan 5. butter 6. slice 7. saucepan 8. cut 9. honey 10. steak
Übung 102: 1. interested in 2. surprised at 3. look forward to 4. keen on 5. consist of
Übung 103: 1. shoot a gun 2. cut with scissors 3. tie something up with strings

4. wrap a present 5. take a photo 6. attend a course 7. invite someone to a party 8. wish someone luck 9. wipe a table clean 10. stir coffee

Übung 104: 1. falsch 2. richtig 3. falsch 4. richtig 5. falsch

Übung 105: 1. day 2. week 3. half an hour 4. month 5. dozen 6. hour 7. year

Übung 106: 1. pile 2. sigh 3. fraud 4. mystery 5. evaluation 6. annoying 7. case 8. avoid 9. file

Übung 107: 1. worker 2. few 3. frown 4. one after the other 5. knowledge 6. healthy 7. lacking

Übung 108: 1. epidemic 2. immune system 3. routine case 4. wit 5. scene of the crime

Übung 109: 2. expert 3. colleagues 4. crime 5. housekeeper 6. receiver

Übung 110: 1. private detective 2. policeman (or police officer) 3. lawyer 4. accountant 5. author (or writer) 6. art dealer 7. judge 8. insurance agent 9. auctioneer

Übung 111: 1. a, f 2. b, g 3. c, d 4. e, h

Übung 112: 1. to 2. in 3. at 4. on 5. with 6. around 7. from

Übung 113: 1. falsch 2. richtig 3. falsch 4. richtig 5. falsch 6. falsch 7. richtig

Übung 114: was – to be, dressed – to dress, stared – to stare, fell – to fall, was – to be, executed – to execute, could – can, was – to be, was – to be, held – to hold, were – to be

Übung 115: 2. mugged 3. struck 4. raped 5. smuggled 6. sought out 7. took revenge 8. kidnapped 9. robbed 10. hijacked 11. swore 12. found a clue 13. dug 14. clung

Übung 116: 1. up-to-date 2. clue 3. inspect 4. damaged 5. unharmed 6. strange

Übung 117: 1. police force 2. keep under observation 3. bank robber 4. genetic fingerprint 5. protection money 6. diplomatic relations 7. secret agent 8. in civilian clothes 9. pistol shot 10. code name 11. sign a treaty 12. fire brigade 13. picture frame 14. oil paint 15. water colour 16. pastel crayon

Übung 118: 1. Because she was an expert on art. 2. Two dice, both showing the number six. 3. Picasso and Monet. 4. Because the painting was not worth as much money as the other two. 5. An anonymous artist. 6. How the thieves entered the building.

Übung 119: 1. c 2. b 3. b 4. c 5. c

Übung 120: 2. The sinks were torn from the walls by the thieves. 3. The hole was inspected by Hudson. 4. The tiles were moved by Elvira. 5. The damage is seen by Mr Blighton. 6. Notes are taken by the inspector.

Übung 121: 1. klettern 2. Loch 3. gefährlich 4. Schacht 5. Taschenlampe 6. folgen 7. feucht 8. klebrig 9. vertraut

Übung 122: 1. forensics 2. clues 3. conspiratorially 4. Then 5. ray 6. choice 7. forward

Übung 123: 1. asked/for help 2. trampled 3. smell 4. shine 5. hesitated 6. crawl

Übung 124: Adverbien: direkt/directly, genau/exactly, endlich/finally
Adjektive: alt/old, dunkel/dark, schmal/narrow, enorm/huge, zurück/back, sprach-

los/speechless

Übung 125: 1. Hudson's hunch was correct. 2. A rat is crawling across the floor. 3. He does not have a torch. 4. The tunnel is dangerous. 5. Who destroyed the bathroom? 6. Almost everyone at Scotland Yard has the flu.

Übung 126: 1. garage 2. reply 3. sculpture 4. safe 5. nervous 6. bar 7. spit

Übung 127: 1. May I compliment you? 2. You look lovely today. 3. How about something to eat? 4. Here's to you!

Übung 128: 1. excursion 2. accompany 3. remain 4. bother 5. surface 6. forensics 7. maternal 8. invitation 9. manners 10. impatient

Übung 129: 1. a sip of tea 2. a gang of thieves 3. sum of money 4. a piece of advice 5. a clump of dirt 6. a spot of paint 7. a glass of wine 8. a pound of butter 9. a gust of wind 10. a ray of light

Übung 130: 1. looked 2. hung 3. seemed 4. make out 5. stared 6. fought

Übung 131: 1. richtig 2. falsch 3. falsch 4. richtig 5. falsch 6. falsch 7. falsch 8. richtig 9. richtig 10. falsch

Übung 132: 1. ghost 2. particular 3. network 4. middle 5. notice 6. replaced 7. entrance 8. perfect 9. building 10. snapped

Übung 133: 1. thieves 2. scenes 3. halves 4. mice 5. wolves 6. lights 7. tunnels 8. loaves

Übung 134: 1. Ich denke da an eine bestimmte Situation. 2. Sie hat es aus Freundschaft getan, nicht des Geldes wegen. 3. Er hat Elviras Bekanntschaft letztes Jahr in London gemacht. 4. Der Detektiv schüttelte den Kopf. 5. Mir wäre es lieber, wenn du zu Hause bliebest. 6. Pass auf dich auf. 7. Miss Paddington lächelte in sich hinein. 8. Der Inspector stottert oft.

Übung 135: 1. intruder 2. resolute 3. baseball bat 4. fear 5. familiar 6. unbearable 7. doorway

Übung 136: 1. prefer 2. fanatical 3. thoughtful 4. purse 5. ghost 6. reach 7. breath 8. bacon 9. intruder 10. frighten 11. recognize 12. smell
Lösung: Ploughbottom

Übung 137: 1. sense 2. afraid 3. circles 4. prison 5. unpleasant 6. looked 7. chest 8. dust

Übung 138: 1. return 2. important 3. incompetent 4. fresh 5. multiple 6. uninterested 7. worthless 8. independent 9. husband 10. breakfast

Übung 139: 1. fence 2. construction site 3. convince 4. search warrant 5. tools 6. skeleton

Übung 140: 1. The inspector climbed the lop-sided steps. 2. The moon bathed the steel girders in light. 3. Hudson did not convince the night watchman. 4. The intruder entered the property. 5. A security company patrolled the construction site. 6. The judge issued a search warrant. 7. Nobody used the machines. 8. The torch shone on the station sign.

Übung 141: 1. c 2. a 3. b 4. a 5. c

Übung 142: 1. socially 2. suspiciously 3. well 4. heartily 5. sinisterly 6. illegally 7. carefully 8. rustily 9. actually 10. regularly

Übung 143: 1. stretch 2. wheel around 3. glow 4. mislead 5. reflect 6. rush

Übung 144: 1. sleepy 2. tune 3. co-workers 4. lately 5. picture 6. asset 7. rich 8. competitor 9. curious

Übung 145: 1. People spend a lot of money on art. 2. Elvira had to wait a long time. 3. She called many art dealers. 4. Hudson doesn't like Picasso. 5. Hudson thought he saw a ghost. 6. A scream was heard. 7. Many collectors shop in London.

Übung 146: another time/again, found/discovered, yelled/shouted, lovely/beautiful, thankful/grateful, thruthful/honest, dreadful/terrible

Übung 147: 1. b 2. c 3. a 4. b 5. c

Übung 148: 1. ranch 2. bricks 3. autumn 4. insurance 5. sympathy 6. country 7. waitress

Übung 149: 1. falsch 2. falsch 3. richtig 4. falsch 5. richtig 6. richtig 7. falsch 8. richtig 9. falsch 10. richtig

Übung 150: 1. nodded 2. course 3. stolen 4. leave 5. expensive 6. miss 7. flight

Übung 151: 1. at 2. at 3. from 4. on 5. in 6. on 7. to 8. to 9. out 10. with

Übung 152: 1. nett, Art 2. Ball, Tanzabend 3. verlassen, Wüste 4. Rennen, Rasse 5. Miene, meines 6. lieben, gleich 7. Kompliment, loben

Übung 153: 1. There must be a logical explanation. 2. Miss Paddington believes in ghosts. 3. The rattle of the train was heard again. 4. Her eyes glowed in the dark. 5. Did anyone see the ghost? 6. Elvira was frightened by Hudson's disguise. 7. Hudson smiled as he saw Elvira coming. 8. Elvira asked questions and waited for the answers. 9. Why is Mr Bixby smiling? 10. He asked the waitress for a whiskey.

Übung 154: 1. That the ghosts of passengers haunted the tunnels. 2. Because he didn't have a search warrant. 3. Because he thought criminals would refuse to give him information if he came to them as a member of Scotland Yard. 4. A ghost. 5. Every time a train passed, the 'ghost' appeared.

Übung 155: 1. quiet/noisy 2. supernatural/normal 3. yell/whisper 4. float/sink 5. appear/vanish 6. logical/irrational 7. coincidental/planned 8. lift/drop 9. effective/useless 10. unwanted/welcome 11. hide/reveal 12. enjoy/dislike 13. worn/new

Übung 156: 1. as 2. to 3. In 4. after 5. to 6. during 7. away 8. from

Übung 157: 1. tube 2. pulse 3. rope 4. draught 5. scarecrow 6. pub 7. hidden 8. owner 9. midnight 10. license

Übung 158: 1. b 2. a 3. c 4. b 5. a 6. b 7. b

Übung 159: hinter/behind, verstummte/fell silent, genannt/alias, ohrenbetäubend/deafening, Gespräche/conversation, fettig/greasy, Kumpel/mate, kahl/bald

Übung 160: 1. catch 2. banknote 3. pickpocket 4. sober 5. wrinkle 6. opportunity 7. pretend 8. drag

Übung 161: 1. replied 2. threw 3. won 4. grabbed 5. besought 6. paid 7. doubted 8. shrank

Übung 162: 1. The bartender offers Hudson a beer. 2. The pickpocket only pretends to be drunk. 3. The thieves ignore the law. 4. Hudson's breath smelled of whiskey. 5. He introduced himself as Matches Marconi.

Übung 163: 1. fingernail 2. predominate 3. earnings 4. reward 5. homeless 6. unnoticed Lösung: London

Übung 164: 1. nice 2. fake 3. suspicious 4. disobey 5. hurrying 6. liked

Übung 165: 1. to 2. behind 3. from 4. against 5. on 6. on 7. in 8. from

Übung 166: 1. Verbrechen zahlt sich nicht aus. 2. Morgenstund hat Gold im Mund. 3. Es lief wie am Schnürchen.

Übung 167: 1. dig 2. empty 3. hide 4. get used to 5. lean 6. shout

Übung 168: 1. b 2. a 3. a 4. b 5. c

Übung 169: 1. literature 2. art 3. science 4. cinema 5. politics 6. music 7. cooking 8. charity 9. nobility

Übung 170: 1. protect 2. dialled 3. harmless 4. punched 5. testimony 6. announce

Übung 171: 1. a 2. b 3. a 4. b 5. b 6. a

Übung 172: 1. pretending 2. poured 3. have attacked 4. caught 5. have associated 6. had called

Übung 173: 1. richtig 2. falsch 3. richtig 4. richtig 5. falsch 6. richtig 7. falsch 8. richtig 9. richtig 10. falsch

Übung 174: 1. c 2. a 3. b 4. c

Übung 175: 1. everything 2. mistake 3. American 4. took 5. sip 6. main 7. Maybe

Übung 176: 1. insult 2. jokingly 3. laughingly 4. understanding 5. never 6. harm 7. everyday 8. ignore

Übung 177: 1. He lied about the painting. 2. Why did he pretend to be a businessman? 3. He is a master of disguise. 4. Mr Bixby and Mr Coltrane are the same person. 5. Hudson was still not satisfied. 6. Have you heard of the Phantom? 7. I have never seen his face.

Übung 178: 1. Gerücht 2. Umlauf 3. verantwortlich 4. zweifelnd 5. gierig 6. blass 7. Sicherheit 8. Grund 9. Gegenteil

Übung 179: 1. keep 2. return 3. chin 4. stole 5. attention 6. packing paper 7. fact 8. more 9. unpack 10. smiled

Übung 180: 1. Because he kept thinking about Jimmy Coltrane. 2. He was a gentleman. He never used a weapon 3. Because he used the word 'autumn' instead of 'fall'. 4. So that they won't be afraid. 5. Lord Ploughbottom holding two dice in his hand.

Übung 181: 1. after 2. in 3. from 4. for 5. from 6. with 7. on

Übung 182: 1. jemanden auf dem Laufenden halten 2. wie ein Blitz aus heiterem Himmel 3. jemandem einen Streich spielen 4. doppeltes Spiel mit jemandem treiben 5. krumme Touren machen

Übung 183: 1. tiny/small 2. disappointingly/frustratingly 3. connection/association 4. sense/meaning 5. help/aid 6. disappear/vanish 7. bound/tied 8. pleasant/nice 9. apartment/flat

Übung 184: 1. sped 2. previous 3. owner 4. weeks 5. property 6. estate 7. drive 8. astonished
Übung 185: 1. copper 2. flawless 3. vainly 4. heir 5. bankrupt 6. estate
Lösung: Elvira
Übung 186: 1. I will inspect the old paintings. 2. He strolled out of the bank. 3. Miss Paddington had a pleasant day. 4. The real doctor was found tied to a chair. 5. When will he retire? 6. This was typical for insurance agents.
Übung 187: 1. c 2. b 3. a 4. c 5. c
Übung 188: 1. empty 2. clue, tip 3. poor, impoverished 4. constantly, regularly 5. property 6. see, note, register
Übung 189: 1. The clue in the painting was found by Hudson. 2. The car was steered by the Phantom. 3. The money was taken by the phony bank director. 4. The Ploughbottom estate is taken care of by Mr Nigma. 5. The book was picked up by Elvira.
Übung 190: 1. Verwalter 2. zittern 3. Glücksspiel 4. Anlass 5. Pech 6. Sucht 7. Umschlag 8. Tagebuch 9. Handschrift 10. verblassen
Übung 191: 1. money 2. tyre 3. heir 4. Impressionism 5. source 6. religion 7. entry 8. cover 9. secretary
Übung 192: 1. tuberculosis 2. The handwriting was different, not so shaky ... 3. "According to the rules of probability, luck must be on my side tonight." 4. a debt certificate 5. Isle of Man
Übung 193: 1. falsch 2. richtig 3. falsch 4. richtig 5. falsch 6. richtig 7. richtig 8. falsch 9. richtig 10. richtig 11. falsch
Übung 194: 1. loses 2. beat 3. forgive 4. devote 5. take over 6. bet 7. supports 8. grabbed 9. presents
Übung 195: 1. b 2. a 3. c 4. a 5. c 6. b
Übung 196: 1. conservative 2. dearest 3. speed 4. moustache 5. glue 6. itches
Übung 197: 1. Mr Nigma really turned out to be the Phantom. 2. No one was to be found in the salon. 3. The discovery appeared to be unbelievable. 4. Hudson could barely understand her. 5. The mobile phone went dead all of a sudden. 6. The drugs made Elvira unconscious.
Übung 198: 1. more expressive 2. younger 3. more evil 4. worse 5. best 6. richer 7. worst 8. funnier 9. more tired 10. sunnier
Übung 199: 1. jacket 2. car 3. rubber 4. television 5. kettle
Übung 200: 1. cut 2. removed 3. feel 4. fell 5. came 6. burn 7. twisted 8. passed
Übung 201: 1. furry 2. taste 3. wrist 4. stable 5. object 6. candy 7. rope 8. fist 9. lighter 10. procedure
Übung 202: 1. ballroom 2. bar stool 3. convention hall 4. couch 5. living room 6. gallery 7. health club 8. stove 9. sink 10. wardrobe
Übung 203: 1. falsch 2. richtig 3. falsch 4. falsch 5. richtig 6. richtig 7. falsch

8. richtig 9. falsch
Übung 204: 1. capital 2. hurry 3. sailor 4. kidnap 5. pant 6. dock 7. firearm
Lösung: Phantom
Übung 205: 1. elegant 2. think 3. holiday 4. conversation 5. compliments 6. way 7. approached 8. polite 9. full 10. wallet
Übung 206: 1. tasty/delicious 2. trick/cheat 3. concerned/worried 4. tell/recount 5. rest/relax 6. admiration/respect 7. signal/indicate 8. gun/firearm 9. precaution/preventative measures 10. believe/trust 11. silhoutte/outline 12. leave/depart 13. endless/eternal 14. far/distant 15. wait/delay
Übung 207: 1. Elvira wanted to read him the diary in person. 2. The sailors stand on the dock. 3. Will you walk the entire way home? 4. Hudson used his mobile phone to book a ticket. 5. The prisoner is led into the court room. 6. The waiter will serve up the dessert.
Übung 208: 1. c 2. c. 3. b 4. a 5. b
Übung 209: 1. you 2. them 3. his 4. he 5. her 6. they 7. she 8. her
Übung 210: 1. paws 2. grace 3. backwards 4. declare 5. tempted 6. struggle 7. club 8. stranger 9. redeem 10. arrest
Übung 211: 1. Elvira's handbag 2. men's suits 3. inspectors' offices 4. James' health 5. children's stories 6. thieves' crimes 7. cell's bars
Übung 212: 1. The Pride of the Sea. 2. No. 3. That Elvira was there. 4. Take a shower and rest.
Übung 213: 1. Es hat Zeit. 2. ab und zu 3. gewaltige Anstrengungen unternehmen 4. Liebhaberwert 5. eine lange Geschichte haben 6. im wahrsten Sinne des Wortes 7. die Suppe versalzen 8. in der Familie liegen 9. auf Holz klopfen 10. wie ein Vogel im Käfig
Übung 214: 1. late 2. hope 3. case 4. mayor 5. debt 6. satisfied 7. enough 8. bad
Übung 215: 1. play it by ear 2. failsafe 3. get lucky 4. by chance 5. at sixes and sevens 6. cost an arm and a leg 7. put oneself out 8. sold up the river 9. not my cup of tea
Übung 216: 1. villain/hero 2. unscrupulous/moral 3. asleep/awake 4. rapid/slow 5. muscular/flabby 6. undecided/firm 7. restrain/release 8. smooth/uneven 9. tranquil/stormy 10. worried/carefree
Übung 217: 1. Mr Nigma viciously attacked Elvira. 2. The Phantom possessed the debt certificate. 3. Hudson carried the gun. 4. An unknown man drugged Elvira. 5. Miss Paddington drives Elvira's car. 6. Matches Marconi will drink the beer in the dive. 7. Who will write the letter?
Übung 218: 1. b 2. a 3. c 4. b 5. b
Übung 219: 1. curls 2. comb 3. relief 4. happy 5. entire
Übung 220: 1. Can 2. May 3. Shall 4. should 5. may 6. shall 7. should 8. may 9. Can 10. Should

Übung 221: 1. richtig 2. falsch 3. richtig 4. falsch 5. richtig 6. falsch 7. richtig 8. falsch 9. richtig 10. falsch

Übung 222: 1. That there was no reception. 2. Because they were seasick. 3. He felt the Phantom still had another trump to play. 4. The mayor was to be guarded day and night. 5. He disguised himself as Elvira.

Übung 223: 1. The conversation was anything but funny. 2. Slowly, he is moving towards the table. 3. Where can I redeem this coupon? 4. Someone stepped out of the shadows. 5. Hudson will use the distraction to his own advantage. 6. We will never catch up with him! 7. He is of French ancestry.

Übung 224: 1. The waves rocked the ferry. 2. Storm clouds gathered in the sky. 3. The phoney Elvira Elliot presented the letter. 4. Are you familiar with the works of Picasso? 5. Sir Reginald wants a full report. 6. The Phantom was good looking but had a scar.

Übung 225: 1. Vermögen 2. verhindern 3. Abstammung 4. verdutzt 5. unwillkürlich 6. falsch 7. anstiften 8. lebensecht 9. Mitleid 10. Boden 11. kaum 12. verzweifelt 13. Freizeichen 14. Bericht 15. Volltreffer 16. Tagebuch 17. süchtig 18. würfeln 19. Bescheinigung 20. Ausnahme

Übung 226: 1. nail 2. access 3. rose 4. sonata 5. power 6. promote 7. staircase

Übung 227: 1. pulled 2. hissed 3. trust 4. turned 5. sprang 6. flew

Übung 228: sighed, closed, listened, tried, grinned, continued, suggested

Übung 229: 1. smiled 2. waited 3. rained 4. did not 5. grumbled 6. went 7. was 8. thought 9. frowned 10. entered 11. laughed 12. answered 13. replied

Übung 230: 1. walk 2. yesterday 3. house 4. search 5. book 6. man 7. dry 8. noise

Übung 231: 1. He lives in a flat in London. 2. Miss Paddington is Hudson's housekeeper. 3. He hears the clock ticking, a crashing sound, the rain, the thump of a newspaper, the squeaking of a bicycle and Miss Paddington's curses. 4. He has tea, toast and marmalade for breakfast. 5. He reads The London Times.

Übung 232: did/do, rang/ring, let/let, had/have, was/be, let/let, thought/think, said/say, knew/know, could/can

Übung 233: 1. clue 2. robbery 3. find out 4. murder 5. police Lösung: crime

Übung 234: 1. a, the 2. a 3. An, a 4. a 5. an 6. – 7. the, a 8. The

Übung 235: 1. newspapers 2. thieves 3. women 4. men 5. potatoes 6. mice 7. knives 8. oxen 9. foxes 10. lobbies

Übung 236: 1. Where does Mr Hudson live? 2. How does he go to work? 3. Whose car is that? 4. What sort of car is it? 5. How often does Mr Hudson read the newspaper? 6. When does the museum close? 7. Who is Miss Paddington? 8. What's this book about? 9. How much does it cost? 10. When did he close his last case? 11. Why does Mr Hudson like his car so much?

Übung 237: 1. building 2. entrance 3. rain 4. museum 5. stopped 6. smell 7. discover

Übung 238: 1. display/exhibit 2. see/look 3. find out/discover 4. make/do

5. help/assist 6. investigate/gather evidence 7. arrest/catch 8. escape/run away 9. steal/rob

Übung 239: 1. caught 2. stole 3. knew 4. shook 5. brought 6. saw 7. came 8. went 9. began 10. won 11. slept 12. took 13. could 14. ate 15. had

Übung 240: constable, room, way, site, crime, pieces, childhood, empire, years, findings, relics

Übung 241: 1. I'm not 2. We aren't 3. He wasn't 4. I won't 5. I didn't 6. She can't 7. He didn't steal 8. You haven't stolen 9. I haven't got 10. He doesn't steal 11. you don't dream

Übung 242: 1. criminal 2. brusque 3. surprised 4. scene 5. grin 6. recalled 7. enquired

Übung 243: 1. lost/lost 2. ring/rung 3. think/thought 4. woke/woken 5. speak/spoken 6. steal/stole 7. shot/shot 8. sit/sat 9. paid/paid 10. hit/hit 11. taught/taught

Übung 244: 1. falsch 2. falsch 3. richtig 4. falsch 5. richtig 6. falsch 7. falsch

Übung 245: 1. an 2. a 3. some 4. a 5. a 6. some 7. an 8. some 9. an 10. some 11. some

Übung 246: 1. reply/ask 2. rainy/dry 3. speak/listen 4. yes/no 5. finish/start 6. sad/happy 7. cold/hot 8. panic/calm 9. sick/healthy

Übung 247: 1. by 2. on 3. at 4. of 5. on 6. with 7. in

Übung 248: 1. Inspector Hudson loved the soft noises. 2. James let the phone ring twice. 3. He read the first page again. 4. A minute later Miss Paddington came into the living room. 5. The constable looked at him confused. 6. Perhaps the mummy had an accomplice. 7. Hudson concentrated on the screen.

Übung 249: 1. any 2. some, any 3. any 4. any 5. some 6. some 7. any

Übung 250: 1. Do you often go to the museum? 2. I never drink tea because I don't like it. 3. Hudson is never late for work. 4. My housekeeper always watches the news in the evening. 5. The inspector rarely has a day off. 6. The old car braked suddenly. 7. The cars hooted at the pedestrians loudly.

Übung 251: violently, similarly, always, obviously, well, proudly, snobbishly

Übung 252: 1. at 2. on 3. at 4. in 5. in 6. at 7. at 8. at 9. on 10. in 11. in 12. at

Übung 253: 1. gut, gesund 2. ziemlich, hübsch 3. nur, einzig 4. gerade, gerecht

Übung 254: 1. caught 2. known 3. shaken 4. brought 5. seen 6. come 7. gone 8. begun 9. won 10. slept 11. taken 12. could

Übung 255: 1. works 2. It's raining 3. lives 4. is drinking 5. is looking 6. brings 7. thinks

Übung 256: 1. drizzling 2. meeting 3. impatiently 4. parties 5. throat 6. tip 7. over

Übung 257: 1. c 2. b 3. c 4. c 5. a 6. b

Übung 258: 1. He would never admit that he liked Elvira. 2. The motive would give Hudson a clue about the thief. 3. Inspector Hudson would be proud of her. 4. He would find out who had stolen the mummy. 5. It was more money than he would ever earn at the Yard. 6. He would work together with her. 7. But Sir Reginald would never find out.

Übung 259: 1. happier/happiest 2. better/best 3. younger/youngest 4. more/most beautiful 5. worse/worst 6. more/most comfortable 7. busier/busiest 8. more/most patient 9. more/most polite 10. further/furthest

Übung 260: 1. anything 2. Nobody 3. Nothing, anything 4. anywhere 5. Nobody, anything 6. nobody 7. anything

Übung 261: Well, what should he do, thought Hudson. – After all, if it hadn't been for Elvira, he might never have known about the other thefts. – It was only fair to let her take part in the investigation. – Sir Reginald must never know of it, though. – Hopefully he would not regret this decision.

Übung 262: 1. straight/crooked 2. back/front 3. wealthy/poor 4. young/elderly 5. freezing/boiling 6. hard-working/lazy 7. laugh/cry 8. outgoing/reserved 9. black/white 10. grow/decrease 11. tumult/calm 12. devil/angel 13. broken/intact 14. diverse/identical 15. seldom/often

Übung 263: 1. defence 2. charge 3. manslaughter 4. sentence 5. stole 6. killed 7. guilty

Übung 264: had not answered the phone, had been sitting, had laid down, had been busy, had not come across, had cheated, had not led, had been stolen

Übung 265: 1. holiday 2. evidence 3. proof 4. the city 5. church 6. a member 7. good old Elvira

Übung 266: 1. Because he wanted Hudson to answer the reporters' questions at the press conference. 2. She was searching for information on the stolen relics. 3. Because he's old-fashioned. In fact he also has an old car.

Übung 267: 1. a swarm of bees 2. a pack of wolves 3. a flight of birds 4. a herd of cattle 5. a pack of hyenas 6. a school of fish 7. a gaggle of geese

Übung 268: 1. pulled 2. sat 3. could 4. was 5. was doing 6. came across 7. took 8. have been stolen

Übung 269: 1. A Bentley is more expensive than a Ford. 2. A clock is bigger than a watch. 3. A pyramid is higher than a sphinx. 4. A town is larger than a village. 5. A lake is deeper than a pond. 6. A tree is taller than a bush. 7. Germany is bigger than England.

Übung 270: 1. broke into 2. came across 3. find out 4. was after 5. looking for 6. take good care of 7. give up

Übung 271: 1. twenty-six 2. second 3. first 4. thirtieth 5. half 6. nineteen thirty-three 7. eight hundred and fifty-three thousand 8. five point seven eight 9. three-quarters

Übung 272: murmured, said, exclaimed, cried, asked

Übung 273: 1. still 2. yet 3. still 4. any more/any longer 5. no longer 6. still

Übung 274: 1. fill in a form 2. put away clothes in a cupboard 3. sort out a problem 4. find out information 5. try on clothes in a shop 6. try out a new idea 7. bring up children 8. take back something you don't want 9. put off a meeting

10. clear up a mess 11. put out a fire
Übung 275: 1. grinned 2. has/possesses 3. relics 4. grave 5. nobleman 6. chance/fluke 7. breathed out
Übung 276: 1. which/that 2. where 3. which 4. who 5. whose 6. which oder nichts 7. when oder nichts 8. which/that
Übung 277: 1. richtig 2. richtig 3. falsch 4. richtig 5. falsch 6. richtig 7. richtig
Übung 278: 1. have announced 2. were stolen 3. were valued 4. were taken 5. did not go off 6. was not discovered 7. have been found
Übung 279: 1. c 2. b 3. a 4. b 5. b 6. c 7. b
Übung 280: "Good afternoon, old chap," he called, "where can I park my car, please?" – "I'm sorry sir, the club and its parking places are for members only."
"Arrogant pig!" whispered Elvira from the passenger seat. – "I don't have a member's card, but perhaps this will open the door to your respectable rooms." – "Scotland Yard? I'm very sorry, sir. I didn't know. You may park directly behind the building in the guests' parking place." – "Now, Elvira," said Hudson regretfully, "I'm afraid the authority of my badge is not enough to get you into the club as well."
Übung 281: James asked where he could park his car. 2. James said he did not have a member's card. 3. James said that perhaps his badge would let him in. 4. The porter said he could park behind the building. 5. Elvira said she would read the diary. 6. Miss Paddington said that he had promised to rest. 7. Elvira asked James what he was looking for.
Übung 282: 1. clue 2. red herring 3. alibi 4. witness 5. inspector 6. Evidence 7. Suspects
Übung 283: 1. give up/surrender 2. imagination/fantasy 3. spirits/morale 4. trace/hint 5. picked up/caught 6. perplexed/puzzled 7. medication/drugs 8. sceptics/doubters
Übung 284: 1. gone 2. been 3. been 4. been 5. gone 6. been 7. gone
Übung 285: 2. Hudson sits in his bureau listening to the radio. 3. Elvira finds out a lot reading the books. 4. Miss Paddington came into the kitchen wanting to cook for dinner. 5. The man walks away looking a little pale.
Übung 286: from … to, around, next to, in, through
Übung 287: 1. wasted 2. well-off 3. will 4. safe 5. salary 6. coin 7. broke
Übung 288: 1. perfectly 2. carefully 3. heavily 4. well 5. fast 6. hard 7. late
Übung 289: 1. something 2. hurry up 3. best 4. direct 5. nice 6. rarely 7. real 8. outside 9. agreement 10. raised
Übung 290: 1. hardly 2. hard 3. Hardly 4. well 5. good 6. lately 7. late
Übung 291: 1. In the meantime, Hudson had had time to brew some tea and serve Elvira a cup. 2. In 1903 Lord Douglas Winterbutton discovered Tut-Enk-Ra's tomb by chance. 3. It rang at least a dozen times before someone picked up the phone at the other end. 4. Inspector Hudson said goodbye and got out the car. 5. A couple of the guests turned around surprised. 6. Mr Cornwall pointed to two free armchairs which were next to each other in the corner of the room. 7. Patience was definitely

not a virtue Elvira possessed.
Übung 292: began, started, was, was heading, aimed at, knew, had existed, was, thought, was, would obtain, squander, regarded, was married, was expecting, was, took, was, had to be transported, were, help, find
Übung 293: 1. hunger 2. friend 3. dizzy 4. widow 5. penguin 6. dish 7. author
Übung 294: 1. falsch 2. falsch 3. richtig 4. falsch 5. richtig 6. falsch 7. richtig
Übung 295: 2. would not be/ate 3. didn't have to work/could meet 4. would taste/had 5. would know/had 6. were/would live 7. would buy/earned 8. listened/would make
Übung 296: 1. bigger, biggest 2. more nervous, most nervous 3. thirstier, thirstiest 4. politer, politest 5. more, most 6. better, best 7. quieter, quietest 8. further, furthest 9. luckier, luckiest 10. more careful, most careful
Übung 297: 2. he were/was here 3. I didn't live there 4. he had a new one 5. he were/was younger 6. he were/was thinner and taller 7. knew
Übung 298: 1. angry 2. beam 3. boiling 4. exhausted 5. shout 6. terrified 7. argue
Übung 299: thin/skin and bones, smiling/beaming, appreciatively/gratefully, lounge/living room, start again/resume, presently/before long, hollow/empty
Übung 300: 1. driving licence 2. steering wheel 3. insurance agent 4. airport 5. birthday card 6. motorway 7. country estate 8. sun glasses 9. headlights
Übung 301: 1. He had to go abroad quite often. 2. The Winterbutton family had been unlucky. 3. The thief must have done it. 4. Hudson may not /is not allowed to drink on duty.
Übung 302: Adverbien: carefully, slowly, gruffly, luckily, probably, really, curiously Adjektive: fast, sporty, unsporty, slower, safe, sound, wrong, moderate
Übung 303: 1. wouldn't have answered 2. hadn't driven/wouldn't have got 3. had given/wouldn't have gone 4. had been/wouldn't have gone 5. hadn't followed/wouldn't have found out 6. hadn't gone/wouldn't have died
Übung 304: 1. ruin 2. prince 3. violence 4. estate 5. suspect 6. tomb 7. coincidence 8. interrogate 9. paperboy 10. descendant 11. die 12. tongue 13. pain
Lösung: investigation
Übung 305: 1. much 2. Many 3. a lot of 4. Many 5. much 6. many 7. a lot 8. a lot of 9. a lot
Übung 306: 1. unless 2. before 3. But 4. too 5. Only
Übung 307: 1. he goes 2. he is going 3. he went 4. he used to go 5. he was going 6. he has gone 7. he has been going 8. he had gone 9. he had been going 10. he is going to go 11. he will go 12 he will have gone 13. he will have been going
Übung 308: 1. ancient/old 2. automobile/car 3. dead/deceased 4. enquire/ask 5. cop/policeman 6. steal/pinch 7. strange/bizzare 8. drink/sip
Übung 309: 1. wasn't listening 2. was staring 3. had rung 4. is 5. took 6. was trying 7. came
Übung 310: 1. His carriers had the symptoms of the fever before they discovered the pyramid and it is highly likely that the lord died of the same fever. 2. Two. The entrance hall and a bedroom on the first floor. 3. The fact that he

limped just like the thief. 4. He was the grandson of the pyramid's discoverer; he had the largest (untouched) collection of relics from Tut-Enk-Ra's tomb; he had access to the museum. 5. Because he wasn't feeling very well, and perhaps he had something to hide!

Übung 311: 1. Hudson 2. she/Elvira 3. She 4. Hudson 5. Hudson 6. he

Übung 312: 1. bump into 2. moaned 3. went after 4. huge 5. looked 6. middle

Übung 313: "The end justifies the means." Der Zweck heiligt die Mittel.

Übung 314: make out, dropped in, calm down, taken aback, brought along

Übung 315: 1. The mummy was stolen from the museum. 2. Some forensic tests are being conducted. 3. The case will have been solved by Hudson. 4. The tomb was opened straight away. 5. Elvira and Hudson have not been invited by the butler.

Übung 316: 1. Lord Winterbutton raised himself tiredly from his pillows. 2. The thief broke into the house. 3. Before going home, he dropped her off. 4. Hudson is looking forward to his day off. 5. Hudson was always assigned the difficult cases. 6. They broke into the house and stole some portraits. 7. Does he know anything about the mummy theft? 8. The Egyptian culture is really interesting.

Übung 317: 1. quickly 2. kept 3. it must be stored 4. than 5. Without waiting 6. next to the door 7. Luckily

Übung 318: 1. c 2. d 3. b 4. e 5. a 6. i 7. f 8. j 9. h 10. g

Übung 319: 2. Elvira is a friend (who) Hudson can always rely on./Elvira is a friend on whom Hudson can always rely. 3. That's the man (who) the police were looking for. 4. That is the mummy the investigator is looking for. 5. Sir Reginald is the boss Hudson listens to. 6. This is a clue (which) Hudson looked for carefully. 7. That's his friend who is sitting next to him.

Übung 320: 1. label 2. taste 3. size 4. trespassing 5. horizontally 6. torch

Übung 321: 1. upright/horizontal 2. right/wrong 3. forwards/backwards 4. laugh/cry 5. approve/disapprove 6. huge/tiny 7. carefully/carelessly 8. steep/gradual 9. narrow/wide

Übung 322: 1. put 2. held 3. gave 4. swung 5. are 6. said 7. froze 8. had been catapulted 9. could 10. were decorated

Übung 323: 2. will she 3. shall we 4. isn't it 5. does he 6. shouldn't she 7. will you 8. aren't I

Übung 324: 1. I'm going to 2. is going to 3. will 4. I'll 5. you'll 6. I'm not going to 7. I'll 8. are you going to 9. will

Übung 325: 1. on 2. between 3. have 4. width 5. depth 6. alive 7. run away 8. policeman

Übung 326: 2. He must be afraid of dying. 3. He might have hidden them. 4. He must have a deadline to meet. 5. Someone could still be awake. 6. He must have used the access card. 7. Lord Winterbutton might be sleeping.8. They must have been unlucky. 9. He could have used the fire escape.

Übung 327: 1. tricks 2. tomb 3. butler 4. authority 5. caught 6. inspector

Übung 328: "With the disappearance of the mummy!" said Elvira angrily "You mean with the theft of the mummy, just like all the other thefts. Half the relics have been stolen from all around the world." – "I'm afraid you're right, sir. But I had my good reasons." – "And I have good reasons to arrest you, Lord Winterbutton!" said Hudson sternly. – "I'm very sorry, but I can't allow that. It would be my death sentence."

Übung 329: 1. change 2. hurt oneself 3. feel 4. remember 5. enjoy oneself 6. look after oneself

Übung 330: 1. of 2. for 3. for 4. of 5. with 6. about 7. to 8. for 9. to 10. about 11. of 12. at

Übung 331: 1. discussion 2. suspicion 3. advice 4. exclamation 5. enquiry 6. imitation 7. employment

Übung 332: 1. grinned 2. measures 3. asked 4. poison 5. lawyer 6. crime 7. clever 8. trust

Übung 333: 1. shouldn't 2. don't have to 3. couldn't 4. won't 5. was able to 6. mustn't 7. should have obtained

Übung 334: 2. of 3. of 4. in 5. on 6. in 7. in 8. of

Übung 335: 1. I'm ashamed of what I have done. 2. Inspector Hudson took a step forward. 3. The main entrance was surrounded by a large crowd of photographers. 4. He seemed rather excited at the idea of helping Scotland Yard in an investigation. 5. The sports car was driven by either a madman or a reporter. 6. All the equipment had to be transported on camels. 7. When they came to the top of the stairs, they saw a long, dark corridor.

Übung 336: 1. An imitation of Tut-Enk-Ra's tomb. 2. The mummy. 3. Elvira knocked him on the floor. 4. To profit from his family. Every time a Winterbutton died, his family kept a lot of the family's fortune. 5. He intended closing them in the tomb.

Übung 337: 1. gave 2. we'll pull 3. doesn't need 4. will eliminate 5. being 6. heard 7. was overjoyed. 8. you'll celebrate 9. went

Übung 338: 1. Elvira had found a half-open window and carefully pushed it open. 2. His eyes slowly got used to the darkness. 3. He was happy for the insurance agent because her clients would save millions of pounds. 4. Hudson could not believe his eyes because instead of a cellar he had found an Egyptian death chamber. 5. Luckily the butler also seemed to be asleep at this late hour. 6. There was some light on the first floor, so both of them were careful. 7. Despite the late hour it took only a few seconds before a man dressed as a butler opened the door.

Übung 339: 1. of 2. from 3. against 4. for 5. in 6. for

Übung 340: 1. he steals 2. he is stealing 3. he stole 4. he used to steal 5. he was stealing 6. he has stolen 7. he has been stealing 8. he had stolen 9. he had been stealing 10. he is going to steal 11. he will steal 12. he will have stolen 13. he will have been stealing

Englisch Grundwortschatz

Abkürzungsverzeichnis:

AE	American English
fam	umgangssprachlich
pl	Plural
s.o.	someone
o.s.	oneself

A

a, an [eɪ, ən]	ein(e)
ability [ə'bɪlɪtɪ]	Fähigkeit
able ['eɪbl]	fähig, in der Lage
about [ə'baʊt]	über, ungefähr, gegen
above [ə'bʌv]	oberhalb, über, darüber
abroad [ə'brɔːd]	ins Ausland, im Ausland
absent ['æbsənt]	abwesend
absolutely [æbsə'luːtli]	völlig
access ['ækses]	Zugang
accessories [æk'sesərɪs] *pl*	Zubehör, Accessoires
accident ['æksɪdənt]	Unfall
accommodation [əkɔmə'deɪʃən]	Unterkunft
according to [ə'kɔːdɪŋ'tuː]	gemäß, laut, entsprechend
account [ə'kaʊnt]	Konto
accuse [ə'kjuːz]	beschuldigen, anklagen
ache [eɪk]	Schmerz
acquaintance [ə'kweɪntəns]	Bekannte(r)
act [ækt]	Akt, handeln, sich aufführen *fam*
action ['ækʃn]	Handlung
active ['æktɪv]	aktiv
activity [æk'tɪvɪtɪ]	Aktivität
actor ['æktə]	Schauspieler
actress ['æktrɪs]	Schauspielerin
actually ['æktjʊəlɪ]	wirklich
ad [æd]	(Zeitungs-)Anzeige
add [æd]	addieren
add up (to) [æd'ʌp(tuː)]	betragen, sich belaufen auf
address [ə'dres]	Adresse
adhesive tape [əd'hiːsɪvteɪp]	Klebeband

adjacent [ə'dʒeɪsənt]	angrenzend
admit [əd'mɪt]	zugeben
adult ['ædʌlt]	Erwachsene(r), erwachsen
advantage [əd'vɑːntɪdʒ]	Vorteil
advert ['ædvɜːt]	(Zeitungs-)Anzeige
advertisement [əd'vɜːtɪzmənt]	Werbung, Anzeige
advice [əd'vaɪs]	Rat
advise [əd'vaɪz]	raten, beraten
affirm [ə'fɜːm]	behaupten
afford [ə'fɔːd]	sich leisten
Africa ['æfrɪkə]	Afrika
after ['ɑːftə]	nach
afternoon [ɑːftə'nuːn]	Nachmittag
afterwards ['ɑːftəwədz]	anschließend, hinterher, nachher
again [ə'gen]	wieder
against [ə'genst]	gegen
age [eɪdʒ]	Alter, altern, älter werden
ago [ə'gəʊ]	vor
agree [ə'griː]	zustimmen, sich einigen
agreeable [ə'griːəbl]	angenehm
agreement [ə'griːmənt]	Vereinbarung
air [ɛə]	Luft
aircraft ['ɛəkrɑːft]	Flugzeug
airline ['ɛəlaɪn]	Fluggesellschaft
airmail ['ɛəmeɪl]	Luftpost
airport ['ɛəpɔːt]	Flughafen
alarm clock [ə'lɑːmklɔk]	Wecker
alcohol ['ælkəhɔl]	Alkohol
alcoholic [ælkə'hɔlɪk]	alkoholisch
A-levels ['eɪlevlz]	Abitur

alike [ə'laɪk]	gleich
alive [ə'laɪv]	lebendig
all [ɔːl]	alle, alles, ganz
all right [ɔːl'raɪt]	in Ordnung
all the same [ɔːlðə'seɪm]	trotzdem
allow [ə'laʊ]	erlauben
almost ['ɔːlməʊst]	beinahe
already [ɔːl'redɪ]	schon, bereits
also ['ɔːlsəʊ]	auch
although [ɔːl'ðəʊ]	obwohl, auch wenn
altogether [ɔːltə'geðə]	zusammen, völlig, alles in allem
always ['ɔːlweɪz]	immer
a.m. [eɪ'em]	morgens, vormittags
ambulance ['æmbjʊləns]	Krankenwagen
America [ə'merɪkə]	Amerika
among [ə'mʌŋ]	unter, inmitten, zwischen
amount [ə'maʊnt]	Menge, Summe, Betrag, betragen, sich belaufen auf
and [ænd]	und
anger ['æŋgə]	Ärger
angry ['æŋgrɪ]	ärgerlich
animal ['ænɪməl]	Tier
anniversary [ænɪ'vɜːsərɪ]	Jahrestag
another [ə'nʌðə]	noch ein(-e, -r)
answer ['ɑːnsə]	Antwort, antworten
answering machine ['ɑːnsərɪŋməʃiːn]	Anrufbeantworter
any ['enɪ]	irgendein(-e, -r)
anybody ['enɪbədɪ]	irgendjemand, jeder
anyone ['enɪwʌn]	irgendjemand, jeder
anything ['enɪθɪŋ]	irgendetwas, alles
anywhere ['enɪweə]	irgendwo

apart [ə'pɑːt]	getrennt, abgesehen von
apartment [ə'pɑːtmənt] *AE*	Wohnung, Etagenwohnung
apologize [ə'pɔlədʒaɪz]	sich entschuldigen
apology [ə'pɔlədʒɪ]	Entschuldigung
apparently [ə'pærəntli]	anscheinend
appear [ə'pɪə]	erscheinen, scheinen
applause [ə'plɔːz]	Applaus
apple ['æpl]	Apfel
application [æplɪ'keɪʃən]	Antrag
apply [ə'plaɪ]	sich bewerben
appointment [ə'pɔɪntmənt]	Verabredung, Termin
apprentice [ə'prentɪs]	Lehrling
apprenticeship [ə'prentɪsʃɪp]	Lehre
approximately [ə'prɔksɪmɪtlɪ]	ungefähr, gegen
apricot ['eɪprɪkɔt]	Aprikose
April ['eɪprɪl]	April
area ['ɛərɪə]	Fläche, Gebiet
Argentina [ɑːdʒən'tiːnə]	Argentinien
argue ['ɑːgjuː]	streiten
argument ['ɑːgjʊmənt]	Streit, Argument
arm [ɑːm]	Arm
around [ə'raʊnd]	ungefähr, gegen
arrange [ə'reɪndʒ]	regeln, arrangieren
arrangement [ə'reɪndʒmənt]	Vereinbarung, Vorbereitung
arrest [ə'rest]	festnehmen
arrival [ə'raɪvəl]	Ankunft
art [ɑːt]	Kunst
article ['ɑːtɪkl]	Artikel
as [æz]	so wie, als, während, wie, da
as … as [æz … æz]	genauso wie
as well as [æz'welæz]	sowohl als auch
Asia ['eɪʃə]	Asien

ask [ɑːsk]	fragen, bitten
assemble [ə'sembl]	aufbauen, montieren
astonish [əs'tɔnɪʃ]	erstaunen
at [æt]	bei, um
at all [æt'ɔːl]	überhaupt
at once [æt'wʌns]	sofort
at the back [ætðə'bæk]	hinten
at the bottom [ætðə'bɒtəm]	unten
at the front [ætðə'frʌnt]	vorne
at the same time [ætðə'seɪm'taɪm]	gleichzeitig
at the side [ætðə'saɪd]	seitlich
at the time [ætðə'taɪm]	damals, als
at the top [ætðə'tɒp]	oben
ATM (automated teller machine) [eɪtiː'em]	Bankautomat
attach [ə'tætʃ]	anhängen
attachment [ə'tætʃmənt]	Anhang
attack [ə'tæk]	Überfall, überfallen
attempt [ə'tempt]	Versuch
attend [ə'tend]	besuchen, teilnehmen
attention [ə'tenʃən]	Aufmerksamkeit
attic ['ætɪk]	Speicher, Mansarde
attractive [ə'træktɪv]	attraktiv
aubergine ['əʊbəʒiːn]	Aubergine
audience ['ɔːdɪəns]	Publikum
August ['ɔːgəst]	August
aunt [ɑːnt]	Tante
Australia [ɔs'treɪlɪə]	Australien
authentic [ɔː'θentɪk]	echt
author ['ɔːθə]	Autor
authority [ɔː'θɔrɪtɪ]	Behörde, Amt
autumn ['ɔːtəm]	Herbst

avoid [ə'vɔɪd] (ver)meiden, ausweichen
awake [ə'weɪk] wach, erwecken
away [ə'weɪ] weg

B

baby ['beɪbɪ] Baby
back [bæk] Rücken
backache ['bækeɪk] Rückenschmerzen
backpack ['bækpæk] *AE* Rucksack
backwards ['bækwədz] rückwärts
bad [bæd] schlecht, böse
bad luck [bæd'lʌk] Pech
bag [bæg] Tasche, Tüte
baggage ['bægɪdʒ] *AE* Gepäck
bake [beɪk] backen
bakery ['beɪkərɪ] Bäckerei
balance ['bæləns] Bilanz
balcony ['bælkənɪ] Balkon
ball [bɔːl] Ball
banana [bə'nɑːnə] Banane
bandage ['bændɪdʒ] Verband
band-aid ['bændeɪd] Pflaster
bank [bæŋk] Bank, Ufer
bank account [bæŋkə'kaʊnt] Konto
bank account statement [bæŋkə'kaʊnt'steɪtmənt] Kontoauszug
bar [bɑː] Bar, Theke
barbecue ['bɑːbɪkjuː] Grill
bargain ['bɑːgɪn] Sonderangebot, Schnäppchen
basic ['beɪsɪk] Basis-, grundlegend
bathe [beɪð] baden

bathroom ['bɑːθruːm]	Badezimmer
bathtub ['bɑːθtʌb]	Badewanne
battery ['bætərɪ]	Batterie
be [biː]	sein
be afraid [biːə'freɪd]	Angst haben, fürchten
be born [biː'bɔːn]	geboren werden, geboren sein
be careful [biː'kɛəfʊl]	vorsichtig sein
be silent [biː'saɪlənt]	schweigen
be sorry [biː'sɒrɪ]	Leid tun
be surprised [biːsə'praɪzd]	überrascht sein
beach [biːtʃ]	Strand
beach towel ['biːtʃtaʊəl]	Strandtuch
bean [biːn]	Bohne
bear [bɛə]	Bär
beard [bɪəd]	Bart
beat [biːt]	Schlag, schlagen
beautiful ['bjuːtɪfʊl]	schön
beautycase ['bjuːtɪkeɪs]	Kosmetikkoffer
because [biː'kɒz]	weil
become [bɪ'kʌm]	werden
bed [bed]	Bett
bed and breakfast [bedənd'brekfəst]	Übernachtung mit Frühstück
bedroom ['bedruːm]	Schlafzimmer
bee [biː]	Biene
beef [biːf]	Rindfleisch
beer [bɪə]	Bier
before [bɪ'fɔː]	vor, vorher
begin [bɪ'gɪn]	anfangen, beginnen
beginning [bɪ'gɪnɪŋ]	Anfang
behind [bɪ'haɪnd]	hinter, dahinter
belief [bɪ'liːf]	Glaube

believe [bɪ'liːv]	glauben
bell [bel]	Glocke, Klingel
belong [bɪ'lɒŋ]	gehören
below [bɪ'ləʊ]	unter, unterhalb, darunter
belt [belt]	Gürtel
bend [bend]	Kurve
benefit ['benɪfɪt]	Nutzen, profitieren
beside [bɪ'saɪd]	neben
better ['betə]	besser
between [bɪ'twiːn]	zwischen
bicycle ['baɪsɪkl]	Fahrrad
big [bɪg]	groß
bike [baɪk]	Fahrrad
bill [bɪl]	Rechnung
billion ['bɪlɪən]	Milliarde
bird [bɜːd]	Vogel
birth [bɜːθ]	Geburt
birthday ['bɜːθdeɪ]	Geburtstag
biscuit ['bɪskɪt]	Keks
bit [bɪt]	Stück
bitter ['bɪtə]	bitter
black [blæk]	schwarz
blackberry ['blækberɪ]	Brombeere
blanket ['blæŋkɪt]	Bettdecke
blood [blʌd]	Blut
blood pressure ['blʌdpreʃə]	Blutdruck
blossom ['blɒsəm]	Blüte
blouse [blaʊz]	Bluse
blow [bləʊ]	wehen
blue [bluː]	blau
blueberry ['bluːberɪ]	Heidelbeere
board [bɔːd]	Brett, Tafel

boat [bəʊt]	Boot
body ['bɒdɪ]	Körper
boil [bɔɪl]	kochen, sieden
bomb [bɒm]	Bombe
bone [bəʊn]	Knochen
book [bʊk]	Buch, buchen
boot [buːt]	Stiefel
border ['bɔːdə]	Grenze
bordering ['bɔːdərɪŋ]	angrenzend
boring ['bɔːrɪŋ]	langweilig
borrow ['bɒrəʊ]	leihen
boss [bɒs]	Vorgesetzte(r)
both [bəʊθ]	beide
bother ['bɒðə]	belästigen, aufregen
bottle ['bɒtl]	Flasche
bottle-opener ['bɒtləʊpnə]	Flaschenöffner
bottom ['bɒtəm]	Boden, Grund, Unterseite, Gesäß
bouquet (of flowers) ['bʊkeɪ(ɒv'flaʊəz)]	Blumenstrauß
bow [bəʊ]	Bogen
bowl [bəʊl]	Schüssel
box [bɒks]	Schachtel, Kiste
boxroom ['bɒksruːm]	Abstellkammer
boy [bɔɪ]	Junge
boyfriend ['bɔɪfrend]	fester Freund
bracelet ['breɪslɪt]	Armband, Armreif
brain [breɪn]	Gehirn
branch [brɑːntʃ]	Ast, Zweig
brave [breɪv]	tapfer
Brazil [brə'zɪl]	Brasilien
bread [bred]	Brot

break [breɪk]	Pause, (sich) brechen
breakfast ['brekfəst]	Frühstück
breast [brest]	Brust
breath [breθ]	Atem, atmen
bridge [brɪdʒ]	Brücke
bring [brɪŋ]	bringen
British ['brɪtɪʃ]	britisch
broad [brɔːd]	breit, weit
brochure ['brəʊʃʊə]	Broschüre, Prospekt
broken ['brəʊkən]	kaputt
brooch [brəʊtʃ]	Brosche
broom [bruːm]	Besen
brother ['brʌðə]	Bruder
brother-in-law ['brʌðərɪnlɔː]	Schwager
brothers and sisters ['brʌðəzænd'sɪstəz] *pl*	Geschwister
brown [braʊn]	braun
brush [brʌʃ]	Bürste, bürsten
bucket ['bʌkɪt]	Eimer
buddy ['bʌdɪ] *fam*	Kumpel *fam*
build [bɪld]	bauen
building ['bɪldɪŋ]	Gebäude
bull [bʊl]	Bulle
bunch (of flowers) [bʌntʃ(ɒv'flaʊəz)]	Blumenstrauß
bureaucracy [bjuː'rɒkrəsɪ]	Bürokratie
burn [bɜːn]	brennen, verbrennen
bus [bʌs]	Bus
bush [bʊʃ]	Busch, Strauch
business ['bɪznɪs]	Geschäft, geschäftlich
busy ['bɪzɪ]	beschäftigt
but [bʌt]	aber, sondern

butcher's (shop) ['bʊtʃəz(ʃɒp)]	Metzgerei
butter ['bʌtə]	Butter
button ['bʌtn]	Knopf
buy [baɪ]	kaufen
by [baɪ]	von, bei, bis, mit, spätestens
bye [baɪ]	tschüss

C

cab [kæb] *AE*	Taxi
cabbage ['kæbɪdʒ]	Kohl
cable ['keɪbl]	Kabel
cactus ['kæktəs]	Kaktus
café ['kæfeɪ]	Café, Restaurant
cake [keɪk]	Kuchen
calculate ['kælkjʊleɪt]	rechnen
calculator ['kælkjʊleɪtə]	Taschenrechner
call ['kɔːl]	Anruf, anrufen
call back [kɔːl'bæk]	zurückrufen
caller ['kɔːlə]	Anrufer
calm [kɑːm]	ruhig, sich beruhigen
camera ['kæmərə]	Kamera
camping site ['kæmpɪŋsaɪt]	Campingplatz
can [kæn]	Dose, können
can opener ['kænəʊpənə]	Dosenöffner
Canada ['kænədə]	Kanada
cancel ['kænsəl]	absagen, stempeln, entwerten
candle ['kændl]	Kerze
cap [kæp]	Mütze, Kappe
capital ['kæpɪtl]	Hauptstadt
car [kɑː]	Auto
car park ['kɑːpɑːk]	Parkplatz

card [kɑːd]	Karte
care [kɛə]	Sorgfalt, Pflege, sich kümmern
career [kə'rɪə]	Karriere
careful ['kɛəfʊl]	sorgfältig, vorsichtig
careless ['kɛəlɪs]	leichtsinnig
carpet ['kɑːpɪt]	Teppich
carrot ['kærət]	Karotte
carry ['kærɪ]	tragen
case [keɪs]	Fall, Kiste, Koffer
cash [kæʃ]	Bargeld, Barzahlung
cash in [kæʃ'ɪn]	einlösen
cash-desk ['kæʃdesk]	Kasse
cassette [kə'set]	Kassette
castle ['kɑːsl]	Burg, Schloss
cat [kæt]	Katze
catch [kætʃ]	fangen
cauliflower ['kɒlɪflaʊə]	Blumenkohl
cause [kɔːz]	Ursache, verursachen
cautious ['kɔːʃəs]	vorsichtig
ceiling ['siːlɪŋ]	Decke
celebrate ['selɪbreɪt]	feiern
celebration [selɪ'breɪʃən]	Fest, Feier
cellar ['selə]	Keller
cemetery ['semɪtrɪ]	Friedhof
centimetre ['sentɪmiːtə]	Zentimeter
central ['sentrəl]	Zentrale, zentral
centre ['sentə]	Innenstadt, Zentrum
century ['sentjʊrɪ]	Jahrhundert
certain ['sɜːtən]	sicher, gewiss, zuverlässig
certainly ['sɜːtənlɪ]	sicherlich, natürlich
certificate [sɜ'tɪfɪkɪt]	Zeugnis, Urkunde
chair [tʃɛə]	Stuhl

chance [tʃɑːns]	Chance
change [tʃeɪndʒ]	Kleingeld, Wechselgeld, wechseln
character ['kærɪktə]	Charakter, Original
characteristic [kærɪktə'rɪstɪk]	Eigenschaft
charge [tʃɑːdʒ]	berechnen
charming ['tʃɑːmɪŋ]	charmant, reizend
cheap [tʃiːp]	billig
check [tʃek]	(über)prüfen, kontrollieren
check [tʃek] *AE*	Scheck
check in [tʃek'ɪn]	(sich) anmelden, einchecken
check-out ['tʃekout]	Kasse
cheese [tʃiːz]	Käse
chemist ['kemɪst]	Drogerie, Apotheker(in)
cheque [tʃek]	Scheck
cherry ['tʃerɪ]	Kirsche
chest of drawers [tʃestɒv'drɔːz]	Kommode
chicken ['tʃɪkən]	Huhn
child [tʃaɪld], **children** ['tʃɪldrən] *pl*	Kind, Kinder
childhood ['tʃaɪldhʊd]	Kindheit
children's room ['tʃɪldrənsruːm]	Kinderzimmer
chin [tʃɪn]	Kinn
china ['tʃaɪnə]	Porzellan
China ['tʃaɪnə]	China
chips [tʃɪps]	Pommes frites
chocolate ['tʃɒklɪt]	Schokolade
choice [tʃɔɪs]	Wahl
choose [tʃuːz]	wählen, auswählen, aussuchen
chop [tʃɒp]	hacken
christian name ['krɪstʃənneɪm]	Vorname
Christmas ['krɪsməs]	Weihnachten

church [tʃɜːtʃ]	Kirche
cigar [sɪ'gɑː]	Zigarre
cigarette [sɪgə'ret]	Zigarette
cinema ['sɪnəmə]	Kino
circle ['sɜːkl]	Kreis
citizen ['sɪtɪzn]	Bürger
citizenship ['sɪtɪznʃɪp]	Staatsangehörigkeit
city ['sɪtɪ]	Stadt
city map ['sɪtɪmæp]	Stadtplan
city tour ['sɪtɪtʊə]	Stadtrundfahrt
civil servant ['sɪvl 'sɜːvənt]	Beamter, Beamtin
class [klɑːs]	Klasse
classroom ['klɑːsruːm]	Klassenzimmer
clean [kliːn]	aufräumen, putzen, sauber
clear [klɪə]	klar, deutlich
clerk [klɑːk]	(Büro-)Angestellte(r)
clever ['klevə]	klug
climate ['klaɪmɪt]	Klima
climb [klaɪm]	klettern, besteigen
clock [klɒk]	Uhr
close [kləʊs]	schließen, nahe
closed [kləʊzd]	zu, geschlossen
cloth [klɒθ]	Stoff, Gewebe, Putzlappen
clothes [kləʊz] *pl*	Kleidung
cloud [klaʊd]	Wolke
club [klʌb]	Klub, Verein
coach [kəʊtʃ]	Reisebus, Trainer
coal [kəʊl]	Kohle
coast [kəʊst]	Küste
coat [kəʊt]	Mantel, Jacke
coffee ['kɒfɪ]	Kaffee
coin [kɔɪn]	Münze

colander ['kɒləndə]	Sieb
cold [kəʊld]	Erkältung, kalt
cold meat [kəʊld'miːt]	Wurst, Aufschnitt
collar ['kɒlə]	Kragen
colleague ['kɒliːg]	Kollege, Kollegin
collect [kə'lekt]	sammeln
collection [kə'lekʃən]	Sammlung
college ['kɒlɪdʒ]	College, Universität, Hochschule
colour ['kʌlə]	Farbe
comb [kəʊm]	Kamm, kämmen
come [kʌm]	kommen
comfortable ['kʌmfətəbl]	bequem
commerce ['kɒmɜːs]	Handel
commercial [kə'mɜːʃəl]	Handels-, gewerblich
common ['kɒmən]	gemeinsam, üblich
communication [kəmjuːnɪ'keɪʃən]	Kommunikation
company ['kʌmpənɪ]	Unternehmen, Firma
compare [kəm'pɛə]	vergleichen
complain [kəm'pleɪn]	sich beschweren
complaint [kəm'pleɪnt]	Beschwerde
complete [kəm'pliːt]	völlig, vollständig
computer [kəm'pjuːtə]	Computer
concert ['kɒnsət]	Konzert
condition [kən'dɪʃən]	Bedingung, Zustand
conductor [kən'dʌktə]	Schaffner(in)
confirm [kən'fɜːm]	bestätigen
confirmation [kɒnfə'meɪʃən]	Bestätigung
confuse [kən'fjuːz]	verwechseln, durcheinander bringen, verwirren
congestion [kən'dʒestʃən]	Stau

congratulate [kən'grætjʊleɪt]	gratulieren
connect [kə'nekt]	verbinden
connection [kə'nekʃən]	Anschluss
consider [kən'sɪdə]	überlegen, erwägen, betrachten, prüfen
consideration [kənsɪdə'reɪʃən]	Rücksicht, Berücksichtigung
contest ['kɒntest]	Wettkampf, Wettbewerb
continent ['kɒntɪnənt]	Kontinent
continue [kən'tɪnjuː]	fortfahren, weitermachen
contract ['kəntrækt]	Vertrag
contradict [kɒntrə'dɪkt]	widersprechen
control [kən'trəʊl]	Kontrolle, Beherrschung, kontrollieren, beherrschen
conversation [kɒnvə'seɪʃən]	Gespräch, Unterhaltung
convict [kən'vɪkt]	verurteilen
convince [kən'vɪns]	überzeugen
cook [kʊk]	Koch, Köchin, kochen
cookie ['kʊkɪ] *AE*	Keks
cooking spoon ['kʊkɪŋspuːn]	Kochlöffel
cool [kuːl]	kühl
copy ['kɒpɪ]	Kopie, Exemplar
copying machine ['kɒpiɪŋmə'ʃiːn]	Kopiergerät
corkscrew ['kɔːkskruː]	Korkenzieher
corn [kɔːn] *AE*	Mais
corner ['kɔːnə]	Winkel, Ecke
corporate ['kɔːpərɪt]	Firmen-
corporation [kɔːpə'reɪʃən]	Unternehmen, Firma
correct [kə'rekt]	korrigieren, richtig, korrekt
corridor ['kɒrɪdə]	Flur
cost [kɒst]	kosten
costume ['kɒstjuːm]	Kostüm

cosy ['kəʊzɪ]	gemütlich
cotton ['kɒtn]	Baumwolle
cough [kɒf]	Husten, husten
could [kəʊld]	könnte, könntest, könntet, könnten
council ['kaʊnsl]	Rat, Ausschuss, Verwaltung
count [kaʊnt]	zählen
counter ['kaʊntə]	Ladentheke, Schalter
country ['kʌntrɪ]	Land
country road ['kʌntrɪrəʊd]	Landstraße
countryside ['kʌntrɪsaɪd]	Landschaft
couple ['kʌpl]	Paar
couple of ['kʌpləv]	paar
courageous [kə'reɪdʒəs]	mutig
courgette [kɔː'ʒet]	Zucchini
course [kɔːs]	Kurs
court [kɔːt]	Gericht
cousin ['kʌzn]	Cousin, Cousine
cow [kaʊ]	Kuh
cowardly ['kaʊədlɪ]	feige
co-worker ['kəʊwɜːkə]	Mitarbeiter(in)
cozy ['koʊzɪ]	gemütlich
cream [kriːm]	Creme, Sahne
credit ['kredɪt]	Darlehen, Kredit
credit card ['kredɪtkɑːd]	Kreditkarte
crime [kraɪm]	Straftat
criminal ['krɪmɪnl]	Kriminelle(r), kriminell
criticism ['krɪtɪsɪzəm]	Kritik
criticize ['krɪtɪsaɪz]	kritisieren
crooked ['krʊkɪd]	schief
cross [krɒs]	Kreuz, überqueren
crossing ['krɒsɪŋ]	Kreuzung
crowd [kraʊd]	(Menschen-)Menge

crucifix ['kruːsɪfɪks]	Kruzifix
cruise [kruːz]	Kreuzfahrt
cucumber ['kjuːkʌmbə]	Gurke
culture ['kʌltʃə]	Kultur
cup [kʌp]	Tasse
cupboard ['kʌbəd]	Schrank
cure [kjʊə]	Kur, kurieren
currency ['kʌrənsɪ]	Währung
current ['kʌrənt]	aktuell
curriculum vitae, **CV** [kə'rɪkjʊləm'vaɪtiː]	Lebenslauf
curtain ['kɜːtn]	Gardine
custom ['kʌstəm]	Sitte, Brauch
customer ['kʌstəmə]	Kunde, Kundin
customs ['kʌstəmz]	Zoll
cut [kʌt]	Schnitt, schneiden
cutlery ['kʌtlərɪ]	Besteck
Czech Republic [tʃekrɪ'pʌblɪk]	Tschechien

D

daily ['dælɪ]	täglich
daily (news)paper ['deɪlɪ(njuːz)'peɪpə]	Tageszeitung
damage ['dæmɪdʒ]	Schaden
dance [dɑːns]	Tanz, tanzen
danger ['deɪndʒə]	Gefahr
dangerous ['deɪndʒərəs]	gefährlich
dark [dɑːk]	Dunkelheit, dunkel
data ['deɪtə]	Daten
date [deɪt]	Datum, Verabredung, mit jmdm. gehen

daughter ['dɔːtə]	Tochter
day [deɪ]	Tag
day after tomorrow ['deɪ'aːftatə'mɒrəʊ]	übermorgen
day before yesterday ['deɪbɪ'fɔː'jestədeɪ]	vorgestern
dear [dɪə]	lieb, geehrt
death [deθ]	Tod
debts [dets] *pl*	Schulden
decade ['dekeɪd]	Jahrzehnt
December [dɪ'sembə]	Dezember
decide [dɪ'saɪd]	entscheiden
decision [dɪ'sɪʒən]	Entscheidung
deep [diːp]	tief
defend [dɪ'fend]	verteidigen
defense [dɪ'fens]	Verteidigung
definitely ['defɪnɪtlɪ]	sicherlich, zweifellos
degree [dɪ'griː]	Abschluss
delay [dɪ'leɪ]	Verspätung
delayed [dɪ'leɪd]	verspätet
delicious [dɪ'lɪʃəs]	wunderbar, köstlich
demand [dɪ'mɑːnd]	verlangen, fordern
democracy [dɪ'mɒkrəsɪ]	Demokratie
Denmark ['denmɑːk]	Dänemark
dentist ['dentɪst]	Zahnarzt, Zahnärztin
deodorant [diː'əʊdərənt]	Deo
department [dɪ'pɑːtmənt]	Ministerium, Abteilung
department store [dɪ'pɑːtməntstɔː]	Kaufhaus
departure [dɪ'pɑːtʃə]	Abreise
depend [dɪ'pend]	abhängen, sich verlassen auf
depth [depθ]	Tiefe

describe [dɪs'kraɪb]	beschreiben
description [dɪs'krɪpʃən]	Beschreibung
desk [desk]	Schreibtisch
dessert [dɪ'zɜːt]	Dessert
detail ['diːteɪl]	Einzelheit
detergent [dɪ'tɜːdʒənt]	Putzmittel
develop [dɪ'veləp]	entwickeln, sich entwickeln
development ['dɪveləpmənt]	Entwicklung
device [dɪ'vaɪs]	Gerät, Vorrichtung, Trick
diagonal [daɪ'ægənl]	diagonal
dial [daɪl]	wählen
dictatorship [dɪk'teɪtəʃɪp]	Diktatur
dictionary ['dɪkʃənrɪ]	Wörterbuch
die [daɪ]	sterben
diet ['daɪət]	Abmagerungskur, Diät
difference [vdɪfrəns]	Unterschied
different ['dɪfrənt]	unterschiedlich
difficult ['dɪfɪkəlt]	schwierig
difficulty ['dɪfɪkəltɪ]	Schwierigkeit, Mühe
digit ['dɪdʒɪt]	Zahl
dining room ['daɪnɪŋruːm]	Esszimmer
dinner ['dɪnə]	Abendessen
diploma [dɪp'ləʊmə]	Diplom
direct [dɪ'rekt]	direkt
direction [dɪ'rekʃən]	Richtung
director [daɪ'rektə]	Direktor(in)
dirty ['dɜːtɪ]	schmutzig
disabled [dɪs'eɪbld]	behindert
disadvantage [dɪsəd'vɑːntɪdʒ]	Nachteil
disagree [dɪsə'griː]	nicht einverstanden sein, nicht einer Meinung sein
disagreement [dɪsə'griːmənt]	Meinungsverschiedenheit

disappear [dɪsə'pɪə]	verschwinden
disappoint [dɪsə'pɔɪnt]	enttäuschen
disassemble [dɪsə'sembl]	zerlegen
discount ['dɪskaʊnt]	Rabatt
discriminate [dɪ'skrɪmɪneɪt]	benachteiligen, diskriminieren
discrimination [dɪskrɪmɪ'neɪʃən]	Benachteiligung, Diskriminierung
discuss [dɪs'kʌs]	diskutieren
discussion [dis'kʌʃən]	Diskussion
disease [dɪ'zi:z]	Krankheit
dish [dɪʃ]	Speise
dishes [dɪʃɪz]	Geschirr
dishwasher ['dɪʃwɒʃə]	Geschirrspüler
disk [dɪsk]	Diskette
dismiss [dɪs'mɪs]	entlassen
distance ['dɪstəns]	Distanz, Entfernung, Strecke
distant ['dɪstənt]	entfernt
divide [dɪ'vaɪd]	dividieren, teilen
divorce [dɪ'vɔ:s]	Scheidung, sich scheiden lassen
do [du:]	tun
doctor ['dɒktə]	Arzt, Ärztin
document ['dɒkjʊmənt]	Dokument
dog [dɒg]	Hund
door [dɔ:]	Tür
doorbell ['dɔ:bel]	Klingel
double ['dʌbl]	doppelt
doubt [daʊt]	Zweifel, zweifeln
down [daʊn]	herunter, hinunter, nieder
downstairs [daʊn'stɛəz]	unten
downtown ['daʊntaʊn]	Innenstadt, Zentrum
downwards ['daʊnwədz]	nach unten, abwärts
dozen ['dʌzn]	ein Dutzend

draw [drɔː]	zeichnen
drawer [drɔː]	Schublade
dream [driːm]	Traum, träumen
dress [dres]	Kleid, sich anziehen
drill [drɪl]	Bohrer, bohren
drink [drɪŋk]	Getränk, trinken
drive [draɪv]	fahren
driving license ['draɪvɪŋ'laɪsəns]	Führerschein
drop [drɒp]	Tropfen, fallen lassen
drug [drʌg]	Medikament, Droge
drums [drʌmz]	Schlagzeug
dry [draɪ]	abwischen, abtrocknen, trocken
duck [dʌk]	Ente
due [djuː]	fällig, aufgrund, wegen
during ['djʊrɪŋ]	während
dust [dʌst]	Staub, abstauben
duty ['djuːtɪ]	Pflicht, Dienst

E

each [iːtʃ]	jede(-r, -s) (einzelne)
each other [iːtʃ'ʌðə]	einander, (sich) gegenseitig
ear [ɪə]	Ohr
earache ['ɪəreɪk]	Ohrenschmerzen
early ['ɜːlɪ]	früh
earn [ɜːn]	verdienen
earring ['ɪərɪŋ]	Ohrring
earth [ɜːθ]	Erde
east [iːst]	Ost
Easter ['iːstə]	Ostern
easy ['iːzɪ]	leicht
eat [iːt]	essen

economic [iːkə'nɒmɪk]	preiswert
economy [iː'kɒnəmɪ]	Wirtschaft
edge [edʒ]	Kante
education [edjʊ'keɪʃən]	Bildung, Ausbildung
effect [ɪ'fekt]	Wirkung, Auswirkung, Effekt
effort ['efət]	Anstrengung, Bemühung
egg [eg]	Ei
eight [eɪt]	acht
eighteen [eɪ'tiːn]	achtzehn
eighteenth [eɪ'tiːnθ]	achtzehnte(-r, -s)
eighth [eɪtθ]	achte(-r, -s)
eighty ['eɪtɪ]	achtzig
either … or ['aɪðə … ɔː]	entweder … oder
elect [ɪ'lekt]	wählen
election [ɪ'lekʃən]	Wahl
electricity [ɪlek'trɪsɪtɪ]	Strom, Elektrizität
elementary school [elɪ'mentərɪskuːl]	Grundschule
elephant ['elɪfənt]	Elefant
eleven [ɪ'levn]	elf
eleventh [ɪlevnθ]	elfte(-r, -s)
else [els]	sonst, außerdem
e-mail ['iːmeɪl]	E-Mail
embarrassing [ɪm'bærəsɪŋ]	peinlich, unangenehm
emergency [ɪ'mɜːdʒənsɪ]	Notfall
employ [ɪm'plɔɪ]	beschäftigen
employee [emplɔɪ'iː]	Angestellte(r)
employer [ɪm'plɔɪə]	Arbeitgeber(in)
empty ['emptɪ]	leer
end [end]	Ende, aufhören, beenden
enemy ['enɪmɪ]	Feind(in), feindlich
energy ['enədʒɪ]	Energie

engaged [ɪn'geɪdʒd]	verlobt, besetzt
engine ['endʒɪn]	Motor, Lokomotive
engineer [endʒɪ'nɪə]	Ingenieur(in), Techniker(in)
engineering [endʒɪ'nɪərɪŋ]	Ingenieurwesen, Maschinenbau
England ['ɪŋlənd]	England
English ['ɪŋglɪʃ]	Englisch, englisch
enjoy [ɪn'dʒɔɪ]	genießen, gerne tun
enough [ɪ'nʌf]	genug, ausreichend
enquire [ɪn'kwaɪə]	sich erkundigen, anfragen
enquiries [ɪn'kwaɪəriːs]	Erkundigungen, Auskunft
enquiry [ɪn'kwaɪərɪ]	Anfrage
enter ['entə]	eingeben
entertain [entə'teɪn]	unterhalten
entertainment [entə'teɪnmənt]	Vergnügen, Unterhaltung
entire [ɪn'taɪə]	ganz, gesamt
entrance ['entrəns]	Eingang
entry ['entrɪ]	Einfahrt
envelope ['envələʊp]	Umschlag
environment [ɪn'vaɪərənmənt]	Umwelt
environment protection [ɪn'vaɪərənməntprə'tekʃn]	Umweltschutz
equal ['iːkwəl]	gleich
equality [iː'kwɒlɪtɪ]	Gleichheit
equipment [ɪ'kwɪpmənt]	Anlage, Ausstattung, Einrichtung
erase [ɪ'reɪz]	löschen
error ['erə]	Irrtum
especially [ɪs'peʃəlɪ]	besonders
Europe ['jʊərəp]	Europa
even ['iːvən]	gleichmäßig, ebenmäßig
evening ['iːvnɪŋ]	Abend
event [ɪ'vent]	Ereignis, Veranstaltung

eventually [ɪ'ventʃʊəlɪ]	endlich, schließlich
ever ['evə]	je(mals), immer
every ['evrɪ]	jede(-r, -s)
everybody ['evrɪbɒdɪ]	jeder, alle
everyone ['evrɪwʌn]	jeder, alle
everything ['evrɪθɪŋ]	alles
everywhere ['evrɪwɛə]	überall
exact [ɪg'zækt]	genau, gerade
exam [ɪg'zæm]	Examen, Prüfung
examine [ɪg'zæmɪn]	untersuchen
example [ɪg'zɑːmpl]	Beispiel, Vorbild
excellent ['eksələnt]	ausgezeichnet
except [ɪk'sept]	außer
exception [ɪk'sepʃən]	Ausnahme
exchange [ɪk'tʃeɪndʒ]	Tausch, tauschen, austauschen, umtauschen
exciting [ɪk'saɪtɪŋ]	aufregend, spannend
excuse [ɪk'skjuːz]	Entschuldigung, entschuldigen
exercise ['eksəsaɪz]	Übung
exhibition [eksɪ'bɪʃən]	Ausstellung
exit ['egzɪt]	Ausgang, Ausfahrt
expect [ɪk'spekt]	erwarten
expensive [ɪk'spensɪv]	teuer
experience [ɪk'spɪərɪəns]	erleben
expert ['ekspɜːt]	Fachmann, Experte, Expertin
expire [ɪk'spaɪə]	ablaufen
explain [ɪk'spleɪn]	erklären
explanation [eksplə'neɪʃən]	Erklärung
express [ɪk'spres]	ausdrücken
express delivery [ɪk'spresdɪ'lɪvərɪ]	Eilsendung
expression [ɪk'spreʃən]	Ausdruck

extraordinary [ɪk'strɔːdnrɪ]	außergewöhnlich
eye [aɪ]	Auge

F

fabric ['fæbrɪk]	Stoff, Gewebe
face [feɪs]	Gesicht, gegenüberliegen, gegenüberstehen, sich stellen
factory ['fæktərɪ]	Fabrik
fade [feɪd]	welken
fail [feɪl]	durchfallen, scheitern
failure ['feɪljə]	Misserfolg, Niederlage
fair [fɛə]	hell
fairly ['fɛəlɪ]	ziemlich
faithful ['feɪθfʊl]	treu
fake [feɪk]	unecht
fall [fɔːl]	fallen
fall in love [fɔːlin'lʌv]	sich verlieben
family ['fæmɪlɪ]	Familie
famous ['feɪməs]	berühmt
far (away) [fɑː(ə'weɪ)]	(weit) entfernt
fare [fɛə]	Tarif
farm [fɑːm]	Bauernhof
farmer [fɑːmə]	Bauer, Bäuerin
fashion ['fæʃən]	Mode
fashionable ['fæʃənəbl]	modisch
fast [fɑːst]	schnell
fat [fæt]	dick
father ['fɑːðə]	Vater
father-in-law ['fɑːðərɪnlɔː]	Schwiegervater
fault [fɔːlt]	Fehler, Schuld
favour ['feɪvə]	Gefallen, Gefälligkeit

favourite ['feɪvərɪt]	Lieblings-
fax [fæks]	Fax, faxen
fear [fɪə]	Angst, Befürchtung, fürchten
February ['febrʊərɪ]	Februar
fee [fiː]	Gebühr
feed [fiːd]	füttern
feel [fiːl]	fühlen
feeling ['fiːlɪŋ]	Gefühl
female ['fiːmeɪl]	weiblich
fence [fens]	Zaun
ferry ['ferɪ]	Fähre
fetch [fetʃ]	holen
fever ['fiːvə]	Fieber
few [fjuː]	wenig, wenige
field [fiːld]	Feld
fifteen [fɪf'tiːn]	fünfzehn
fifteenth [fɪf'tiːnθ]	fünfzehnte(-r, -s)
fifth [fɪfθ]	fünfte(-r, -s)
fifty ['fɪftɪ]	fünfzig
fight [faɪt]	Kampf, kämpfen
figure ['fɪgə]	Zahl
file [faɪl]	Datei, Aktenordner
fill [fɪl]	füllen
filling station ['fɪlɪŋsteɪʃən]	Tankstelle
film [fɪlm]	Film
final destination ['faɪnldestɪ'neɪʃən]	Endstation
finally ['faɪnəlɪ]	endlich, schließlich
finance ['faɪnæns]	finanzieren
finances ['faɪnænsɪz] *pl*	Finanzen
find [faɪnd]	finden
fine [faɪn]	Geldstrafe, ausgezeichnet, schön

finger ['fɪŋgə]	Finger
fingerprint ['fɪŋgəprɪnt]	Fingerabdruck
finish ['fɪnɪʃ]	erledigen, fertig stellen, enden
fire ['faɪə]	Feuer, Brand, entlassen
fire brigade ['faɪəbrɪgeɪd]	Feuerwehr
fireman ['faɪəmən]	Feuerwehrmann
firm [fɜːm]	Unternehmen, Firma
first [fɜːst]	zuerst, als Erste(r), erste(-r, -s)
fish [fɪʃ]	Fisch
fit [fɪt]	passen, fit
fitness ['fɪtnɪs]	Fitness, Kondition
five [faɪv]	fünf
fix [fɪks] *fam*	reparieren
flat [flæt]	Wohnung, flach, eben, niedrig
flexi-time ['fleksɪtaɪm]	Gleitzeit
flight [flaɪt]	Flug
floor [flɔː]	Stockwerk, Etage, Fußboden
flour ['flaʊə]	Mehl
flower ['flaʊə]	Blume
flower-bed ['flaʊəbed]	Blumenbeet
flowerpot ['flaʊəpɒt]	Blumentopf
flu [fluː] *fam*	Grippe
fluent ['fluːənt]	fließend
flunk [flʌŋk] *fam*	durchfallen
flute [fluːt]	Flöte
fly [flaɪ]	Fliege, fliegen
fog [fɒg]	Nebel
follow ['fɒləʊ]	(be)folgen
food [fuːd]	Lebensmittel, Essen
foot [fʊt], **feet** [fiːt] *pl*	Fuß
football ['fʊtbɔːl]	Fußball
for [fɔː]	für, zu, seit, nach

for free [fɔː'friː]	kostenlos, gratis
forbid [fə'bɪd]	verbieten
forehead ['fɔːhed]	Stirn
foreign ['fɒrən]	ausländisch, fremd
foreigner ['fɒrənə]	Ausländer(in)
forest ['fɔrɪst]	Wald
forget [fə'get]	vergessen
forgive [fə'gɪv]	verzeihen
fork [fɔːk]	Gabel
form [fɔːm]	Form, Formular, bilden
formal ['fɔːməl]	formell, offiziell
former ['fɔːmə]	ehemalige(r), frühere(r)
fortnight ['fɔːtnaɪt]	zwei Wochen, vierzehn Tage
fortunately ['fɔːtʃənɪtlɪ]	glücklicherweise, zum Glück
fortune ['fɔːtʃən]	Vermögen
forty ['fɔːtɪ]	vierzig
forwards ['fɔːwədz]	vorwärts
four [fɔː]	vier
fourteen [fɔː'tiːn]	vierzehn
fourteenth [fɔː'tiːnθ]	vierzehnte(-r, -s)
fourth [fɔːθ]	vierte(-r, -s)
frame [freɪm]	Bilderrahmen, rahmen
France [frɑːns]	Frankreich
free [friː]	frei
freedom ['friːdəm]	Freiheit
freeze [friːz]	frieren
freezer ['friːzə]	Tiefkühltruhe
French [frentʃ]	Französisch, französisch
frequently ['friːkwəntlɪ]	oft, häufig
fresh [freʃ]	frisch
Friday ['fraɪdeɪ]	Freitag
fridge [frɪdʒ] *fam*	Kühlschrank

friend [frend]	Freund, Freundin
friendly ['frendlɪ]	freundlich
frighten ['fraɪtn]	ängstigen, Angst machen
frog [frɒg]	Frosch
from ... until [frɒm … ən'tɪl]	von ... bis
front [frʌnt]	Vorderseite, Vorder-, vordere(-r, -s)
fruit [fru:t]	Obst, Früchte
fry [fraɪ]	braten
frying-pan ['fraɪɪŋpæn]	Pfanne
full [fʊl]	satt, voll
full board ['fʊlbɔ:d]	Vollpension
full-time ['fʊltaɪm]	Vollzeit
fun [fʌn]	Spaß
funny ['fʌnɪ]	komisch, lustig
furniture ['fɜ:nɪtʃə]	Möbel
fury ['fjʊərɪ]	Wut
future ['fju:tʃə]	Zukunft, zukünftig

G

gallery ['gælerɪ]	Galerie
game [geɪm]	Spiel
garage ['gærɑ:ʒ]	Garage
garden ['gɑ:dn]	Garten
garlic ['gɑ:lɪk]	Knoblauch
gas [gæs]	Gas
gate [geɪt]	Tor, Flugsteig
general ['dʒenərəl]	allgemein
gentleman ['dʒentlmən]	Herr
genuine ['dʒenjʊɪn]	echt
German ['dʒɜ:mən]	Deutsch, deutsch

Germany ['dʒɜːmənɪ]	Deutschland
get [get]	bekommen
get old [get'əʊld]	altern, älter werden
get up [get'ʌp]	aufstehen
gift [gɪft]	Geschenk
girl [gɜːl]	Mädchen
girlfriend ['gɜːlfrend]	feste Freundin
give [gɪv]	geben
glad [glæd]	froh
glass [glɑːs]	Glas
glass cabinet [glɑːs'kæbɪnet]	Vitrine
glasses ['glɑːsɪz] *pl*	Brille
globalization [gləubəlaɪ'zeɪʃən]	Globalisierung
glove [glʌv]	Handschuh
glue [gluː]	Klebstoff
go [gəʊ]	gehen
go bad [gəʊ'bæd]	verderben
go out [gəʊ'aʊt]	ausgehen
goat [gəʊt]	Ziege
God [gɒd]	Gott
gold [gəʊld]	Gold
gone [gɒn]	weg(gegangen)
Good afternoon. [gʊdɑːftə'nuːn]	Guten Tag.
Good bye. [gʊd'baɪ]	Auf Wiedersehen.
Good evening. [gʊd'iːvnɪŋ]	Guten Abend.
good looking [gʊd'lʊkɪŋ]	gut aussehend
Good morning. [gʊd'mɔːnɪŋ]	Guten Morgen.
Good night. [gʊd'naɪt]	Gute Nacht.
goose [guːs], **geese** [giːs] *pl*	Gans
govern ['gʌvən]	regieren
government ['gʌvənmənt]	Regierung
grab [græb]	greifen

grade [greɪd]	Note
grammar ['græmə]	Grammatik
grammar school ['græməsku:l]	Gymnasium
gramme [græm]	Gramm
grandchild ['grændtʃaɪld]	Enkel(in)
granddaughter ['grænddɔ:tə]	Enkelin
grandfather ['grændfɑ:ðə]	Großvater
grandmother ['grændmʌðə]	Großmutter
grandparents ['grændpeərənts]	Großeltern
grandson ['grændsʌn]	Enkel(sohn)
grape [greɪp]	Traube
grapefruit ['greɪpfru:t]	Grapefruit, Pampelmuse
grass [grɑ:s]	Gras
great [greɪt]	großartig
Great Britain [greɪt'brɪtn]	Großbritannien
Greece [gri:s]	Griechenland
green [gri:n]	grün
greet [gri:t]	begrüßen
grey [greɪ]	grau
grief [gri:f]	Trauer
grill [grɪl]	grillen
ground [graʊnd]	Boden, Erde
ground floor ['graʊndflɔ:]	Erdgeschoss
group [gru:p]	Gruppe
grow (up) [grəʊ(ʌp)]	(auf)wachsen
grown-up ['grəʊnʌp]	Erwachsene(r), erwachsen
guess [ges]	raten, erraten, vermuten
guest [gest]	Gast
guest-house ['gesthaʊs]	Pension
guide [gaɪd]	Fremdenführer(in), Reiseführer
guilty ['gɪltɪ]	schuldig
guitar [gɪ'tɑ:]	Gitarre

gun [gʌn]	Gewehr, Pistole, Revolver
guy [gaɪ]	Typ

H

habit ['hæbɪt]	Gewohnheit
hail [heɪl]	Hagel
hair [hɛə]	Haare
hair slide ['hɛəslaɪd]	Haarspange
haircut ['hɛəkʌt]	Haarschnitt
hairdresser ['hɛədresə]	Friseur(in)
hair-dryer ['hɛədraɪə]	Fön
half [hɑːf]	Hälfte, halb
half board ['hɑːfbɔːd]	Halbpension
hall [hɔːl]	Hausflur
ham [hæm]	Schinken
hammer ['hæmə]	Hammer
hand [hænd]	Hand
hand luggage ['hændlʌgɪdʒ]	Handgepäck
handbag ['hændbæg]	Handtasche
handful ['hændfʊl]	eine Hand voll
handicapped ['hændɪkæpt]	behindert
handkerchief ['hæŋkətʃɪf]	Taschentuch
handsome ['hænsəm]	gut aussehend
hang up [hæŋ'ʌp]	auflegen
happen ['hæpən]	passieren, sich ereignen, geschehen
happiness ['hæpɪnɪs]	Glück
happy ['hæpɪ]	glücklich
harbour ['hɑːbə]	Hafen
hard [hɑːd]	hart, schwer
hardly ['hɑːdlɪ]	kaum

hardware ['hɑːdwɛə]	Hardware
hard-working [hɑːd'wɜːkɪŋ]	fleißig
hare [hɛə]	Hase
hat [hæt]	Hut
hate [heɪt]	Hass, hassen
have [hæv]	haben
have to ['hævtuː]	müssen
he [hiː]	er
head [hed]	Kopf
headache ['hedeɪk]	Kopfschmerzen
heal [hiːl]	heilen
health [helθ]	Gesundheit
healthy ['helθɪ]	gesund
hear [hɪə]	hören
heart [hɑːt]	Herz
heat [hiːt]	Hitze
heating ['hiːtɪŋ]	Heizung
heavy ['hevɪ]	schwer
height [haɪt]	Höhe
help [help]	Hilfe, helfen
helpful ['helpfʊl]	hilfsbereit
her [hɜː]	ihr(-e, -r), sie
here [hɪə]	hier
hers [hɜːz]	ihr(-e, -r, -s)
herself [hɜː'self]	sie/sich selbst
hesitate ['hezɪteɪt]	zögern
hide [haɪd]	verstecken
high [haɪ]	hoch
high season [haɪ'siːzn]	Hauptsaison
high-rise ['haɪraɪz]	Hochhaus
hill [hɪl]	Hügel
him [hɪm]	ihm, ihn, er

himself [hɪm'self]	er/sich selbst
hint [hɪnt]	Hinweis, Tipp
hire [haɪə]	einstellen
his [hɪz]	sein(-e, -r)
history ['hɪstərɪ]	Geschichte
hit [hɪt]	schlagen, treffen
hobby ['hɒbɪ]	Hobby
hold [həʊld]	halten
hole [həʊl]	Loch
holiday ['hɒlɪdeɪ]	Urlaub, Ferien
home [həʊm]	Wohnung, Zuhause
home(town) [həʊm(taʊn)]	Heimat(stadt)
homework ['həʊmwɜːk]	Hausaufgaben
honest ['ɒnɪst]	ehrlich
honestly ['ɒnɪstlɪ]	wirklich, tatsächlich
honey ['hʌnɪ]	Honig
honeymoon ['hʌnɪmuːn]	Flitterwochen
hook [hʊk]	Haken
hoover® ['huːvə]	Staubsauger, staubsaugen
hope [həʊp]	Hoffnung, hoffen
hopefully ['həʊpfəlɪ]	hoffentlich
horrible ['hɒrɪbl]	schrecklich
horse [hɔːs]	Pferd
horse riding ['hɔːsraɪdɪŋ]	Reiten
hospital ['hɒspɪtl]	Krankenhaus
hot [hɒt]	heiß, scharf
hotel [həʊ'tel]	Hotel
hour [aʊə]	Stunde
hourly ['aʊəlɪ]	stündlich
house [haʊs]	Haus
household ['haʊshəʊld]	Haushalt
housewife ['haʊswaɪf]	Hausfrau

housework ['haʊswɜːk]	Hausarbeit
how [haʊ]	wie
however [haʊ'evə]	jedoch
human ['hjuːmən]	menschlich
human being ['hjuːmən'biːɪŋ]	Mensch, Wesen
humid ['hjuːmɪd]	feucht, schwül
humour ['hjuːmə]	Humor
hundred ['hʌndrɪd]	hundert
hundred thousand ['hʌndrɪd'θaʊzənd]	hunderttausend
Hungary ['hʌŋgərɪ]	Ungarn
hungry ['hʌŋgrɪ]	hungrig
hurt [hɜːt]	verletzen
husband ['hʌzbənd]	Ehemann

I

I [aɪ]	ich
ice [aɪs]	Eis, Glätte
ice cream ['aɪskriːm]	Eis(creme)
icon ['aɪkɒn]	Symbol
idea [aɪ'dɪə]	Idee, Einfall
identity [aɪ'dentɪtɪ]	Identität
identity card [aɪ'dentɪtɪkɑːd]	Personalausweis
if [ɪf]	wenn, falls, ob
ignore [ɪg'nɔː]	ignorieren, nicht beachten
ill [ɪl]	krank
illegal [ɪ'liːgəl]	illegal
illness ['ɪlnɪs]	Krankheit
imagination [ɪmædʒɪ'neɪʃən]	Einbildungskraft, Fantasie
imagine [ɪ'mædʒɪn]	sich vorstellen, sich denken
immediately [ɪ'miːdɪətlɪ]	sofort, unmittelbar

immigration [ɪmɪ'greɪʃən]	Einwanderung
impatient [ɪm'peɪʃənt]	ungeduldig
importance [ɪm'pɔːtəns]	Wichtigkeit, (große) Bedeutung
important [ɪm'pɔːtənt]	wichtig
impossible [ɪm'pɒsəbl]	unmöglich
impression [ɪm'preʃən]	Eindruck
improve [ɪm'pruːv]	verbessern
improvement [ɪm'pruːvmənt]	Verbesserung
in [ɪn]	in
in charge [ɪn'tʃɑːdʒ]	zuständig
in fact [ɪn'fækt]	eigentlich
in front [ɪn'frʌnt]	vorne
in front of [ɪn'frʌntɒf]	vor
in general [ɪn'dʒeneral]	im Allgemeinen
in good time [ɪngʊd'tɑɪm]	frühzeitig
in order to [ɪn'ɔːdətuː]	um zu
in person [ɪn'pɜːsn]	persönlich
in the year [ɪnðə'jɪə]	im Jahr
in time [ɪn'tɑɪm]	rechtzeitig
inch [ɪntʃ]	Zoll
include [ɪn'kluːd]	einschließen, enthalten
inclusive [ɪn'kluːsɪv]	inklusive
increase [ɪn'kriːs]	vergrößern, vermehren, zunehmen
indebted [ɪn'detɪd]	verschuldet
India ['ɪndɪə]	Indien
industry ['ɪndəstrɪ]	Industrie, Branche
influenza [ɪnflʊ'enzə]	Grippe
inform [ɪn'fɔːm]	mitteilen, informieren
information [ɪnfə'meɪʃən]	Information
injection [ɪn'dʒekʃən]	Spritze
injured ['ɪndʒəd]	verletzt

injury ['ındʒərı]	Verletzung
innocent ['ınəsənt]	unschuldig
inquire [ın'kwaıə]	sich erkundigen, anfragen
inquiry [ın'kwaıərı]	Anfrage
insect ['ınsekt]	Insekt
inside [ın'saıd]	innen, drinnen
installment [ın'stɔːlmənt]	Rate
instead [ın'sted]	statt, stattdessen
instruct [ın'strʌkt]	anleiten, einweisen
instruction [ın'strʌkʃən]	Anweisung, Anleitung
instrument ['ınstrʊmənt]	Instrument, Gerät
insurance [ın'ʃʊərəns]	Versicherung
intelligence [ın'telıdʒəns]	Intelligenz
intelligent [ın'telıdʒənt]	intelligent
intention [ın'tenʃən]	Absicht
interest ['ıntrıst]	Zinsen
interesting ['ıntrıstıŋ]	interessant
internet ['ıntənet]	Internet
interrupt [ıntə'rʌpt]	unterbrechen
interruption [ıntə'rʌpʃən]	Unterbrechung
into ['ıntʊ]	gegen, hinein
introduce [ıntrə'djuːs] *o.s.*	sich vorstellen
introduce [ıntrə'djuːs] *s.o.*	jmd. vorstellen
invest [ın'vest]	investieren
invitation [ınvı'teıʃən]	Einladung
invite [ın'vaıt]	einladen
Ireland ['aıələnd]	Irland
iron ['aıən]	Eisen, Bügeleisen, bügeln
irregular [ı'regjʊlə]	unregelmäßig
it [ıt]	es
island ['aılənd]	Insel
Italian [ı'tælıən]	Italienisch, italienisch

Italy ['ɪtəlɪ] Italien
its [ɪts] sein(-e, -r, -s)
itself [ɪt'self] es/sich selbst

J

jacket ['dʒækɪt] Jacke, Jackett
jam [dʒæm] Marmelade
January ['dʒænjʊərɪ] Januar
Japan [dʒə'pæn] Japan
jewellery ['dʒuːələrɪ] Schmuck
job [dʒɒb] Beruf, Arbeitsstelle
job advertisement ['dʒɒbəd'vɜːtɪzmənt] Stellenangebot
job application ['dʒɒbæplɪ'keɪʃən] Bewerbung
job interview ['dʒɒb'ɪntəvjuː] Vorstellungsgespräch
join [dʒɒɪn] mitkommen, teilnehmen
joke [dʒəʊk] Witz, Witze machen
journey ['dʒɜːnɪ] Reise
joy [dʒɔɪ] Freude
judge [dʒʌdʒ] Richter(in)
juice [dʒuːs] Saft
July [dʒuː'laɪ] Juli
jump [dʒʌmp] Sprung, springen
junction ['dʒʌnkʃən] Kreuzung
June [dʒuːn] Juni
just [dʒʌst] gerade, nur, einfach

K

keep [kiːp] halten, behalten
key [kiː] Schlüssel

keyboard ['kiːbɔːd]	Tastatur
kill [kɪl]	töten, ermorden
kilogramme ['kɪləʊgræm]	Kilogramm
kilometre ['kɪləʊmiːtə]	Kilometer
kind [kaɪnd]	Art, freundlich
kindergarten ['kɪndəgɑːtn]	Kindergarten
king [kɪŋ]	König
kiss [kɪs]	Kuss, küssen
kitchen ['kɪtʃɪn]	Küche
kitchen cupboard ['kɪtʃɪn'kʌbəd]	Küchenschrank
kiwi ['kiːwiː]	Kiwi
knee [niː]	Knie
knife [naɪf]	Messer
knock [nɒk]	klopfen
know [nəʊ]	wissen
knowledge ['nɒlɪdʒ]	Wissen

L

lady ['leɪdɪ]	Dame
lake [leɪk]	See
lamb [læm]	Lamm
lamp [læmp]	Lampe
land [lænd]	Land, landen
landlord ['lændlɔːd]	Vermieter
language ['læŋgwɪdʒ]	Sprache
laptop ['læptɒp]	Laptop
large [lɑːdʒ]	groß
last [lɑːst]	zuletzt, letzte(-r, -s)
last name ['lɑːstneɪm]	Nachnahme
late [leɪt]	spät

lately ['leɪtlɪ]	neulich, kürzlich
later ['leɪtə]	später
lateral ['lætərəl]	seitlich
latest ['leɪtɪst]	letzte(-r, -s), neueste(-r,-s)
laugh [lɑːf]	lachen
laundry ['lɔːndrɪ]	Wäsche, Reinigung
law [lɔː]	Recht, Gesetz
lawn [lɔːn]	Rasen
lawyer ['lɔːjə]	Rechtsanwalt, Rechtsanwältin
laze about [leɪzə'baʊt]	faulenzen
lazy ['leɪzɪ]	faul
lead [liːd]	führen, leiten
learn [lɜːn]	lernen
least [liːst]	am wenigsten, geringste(-r, -s)
leather ['leðə]	Leder
leave [liːf]	Blatt, verlassen
left [left]	links
leg [leg]	Bein
legal ['liːgl]	legal
leisure time ['leʒətaɪm]	Freizeit
lemon ['lemən]	Zitrone
lend [lend]	leihen
length [leŋθ]	Länge
less [les]	weniger
lesson ['lesn]	Unterrichtsstunde
let [let]	lassen, zulassen
letter ['letə]	Brief
letterbox ['letəbɒks]	Briefkasten
liberty ['lɪbətɪ]	Freiheit
library ['laɪbrərɪ]	Bibliothek
licence ['laɪsəns]	Erlaubnis, Genehmigung, Lizenz

lid [lɪd]	Deckel
lie [laɪ]	Lüge, lügen, liegen
life [laɪf]	Leben
lift [lɪft]	Aufzug
light [laɪt]	Licht, hell, leicht
light switch ['laɪtswɪtʃ]	Lichtschalter
lighter ['laɪtə]	Feuerzeug
lightning ['laɪtnɪŋ]	Blitz
like [laɪk]	mögen, wie, ähnlich, gleich
likely ['laɪklɪ]	wahrscheinlich
line [laɪn]	Leitung, Linie
linen ['lɪnɪn]	Leinen
lion ['laɪən]	Löwe
lip [lɪp]	Lippe
list [lɪst]	Liste, Verzeichnis
listen ['lɪsn]	zuhören
literature ['lɪtrətʃə]	Literatur
litre ['liːtə]	Liter
little ['lɪtl]	klein, wenig, kaum
little bit [ə'lɪtl'bɪt]	ein bisschen
live [lɪv]	leben
living ['lɪvɪŋ]	Lebensunterhalt
living room ['lɪvɪŋruːm]	Wohnzimmer
loan [ləʊn]	Darlehen, Anleihe
local ['ləʊkəl]	örtlich, Orts-
location [ləʊ'keɪʃən]	Ort, Platz, Stelle
lock [lɒk]	Schloss, schließen, abschließen
lonely ['ləʊnlɪ]	einsam
long [lɒŋ]	lang
look [lʊk]	sehen, schauen, aussehen
look after [lʊk'ɑːftə]	sich kümmern (um)
look for [lʊk'fɔː]	suchen

look forward to [lʊk]	sich freuen auf
look into [lʊk]	untersuchen
look out [lʊk]	aufpassen
loose [luːs]	locker, lose
lopsided ['lɒpsaɪdɪd]	schief
lorry ['lɒrɪ]	Lastwagen
lose [luːz]	verlieren
loser ['luːzə]	Verlierer(in)
loss [lɒs]	Verlust
lot [lɒt]	viel
lotion ['ləʊʃən]	Lotion
lots [lɒts]	viele
loud [laʊd]	laut
lounge [laʊndʒ]	Aufenthaltsraum, Hotelhalle
love [lʌv]	Liebe
lovely ['lʌvlɪ]	herrlich, großartig, schön
low [ləʊ]	niedrig
low season [ləʊ'siːzn]	Nebensaison
luck [lʌk]	Glück
lucky ['lʌkɪ]	Glück haben
luggage ['lʌgɪdʒ]	Gepäck
lunch [lʌntʃ]	Mittagessen
lunchtime ['lʌntʃtaɪm]	Mittag(szeit)

M

machine [mə'ʃiːn]	Maschine
mad [mæd]	verrückt
made of ['meɪdəv]	aus
magazine ['mægəziːn]	Zeitschrift, Magazin
main [meɪn]	Haupt-, hauptsächlich
main course ['meɪnkɔːs]	Hauptspeise

main street ['meɪnstriːt]	Hauptstraße
maize [meɪz]	Mais
majority [mə'dʒɒrɪtɪ]	Mehrheit
make [meɪk]	machen
make an effort [meɪkæn'efət]	sich bemühen, sich anstrengen
make money [meɪk'mʌnɪ]	Geld verdienen
make-up ['meɪkʌp]	Make-up
male [meɪl]	männlich
man [mæn]	Mann, Mensch
manage ['mænɪdʒ]	leiten, zurechtkommen, bewältigen
management ['mænɪdʒmənt]	Geschäftsführung
manager ['mænɪdʒə]	Manager(in)
many ['menɪ]	viele
map [mæp]	(Land-)Karte, Stadtplan
March [mɑːtʃ]	März
mark [mɑːk]	Note
market ['mɑːkɪt]	Markt
marriage ['mærɪdʒ]	Ehe
married ['mærɪd]	verheiratet
marry ['mærɪ]	heiraten
marvellous ['mɑːvələs]	wunderbar, fantastisch
match [mætʃ]	Spiel
matches ['mætʃɪz] *pl*	Streichhölzer
material [mə'tɪərɪəl]	Material, Stoff
matter ['mætə]	Sache, Angelegenheit
maximum ['mæksɪməm]	Maximum
may [meɪ]	dürfen, können
May [meɪ]	Mai
maybe ['meɪbɪ]	vielleicht
mayor ['meə]	Bürgermeister(in)
me [miː]	mich, mir, ich

meadow ['medəʊ]	Wiese
meal [miːl]	Mahlzeit
mean [miːn]	meinen, gemein, niederträchtig
meaning ['miːnɪŋ]	Bedeutung
measure ['meʒə]	Maßnahme
meat [miːt]	Fleisch
medal ['medl]	Medaille
media ['miːdɪə]	Medien
medical ['medɪkəl]	medizinisch, ärztlich
medicament [me'dɪkəmənt]	Medikament
medicine ['medɪsɪn]	Medizin
meet [miːt]	kennen lernen, treffen
meeting ['miːtɪŋ]	Sitzung, Besprechung
melody ['melədɪ]	Melodie
melon ['melən]	Melone
member ['membə]	Mitglied
memory ['memərɪ]	Gedächtnis, Erinnerung
mention ['menʃən]	erwähnen
menu ['menjuː]	Speisekarte, Menü
merry ['merɪ]	fröhlich
mess [mes]	Unordnung, Durcheinander
message ['mesɪdʒ]	Nachricht
metal ['metl]	Metall
meter ['miːtə]	Maß, Zähler
method ['meθəd]	Methode
metre ['miːtə]	Meter
microwave ['maɪkrəʊweɪv]	Mikrowelle
midday ['mɪddeɪ]	Mittag, zwölf Uhr
middle ['mɪdl]	Mitte
midnight ['mɪdnaɪt]	Mitternacht, 24 Uhr
might [maɪt]	könnte, könntest, könntet, könnten

mild [maɪld]	mild
mile [maɪl]	Meile
military ['mɪlɪtərɪ]	Militär
milk [mɪlk]	Milch
millennium [mɪ'lenɪəm]	Jahrtausend
millimetre ['mɪlɪmiːtə]	Millimeter
million ['mɪljən]	Million
mince [mɪns]	hacken
mind [maɪnd]	Verstand, Erinnerung
mine [maɪn]	mein(-e, -r, -s)
mineral water ['mɪnərəl'wɔːtə]	Mineralwasser
minimum ['mɪnɪməm]	Minimum
minister ['mɪnɪstə]	Minister(in)
ministry ['mɪnɪstrɪ]	Ministerium
minority [maɪ'nɒrɪtɪ]	Minderheit
minus ['maɪnəs]	Minus, minus
minute ['mɪnɪt]	Minute
miracle ['mɪrəkəl]	Wunder
mirror ['mɪrə]	Spiegel
misfortune [mɪs'fɔːtʃən]	Unglück
Miss [mɪs]	Fräulein
mis [mɪs]	verfehlen, versäumen
mistake [mɪs'teɪk]	Fehler
mix [mɪks]	mischen, vermischen, mixen
mix up [mɪks'ʌp]	verwechseln, durcheinander bringen, verwirren
mixture ['mɪkstʃə]	Mischung
mobile phone ['məʊbaɪlfəʊn]	Mobiltelefon
moment ['məʊmənt]	Moment, Augenblick
monarchy ['mɒnəkɪ]	Monarchie
Monday ['mʌndeɪ]	Montag

money ['mʌnɪ]	Geld
month [mʌnθ]	Monat
monument ['mɒnjʊmənt]	Denkmal
mood [muːd]	Laune
moon [muːn]	Mond
more [mɔː]	mehr
morning ['mɔːnɪŋ]	Morgen
mosquito bite [məs'kiːtəʊbaɪt]	Mückenstich
most [məʊst]	meist, (die) meisten
mostly ['məʊstlɪ]	meistens
mother ['mʌðə]	Mutter
mother-in-law ['mʌðərɪnlɔː]	Schwiegermutter
motorbike ['məʊtəbaɪk]	Motorrad
motorcycle ['məʊtəsaɪkl]	Motorrad
motorway ['məʊtəweɪ]	Autobahn
mountain ['maʊntɪn]	Berg
mountains ['maʊntɪns] *pl*	Gebirge
mourn [mɔːn]	trauern
mouse [maʊs], **mice** [maɪs] *pl*	Maus
mouth [maʊθ]	Mund
move [muːv]	Umzug, bewegen
move in [muːv'ɪn]	einziehen
move out [muːv'aʊt]	ausziehen
movement ['muːvmənt]	Bewegung
movie ['muːvɪ] *AE*	Film
movie theatre ['muːvɪ'θɪətə] *AE*	Kino
Mr ['mɪstə]	Herr
Mrs ['mɪsɪz]	Frau
Ms [mɪz]	Frau
much [mʌtʃ]	viel
mug [mʌg]	Becher
multiply ['mʌltɪplaɪ]	multiplizieren

multi-storey building [mʌltɪ'stɔːrɪ'bɪldɪŋ]	Hochhaus
multi-storey car parking [mʌltɪ'stɔːrɪ'kɑːpɑːkɪŋ]	Parkhaus
murder ['mɜːdə]	Mord, ermorden
murderer ['mɜːdərə]	Mörder(in)
museum [mjuː'zɪəm]	Museum
mushroom ['mʌʃruːm]	Pilz
music ['mjuːzɪk]	Musik
must [mʌst]	müssen
must not ['mʌsnt]	nicht dürfen
my [maɪ]	mein(-e, -r)
myself [maɪ'self]	mir/ich (selbst)

N

nail [neɪl]	Nagel
name [neɪm]	Name, nennen
napkin ['næpkɪn]	Serviette
narrow ['nærəʊ]	eng, schmal
nation ['neɪʃən]	Nation, Volk
national ['næʃənl]	national, National-
nationality [næʃə'nælɪtɪ]	Nationalität
native ['neɪtɪv]	Mutter-
natural ['nætʃrəl]	natürlich
natural resources ['nætʃrəlrɪ'sɔːsɪz]	Bodenschätze
nature ['neɪtʃə]	Natur
near [nɪə]	nahe, in der Nähe
nearby ['nɪəbaɪ]	in der Nähe
nearly ['nɪəlɪ]	beinahe, fast
neat [niːt]	ordentlich, sauber

necessary ['nesɪsərɪ]	nötig, notwendig
neck [nek]	Hals, Nacken
necklace ['neklɪs]	Kette
need [niːd]	brauchen
needle ['niːdl]	Nähnadel
needn't [niːdnt]	nicht müssen, nicht brauchen
neighbour ['neɪbə]	Nachbar(in)
neither ... **nor** ['naɪðə ... nɔː]	weder ... noch
nephew ['nefjuː]	Neffe
nervous ['nɜːvəs]	nervös, Nerven-
never ['nevə]	nie
new [njuː]	neu
New Zealand [njuː'ziːlənd]	Neuseeland
news [njuːz]	Nachrichten, Neuigkeiten
newspaper ['njuːzpeɪpə]	Zeitung
next [nekst]	nächste(-r, -s)
next to ['nekstuː]	neben
nice [naɪs]	nett
niece [niːs]	Nichte
night [naɪt]	Nacht
nine [naɪn]	neun
nineteen [naɪn'tiːn]	neunzehn
nineteenth [naɪn'tiːnθ]	neunzehnte(-r, -s)
ninety ['naɪntɪ]	neunzig
ninth [naɪnθ]	neunte(-r, -s)
no [nəʊ]	nein, kein
no one ['nəʊwʌn]	niemand
nobody ['nəʊbədɪ]	niemand
noise [nɔɪz]	Lärm, Geräusch
noisy ['nɔɪzɪ]	laut, geräuschvoll
none [nʌn]	keine(-r, -s)
nonsense ['nɒnsəns]	Unsinn, Quatsch

noodle ['nuːdl]	Nudel
noon [nuːn]	Mittag, zwölf Uhr
nor [nɔ]	noch, auch nicht
normal ['nɔːməl]	normal
north [nɔːθ]	Nord
North America [nɔːθə'merɪkə]	Nordamerika
northeast [nɔːθ'iːst]	Nordost
northern ['nɔːðən]	nördlich
northwest [nɔːθ'west]	Nordwest
Norway ['nɔːweɪ]	Norwegen
nose [nəʊz]	Nase
not [nɒt]	nicht
note [nəʊt]	(Geld-)Schein, Note, Notiz, aufschreiben
notepad ['nəʊtpæd]	Notizblock
nothing ['nʌθɪŋ]	nichts
notice ['nəʊtɪs]	Bescheid, bemerken, beachten
November [nəʊ'vembə]	November
now [naʊ]	jetzt
nowhere ['nəʊwɛə]	nirgendwo
number ['nʌmbə]	Nummer
nurse [nɜːs]	Krankenschwester
nursery school ['nɜːsərɪskuːl]	Kindergarten
nut [nʌt]	Nuss
nylon stocking ['naɪlɒn'stɒkɪŋ]	Nylonstrumpf

O

o'clock [ə'klɒk]	Uhr
object ['ɒbdʒɪkt]	Gegenstand, Objekt
objective [əb'dʒektɪv]	Ziel

observe [əb'zɜːv]	beobachten
obvious ['ɒbvɪəs]	offensichtlich
occasionally [ə'keɪʒənəlɪ]	gelegentlich, ab und zu
occupied ['ɒkjʊpaɪd]	besetzt, belegt
ocean ['əʊʃən]	Ozean
October [ɒk'təʊbə]	Oktober
of [ɒv]	von
of course [ɒv'kɔːs]	natürlich, selbstverständlich
off [ɒf]	aus
offer ['ɒfə]	Angebot, anbieten
office ['ɒfɪs]	Büro
office building ['ɒfɪs'bɪldɪŋ]	Bürogebäude
officer ['ɒfɪsə]	Beamter, Beamtin
official [ə'fɪʃəl]	Beamter, Beamtin, offiziell
often ['ɒfən]	oft, häufig
oil [ɒɪl]	Öl
old [əʊld]	alt
old-fashioned [əʊld'fæʃənd]	altmodisch
on [ɒn]	ein(geschaltet), auf, an, über
on foot [ɒn'fʊt]	zu Fuß
on one hand ... on the other hand [ɒn'wʌnhænd … ɒnðiː'ʌðəhænd]	einerseits ... andererseits
on sale [ɒn'seɪl]	heruntergesetzt
one [wʌn]	eins, eine(-r, -s)
oneself [wʌn'self]	sich/man selbst/selber
one-way street ['wʌnweɪstriːt]	Einbahnstraße
onion ['ʌnjən]	Zwiebel
only ['əʊnlɪ]	nur, einzig
open ['əʊpən]	öffnen, offen, auf
opera ['ɒpərə]	Oper
operation [ɒpə'reɪʃən]	Operation, Unternehmung

operator ['ɒpəreɪtə]	Vermittler(in)
opinion [ə'pɪnjən]	Meinung
opportunity [ɒpə'tjuːnɪtɪ]	Gelegenheit
opposite ['ɒpəzɪt]	entgegengesetzt, gegenüber
opposition [ɒpə'zɪʃən]	Opposition
or [ɔː]	oder
orange ['ɒrɪndʒ]	Orange, orange
order ['ɔːdə]	Gesetz, Bestellung, Auftrag, befehlen, bestellen
orderly ['ɔːdəlɪ]	ordentlich, sauber
ordinary ['ɔːdɪnərɪ]	gewöhnlich, normal
organisation [ɔːgənaɪ'zeɪʃən]	Organisation
organize ['ɔːgənaɪz]	organisieren
original [ə'rɪdʒɪnl]	Original
other ['ʌðə]	andere(-r, -s)
otherwise ['ʌðəwaɪz]	sonst
ought to ['ɔːttʊː]	sollte, solltest, sollte, sollten
our [aʊə]	unser(-e, -r)
ours ['aʊəz]	unser(-e, -r, -s)
ourself [aʊə'self]	wir/uns selbst
out [aʊt]	hinaus, heraus, aus, außen, draußen
outside [aʊt'saɪd]	außen, draußen
oval ['əʊvəl]	oval
oven ['ʌvn]	Ofen
over ['əʊvə]	über
overdraw [əʊvə'drɔː]	überziehen
overweight [əʊvə'weɪt]	übergewichtig
own [əʊn]	besitzen, eigene(-r, -s)
owner ['əʊnə]	Eigentümer(in), Inhaber(in), Besitzer(in)
ox [ɒks], **oxen** ['ɒksn] *pl*	Ochse

P

pack [pæk]	packen
package ['pækɪdʒ]	Paket
package holiday ['pækɪdʒ'hɒlɪdeɪ]	Pauschalreise
package tour ['pækɪdʒtʊə]	Pauschalreise
packet ['pækɪt]	Paket, Päckchen, Packung
page [peɪdʒ]	Seite
pain [peɪn]	Schmerz, Schmerzen
paint [peɪnt]	streichen, malen
painting ['peɪntɪŋ]	Gemälde
pair of ['pɛəv]	Paar
pale [peɪl]	blass
palm [pɑːm]	Palme
paper ['peɪpə]	Papier
paper clip ['peɪpəklɪp]	Büroklammer
parcel ['pɑːsl]	Paket, Päckchen
Pardon? ['pɑːdn]	Wie bitte?
parents ['peərənts]	Eltern
parents-in-law ['peərəntsɪnlɔː]	Schwiegereltern
park [pɑːk]	Park
parliament ['pɑːləmənt]	Parlament
part [pɑːt]	Teil, teilen, einteilen, aufteilen
particular [pə'tɪkjʊlə]	besonders
partner ['pɑːtnə]	Partner(in)
part-time ['pɑːt'taɪm]	Teilzeit
party ['pɑːtɪ]	Partei, Party
pass [pɑːs]	bestehen
passenger ['pæsɪndʒə]	Passagier(in)
passion ['pæʃən]	Leidenschaft
passive ['pæsɪv]	passiv

passport ['pɑːspɔːt]	Pass
past [pɑːst]	Vergangenheit
pasta ['pæstə]	Nudeln
paste [peɪst]	Leim, Paste, einfügen
path [pɑːθ]	Pfad, Weg
patience ['peɪʃəns]	Geduld
patient ['peɪʃənt]	Patient(in), geduldig
pavement ['peɪvmənt]	Bürgersteig
pay [peɪ]	bezahlen
pay in [peɪ'ɪn]	einzahlen
payment ['peɪmənt]	Zahlung
pea [piː]	Erbse
peace [piːs]	Frieden
peach [piːtʃ]	Pfirsich
peak [piːk]	Gipfel
peak hour ['piːkaʊə]	Hauptverkehrszeit
pear [pɛə]	Birne
pedestrian [pɪ'destrɪən]	Fußgänger(in)
pen [pen]	Kugelschreiber
pencil ['pensl]	Bleistift
penitence ['penɪtəns]	Buße
pension ['penʃən]	Rente, Pension
pensioner ['penʃənə]	Rentner(in)
Pentecost ['pentɪkɒst]	Pfingsten
people ['piːpl]	Menschen, Leute
pepper ['pepə]	Pfeffer, Paprika
per cent [pə'sent]	Prozent
perceive [pə'siːv]	wahrnehmen
perfect [pə'fekt]	vollkommen, perfekt
perform [pə'fɔːm]	aufführen
performance [pə'fɔːməns]	Aufführung
perhaps [pə'hæps]	vielleicht

period (of time) ['pɪərɪəd(of'taɪm)]	Zeitraum
permit [pə'mɪt]	Genehmigung, Erlaubnis, erlauben
person ['pɜːsn]	Person
personal ['pəːsənl]	persönlich
personal computer, **PC** ['pɜːsənlkəm'pjuːtə]	Computer, PC
personnel [pɜːsə'nel]	Belegschaft, Personal
pet [pet]	Haustier
petrol station ['petrəlsteɪʃən]	Tankstelle
pharmacy ['fɑːməsɪ]	Apotheke
phone [fəʊn]	Telefon, anrufen
photo ['fəʊtəʊ]	Fotografie
physician [fɪ'zɪʃən]	Arzt, Ärztin
piano ['pjɑːnəʊ]	Klavier
pick up [pɪk'ʌp]	(den Hörer) abnehmen, abholen
picture ['pɪktʃə]	Bild, Foto
piece [piːs]	Stück
pig [pɪg]	Schwein
pill [pɪl]	Pille, Tablette
pillow ['pɪləʊ]	Kopfkissen
pin [pɪn]	Stecknadel
pine [paɪn]	Tanne
pineapple ['paɪnæpl]	Ananas
pink [pɪŋk]	rosa
pint [paɪnt]	großes Bier, Pint (ca. 0,57 l)
pipe [paɪp]	Pfeife
pity ['pɪtɪ]	Mitleid, bemitleiden, bedauern
place [pleɪs]	Ort, Platz, Stelle
plan [plæn]	Plan, Entwurf
plane [pleɪn]	Flugzeug

planet ['plænɪt]	Planet
plant [plɑːnt]	Pflanze, Fabrik
plastic ['plæstɪk]	Plastik
plate [pleɪt]	Teller
platform ['plætfɔːm]	Plattform
play [pleɪ]	Theaterstück, spielen
player ['pleɪə]	Spieler(in)
pleasant ['pleznt]	angenehm
please [pliːz]	bitte, gefallen
pleasure ['pleʒə]	Vergnügen
plenty of ['plentɪəv]	viel
pliers ['plaɪəz] *pl*	Zange
plug [plʌg]	Stecker, anschließen, einstecken
plus [plʌs]	Plus, plus
p.m. [piː'em]	nachmittags, abends
pocket ['pɒkɪt]	Tasche
poem ['pəʊəm]	Gedicht
point [pɔɪnt]	Punkt
point of time [pɔɪntɒv'taɪm]	Zeitpunkt
point of view [pɔɪntɒv'vjuː]	Standpunkt
pointed ['pɔɪntɪd]	spitz
poisonous ['pɔɪznous]	giftig
Poland ['pəʊlənd]	Polen
police [pə'liːs]	Polizei
policeman [pə'liːsmən]	Polizist
polite [pə'laɪt]	höflich
politics ['pɒlətɪks]	Politik
pollution [pə'luːʃn]	Umweltverschmutzung
pond [pɒnd]	Teich
poor [pʊə]	arm
popular ['pɒpjʊlə]	populär, beliebt
pork [pɔːk]	Schweinefleisch

port [pɔːt]	Hafen
position [pə'zɪʃən]	Lage, Stellung, Position
possibility [pɒsə'bɪlɪtɪ]	Möglichkeit
possible ['pɒsəbl]	möglich
post [pəʊst]	Post
post office ['pəʊstɒfɪs]	Postamt
postbox ['pəʊstbɒks]	Post-, Briefkasten
postcard ['pəʊstkɑːd]	Postkarte
postman ['pəʊstmən]	Briefträger
pot [pɒt]	Topf, Kanne
potato [pə'teɪtəʊ]	Kartoffel
poultry ['pəʊltrɪ]	Geflügel
pound [paʊnd]	Pfund
powder ['paʊdə]	Pulver, Puder
power [paʊə]	Kraft, Macht, Strom, Energie
practice ['præktɪs]	Praxis, Übung
praise [preɪz]	Lob, loben
pray [preɪ]	beten
prayer [prɛə]	Gebet
predict [prɪ'dɪkt]	voraussagen, vorhersagen
prefer [prɪ'fɜː]	vorziehen
preference ['prefərəns]	Vorliebe
pregnancy ['pregnənsɪ]	Schwangerschaft
pregnant ['pregnənt]	schwanger
prepare [prɪ'pɛə]	zubereiten
prescribe [prɪs'kraɪb]	verschreiben
prescription [prɪs'krɪpʃən]	Rezept
presence ['prezns]	Gegenwart
present ['preznt]	Gegenwart, Geschenk
present [prɪ'zent]	anwesend
president ['prezɪdənt]	Präsident(in)
press [pres]	Presse, drücken

pretty ['prɪtɪ]	hübsch, ganz, ziemlich
price [praɪs]	Preis
pride [praɪd]	Stolz
priest [priːst]	Pfarrer
prime minister [praɪm'mɪnɪstə]	Premierminister
print [prɪnt]	drucken
printer ['prɪntə]	Drucker
prison ['prɪzn]	Gefängnis
private ['praɪvɪt]	privat
probably ['probəblɪ]	wahrscheinlich
problem ['prɒbləm]	Problem
process ['prəʊses]	Prozess
product ['prɒdʌkt]	Produkt
production [prə'dʌkʃən]	Produktion
profession [prə'feʃən]	Beruf
professional education [prə'feʃənledjʊ'keɪʃən]	Berufsausbildung
profit ['prɒfɪt]	Gewinn
programme ['prəʊgræm]	Progamm, Sendung
progress [prə'gres]	Fortschritt
promise ['prɒmɪs]	Versprechen, versprechen
promote [prə'məʊt]	befördern
promotion [prə'məʊʃən]	Beförderung
pronounce [prə'naʊns]	aussprechen
proof [pruːf]	Beweis
property ['prɒpətɪ]	Eigentum, Besitz
protection [prə'tekʃən]	Schutz
proud [praʊd]	stolz
prove [pruːv]	beweisen
provide [prə'vaɪd]	zur Verfügung stellen, versorgen
prune [pruːn]	Pflaume

public ['pʌblɪk]	Öffentlichkeit, öffentlich, staatlich
public holiday ['pʌblɪk'hɒlɪdeɪ]	Feiertag
public transport ['pʌblɪk'trænspɔːt]	öffentliche Verkehrsmittel
pull [pʊl]	ziehen
pullover ['pʊləʊvə]	Pullover
punch [pʌntʃ]	Locher
punctual ['pʌŋktjʊəl]	pünktlich
punish ['pʌnɪʃ]	bestrafen
pupil ['pjuːpl]	Schüler(in)
purpose ['pɜːpəs]	Zweck, Absicht
purse [pɜːs]	Geldbeutel
push [pʊʃ]	schieben, drücken
put [pʊt]	stellen, legen, setzen
put through [pʊt'θruː]	verbinden, durchstellen

Q

quality ['kwɒlɪtɪ]	Qualität
quantity ['kwɒntɪtɪ]	Menge
quarter ['kwɔːtə]	(ein) Viertel
queen [kwiːn]	Königin
question ['kwestʃən]	Frage, fragen
queue [kjuː]	Schlange
queue up [kjuː'ʌp]	Schlange stehen
quick [kwɪk]	schnell

R

rabbit ['ræbɪt]	Kaninchen
race [reɪs]	Rennen
racket ['rækɪt]	Schläger

radio ['reɪdɪəʊ]	Radio
rage [reɪdʒ]	Zorn, Wut, wettern *fam*
rail [reɪl]	Schiene
railway ['reɪlweɪ]	Eisenbahn
railway station ['reɪlweɪ'steɪʃən]	Bahnhof
rain [reɪn]	Regen, regnen
rainbow ['reɪnbəʊ]	Regenbogen
rarely ['reəlɪ]	selten
raspberry ['rɑːzbərɪ]	Himbeere
rather ['rɑːðə]	eher, lieber, ziemlich
reach [riːtʃ]	erreichen
read [riːd]	lesen
ready ['redɪ]	fertig, bereit
real ['rɪəl]	echt
realize ['rɪəlaɪz]	verstehen, begreifen, erkennen
really ['rɪəlɪ]	wirklich
reason ['riːzn]	Grund, Ursache, Vernunft
reasonable ['riːznəbl]	vernünftig
receipt [rɪ'siːt]	Kassenzettel
receive [rɪ'siːv]	erhalten, bekommen
recently ['riːsəntlɪ]	kürzlich, vor Kurzem
reception [rɪ'sepʃən]	Empfang
recipe ['resɪpɪ]	Rezept
recipient [rɪ'sɪpɪənt]	Empfänger(in)
recognize ['rekəgnaɪz]	erkennen
recommend [rekə'mend]	empfehlen
recommendation [rekəmen'deɪʃən]	Empfehlung
record ['rekɔːd]	Rekord, Schallplatte
recreation [rekrɪ'eɪʃən]	Erholung
red [red]	rot
reflect [rɪ'flekt]	nachdenken

reform [rɪ'fɔːm]	Reform
refrigerator [rɪ'frɪdʒəreɪtə]	Kühlschrank
refusal [rɪ'fjuːzəl]	Ablehnung
refuse [rɪ'fjuːz]	ablehnen, verweigern
regards [rɪ'gɑːds] *pl*	Grüße
regret [rɪ'gret]	Bedauern, Reue, bedauern, bereuen
regular ['regjʊlə]	regelmäßig, normal
reject [rɪ'dʒekt]	ablehnen
relationship [rɪ'leɪʃənʃɪp]	Beziehung, Verhältnis
relative ['relətɪv]	Verwandte(r)
relax [rɪ'læks]	sich entspannen, sich erholen
religion [rɪ'lɪdʒən]	Religion
remember [rɪ'membə]	sich erinnern
remind [rɪ'maɪnd]	jmd. erinnern
remote control [rɪ'məʊtkən'trəʊl]	Fernbedienung
renew [rɪ'njuː]	erneuern, verlängern
renovate ['renəveɪt]	renovieren
rent [rent]	Miete, mieten
rental car ['rentəlkɑː]	Mietwagen
repair [rɪ'pεə]	reparieren
repeat [rɪ'piːt]	wiederholen
reply [rɪ'plaɪ]	Antwort, Erwiderung, antworten, erwidern
report [rɪ'pɔːt]	Bericht, berichten, melden
reproach [rɪ'prəʊtʃ]	vorwerfen
request [rɪ'kwest]	Bitte, Wunsch, Antrag, Ersuchen, bitten, ersuchen
reserve [rɪ'zɜːv]	reservieren
residence permit ['rezɪdəns'pɜːmɪt]	Aufenthaltserlaubnis

respect [rɪs'pekt]	Respekt
responsibility [rɪspɒnsə'bɪlɪtɪ]	Verantwortung
rest [rest]	Rest, sich ausruhen
restaurant ['restərənt]	Restaurant
result [rɪ'zʌlt]	Ergebnis, Resultat
return [rɪ'tɜːn]	zurückkommen
return ticket [rɪ'tɜːn'tɪkɪt]	Rückfahrkarte
revenue ['revənjuː]	Umsatz
rice [raɪs]	Reis
rich [rɪtʃ]	reich
ride [raɪd]	Fahrt, fahren, reiten
right [raɪt]	richtig, rechts
ring [rɪŋ]	Ring, klingeln
risk [rɪsk]	Risiko
river ['rɪvə]	Fluss
road [rəʊd]	Straße
roast [rəʊst]	Braten, braten
rock [rɒk]	Felsen, Felsbrocken
roll [rəʊl]	Brötchen
roof [ruːf]	Dach
room [ruːm]	Zimmer, Raum, Platz
root [ruːt]	Wurzel
rose [rəʊz]	Rose
rotten ['rɒtn]	verdorben
rough [rʌf]	rau, grob, ungefähr
round [raʊnd]	rund
roundtrip ['raʊndtrɪp]	Rundreise, Hin- und Rückfahrt
row [rəʊ]	Reihe
rubber ['rʌbə]	Gummi, Radiergummi
rucksack ['rʌksæk]	Rucksack
rule [ruːl]	Regel
run [rʌn]	laufen, rennen

rush hour ['rʌʃaʊə]	Hauptverkehrszeit
Russia ['rʌʃə]	Russland

S

sad [sæd]	traurig
sadness ['sædnɪs]	Traurigkeit
safety ['seɪftɪ]	Sicherheit
sail [seɪl]	Segel, segeln
salad ['sæləd]	(angemachter) Salat
salary ['sælərɪ]	Gehalt, Lohn
sale [seɪl]	Verkauf
sales [seɪlz]	Ausverkauf, Schlussverkauf
salesman [seɪlzmən]	Verkäufer, Vertreter
salt [sɔːlt]	Salz
salty ['sɔːltɪ]	salzig
same [seɪm]	gleich, derselbe, dieselbe, dasselbe
sand [sænd]	Sand
satisfied ['sætɪsfaɪd]	zufrieden
Saturday ['sætədeɪ]	Samstag
sauce ['sɔːs]	Soße, Sauce
saucer ['sɔːsə]	Untertasse
sausage ['sɒsɪdʒ]	Würstchen
save [seɪv]	retten, sparen, speichern
saw [sɔː]	Säge
say [seɪ]	sagen
say goodbye [seɪgʊd'baɪ]	verabschieden
scarf [skɑːf]	Schal, Halstuch
scenery ['siːnərɪ]	Landschaft
school [skuːl]	Schule
science ['saɪəns]	(Natur-)Wissenschaft

scissors ['sɪzəz] *pl*	Schere
Scotland ['skɒtlənd]	Schottland
scream [skriːm]	Schrei, schreien
screen [skriːn]	Bildschirm
screw [skruː]	Schraube
screwdriver ['skruːdraɪvə]	Schraubenzieher
sculpture ['skʌlptʃə]	Skulptur, Plastik
sea [siː]	Meer
sea view ['siːvjuː]	Meerblick
seam [siːm]	Saum
search [sɜːtʃ]	Suche, suchen
search engine ['sɜːtʃ'endʒɪn]	Suchmaschine
season ['siːzn]	Jahreszeit
seat [siːt]	Sitzplatz
second ['sekənd]	Sekunde, zweite(-r, -s)
secret ['siːkrət]	Geheimnis, geheim, heimlich
secretary ['sekrətrɪ]	Sekretariat, Sekretärin, Minister(in)
security [sɪ'kjʊrɪtɪ]	Sicherheit
see [siː]	sehen
seem [siːm]	scheinen
seed [siːd]	Samen
seldom ['seldəm]	selten
self-confident [self'kɒnfɪdənt]	selbstbewusst
self-service [self'sɜːvɪs]	Selbstbedienung
sell [sel]	verkaufen
send [send]	senden, verschicken
sender ['sendə]	Absender(in)
sense [sens]	Sinn
sensible ['sensɪbl]	vernünftig
sensitive ['sensɪtɪv]	empfindlich
sentence ['sentəns]	Satz, Strafe
separate ['sepəreɪt]	sich trennen

September [sep'tembə]	September
serious ['sɪərɪəs]	ernst
serve [sɜːv]	bedienen, bringen
service ['sɜːvɪs]	Dienst, Dienstleistung, Bedienung, Service, Gottesdienst
set meal ['setmiːl]	Menü
seven ['sevn]	sieben
seventeen [sevn'tiːn]	siebzehn
seventeenth [sevn'tiːnθ]	siebzehnte(-r, -s)
seventh ['sevnθ]	siebte(-r, -s)
seventy ['sevntɪ]	siebzig
several ['sevrəl]	mehrere, verschiedene
sex [seks]	Geschlecht, Sex
shake [ʃeɪk]	schütteln
shall [ʃæl]	sollen, werden
shape [ʃeɪp]	Gestalt, Form
share [ʃɛə]	Aktie, Anteil, teilen
sharp [ʃɑːp]	scharf, genau um, Punkt
sharpener ['ʃɑːpnə]	Bleistiftspitzer
shave [ʃeɪv]	rasieren
shaver ['ʃeɪvə]	Rasierapparat
sheep [ʃiːp]	Schaf
sheet [ʃiːt]	Blatt, Bettlaken
shelf [ʃelf], **shelves** [ʃelvz] *pl*	Regal
shine [ʃaɪn]	scheinen, leuchten, glänzen
ship [ʃɪp]	Schiff
shirt [ʃɜːt]	Hemd
shoe [ʃuː]	Schuh
shoemaker ['ʃuːmeɪkə]	Schuster(in)
shoot [ʃuːt]	schießen
shop [ʃɒp]	Geschäft, einkaufen
shop assistant [ʃɒpə'sɪstənt]	Verkäufer(in)

shopping list ['ʃɒpɪŋlɪst]	Einkaufsliste
short [ʃɔːt]	kurz, klein
shot [ʃɒt]	Spritze
should [ʃʊd]	sollte, solltest, solltet, sollten
shoulder ['ʃəʊldə]	Schulter
shout [ʃaʊt]	Ruf, rufen
show [ʃəʊ]	Show, Vorstellung, zeigen
shower ['ʃaʊə]	Schauer, Dusche, duschen
shower gel ['ʃaʊədʒel]	Duschgel
shut [ʃʌt]	schließen
sick [sɪk]	(leicht) krank
sickness ['sɪknɪs]	Übelkeit
side [saɪd]	Seite, Seiten-
side dish ['saɪddɪʃ]	Beilage
sights [saɪtz] *pl*	Sehenswürdigkeiten
sightseeing ['saɪtsiːɪŋ]	Besichtigung
sign [saɪn]	Schild, Zeichen, unterschreiben
signature ['sɪgnətʃə]	Unterschrift
silence ['saɪləns]	Stille, Ruhe
silent ['saɪlənt]	still, leise
silk [sɪlk]	Seide
silver ['sɪlvə]	Silber
similar ['sɪmɪlə]	ähnlich
simple ['sɪmpl]	einfach
since [sɪns]	seit, seitdem
sincere [sɪn'sɪə]	aufrichtig
sing [sɪŋ]	singen
singer ['sɪŋə]	Sänger(in)
single ['sɪŋgl]	Single, Einzel-, einzeln, ledig, ungebunden
sink [sɪŋk]	Spülbecken
sister ['sɪstə]	Schwester

sister-in-law ['sɪstərɪnlɔː]	Schwägerin
sit [sɪt]	sitzen
six [sɪks]	sechs
sixteen [sɪk'stiːn]	sechzehn
sixteenth [sɪks'tiːnθ]	sechzehnte(-r, -s)
sixth [sɪksθ]	sechste(-r, -s)
sixty ['sɪkstɪ]	sechzig
size [saɪz]	Größe
ski [skiː]	Ski, Ski fahren
skill [skɪl]	Geschick, Fertigkeit, Kenntnis
skilful ['skilfʊl]	geschickt
skin [skɪn]	Haut
skirt [skɜːt]	Rock
sky [skaɪ]	Himmel
sleep [sliːp]	Schlaf, schlafen
sleeve [sliːv]	Ärmel
slice [slaɪs]	Scheibe, durchschneiden
slim [slɪm]	schlank
slow [sləʊ]	langsam
small [smɔːl]	klein
small money [smɔːl'mʌnɪ]	Kleingeld, Wechselgeld
smart [smɑːt]	schlau
smell [smel]	Geruch, riechen
smile [smaɪl]	Lächeln, lächeln
smoke [sməʊk]	Rauch, rauchen
smooth [smuːð]	glatt
snack [snæk]	Imbiss, Snack
snow [snəʊ]	Schnee
so [səʊ]	so, deshalb, daher
so that [səʊ'ðæt]	dass
soap [səʊp]	Seife
society [sə'saɪətɪ]	Gesellschaft

sock [sɒk]	Socke
socket ['sɒkɪt]	Steckdose
sofa ['səʊfə]	Sofa
soft [sɒft]	weich, sanft
software ['sɒftwɛə]	Software
soil [sɔɪl]	Boden, Erde
soldier ['səʊldʒə]	Soldat(in)
solid ['sɒlɪd]	fest, solide, massiv
solution [sə'luːʃən]	Lösung
some [sʌm]	einige
somebody ['sʌmbədɪ]	jemand
somehow ['sʌmhaʊ]	irgendwie
someone ['sʌmwʌn]	jemand
something ['sʌmθɪŋ]	etwas
sometimes ['sʌmtaɪmz]	manchmal
somewhere ['sʌmwɛə]	irgendwo
son [sʌn]	Sohn
song [sɒŋ]	Lied
soon [suːn]	bald
sore [sɔː]	wund, weh, schlimm
sorrow ['sɒrəʊ]	Trauer, Sorge
Sorry! ['sɒrɪ]	Entschuldigung!
sort [sɔːt]	Art, Sorte
soul [səʊl]	Seele
sound [saʊnd]	Klang, Ton, Laut, klingen
soup [suːp]	Suppe
soup plate ['suːppleɪt]	Suppenteller
sour [saʊə]	sauer
source [sɔːs]	Quelle
south [saʊθ]	Süd
South America [saʊθə'merɪkə]	Südamerika
southeast [saʊθ'iːst]	Südost

southern ['sʌðən]	südlich, Süd-
southwest [saʊθ'west]	Südwest
space [speɪs]	Raum, Platz
Spain [speɪn]	Spanien
Spanish ['spænɪʃ]	Spanisch, spanisch
speak [spiːk]	sprechen
special ['speʃəl]	besonders
speech [spiːtʃ]	Ansprache, Rede
speed [spiːd]	Geschwindigkeit
spell [spel]	buchstabieren
spend [spend]	ausgeben, verbringen
spice [spaɪs]	Gewürz
spicy ['spaɪsɪ]	würzig
spider ['spaɪdə]	Spinne
spinach ['spɪnɪtʃ]	Spinat
spirit ['spɪrɪt]	Laune
split up [splɪt'ʌp]	sich trennen
spoil [spɔɪl]	verderben, verwöhnen
spoon [spuːn]	Löffel
sport [spɔːt]	Sport(art)
spot [spɒt]	Fleck
spring [sprɪŋ]	Frühling
square [skwɛə]	Platz, Quadrat, quadratisch, eckig
stadium ['steɪdɪəm]	Stadion
staff [stɑːf]	Belegschaft, Personal
stage [steɪdʒ]	Bühne
stair [stɛə]	Treppe
staircase ['stɛəkeɪs]	Treppenhaus
stamp [stæmp]	Briefmarke, Stempel
stand [stænd]	stehen
stand up [stænd'ʌp]	aufstehen

standpoint ['stændpɔɪnt]	Standpunkt
stapler ['steɪplə]	Hefter
star [stɑː]	Stern
start [stɑːt]	Anfang, Beginn, Start
starter ['stɑːtə]	Vorspeise
state [steɪt]	Staat
station ['steɪʃən]	Haltestelle, Bahnhof, Sender
stay [steɪ]	Aufenthalt, sich aufhalten
steal [stiːl]	stehlen
steam [stiːm]	Dampf
steep [stiːp]	steil
step [step]	Schritt, Stufe
stick [stɪk]	Stock, (an-, auf-)kleben
sticky tape ['stɪkɪteɪp]	Klebeband
stiff [stɪf]	steif
still [stɪl]	immer noch
stir [stɜː]	umrühren
stock [stɒk]	Aktie, Aktien, Lager, Vorrat
stocking ['stɒkɪŋ]	Strumpf
stock market ['stɒk'mɑːkɪt]	Börse
stomach ['stʌmək]	Bauch, Magen
stomachache ['stʌməkeɪk]	Bauchschmerzen
stone [stəʊn]	Stein
stop [stɒp]	Haltestelle
store [stɔː]	Laden, Kaufhaus
storm [stɔːm]	Sturm
story ['stɔːrɪ]	Geschichte
stove [stəʊv]	Herd
straight [streɪt]	gerade
strange [streɪndʒ]	sonderbar, merkwürdig
stranger ['streɪndʒə]	Fremde(r)
straw [strɔː]	Strohhalm

strawberry ['strɔːbərɪ]	Erdbeere
street [striːt]	Straße
strike [straɪk]	Streik
string [strɪŋ]	Schnur
strong [strɒŋ]	kräftig, stark
student ['stjuːdənt]	Student(in)
study ['stʌdɪ]	Arbeitszimmer, studieren
stuff [stʌf]	Zeug, Sachen
stupid ['stjuːpɪd]	dumm
subject ['sʌbdʒɪkt]	Fach, Thema
subtract [səb'trækt]	subtrahieren, abziehen
suburb ['sʌbɜːb]	Vorort, Stadtrand
success [sək'ses]	Erfolg
such [sʌtʃ]	solche(-r, -s)
sudden ['sʌdn]	plötzlich, unerwartet
suffer ['sʌfə]	leiden
sugar ['ʃʊgə]	Zucker
suggest [sə'dʒest]	vorschlagen
suggestion [sə'dʒestʃən]	Vorschlag
suit [suːt]	Anzug, gut stehen
suitcase ['suːtkeɪs]	Koffer
sum [sʌm]	Summe, Betrag
summer ['sʌmə]	Sommer
sun [sʌn]	Sonne
sun protection ['sʌnprə'tekʃən]	Sonnenschutz
sun tan ['sʌntæn]	Sonnenbräune
sunburn ['sʌnbɜːn]	Sonnenbrand
Sunday ['sʌndeɪ]	Sonntag
sunglasses ['sʌnglɑːsɪz] *pl*	Sonnenbrille
sunrise ['sʌnraɪz]	Sonnenaufgang
sunset ['sʌnset]	Sonnenuntergang
sunshine ['sʌnʃaɪn]	Sonnenschein

supermarket ['su:pəmɑ:kɪt]	Supermarkt
supper ['sʌpə]	Abendessen
support [sə'pɔ:t]	Unterstützung, unterstützen
suppose [sə'pəʊz]	annehmen, vermuten
sure [ʃʊə]	sicher, gewiss
surface ['sɜ:fɪs]	Oberfläche
surname ['sɜ:neɪm]	Nachname
surprise [sə'praɪz]	Überraschung, überraschen
sweater ['swetə]	Pullover
Sweden ['swi:dn]	Schweden
sweep [swi:p]	fegen, wischen
sweet [swi:t]	süß
sweets [swi:ts] *pl*	Süßigkeiten
swim [swɪm]	schwimmen
swimming-pool ['swɪmɪŋpu:l]	Swimmingpool
swimsuit ['swɪmsu:t]	Badeanzug
switch [swɪtʃ]	Schalter, einschalten
sympathy ['sɪmpəθɪ]	Mitleid

T

table ['teɪbl]	Tisch
table cloth ['teɪblklɒθ]	Tischdecke
tableware ['teɪblwɛə]	Geschirr
take [teɪk]	nehmen
take care of [teɪk'kɛəv]	sich kümmern um
take off [teɪk'ɒv]	ausziehen, starten
take part [teɪk'pa:t]	teilnehmen
take place [teɪk'pleɪs]	stattfinden
talent ['tælənt]	Begabung
talk [tɔ:k]	Gespräch, Unterredung, sprechen

tall [tɔːl]	groß
tape [teɪp]	Band
tariff ['tærɪf]	Tarif
task [tɑːsk]	Aufgabe
taste [teɪst]	Geschmack, probieren, schmecken
tax [tæks]	Steuer
taxi ['tæksɪ]	Taxi
tea [tiː]	Tee
teach [tiːtʃ]	lehren
teacher ['tiːtʃə]	Lehrer(in)
team [tiːm]	Team, Mannschaft
teenager ['tiːneɪdʒə]	Jugendliche(r)
telephone ['telɪfəʊn]	Telefon
telephone box ['telɪfəʊnbɒks]	Telefonzelle
television ['telɪvɪʒn]	Fernsehen
tell [tel]	erzählen
temperature ['temprɪtʃə]	Fieber, Temperatur
ten [ten]	zehn
ten thousand [ten'θaʊzənd]	zehntausend
tennis ['tenɪs]	Tennis
tent [tent]	Zelt
tenth [tenθ]	zehnte(-r, -s)
terrible ['terɪbl]	schrecklich
test [test]	Test, Prüfung
text [tekst]	Text
thank you ['θaŋkjuː]	danke
thankful ['θæŋkfʊl]	dankbar
that [ðæt]	diese(-r, -s), jene(-r, -s), der, die, das, dass
The Netherlands [ðə'neðələndz]	die Niederlande

theatre ['θɪətə]	Theater
theft [ðeft]	Diebstahl
their [ðɛə]	ihr(-e, -r)
theirs [ðɛəz]	ihr(-e, -r, -s)
them [ðem]	ihnen, sie
themselves [ðəm'selvz]	sie/sich selbst
then [ðen]	dann, damals
there [ðɛə]	da, dort
thermometer [θə'mɒmɪtə]	Thermometer
these [ði:z]	diese
they [ðeɪ]	sie
thick [θɪk]	dick, dicht
thief [θi:f]	Dieb(in)
thin [θɪn]	dünn
thing [θɪŋ]	Ding, Sache
think [θɪŋk]	denken
third [θɜ:d]	dritte(-r, -s)
thirsty ['θɜ:stɪ]	durstig
thirteen [θɜ:'ti:n]	dreizehn
thirteenth [θɜ:'ti:nθ]	dreizehnte(-r, -s)
thirty ['θɜ:tɪ]	dreißig
this [ðɪs]	dies, das, dieser, dieses
thoroughly ['θʌrəlɪ]	gründlich
those [ðəʊz]	diese (da), jene, die(jenigen)
though [ðəʊ]	obwohl, obgleich, allerdings
thought [θɔ:t]	Gedanke
thoughtless ['θɔ:tlɪs]	gedankenlos
thousand ['θaʊzənd]	tausend
three [θri:]	drei
throat [θrəʊt]	Hals, Kehle
through [θru:]	von, durch, mittels, per
throw [θrəʊ]	werfen

thunder ['θʌndə]	Donner
thunderstorm ['θʌndəstɔːm]	Gewitter
Thursday ['θɜːzdeɪ]	Donnerstag
ticket ['tɪkɪt]	Ticket, Fahrkarte, Strafzettel
tidy ['taɪdɪ]	ordentlich, sauber
tie [taɪ]	Krawatte
tiger ['taɪgə]	Tiger
tight [taɪt]	dicht, fest, eng
tights ['taɪts] *pl*	Strumpfhose
till [tɪl]	bis
time [taɪm]	Zeit
timetable [ðətaɪmteɪbl]	Fahrplan
tin [tɪn]	Dose
tin-opener ['tɪnəʊpənə]	Dosenöffner
tip [tɪp]	Trinkgeld, Trinkgeld geben
tired ['taɪəd]	müde
tissue ['tɪʃuː]	Kosmetiktuch
title ['taɪtl]	Titel, Überschrift
to [tuː]	zu, bis, nach, in, an vor
tobacco [tə'bækəʊ]	Tabak
today [tə'deɪ]	heute
toe [təʊ]	Zehe
together [tə'geðə]	gemeinsam, zusammen
toilet ['tɔɪlɪt]	Toilette, Gäste-WC
toilet paper ['tɔɪlɪtpeɪpə]	Toilettenpapier
tomato [tə'mɑːtəʊ]	Tomate
tomorrow [tə'mɒrəʊ]	morgen
ton [tʌn]	Tonne
tongue [tʌŋ]	Zunge
tonight [tə'naɪt]	heute Abend, heute Nacht
too [tuː]	auch
toolbox ['tuːlbɒks]	Werkzeugkasten

tools [tuːlz] *pl*	Werkzeug
tooth [tuːθ], **teeth** [tiːð] *pl*	Zahn
toothache ['tuːθeɪk]	Zahnschmerzen
toothbrush ['tuːθbrʌʃ]	Zahnbürste
toothpaste ['tuːθpeɪst]	Zahnpasta
top [tɒp]	Spitze
top floor ['tɒpflɔː]	Dachgeschoss
topic ['tɒpɪk]	Thema
torch [tɔːtʃ]	Taschenlampe
total ['təʊtl]	Gesamtbetrag
touch [tʌtʃ]	Berührung, tasten, berühren, rühren
tourist ['tʊərɪst]	Tourist
towards [tə'wɔːd]	nach, gegen
towel ['taʊəl]	Handtuch
town [taʊn]	Stadt
town hall ['taʊnhɔːl]	Rathaus
track [træk]	Bahngleis
trade [treɪd]	Handel, Handwerk, handeln
trade union ['treɪdjuːnɪən]	Gewerkschaft
traffic ['træfɪk]	Verkehr
traffic jam ['træfɪkdʒæm]	Stau
traffic light ['træfɪklaɪt]	Ampel
traffic sign ['træfɪksaɪn]	Straßenschild
train [treɪn]	Zug, ausbilden, trainieren
train station ['treɪnsteɪʃən]	Bahnhof
trainer ['treɪnə]	Turnschuh, Trainer(in)
tram [træm]	Straßenbahn
transfer [træns'fɜː]	Überweisung, überweisen
translate [trænz'leɪt]	übersetzen
transport ['trænspɔːt]	Transport
travel ['trævl]	Reise, reisen

travel agency ['trævl'eɪdʒənsɪ]	Reisebüro
travel guide ['trævlgaɪd]	Reiseleiter(in)
traveller ['trævla]	Reisende(r)
treat [triːt]	behandeln
tree [triː]	Baum
trendy ['trendɪ]	modisch
trip [trɪp]	Reise, Ausflug
trouble ['trʌbl]	Schwierigkeiten, Ärger, Probleme
trousers ['traʊzəz] *pl*	Hose
truck [trʌk] *AE*	Lastwagen
true [truː]	wahr
try [traɪ]	probieren, versuchen
trust [trʌst]	trauen, vertrauen
truth [truːθ]	Wahrheit
t-shirt ['tiːʃɜːt]	T-Shirt
Tuesday ['tjuːzdeɪ]	Dienstag
tulip ['tjʊlɪp]	Tulpe
tune [tjuːn]	Melodie
Turkey ['tɜːkɪ]	Türkei
turn [tɜːn]	drehen, umdrehen, abbiegen
turn off [tɜːn'ɒv]	ausmachen
turn on [tɜːn'ɒn]	anmachen
turn round [tɜːn'raʊnd]	umkehren
twelve [twelv]	zwölf
twelfth [twelfθ]	zwölfte(-r, -s)
twentieth ['twentɪθ]	zwanzigste(-r, -s)
twenty ['twentɪ]	zwanzig
twenty-first [twentɪ'fɜːst]	einundzwanzigste(-r, -s)
twice [twaɪs]	zweimal, doppelt
twin [twɪn]	Zwilling, Partner(in), Paar
two [tuː]	zwei

upstairs [ʌp'stɛəz]	oben
upwards ['ʌpwədz]	nach oben, aufwärts
urgent ['ɜːdʒənt]	dringend, eilig
us [ʌs]	uns, wir
use [juːz]	Gebrauch, benutzen, verwenden
used [juːzt]	gebraucht
useful ['juːsfʊl]	nützlich
useless ['juːslɪs]	nutzlos
user [juːzə]	Benutzer(in)
usual ['juːʒʊəl]	üblich, gewöhnlich

V

vacancy ['veɪkənsɪ]	freie Stelle
vacuum ['vækjʊm]	staubsaugen
vacuum cleaner ['vækjʊmkliːnə]	Staubsauger
valley ['vælɪ]	Tal
value ['væljuː]	Wert
van [væn]	Lieferwagen
various ['vɛərɪəs]	verschieden
veal [viːl]	Kalbfleisch
vegetable ['vedʒtəbl]	Gemüse
verdict ['vɜːdɪkt]	Urteil
very ['verɪ]	sehr
video ['vɪdɪəʊ]	Video
view [vjuː]	Aussicht
village ['vɪlɪdʒ]	Dorf
vinegar ['vɪnɪgə]	Essig
violin [vaɪə'lɪn]	Geige
visit ['vɪzɪt]	Besuch, besuchen
visitor ['vɪzɪtə]	Besucher(in)
vomit ['vɒmɪt]	sich übergeben

vote [vəʊt]	wählen, stimmen für
voter [vəʊtə]	Wähler(in)

W

wage [weɪdʒ]	Gehalt, Lohn
wait [weɪt]	warten
waiter ['weɪtə]	Kellner
waitress ['weɪtrɪs]	Kellnerin
wake up ['weɪkʌp]	aufwachen, aufwecken
walk [wɔːk]	Spaziergang, spazieren gehen, laufen
wall [wɔːl]	Mauer, Wand
wallet ['wɒlɪt]	Brieftasche
war [wɔː]	Krieg
warm [wɔːm]	warm
warn [wɔːn]	warnen
wash [wɒʃ]	(sich) waschen
wash basin ['wɒʃbeɪsɪn]	Waschbecken
wash the dishes ['wɒʃðə'dɪʃɪz]	(Geschirr) spülen
washing machine ['wɒʃɪŋmə'ʃiːn]	Waschmaschine
waste [weɪst]	Abfall, verschwenden
waste bin ['weɪstbɪn]	Mülltonne
wastepaper basket ['weɪstpeɪpə'bɑːskɪt]	Papierkorb
watch [wɒtʃ]	Armbanduhr, anschauen, schauen
watch out [wɒtʃ'aʊt]	sich in Acht nehmen, aufpassen
water ['wɔːtə]	Wasser, gießen
way [weɪ]	Weg, Art und Weise
we [wiː]	wir

type [taɪp]	Sorte, Gattung
tyre [taɪə]	Reifen

U

ugly ['ʌglɪ]	hässlich
umbrella [ʌm'brelə]	Regenschirm
unable [ʌn'eɪbl]	unfähig
uncle ['ʌŋkl]	Onkel
uncomfortable [ʌn'kʌmfətəbl]	unbequem
unconscious [ʌn'kɒnʃəs]	bewusstlos
under ['ʌndə]	unter
underground ['ʌndəgraʊnd]	U-Bahn
understand [ʌndə'stænd]	verstehen, begreifen
underwear ['ʌndəwɛə]	Unterwäsche
unemployed ['ʌnɪmplɔɪd]	arbeitslos
unemployment[ʌnɪm'plɔɪmənt]	Arbeitslosigkeit
unfortunately [ʌn'fɔːtʃənətli]	unglücklicherweise, leider
unfriendly [ʌn'frendlɪ]	unfreundlich
unhappy [ʌn'hæpɪ]	unglücklich
union ['juːnjən]	Gewerkschaft, Vereinigung, Union
United States [juː'naɪtɪd'steɪts]	Vereinigte Staaten
university [juːnɪ'vɜːsɪtɪ]	Universität
unless [ʌn'les]	es sei denn, wenn … nicht
unpack [ʌn'pæk]	auspacken
unpleasant [ʌn'pleznt]	unangenehm
untidy [ʌn'taɪdɪ]	unordentlich
until [ən'tɪl]	bis
unusual [ʌn'juːʒʊəl]	ungewöhnlich
up [ʌp]	hinauf, auf, aufwärts, oben
upset [ʌp'set]	aufgeregt, bestürzt, mitgenommen

weak [wiːk]	schwach
wear [wɛə]	tragen
weather ['weðə]	Wetter
weather forecast ['weðə'fɔːkɑːst]	Wettervorhersage
wedding ['wedɪŋ]	Hochzeit
Wednesday ['wenzdeɪ]	Mittwoch
week [wiːk]	Woche
weekday ['wiːkdeɪ]	Wochentag, Werktag
weekend [wiːk'end]	Wochenende
weekly ['wiːklɪ]	wöchentlich
weight [weɪt]	Gewicht
welcome ['welkəm]	Willkommen, willkommen heißen
well [wel]	gut, nun, also
west [west]	West
wet [wet]	nass
what [wɒt]	was
wheel [wiːl]	Rad
when [wen]	wann, wenn, als
where [wɛə]	wo
whether ['weðə]	ob
which [wɪtʃ]	welche
while [waɪl]	während
whisper ['wɪspə]	Flüstern, flüstern
white [waɪt]	weiß
Whitsun ['wɪtsn]	Pfingsten
who [huː]	wer
whole [həʊl]	ganz, ganze
whom [huːm]	wem
whose [huːz]	wessen
why [waɪ]	warum, weshalb
wide [waɪd]	breit, weit

widow ['wɪdəʊ]	Witwe
widower ['wɪdəʊə]	Witwer
width [widθ]	Breite
wife [waɪf]	Ehefrau
wild [waɪld]	wild
will [wɪl]	werde, wirst, wird, werdet, werden
win [wɪn]	gewinnen
wind [wɪnd]	Wind
window ['wɪndəʊ]	Fenster
wine [waɪn]	Wein
winner ['wɪnə]	Sieger
winter ['wɪntə]	Winter
wireless ['waɪəlɪs]	drahtlos
wise [waɪz]	klug
wish [wɪʃ]	wünschen
with [wɪð]	mit
within [wɪ'ðɪn]	innerhalb
withdraw [wɪð'drɔː]	abheben
without [wɪð'aʊt]	ohne
witness ['wɪtnɪs]	Zeuge, Zeugin, Zeuge sein
woman ['wʊmən]	Frau
wonder ['wʌndə]	Wunder, sich fragen, sich wundern
wonderful ['wʌndəfʊl]	wunderbar
wood [wʊd]	Holz
wool [wʊl]	Wolle
work [wɜːk]	Arbeit, arbeiten
worker ['wɜːkə]	Arbeiter(in)
workforce ['wɜːkfɔːs]	Arbeitnehmer *pl*
workman ['wɜːkmæn]	Handwerker
workplace ['wɜːkpleɪs]	Arbeitsplatz
world [wɜːld]	Welt
worm [wɜːm]	Wurm

worry ['wʌrɪ]	Sorge, sich Sorgen machen
worse [wɜːs]	schlechter
worth [wɜːθ]	wert
would [wʊd]	würde, würdest, würdet, würden
wound [wuːnd]	Wunde
wrap [ræp]	einwickeln, verpacken
write [raɪt]	schreiben
write down [raɪt'daʊn]	aufschreiben
wrong [rɒŋ]	falsch

Y/Z

yard [jɑːd]	Yard, Hof
year [jɪə]	Jahr
yeast [jiːst]	Gips
yell [jel]	Schrei, schreien
yellow ['jeləʊ]	gelb
yesterday ['jestədeɪ]	gestern
yet [jet]	schon, noch
yog(h)urt ['jəʊgɜːt]	Jogurt
you [juː]	du, dich, dir, euch, ihr, Sie, man
young [jʌŋ]	jung
your [jʊə]	dein(-e, -r), euer(-e)
yours [jʊəz]	dein(-e, -r, -s), euer(-e, -es)
yourself [jə'self]	dir/du selbst
yourselves [jə'selvz]	ihr/euch selbst
youth [juːθ]	Jugend
youth hostel ['juːθhɒstəl]	Jugendherberge
zero ['zɪərəʊ]	null
zipper ['zɪpə]	Reißverschluss
zoo [zuː]	Zoo
zucchini [zuː'kiːnɪ] *AE*	Zucchini